CHRISTIANITY
AND THE
SOCIAL REVOLUTION

CHRISTIANITY
AND THE
SOCIAL REVOLUTION

Edited by
JOHN LEWIS
KARL POLANYI
DONALD K. KITCHIN

Editorial Board
JOSEPH NEEDHAM

CHARLES E. RAVEN

JOHN MACMURRAY

BOOKS FOR LIBRARIES PRESS
FREEPORT, NEW YORK

First Published 1935
Reprinted 1972

INTERNATIONAL STANDARD BOOK NUMBER:
0-8369-6729-1

LIBRARY OF CONGRESS CATALOG CARD NUMBER:
79-37892

PRINTED IN THE UNITED STATES OF AMERICA
BY
NEW WORLD BOOK MANUFACTURING CO., INC.
HALLANDALE, FLORIDA 33009

CONTENTS

6 CONTENTS

PART II

COMMUNISM AND RELIGION

PART III

DIES IRÆ

PREFACE

THIS VOLUME OF ESSAYS has a definite purpose, and its plan follows from the purpose. It challenges the traditional attitude of Christianity towards the question of radical social change. It also challenges the orthodox attitude of Communism to Religion.

In Part I. the authors reconsider the life and teaching of Jesus and the history of the Church in the closest relation to the social background of the times and current social problems.

It is a study of the Communism in Christianity. Conrad Noel, the Vicar of Thaxted, represents a movement, within the Church of England, and orthodox in its theology, which is nevertheless (or as Conrad Noel himself would say, *therefore*) not only Socialist, but revolutionary. The Rev. Clive Binyon has long been known as a courageous and devout representative of a quite different stream of Socialist conviction in the English Church. Continental Socialism finds it extremely difficult to believe in the existence of genuine Socialism which is at the same time orthodox and ecclesiastical. Here it is, and the Society of Socialist Christians could add the names of many prominent Free Church ministers and many other Anglican priests. It is the contention of most of the authors of this book that Christianity cannot be ignored by Socialists. It is, in this country, too virile, in spite of all its defects, and too deeply penetrated with social idealism to be scorned either as a foe or an ally.

The other essays in this Part are both more objective and more critical in their treatment of historical Christianity, and it is clear that their authors, with whatever measure of sympathy they might regard the Christian

Socialism of Conrad Noel and Clive Binyon, would disagree profoundly with their exposition of the Christian
Religion.

The second Part of this book needs a few words of
explanation. The intention here is to allow Marxism to
speak for itself without editorial censorship or any reluctance
to hit as hard as it likes. John Macmurray lets us see what
the early Marx thought of religion ; the remaining essays
are from the hands of avowed Communists. Inexcusable
though it is, even the more responsible ethical and religious
criticisms of Communism are usually ignorant of the system
of thought and practice with which they disagree. For
example, Mr. Kenneth Ingram, in his recent Broadcast
Addresses on " Can We Be Materialists ? " assumes that
Communism reduces all phenomena to physical and
chemical factors, and professes a mechanistic determinism.
No one who reads this section will have any excuse for such
mistakes.

In the preparation of the essay on Communism and
Religion considerable help was derived from an unpub-
lished essay by Professor Lukachevsky, Vice-President of
the Anti-God Society, who, together with several colleagues, would have made himself responsible for this
section but for insurmountable difficulties in the way of
exchange of manuscripts. The Russians very properly
would have preferred to receive all the other contributions
first, in order to base their own essays upon them. The
Editorial Board found no objections to this course, except
that it would have delayed publication yet another twelve
months.

In the third, and final, Part the relation of Christianity
to the emergent society of to-morrow and to the acute
problems of transition is discussed from different points of
view. There has been no attempt to dovetail or harmonise
these five vigorous and challenging essays, nor do they by
any means reach a unanimous conclusion. There is no easy
optimism about any of them. No doubt they will prove
disturbing and unacceptable both to many Christians and

to many Communists. We would pray them, in all humility, not to think that the future will necessarily fall out as they suppose, but to prepare their minds for the unexpected, and to beware, amid the complexities of a dissolving world, of the perils of a full, and false, explanation.

Many unexpected difficulties have delayed the publication of this work, which was conceived in the summer of 1933. To Mr. Donald Kitchin's enthusiasm and energy the launching of the project and the gathering of the early contributors was due. Dr. Karl Polanyi took up the task when illness prevented Mr. Kitchin from carrying on with the work, but his long visit to America rendered it necessary for the present editor to assume final responsibility.

JOHN LEWIS

INTRODUCTION
by Charles E. Raven
Regius Professor of Divinity, Cambridge University

I. THE PRESENT CONFUSION

IN ONE OF THE WORLD'S greatest cities they have
been building a cathedral. Originally it was intended to
produce a vast auditorium in which the civic life could
find space to demonstrate its unity. This was to be supple-
mented by a series of ancillary chapels appropriate to the
particular interests of sections of the community. A Renaissance design was chosen, and the builders set vigorously
to work. Then doubts arose. Was it consistent with tradition to provide for such cosmopolitan assemblies ? Was it
loyal to the Church to offer hospitality and a chapel to
other denominations ? Could the sense of worship be cultivated under a vast dome ? Was not the architecture unsuitable ? Was not the design bad ? So a change was made.
A new architect was appointed ; Gothic was to be the
mode of the edifice ; the existing structure must be recon-
ditioned ; a nave in decorated style should be the dominant
feature. Renaissance pillars were overlaid with Gothic
capitals ; round arches were filled in and pointed ; a
modernised version of the Lady Chapel at Ely was appended
to the existing dome. In the finished building the only
point that a harassed visitor could decently praise was the
ingenuity of the second architect, and, rather tentatively,
the symbolic interest of his performance.

For this is a story typical of our present position. We
all desire to build a house for humanity. Large vague
dreams of a new world occupy what time we can spare from
the serious business of amusement or money-making.

Renaissance—an epoch of rebirth—a recognition of the unity and mutual interdependence of mankind—a social order international in scope and generous in design—such we desire, and for such we would labour. Enthusiasm is not lacking. There are multitudes of individuals and groups, world over, eager to hew stone and lay bricks. There is need for haste, and, of course, we are practical folk in a practical age. Let us to the work.

After the war there was throughout our civilisation a spasm of constructive activity. Unfortunately it hardly occurred to us to consider the problems of lay-out and architecture. Renaissance style would suffice ; or, if not, any other conventional mode : the house would be so large that any sort of structure could find a place in it. Why waste time worrying about general principles ? Philosophy, ethics, religion, could be left to the common sense of mankind, enlightened or bewildered by self-appointed guides and prophets. Experiment was inevitable ; delay would be disastrous. Let us to the work.

The result of our energies soon became plain. This tower of Babel, this hotchpotch of inconsistencies, of make-shifts and improvisations, was a monument to the futility of good intentions—a testimony to the vital importance of an agreed programme. We must decide what sort of life the inhabitants of Mansoul should be helped to live ; what sort of social, moral, and spiritual values were to be realised ; what were the sanctions and inspirations of full personal development ; what was the permanent significance of human existence. Religion in its broad sense could not be ignored, must, indeed, be given a place of primary importance in our planning.

So a reaction set in. Men felt the difficulty of formulating an ideal adequate to the character of the times. They found philosophy, psychology, economics, and political science in a state of confusion. It would take a generation to disentangle the chaos created by the speed and scope of the changes that had affected man's outlook and way of life. Renaissance was unsuitable. Better to fall back upon some more definite and rigid system. Roman Catholicism and the revived Calvinism of Dr. Barth among the Christian groups, nationalism rejuvenated by myths of blood and the cult of a hero among the non-Christian, are typical of the tendency in times of stress to revert to methods which if manifestly anachronisms yet promise at worst a refuge from bewilderment and at best an inspiration to action. We are in the midst of an epoch of revolution ; we have discovered the necessity for the unifying power of an ideal : if we cannot agree as to the new form which that ideal should take, let us fall back upon one of the more striking of its earlier manifestations.

Yet for those who find little satisfaction in any of these temporary revivals there is emerging a tolerably plain alternative. To say that it is a choice between Christianity or Communism is misleading, since Christianity to-day covers a wide variety of faith and practice, and since such a statement suggests a clear-cut antithesis. But if one may judge by the attitude of the more thoughtful and sensitive of the younger generation, whose minds, if inexperienced, are at least free from obsession with tradition, it seems evident that, in the English-speaking world at least, the two serious claimants for attention are roughly the Christian way of life as seen in the records of Christ and interpreted by the forward-looking thought of His modern followers, and that developed by the succession of workers who have shaped the social revolution in Russia and formulated the philosophy or religion that inspires it. It is between these two loyalties that the conflict for the dominance of the future would appear to lie. When the facts and crazes of the moment and the survivals and makeshifts of the past are sifted, these two alone seem to show signs of a more permanent vitality.

II. THE APPARENT CONFLICT

To many minds the issue presents itself in a different form. They see the general and abiding tradition which has persisted for nearly two thousand years in Western Europe, and which, despite its variety of detail and indebtedness to other sources, may loosely be described as Christian, subjected for the first time for many centuries to the challenge of a rival. Here, in these latter days, is the authentic Antichrist, capable of arousing a real and passionate religious fervour, equipped with a synthetic philosophy at once clear in its fundamental tenets and capable of vital expansion, and expressed in a system of social order which takes account of modern economic and scientific realities and gives coherence to the vague, and often compromising, aspirations after equality which have underlain the Socialisms of the past century ; an Antichrist whose name has been triumphantly proclaimed by the persecution of the Church and the propaganda of the Anti-God Movement.

The Communist challenge, when it first became articulate and familiar, had two powerful and obvious commendations —its novelty and its efficiency. During the war we had all been sustained by belief in the coming of a brave new world. It had seemed as if out of so great a travail some fresh birth of brotherhood and hope must emerge. We had seen the foundations laid for such a world by the three great events which signalised the time of conflict—the emancipation of woman, giving promise of a fresh epoch in human social and political history ; the discovery of the enormous resources of modern scientific production, holding out hopes of the banishment of poverty and the raising of the standards of life to levels hitherto unbelievable ; the development of international unity, due to the transformation of the means of communication by aeroplanes and wireless, which called for a federalising of peoples and forecast the speedy achievement of a cosmopolitan civilisation. With such a faith we faced the coming of peace—only to find that every sort of leader, spiritual, economic, political, was content to repeat ancient moralisings, patch up dilapidated systems of credit and exchange, and revive the nationalistic and aggressive ambitions of which war should have purged us. Within a few months of the Armistice it became clear to any tolerably far-sighted observer that the Western world was not capable of formulating anything creative or fresh, and would relapse into its habit of adapting out-of-date formulæ to new uses, into its enthusiastic regard for vested interests, and into its pre-war ambitions and fears. When the reasonable instincts of younger people were leading them to regard antiquity as the hallmark not of worth, but of decrepitude, the sheer novelty of the Communist system gave it an inevitable attraction. Here at least was something which had not made the war, something that spoke in new language and refused to bow down before traditional sanctities.

And it worked. The rest of Europe was paralysed—committed to a vicious treaty, and impotent to carry out the few better elements in it ; cascading from crisis to crisis amid the debates of economists and the enrichment of financiers. The Churches blew hot and cold, one day inviting reunion and the next repudiating it ; gashing themselves with knives and lances in true Baal-worshipping style lest men should discover that they had nothing to say. The man in the street grew poorer and more disillusioned, his dreams denied, his employment insecure, his house-room hard to seek. No one in Church or State found the courage to appeal to the imaginations, to attack the abuses and insist upon the possibilities of the time. No one gave the lie to the increasing conviction that in such a system the individual was helpless, and that out of such a system no fresh vitality could come.

Yet in Russia things were happening—things terrible, perhaps, and terribly distorted in the telling, but things dynamic, dramatic, revolutionary. While Europe muddled and talked, the Soviets planned and acted ; and when soon it appeared that the easy predictions of collapse were being falsified, that a new and permanent society was in being, and that the people, suffering and regimented no doubt, were yet enthusiastic, hopeful, energetic, there was every reason for the West to ask itself what this new force might mean. Even though every artifice of propaganda was employed to influence the public mind against it, the contrast between its achievement and our frustration was enough to overcome prejudice and to compel the enquirer to take the new way of life seriously. Younger and questing minds could hardly fail to be impressed.

Yet for the bulk of the population, especially in the English-speaking world, Bolshevism was a bogey horned and hoofed. The war had demonstrated, mobilised, and exploited the powers of mass-suggestion ; and Communism shocked all the dearest preconceptions of the older civilisation and gave its critics an easy task. It was professedly proletarian ; and, despite the efforts of the Labour movement and the real sympathy of all classes with the depressed, no Britons, and very few Europeans, are free from class-snobbishness or regard themselves as of the common people : there are as clear-cut grades among the unemployed as among the aristocracy ; we all love, or, at least, envy, a lord. It challenged the right to private property ; and, among the heirs of Rome, Christ's warnings against Mammon have never been given general application : indeed the whole force of law, custom, and public opinion estimates a man's worth in terms of his substance. It was bureaucratic and rigidly disciplinary ; and, even if in fact we grumble and accept regimentation, there is no single cause more certain to unite our peoples than a threat to interfere with their privacy or restrict their liberties. It was aggressively atheistic ; and though a flippant agnosticism has now become fashionable in England, convention still looks askance at the atheist and regards any overt attack upon religion as bad form.

Moreover these general characteristics were emphasised by concrete facts. It was not in question that the revolution had taken Russia out of the war at a time when her removal put an intolerable strain upon the Western allies. It was plain that the Tsar and his family had been done to death with ruthless and cold-blooded cruelty ; that multitudes of exiles had been driven, penniless, out of the country, most of them for no fault save that they belonged to the bourgeoisie ; that the Russian Church and clergy were being sternly, and, in some cases, savagely, persecuted ; and that the prime agents in the revolution came from the most unpopular section of Europe's humanity—the cosmopolitan Jews. It did not require much skill in the manipulators of propaganda to create out of such material a widespread reaction of loathing and suspicion. Nothing was too bad to be believed.

Nor could those who desired to study Communism from a more intelligent and detached standpoint escape the conclusion that it threatened not merely the tradition and social order of Europe, but the fundamental spiritual convictions of Christendom. Of this new apocalyptic, Marx was the acclaimed Messiah ; and Marxism, whatever its recent commentators may aver, was to the plain thinker a system of materialistic and economic determinism—materialistic in the ordinary sense of that word as asserting that weight and measurement are the criteria of reality, and economic as Ricardo had expounded the dismal science. As such it not only denied God, but cut away all possibility for a spiritual valuation of the universe, for human personality and freedom. It also restated ideas which had been pulverised with criticism and repudiated by the vast majority of serious students. Christians who had followed the controversies of the past half-century, economists who recognised that the iron law of wages, the keystone of the Ricardian and Marxian theories, had been proved erroneous, could hardly be expected to pay much heed to the confident and rather ill-educated reassertion of these fallacies. Such a philosophy might be put forward to explain and vindicate the Bolshevist régime : that could only confirm Christians in their hostility. With such ideas, as with the practices arising from them, there could be neither compromise nor truce. Rumours of the allegiance of young Oxford to the new system were the final proof that men of sound age need not take its menace very seriously. Even as a bogey it speedily lost its terror.

III. THE GROUNDS FOR
RECONSIDERATION OF THE ISSUES

Christian opinion, and, indeed, the general public mind of the English-speaking world, is probably still convinced that Communism is manifestly opposed to all that it values most in thought and life, and that it must be resisted without further examination. Yet, in fact, there are good grounds for questioning the correctness of that conviction.

In the first place, the Russian experiment, whatever the ruthlessness of its beginning, has falsified the predictions of its critics, and shown a remarkable power not only to establish a new type of social order, but to inspire its people with a zest for life, a loyalty to the community, and a high degree of creative energy. It is still not easy to form a fair estimate of the character of its achievement. In a vast and varied country whose people, formerly known to us by their Westernised intelligentsia, differ widely in temperament, culture, and mode of life from ourselves, the casual visitor, however impartial his outlook, can hardly form a discriminating judgment. But the evidence clearly attests a very remarkable expansion of educational, industrial, artistic, and scientific activities, and a release from the artificialities of class-feeling, a sense of solidarity and comradeship, a contentment and confidence which more than outweigh the privations of a low standard of living. These people believe in their future ; they are planning developments on a scale quite impossible in lands dominated by vested interests : they are prepared to suffer that their dreams may come true.

In the second place, and here we can judge from the Communists of our own country, there is in their movement the authentic exaltation, the generosity, the self-sacrifice of a religion. Indeed, whatever their philosophy, these folk have found a faith to live by, or, what is perhaps more important, a cause to die for. More clearly than any others they reflect the sort of fervour associated with the early days of Christianity when an apocalyptic expectation of the coming Kingdom made the lives of common men thrilling and romantic. For myself, if I may be personal, I am inclined to think that one of my Communist friends among the unemployed dockers of Liverpool was as perfect an example of Christian character as anyone I have known. Certainly when he linked his arm in mine, after a lecture, and said, " I'm a Materialist and you're a Christian : but there's no real difference between us," I felt humbled and glad. His affection, his patience, his sympathy and sensitiveness, his faith in the triumph of good—few churchgoers show more richly what the Apostle calls the fruit of the Spirit.

It is the same with the more educated converts. We may mock at the young men of title who have a way of being Socialists at one-and-twenty and diehards a decade later, and at the intelligentsia who gratify an inferiority complex by flinging themselves into the latest craze. But sincerity and self-sacrifice are proof against contempt ; and when careers are abandoned, fashion defied, and obloquy endured by men of obvious ability and sound character, their evidence cannot be ignored. These men show all the signs of conversion : their lives have been changed ; and along with much that is extravagant and perverse there is genuine conviction and settled purpose. Very certainly in our universities the Christians have begun to ask themselves what these men have got that they have missed, and have been shamed by evidence in them of a courage and devotion such as the Churches should, but too often do not, inspire. These men and their movement are plainly a force which counts in the world. When J. M. Ludlow, shrewdest of social observers, went to Paris in 1849, he came to the conclusion that the Church must take Socialism seriously, and set himself to his life's work of Socialising Christianity and Christianising Socialism. So to-day there are many who feel that unless Christianity can come to an understanding of the power of Communism, and discover and share its secret, the future may well lie rather with the new religion than with the old.

In the third place, and when we examine the quality of Communist enthusiasm, we discover that it can no longer be dismissed as an uprising of the oppressed, nationalised by adoption of a discredited philosophy and an out-of-date economic. From the crude apocalyptic of its early days Dialectic Materialism has developed into a creed which cannot be dismissed by the arguments that would dispose of its original tenets. How far Lenin's version of Marxism is a true interpretation, how far Lenin's commentators and disciples have transformed his views, whether Materialism is any longer a legitimate description of Communist philosophy—these are questions of detail, and could be multiplied many times. What matters is that the original theory which logically left no room for personality or spiritual quality has been drastically reshaped ; that materialistic concepts, in the strict sense of the words, are now anathema ; and that by assimilation to Spinoza, Hegel, and the idealists a fresh and synthetic scheme of thought is being constructed.

So far as my own acquaintance with the writings and speeches of its recent exponents goes, it seems quite clear that the system is at present neither fixed nor coherent. Loyalty to the names of Marx and Lenin forbid any radical re-examination of their tenets, and compel a lip-service to their terminology even when a totally different significance is attached to its leading words. Moreover a synthetic conclusion is not reached by glibly claiming affinity with great thinkers of various schools and interlarding one's exposition by commonplace book extracts from their works. Dialectic Materialism at present is a *synkretismus*, not a synthesis, and, though this may satisfy those who are content to identify philosophy with the rationalisation of conduct, it is a parody of serious thinking for those who believe that the philosopher's task is higher than the provision of plausible arguments to justify lines of action dictated by economic and political expediency.

But however obvious the defects of its present form, what matters is that the cast-iron closed system which rightly or wrongly we have associated with Marxism has been rendered elastic and transformable. We are no longer confronted with a dogma that leaves no room for a spiritual interpretation of life or for any sort of religious experience. Instead it seems as if, in the endeavour to explain their movement, Communists were being led to a radical modification of their philosophy—a modification of which the end is not yet clear. Here are men striving to do justice to the deeper needs and aspirations of their comrades, to interpret the idealism that inspires them, to find sanctions and guidance for their development. We may already wonder whether, in abandoning what alone ought to be called materialism and in finding room for freedom and real creativity, Communists will much longer be able to profess atheism : indeed, some of them are now in fact theists in all but name ; and, though at present they maintain an avowed hostility to Christianity, it will hardly be possible for them to do so consistently unless we admit their claim to identify Christianity with its most obscurantist and static expressions.

Moreover the logic of events is inevitably carrying this process of adaptation forward. The simple formulæ of the class-war which sufficed to explain the revolution drew their strength from a crude determinism. Like most youthful enthusiasts the earlier Bolshevists felt that they had found an obvious and elementary explanation of the true character of human society and of the universe. Experience has raised doubts as to its universal applicability ; concessions in matters of practice have led to modifications of doctrine ; compromises, such as have recently put their French comrades in an unenviable dilemma, have become more and more inevitable. As the régime establishes itself, contact with other, older and not altogether contemptible, civilisations will compel modifications both of policy and of theory. " There is good in growing old "—even if we look back on occasion wistfully to the days when we saw ourselves armed cap-à-pie in a panoply adequate against all comers.

Nor, if Communism is in transition, can any thoughtful Christian doubt that the influences and discoveries of the last century are imposing upon the Churches a similar task of re-examination and restatement. Appeals to them to undertake this task may be stifled or evaded ; attempts upon it may be criticised and condemned : but it remains plain that recent developments in knowledge and way of life cannot be much longer ignored, and that unless Christianity is to be irrevocably associated with a past phase of human history it must be set free from much that is no longer worthy either of an enlightened intelligence or of a sensitive conscience. Something has been done in the realms both of doctrine and of practice. Indeed, in both spheres the past generation has seen more rapid movement than any previous period in the history of organised Christianity. But hitherto most of the progress has been timid and tentative, and, even so, has been made in face of calumny and by a small number of lonely adventurers.

Considering the gravity of the times, the proven inadequacy of out-of-date sanctions, and the evident need for clear principles and a coherent religion, it is surely worth considering whether the traditional system can afford to oppose a blind resistance to an experiment in which many are discovering a new hope and a profound satisfaction. Whether or no Christianity and Communism can come together, it will certainly be of advantage to those Christians who realise the need for re-interpretation and reform, to study carefully the lines of Communist thought and of its criticism of Christian faith and practice.

IV. THE PURPOSE OF THE PRESENT STUDY

It is on these grounds that the contributors to the present volume would ask for a hearing. They agree that Communism is far too vital and vitalising an influence to be ignored ; they are convinced that, whatever the crimes and tragedies of the revolution which initiated its régime in

Russia, its achievements testify to its importance and give it promise of increasing power ; they recognise that those achievements display many characteristics which Christians must approve and desire to share ; they desire to promote a better mutual understanding and in the Churches a more sympathetic approach to Communists and their creed.

In addition the Christians among them wish to point out that although it is probably true that in the more orthodox and general forms, both of its theology and of its ethics, Christianity is committed to an implacable opposition, there are, and have continuously been, within Christendom elements of belief and movements of reform closely akin to Communism. It is simply not true that Christ's religion has always been an opiate to the people, or that it is, as Communists are apt to aver, committed to a rigidly dualistic supernaturalism and therefore indifferent or opposed to an active and revolutionary sociology. No doubt there have been times when its emphasis has been exaggeratedly other-worldly ; times when it has played the sycophant to the established order ; times when its thought and life have become static and therefore reactionary. But these are not typical characteristics either of its origins or of its history ; and recent developments have underlined the extent to which they falsify its whole spirit. We have seen in the past decades plain proof of the importance of apocalyptic in its early years, a recovery not yet complete of the immanentism involved in its belief in the Holy Spirit, and a widespread recognition that the Christian is committed not only to the re-interpretation of his faith, but to revolutionary changes both in personal conduct and in the social order. If, in a time of admitted perplexity, many Christians cling timidly to the Catholic tradition, or to the Victorian ethic, or, like the Archbishop of York, to the plenary inspiration of the Nicene Creed, there are others, and, outside the ranks of the hierarchy, many others, who see in the secular movements of the time not a threat, but an opportunity, who have learnt from them a new appreciation of neglected elements in their own heritage, and who are prepared not merely to denounce much that passes for Christian civilisation as a caricature and an apostasy, but to join hands with any who are working for drastic reform.

Our intention, therefore, in these papers is to give emphasis to the revolutionary character of the Christian faith, and to demonstrate that it has always contained strongly Communistic elements ; to set out the grounds of the Communist opposition to religion and the Church ; and to advance considerations which suggest that it is in the better mutual understanding of the two movements, and even, perhaps, in their synthesis, that the hope of the future lies.

It is, I think, only fair to the editors and contributors to say that the preparation of the volume has been carried out under serious and unforeseeable difficulties ; that we had hoped to include in it a larger number of essays from active Russian Communists, and that, in consequence of their withdrawal, the presentation of the Communist position is less full and less responsible than we desired. Of the gravity of the issues under discussion we are profoundly convinced : of our own capacity to do justice to them we are much less confident ; but at least we believe that the material here collected deserves very serious discussion, and we hope that it may have some effect in overcoming prejudices and promoting a clearer and more sympathetic understanding.

The interesting essay on Moral Sanctions and the Social Function of Religion is from the pen of a distinguished Continental scholar who wishes to remain pseudonymous.

PART I

SOCIALISM IN
HISTORICAL CHRISTIANITY

I

THE GOOD LIFE
by *Wystan Auden*

MAN IS AN ORGANISM with certain desires existing
in an environment which fails to satisfy them fully. His
theories about the universe are attempts, whether religious,
scientific, philosophical, or political, to explain or overcome
this tension. If we regard the environment as static, then the
problem is one of modifying our desires ; if we take the
organism as static, one of modifying the environment.
Religion and psychology begin with the first ; science and
politics with the second.

If we choose the first, we have to answer three
questions :

(1) What are our desires ? Why do we do what we do do ?

(2) If our desires are mutually incompatible, which are we
to choose ? i.e. what ought we to desire and do, and what
ought we not to desire and do ?

(3) How are we to desire what we ought to desire ?

If we choose the second, the questions are :

(1) In what respects does our environment fail to satisfy us ?

(2) How can we change it ?

Further, whichever side we approach the problem from,
there are three possible kinds of resolution :

(1) Those which assert that what is, must be, and that
progress of any kind is a vain delusion. This defeatist view
appears in Stoicism and in Fascist ideology, and is in
general associated with a ruling class which is losing

ground. Oppressed classes without hope, desire vengeance, and may easily adopt a blind eschatology.

(2) The contradiction between what is, and what ought to be, is an illusion arising from the finite nature of human knowledge. In reality there is no Good and Bad.

(3) What is, is a necessary stage in the realisation of what ought to be.

This realisation may be :

(*a*) Sudden and catastrophic.

(*b*) A slow evolution.

(*x*) Voluntary—depending on the determination of the majority of individuals, i.e. it is possible for the consummation to be rejected.

(*y*) Determined—though the individual can accept or reject it ; if he rejects it he joins the losing side.

Christianity is undecided about (*a*) and (*b*), but holds (*y*) not (*x*).

Social Democracy holds (*b*), and is undecided about (*x*) and (*y*).

Psychology, on the whole, holds (*b*) and (*x*).

Communism holds (*a*) and (*y*).

I. THE POLITICS OF THE GOSPELS

(1) *God or Cæsar ?* To extract a political theory from the teaching of Jesus requires the ingenuity of a Seventh-Day Adventist. The suggestion that the cleansing of the Temple is a watered-down version of a revolutionary act—that the disciples were to form the corps of a militant International, that Jesus was really a Communist, can only be maintained by entirely unjustifiable manipulation of the evidence, which on the contrary, as in the account of the Temptation, Cæsar's coin, or the Trial, states that He decisively rejected the political solution. The whole of His direct teaching is concerned with the relation of the individual to God and to his neighbour, irrespective of the

political system under which he may happen to live—though, as in the parables of the Pharisee and the publican, and the Good Samaritan, or the story of the healing of the centurion's daughter, He demonstrates the evil and absurdity of class and racial prejudice ; but the emphasis is laid, not on the necessity for consciously setting out to abolish these, but on behaving as if class and race did not exist, on the supposition that if we so live, they will automatically disappear.

In this sense the teaching of Jesus is fundamentally non-political in that it regards all institutions as a product of the heart, the form of which can be changed, and only changed by a change in the latter. The parable of the house swept and garnished emphasises this.

(2) *Economic inequality.* The cause of inequality is Greed. The cure is the abandonment of money-getting as a motive.

(3) *Eschatology.* It is possible for the historian to say that, even supposing Jesus to have believed the ideal society to be a Communist one, the circumstances and date of His birth would have made revolutionary advice to His disciples both foolish and immoral. A militant Communist movement at such a period of technological advance would have been destroyed as quickly and brutally as the Anabaptists were later, but the eschatological teaching of Jesus makes such reflections irrelevant, e.g. Mark ix. 1, viii. 26, xiv. 62, despite the efforts of Jerome, Origen, and others to explain them away, making a distinction, for example, between " tasting " and " seeing " death, cannot mean anything except that Jesus Himself believed : (i) That the Parousia[1] was imminent, an event to take place within the disciples' lifetime. (ii) That even before the final consummation the Kingdom of God is present on earth in the remnant of which He Himself is the head, the *saving* remnant of Deutero-Isaiah, that is, rather than the saved remnant of earlier prophecies. (iii) That it is not a compensation for

---

[1] The *Parousia* or second advent introduces the consummation of the divine Kingdom founded by the Messiah. [Ed.]

BR

the sufferings of the remnant, but the result of them.
(iv) That it will come suddenly and not by a slow
evolution. (Parable of the robbed householder in Luke
xii.) (v) It will be a judgment at which the principal
criterion will be the attitude taken up by men to Jesus
Himself, or, in a general sense, each individual is judged
on his merits as determined by the disposition of his
will towards the Kingdom of God, as manifest in his
day and generation. (vi) It will be a moral, not a
political, victory. The world powers are not to be
overthrown by earthly or supernatural weapons. (vii)
It marks the division between the past age and the age
to come. It ushers in a universe purged of evil.

To such beliefs politics can have no meaning. All through
history men have attempted to prove that Christianity stood
for Feudalism, Absolute Monarchy, Democracy, and what
not, and the political activities of the Church remain
obscure until we see them as those of an organised and
therefore political society professing an a-political faith.

Christianity, then, like most religions, is one which accepts
the environment as given and concerns itself with controlling man's behaviour towards it.

What our desires are. Since the cause and sustainer of the
universe is God, who is good : our real desire is to be at one
with Him. When human the relationship between ourselves
and Him is one of father to son. Ultimately that is the purpose of our actions.

What we ought to desire. In practice we desire all sorts of
other things. Some of these may be explained as being
modes of desiring God—immature stages in development,
good in so far as they lead us to God. Others are evil—evil
being anything that is self-centred. To them must be attributed the overt symptoms of suffering that we experience. Their existence in us is to be explained by the
Fall—an inherited defect in our nature, which, since God
is good, must be attributed to a volitional act of rebellion

at some period of human development. Further, there is in the universe an evil principle—Satan—hostile to good—but finally inevitably to be vanquished.

1639822

II. THE MEANS OF REALISATION

The teaching of Jesus is unique in that it is absolutely non-moralistic. It contains little dogmatic teaching about the nature of evil, but, as regards the methods of overcoming it, He is very definite. His repeated attacks on the scribes and Pharisees, not as individuals, but as a class (except your righteousness exceed the righteousness of the scribes and Pharisees, ye shall in no wise enter the Kingdom of Heaven), His verdict on John the Baptist (nevertheless · I say unto you, the least in the Kingdom of God is greater than he), and the sayings about resisting evil, and those who take the sword, condemn as useless—and, more than that, as provoking those very evils it is designed to cure—the whole intellectual system of moral imperatives which had governed human life up to this time and has continued to govern it. The two commandments of loving God and thy neighbour imply that the good life is a product, and only a product, of an attitude of complete love and faith toward both. On repeated occasions He indicated that the term neighbour admits of no distinction or qualification whatever. Every individual is of equal value.

" If a man love not his brothers whom he hath seen, how shall he love God whom he hath not seen ? "

" Not everyone that saith unto Me, ' Lord, Lord,' shall enter into the Kingdom of Heaven ; but he that doeth the will of My Father which is in Heaven."

" Inasmuch as ye did it unto the least of these My brethren, ye did it unto Me."

" Every good tree bringeth forth good fruit, but a corrupt tree bringeth forth a corrupt fruit."

Christianity is not a quietist religion—it does not in fact

really take the environment as given and static, but states that a change of heart can, and must, bring about a change in the environment. The test of the former, indeed, is the latter. Behaviour—and behaviour is always material action —is the only criterion. Whatever creed or social code men profess, if the results are evil, either the creed or code, or men's interpretation of it, is condemned. Faith and works —which last cannot possibly be construed to mean " works " in the district-visitor sense—are not independent. A faith stands or falls by its results.

" Except ye be born again, ye cannot enter into the Kingdom of Heaven."

" Be ye perfect—even as your Father in Heaven is perfect."

Christianity is a twice-born catastrophic religion. Jesus teaches that a real conversion is required, not a slow amelioration. Further, that the good life is possible here and now. The call to enter the Kingdom is an immediate one, not a reference to something which may take place after death. A theology which stresses an absolute gulf between God and man, and the *inevitable* corruption of the world is not really consonant with his teaching.

PSYCHOLOGY

Psychology is principally an investigation into the nature of evil. Its essential problem is to discern what it is that prevents people having the good will. It holds :

(1) The driving force in living things is a *libido* which is unconscious and creative—Dante's " Amor Naturale " which is always without error. Beyond that psychology does not go—that is to say, it is a naturalistic theory which refuses to raise the question of the Unmoved Mover, which it would say is not a real question at all. " No intelligent question can be framed concerning causality unless there exist two co-isolates of a larger neutral isolate.

The question, " What is the cause of the changing universe ? accepts the existence of a co-isolate of the universe " (Professor Levy). When we ask the question, " Who made the world ? " we are really asking, " Why isn't it made as we should like it ? "

It does not conceive of this *libido* apart from matter or having a personality other than that it acquires in individual consciousness. The psychologist's unconscious could only be equated with a God of Blake's kind " which only acts and is in existing beings and men."

(2) The development of self-consciousness in man marked a break with the rest of the organic world. Henceforward the conscious image or idea could interfere and govern[1] the unconscious impulse which had hitherto governed it. What we call evil is a consequence of this. Man developed a personal unconscious. As D. H. Lawrence wrote, in *Psycho-Analysis and the Unconscious*, Adam and Eve fell, not because they had sex or even because they committed the sexual act, but because they became aware of their sex and of the possibility of the act. When sex became to them a mental object—that is, when they discovered that they could deliberately enter upon and enjoy and even provoke sexual activity in themselves—then they were cursed and cast out of Eden. Then man became self-responsible ; he entered on his own career. When the analyst discovers the incest motive in the unconscious, surely he is only discovering a term of humanity's repressed *idea* of sex. It is not even suppressed sex-consciousness, but *repressed*—that is, it is nothing pristine and anterior to mentality. It is in itself the mind's ulterior motive—that is, the incest motive is propagated in the pristine unconscious by the mind itself, and in its origin is not a pristine impulse but a logical extension of the existent idea of sex and love. Or more succinctly : "Man is immoral because he has got a mind and can't get used to the fact." Such a theory differs sharply from

[1] See *The Science of Character*, by Klages: Allen & Unwin.

the nineteenth-century evolutionary doctrine of man moving

> *Upward, working out the beast,*
> *And let the ape and tiger die.*

On the contrary it suggests that most of what we call evil is not primitive at all. The " cave man "—and recent anthropology confirms this—is a product of a relatively high civilisation. The Garden of Eden has more historical justification than is usually believed.

Again, it is opposed to Rousseau in that it regards evil as being due to more than immediate environmental conditions, and differs from the theological doctrine, at least in its Augustinian form, in that it does not make the Fall the result of a conscious moral choice, but regards it as inevitable. It denies original guilt.

(3) What we call evil is something that was once good but has been outgrown. Ignorance begets the moralistic censor as the only means of control. Impulses which are denied expression remain undeveloped in the personal unconscious. From this it follows that the impulse behind all acts which we term evil is good. Psychology will have nothing to do with dualistic theories of Satan or the higher and lower self.

(4) What can be loved can be cured. The two chief barriers are ignorance and fear. Ignorance must be overcome by confession—i.e. drawing attention to unnoticed parts of the field of experience ; fear by the exercise of *caritas* or *eros paidogogos.*

Psychology, like Christianity, is pacifist, with a pacifism that enjoins abstention not only from physical violence, but also from all kinds of dogmatic generalisation and propaganda—from spiritual coercion. The only method of teaching it recognises is parabolic. You cannot convince anyone of anything until they have reached the stage in development when they can relate it to their personal experience—i.e. until they can convince themselves.

You must never tell people what to do—only tell them particular stories of particular people with whom they may voluntarily identify themselves, and from which they voluntarily draw conclusions. A dogmatic intellectual expression of a truth can be accepted consciously by those who have not related it to their experience, but this always results either in their holding it in a simplified view, which, when it is met by facts they had not envisaged, is rejected (the parable of the man who built on sand), or its meaning is twisted to suit the personal unconscious (Satan in the Temptation). People are not cured by reading psychological textbooks. The mistake of liberalism was imagining that free discussion was all that was needed to let truth triumph, whereas, unless people have substantially the same experience, logical controversy is nothing more than systemised misunderstanding.[1] The task of revealing the hidden field of experience, of understanding and curing by love, is a very slow, but ultimately the only satisfactory, one. " The chief sin," wrote Kafka, in one of his aphorisms, " is impatience. Through impatience man lost Eden, and it is impatience that prevents him from regaining it." People take to violence because they haven't the strength and nerve to be absorbent.

(5) Psychology is fundamentally a rationalist movement. It does not say, as some, like Lawrence, have been inclined to say, " Trust your instincts blindly." Just because it believes that the exercise of the reason is the only way through, its first task is to show how little the reason is able to effect directly. Nor does it deny the possibility of free will, except in a sense which is also true of Christian theology. Just as the theologian says that every man is fallen and in bondage to Satan, so the psychologist says that everyone is neurotic, at the mercy therefore of his repressed impulses, and unable to escape from his image. At the same time his aim is to release his

[1] See *Mencius on the Mind*, by I. A. Richards.

patient through increased self-knowledge, so that he may really exercise his reason and make a genuine choice. The ideally " cured " patient would be one in whom the unconscious and the conscious were at one, and who would obey his impulses—which is only deterministic in the sense of " in his will is our peace." No more than Communism rejects Capitalism does psychology reject self-consciousness and reason. Both theories believe in the law of the negation of the negation, and that attempts to put the clock back, either in economic or psychical life, are reactionary and disastrous.

(6) Lastly, psychology does not wish, as both it and Communism have been accused of wishing, to make everyone the same. It has no conception of normality. Like both Communism and Christianity, it believes in the equal value of every individual—i.e. potential value. It does not claim to turn all the geese into swans. It aims at making each discover for himself his unique treasure. What you lose on the swings you gain on the roundabouts, and, further, you can *only* gain on the roundabouts if you lose on the swings.

THE CHURCH

As long as Christianity remained the religion of small " converted " groups, expecting an imminent second coming, in an empire to which it was conscientiously bound to refuse allegiance, it could preserve its enthusiastic, non-economic, anarchic character. But as it grew in numbers and importance, as it became the recognised State religion, as whole countries became converted *en bloc*— sometimes, as in Norway, extremely forcibly—this became impossible. Augustine's *communio sanctorum*, whose minds and lives were directed towards God instead of self, could no longer be identified with the baptised, or even with the Church. Dante was not unorthodox in placing a pope in Hell. It became organised, wealthy, and powerful, and no

society which is these, however unworldly its final ends,
can be anything but worldly in its immediate ends (which,
as the hope of an immediate Parousia faded, became more
important) ; it will favour those forces and persons who
favour its organisation, wealth, and power, and oppose
those which oppose it, without considering too closely their
individual moral value. However much it seeks to define in
theory what belongs to God and what to Cæsar, in practice
it is obliged not only to make generous terms with Cæsar,[1]
but itself to make Cæsar's claims. Offering a socially
honourable career, it offers worldly inducement. And, as
the standard religion, it ceases to demand conversion as
a condition of membership. Men are Christian, not necessarily because of a revelation, but because their parents
were. As Professor Powicke says, " What we call abuses or
superstition in the medieval Church, were part of the price
paid for, not obstacles to, its universality. They were due to
the attempt of pagans to appropriate a mystery. If the
people paid, so did the Church. We distort the facts if we
try to separate clergy and laity too sharply, for paganism
was common to both. By paganism, I mean a state of
acquiescence, a merely professional activity unaccompanied
by sustained religious experience or inward discipline. It
is not a state of vacancy and scepticism. It is confined to
no class of persons, and is not hostile to, though it is easily
wearied by, religious observance. It accepts what is offered
without any sense of responsibility, and easily recovers from
twinges of conscience. At the same time it is full of curiosity,
and is easily moved by what is now called the group-mind.
It is sensitive to the activities of the crowd, is often emotional, and can be raised to those moods of passion, superstition, and love of persecution into which religion, on its
side, can degenerate. A medieval remained a Christian because he was born a Christian and most medieval Christians
were probably men of this kind. In the eleventh century
Cardinal Peter Damiani pointed out, in his lurid way, that
it was no use to try to keep the clergy apart from the laity

[1] e.g. the modification of the strict theological condemnation of usury.

unless strict evangelical poverty were insisted upon for all clergy alike. But Damiani and all the preachers of evangelical poverty who came after him were entangled on the horns of a dilemma. If it is the function of the Church to drive out sin, it must separate itself from sin ; if the Church separates itself from sin it becomes a ' clique.' " (*Legacy of the Middle Ages.*)

The task of the Church became to act for the mass of more or less pagan and ignorant people as a spiritual pacifier ; to protect them from their terrors, and to provide the opportunities for those who wished to live a genuinely Christian life, to do so.

Hence the problem of dogma and the liberty of the private conscience. Divergent theoretical views, whether religious or political, result in divergent actions. What at first seems to be a merely academic difference of opinion may finally land the disputants on opposite sides of the barricade. " The records of the Holy Inquisition are full of histories which we dare not give to the world, because they are beyond the belief of honest men and innocent women ; yet they all began with saintly simpletons. Mark what I say : the woman who quarrels with her clothes and puts on the dress of a man, is like the man who throws off his fur gown and dresses like John the Baptist ; they are followed, as surely as the night follows the day, by bands of wild women and men, who refuse to wear any clothes at all." (*St. Joan.*)

So the Catholic. The Protestant can retort, and with equal truth, that orthodoxy does not necessarily result in goodness, that many of the orthodox are more wicked than those whom they persecute. In fact, such an orthodoxy is extremely rare ; the intellectual acceptance of an idea, without its experience, is no guarantee of its effectiveness. There is little doubt, for example, that, whatever the correct theological attitude, a great many people regard Heaven as a good time, and a reward for not having a good time in this world (i.e. you mustn't enjoy yourself in this world ; i.e. the working classes should congratulate themselves) ; and infer from the doctrine of the Virgin Birth that sexual intercourse is wicked.

III. THE POLITICAL MIND

No politician can really be a liberal in practice, for no society can be liberal unless membership is voluntary ; we become members of a State by birth, and we do not choose to be born. Similarly the governor cannot choose the governed ; he must accept them all—the just and the unjust, the rich and the poor, the selfless and the self-seeking— and the bias of his own mind, for he himself is within the State.

Many political theories are vitiated, either :

(1) By confusing what the State is with what it ought to be. Few people, for example, consciously desire Dante's *vita felice*, the actualising of the potential intellect, or, with Aristotle, to live virtuously. The majority want security, to be free from material and psychological anxiety, to be liked, and to feel of some importance.

(2) By assuming that there is in fact a community of will. The social contract is a grotesque simplification. In animal herds, or Dr. Rivers' boat crew, the unconscious formation of a group pattern, a united will, may be an adequate description of what happens, but in any more conscious and specialised community the social order is accepted ;

    (*a*) Because it is customary ;

    (*b*) Because one is fortunately placed ;

    (*c*) Because, though unfortunately placed, one lacks the knowledge and power to change it.

There is no such thing as a community of will, nor has the will of the majority any effectiveness apart from the material power it is able to wield. A successful change depends on the support of the armed forces.

(3) By using false analogies, e.g. the biological theory of the State (the story of the belly and the members), a theory

which could only be invented by a cell in the central nervous system. Every unit in the State is a conscious one and capable of different functions. Since the governor has always immediate ends to consider, and since the unity of will is a fiction, he cannot afford to wait until this unity is voluntarily reached—i.e. he must coerce either physically, or by the propagandist organisation of public opinion. He may believe, and most of the experimental evidence in the treatment of individuals, either in education, medicine,[1] or the training of animals, will confirm this belief, that violence is inefficient ; but he will point to history to refute the view that violence has never accomplished anything, and he knows that he is compelled to use it, to bring about that organisation of society which can make a real unity of will possible.

Ruling a mass, and knowing that you cannot convert a mass as a mass, because they are individually at different stages and in different positions, he must accept the actual rather than the potential character of the governed, and attempt to modify them by modifying those things which are alone in his power to modify—material conditions and social structure. His view of morality must be one of social utility. For him, that is immoral, and that only, which causes a conflict of will—e.g. theft or ownership relations are rightly a matter of legal regulation, but sexual behaviour, which is by mutual consent, is not. The authoritative exercise of what we usually call moral judgment is only justifiable in a society where membership is entirely voluntary.

IV. PSYCHOLOGY AND RELIGION

Psychology does not deny the fact of religious experience, the usefulness of religious theory, in the past, to assist men to live well. In offering an explanation of the idea of God

[1] *See* a very interesting essay on Constipation, in Dr. Groddeck's *Exploring the Unconscious*, on the evils of forcible purgative treatment.

as a projection of parental images, or as what is left over of the sense of group identity after the individual has taken his lion's share, or of the mystical experience as an eruption from the subconscious, and in condemning the religious explanation as one which the world has outgrown, it asks to be tested by results. It believes that it has a more scientific theory—i.e. one which will work better—and claims that, given a free hand, and time, more people will lead better lives than they would with the help of religion. The Christian will retort that the findings of psychology do not necessarily invalidate a belief in God—that, for example, there is no reason why the parental relation should not be a symbol of the divine relation, instead of vice versa, and can point to a weak spot in psychology, the problem of transference. In order to free the patient from himself, the psychologist must make his claims in the name of something greater. What is it to be ?

" Every confession, within whatever framework it may be made, passes through two phases of a curative effect. First : that one opens oneself to another person, breaks through those walls of loneliness wherein all guilt, whether in the sense of sacrilege or sin, whether it was due to rebellion, oversight, error, weakness, the lust of destruction, or whatever other incitement, at first imprisons every upright man. Confession, simply as openly answering for oneself, and one's conduct, puts an end to the danger of all self-deception by taking this first step towards a fellow man, and sets foot on the slender ladder of trust in humanity by choosing another as humanity's representative. This step of voluntary surrender, this renunciation of cowardly cunning, and of lying on behalf of one's imposing public façade, as does the man of the world, is like a deep expiration of air. Secondly : into the lungs thus freed there follows, with the second step, a deep inspiration ; the father confessor gives what he has to give. If the answer of the private person with difficulty conceals his lower thoughts of tricks and power policy even to active intrigue, so that the sensitive person is stricken with horror, like the bird before the snake—then surely we must introduce poison-gas into the parable. If the private person answers with the fascination of his own ripe and broad humanity, so that the lonely one, suddenly freed, feels, whether he represses it or shows it : ' Thou, my redeemer ! '—then we must speak of intoxicating gas. But when one who knows, answers so that he, with all his private humanity, is as a speaking-tube for something which is not his, but in whose service he is, and in whose name he acts—only then can we say that he pours forth the free strong breath of life, which so fills the lungs of the other, that at one stroke the poison-air is overcome." (Prinzhorn—*Psychotherapy*.)

V. COMMUNISM AND PSYCHOLOGY

Psychology and Communism have certain points in common :

(1) They are both concerned with unmasking hidden conflicts.

(2) Both regard these conflicts as inevitable stages which must be made to negate themselves.

(3) Both regard thought and knowledge not as something spontaneous and self-sufficient, but as purposive and determined by the conflict between instinctive needs and a limited environment. Communism stresses hunger and the larger social mass affected by it ; psychology, love and the small family unit. (Biologically nutrition is anterior to reproduction, so that the Communist approach would seem from this angle the more basic one.) E.g. the psychologist explains the clinging child by the doting mother. Communism explains the doting mother by the social conditions which drive her to be doting.

A discovery, like that of Malinowski, that the typical

Œdipus dream of murdering the father and committing incest with the mother, occurs only in patriarchal communities, while in matriarchal communities it is one of murdering the mother's brother and committing incest with the sister, shows the importance of social structure in influencing character formation.

(4) Both desire and believe in the possibility of freedom of action and choice, which can only be obtained by unmasking and making conscious the hidden conflict.

The hostility of Communism to psychology is that it accuses the latter of failing to draw correct conclusions from its data. Finding the neurotic a product of society, it attempts to adjust him to that society, i.e. it ignores the fact that the neurotic has a real grievance. It should say to him, " Your phantasies are just, but powerless, and a distorted version of something which, if you choose to act, you can alter." The failure to say this has reduced psychology to a quack religion for the idle rich.

VI. COMMUNISM AND RELIGION

The hostility of Communism to religion has two sides :

(1) The religious approach, it says, is the method of those who see no hope of understanding and altering the environment. As long as in one human lifetime no material progress is visible, man is bound to rely upon individual moral progress. The more power he obtains over material objects, the more he finds he is able to make changes which seemed previously to depend solely on moral attitudes—e.g. the influence of the ductless glands on character.

(2) When a religious body becomes an organised Church it becomes a political movement, and the historical evidence can point to no occasion on which the Church has been able to avert either war or economic changes, however contrary to their theories. On the contrary, it has always

made the maintenance of its official position its criterion of conduct, accepted the political *status quo*, shut its eyes to the violence and mad character of its supporters, persistently lent its strength to crush proletarian movements, and whilst preaching the necessity for settlement by agreement, whenever the violent crisis has occurred, has stood by the forces of reaction. A tree must be judged by its fruits.

The contrary objections of the Church to Communism are :

(1) That, without the Christian transcendental beliefs, the Communist will fail to secure the results, in so far as they are good, which he intends. Further, that there is a wretchedness in man's condition without God, that is independent of material conditions.

(2) The Communist use of violence is indefensible.

(3) He wishes to destroy the individual and make a slave State.

(4) That private property is necessary to develop human personality and responsibility.

(5) That he wishes to destroy the family.

(2) *The use of violence.* Unless the Christian denies the value of any Government whatsoever, he must admit, as Schweitzer did when destroying trypanosomes, the necessity for violence, and judge the means by its end. He cannot deny, if he is honest, the reality of the class conflict, and, unless he can offer a better method of surpassing it (supposing that he is not stupid enough to be taken in by the fiction of the corporative State, which is the word and not the thing) than the Communists, he must accept it.

(3) *The individual.* A theory which culminates in the words, " To each according to his needs, from each according to his powers," cannot be accused of denying the individual in intention. In fact Communism is the only political theory that really holds the Christian position of the absolute equality in value of every individual, and the

evil of all State restraint. It is hardly necessary to add that this doctrine of equality does not assert that everyone has the same talents—i.e. that the individual has no uniqueness and is interchangeable with another—nor does it necessarily imply absolute equality of social reward. Communism looks on coercion, the dictatorship of the proletariat, neither as the redemption which it is to the Fascist, nor as an inevitable and perpetual punishment of original sin, but solely as a transitory means to an end.

(4) *Property* has been the subject of subtle and obscure study, particularly by French Catholic writers. Their arguments would be more convincing if they condemned monastic orders, in which the individual's sense of responsibility is developed by the administration of community property. Further, Communism has never suggested that no one should have private belongings ; it only condemns that possession which gives its owner power over the personality of others.

(5) *The family.* Communism has been subjected to the most fantastic attacks, by ignorant and interested persons, on this score. It has no quarrel whatever with the family, as such—only with the narrowing of loyalties to a single one. In depriving the family of economic power, it leaves it free to be what it should be—an emotional bond—instead of what, as psychologists or common-sense observation can testify, it, at present, so often is—a strangling prison, whose walls are not love, but money.

VII. THE CHRISTIAN DILEMMA

In that the Christian is a member of society he must have an attitude towards political movements, and increasingly so as he discovers that many things which he recognised as evil, but believed were unchangeable, the consequences of sin, to be endured, can be changed. The behaviour and utterances of indiscreet Fascists should be enough to disillusion him of that solution, which would otherwise, by its bogus idealist appeal, and its attempt to return to pre-industrial conditions, be a temptation to a religion founded on a pre-industrial event. Social Democracy claims to achieve the same end as the Communist, by non-violent means and with religious tolerance ; it is questionable, however, whether its behaviour in Europe, its pretence that it uses no violence, or its assumption that the possessing classes, however ready to make concessions, will ever voluntarily abdicate, can much longer convince.

At the same time it would be foolish to gloss over the antagonism of Communism to religion, or to suppose that, if Communism were to triumph in England, the Church would not be persecuted. The question for the Christian, however, is not whether Communism is hostile to Christianity, but whether Christianity is less hostile to Communism than to any other political movement—for no political movement is Christian. If it is, then this very persecution is his chance of proving, if he can, that religion is not the opium of the people, not something that has long been outgrown, but a vital truth. Deprived of all economic and social support, with no axe to grind, he can make no illegitimate appeal. The Christian will have to see if what occurred in the first century can occur again in the twentieth. A truth is not tested until, oppressed and illegal, it still shows irresistible signs of growth.

II

JESUS

by Conrad Noel

Vicar of Thaxted, Essex

I. THE WORLD PLAN OF JESUS

WHEN CHRISTIAN PREACHERS tell us that the world
can be saved only by each one of us accepting Jesus as our
personal Saviour, we may justly ask, By which of the many
Christs who are presented to us as the " authentic " Jesus ?
Who in reality is He ? For what does He stand in the world
of our day ? Was He the " final revelation of God " ? He
Himself assumed that after His resurrection He would send
forth His Spirit among men to lead them into further truth,
and promised His disciples : " Greater works than these
shall ye do." It may be, then, that in His " coming again,"
whether in visible and tangible form, or expressed in human
terms when men shall have created the new world, there
may be a further revelation of God.

This question is, anyway, not urgent. In His incarnate
manifestation in Galilee, He was so far ahead, not only of
His own age, but of ours also, that it will take mankind a
good many centuries to catch up with Him. This sketch
of His life and personality and principles will at least
disclose my own reason for believing in His unique importance.

The significance of Jesus is not always fully appreciated.
Someone triumphantly proves that some thought which
occurs to the mind of Jesus Christ is to be found also in
Jewish philosophy, or in a pagan saying. It is conceivable

that every single saying of His can be so paralleled. But the mark of originality is not to think, say, or do something entirely new and alien ; it is to have the power of distilling a food from a poison ; of taking in from the world around one all that is vital, and of rejecting the rest as refuse ; and, finally, of giving out to the world what has been re-created in such a way that people will exclaim, " Never man spake as this man." This is the originality of genius. This is the originality we claim for the Christ.

There is in His life and in His death a sense of compelling truth. This would not have been so, as Bernard Shaw would have it, if He had died comfortably in His bed.[1] To an account of His death, and its tremendous significance, I shall return. I am concerned now with points which suggest His gigantic personality. There have been men down the ages who have had a real love of mankind in the large, and a genius for world statesmanship ; others who have had an intense and burning affection for the individual, and who have devoted themselves to the service of individual cases of hardship and misery. No man has ever, to the same extent as did the Christ, combined genius for world reconstruction with intimate care for the individual. The gospel reveals that Jesus was working against time. There was something like a three-year plan—some say a two- or even a one-year plan—for the propaganda of world redemption. But what is rare and extraordinary is the way in which He would risk the success of His world statesmanship by deliberately stepping out of His plan to give succour bodily, mental, spiritual, to some obscure person ; losing time, expending much energy, as if for the moment the whole world contained but one solitary and helpless soul. It is an amazing thing for a good general to surrender his time-table in the midst of a battle. A Syrophœnician woman[2] calls on Him for help. He is, at the time, in extreme need of rest after a march into exile of twenty miles or more, after a bitter conflict with enemies who were bent on His destruction ; and the publicity which would attend on

[1] Preface to *Androcles and the Lion*.   [2] Mark vii. 24 ff.

healing her daughter would destroy the privacy and rest in which he could re-think His programme. Thwarted by His Galilean enemies, He hesitates, and doubts whether such an expenditure of energy is right—for a foreigner, and at this particular crisis. But the faith of the woman, and the desperate need of her daughter, compel Him to become absorbed in this individual and her misery. At Jericho, on the final march to Jerusalem,[1] Jesus, in spite of the protests of His disciples, held up the progress of Himself and His followers to attend the cry of the blind beggar, Bartimæus, and to give him his sight. In Jerusalem, in immediate danger of arrest and death, in the last and fiercest conflict with the ruling classes, Jesus, hurrying from the city to a place of security for the night, stops, and asks His disciples to notice the act of a widow putting a farthing into the alms chest[2] : the world seems to hold for Him that poor woman and her amazing generosity alone. Nothing else for the moment matters. She has put in more than they all—more than all the plutocrats with their big and much advertised subscriptions. He sees in that act a sign and promise of the final victory of the world plan.

For the Christ, world statesmanship and individual need do not stand in contrast : they are one and the same thing. It is for individuals such as these—the poor, the " unimportant," the people who " don't count "—that world reconstruction on the basis of divine justice is worth while. It is of individuals such as these that the new world shall be built. This is the rock on which He will build His community.

Only when these contrasts and contradictions, these supreme paradoxes in His personality, are understood, can we judge whether the claims glibly made from the pulpit can be substantiated ; whether the pulpit phrase, " Jesus only," means much ; whether He is the supreme master mind of His own time, perhaps of all time.

Christ realised, both in His principles and in His actions,

[1] Luke xviii. 35 ff.
[2] Luke xxi. 1.

the infinite value of each personality, while insisting that individual personality could come into its own only in community, never apart from the realisation of the commonwealth of God here on earth. Mankind, for Him, was a living organism, pervaded by God. As St. Paul put it, " We, the many, are one body."

Now for the main question. What was this commonwealth, this Kingdom of God ? Undoubtedly the Kingdom was the core of His preaching : " Seek ye first the Kingdom of God and His justice " ; " Thy Kingdom come, Thy will be done *on earth* as in heaven." It is the treasure hid in a field for which the seeker is ready to give all that he has.

II. THE TEMPTATIONS

Jesus came into Galilee preaching the Kingdom of God : it was thus that He opened His work.

For thirty years He had lived an obscure life. After Joseph's death, He had taken over the business at Nazareth, making household furniture, ploughs, and various implements for the village and countryside. There must have been much thinking and much talk in the village shop ; news from the caravans along the high roads near by, about the political condition of the country, about the empire, about the hard times, about exploitation by native rulers, and by the Roman (Herodian) tax-gatherers. Abortive risings, and the doings of bandit chieftains, would have been hotly discussed. Gradually there formed in Christ's mind the conviction of the rôle He was destined to play in His nation's history.

But the hour had not yet struck, and still He waited. Suddenly there came to that workshop news of the appearance of John the Baptist in the desert places, in the district near the crowded villages on the hills that formed an embankment to the Jordan. People were flocking from all points to listen, for John answered the popular Messianic prophecies, and fanned the enthusiasm of the folk for a new

order of things to a blaze. He was not the Christ—he was
His necessary herald, an Elijah announcing His approach.

No other leader or group in Palestine had struck that
essential note : it was a call to repentance both individual
and national, an attack upon false patriotism ; and an
appeal to the nation to return to its historic rôle, and to
become again a light to lighten the nations of the world.
" Bring forth fruits springing from a real and drastic
change of mind and will ; lay the axe to the roots of the
evil ; give generously, don't pillage the poor." It was with
simple everyday maxims such as these that John prepared
the way for the Messiah.

Jesus at once perceived that this voice from the wilderness
was indeed destined to prepare the way for the Messiah,
that it was the authentic voice of God. He left the carpenter's bench, identified Himself with John's mission,
and underwent baptism at his hands : thus did He fulfil
all justice—by identifying Himself with a messenger of social
justice in whom He saw the last and greatest of the prophets.

He did not begin His work at once ; He retired to a
lonely spot to think out the principles and the method of the
Kingdom of God, whose Messiah He knew Himself to be.
For forty days and forty nights He fasted, absorbed in these
problems, alone with God.

The keynote of His ministry is struck in the Gospel story
of the Temptations.[1]

According to popular tradition, the Messiah was to be
the bringer of material prosperity, of food in abundance,
the victorious conqueror of foreign powers and the ruler of
an Israel triumphant over the nations—Lord of the world.
These were precisely the temptations which Satan offered
to Christ. After His long fast, He was hungry ; and His
hunger brought home to Him the hunger of His people.
What could be more natural than that He should use His
gigantic powers in giving them bread, in creating fields of
waving corn in barren places, either by a miracle or by
scientific means ? He rejected the temptation as Satanic ;

[1] The best record is given in Matthew.

for men do not live by bread alone, but by every word that proceedeth out of the mouth of God. The words of God had come through Moses and the prophets, who had commanded men to practise justice and generosity, the love of God and of the neighbour. First convert the people to the Divine Justice. As fruits of conversion, let them regain their liberties and till their lands to bring forth abundantly. Besides, what practical statesman would put the food supply in the forefront of his programme when the Romans and their native satellites were in possession, and would drain off by exploitation or by commandeering the new supplies all that had been gained by this extra fruitfulness in Palestine ? So the next suggestion is for the Messiah to put Himself at the head of any available forces, however small, and to hurl Himself against the Roman imperial invaders, and to drive them from the soil. Had not God promised to come to the aid of so valiant an endeavour, and had He not actually done so almost within living memory, at the time of the Maccabean victories ?

Put yourself, runs this next temptation, at the pinnacle of the Temple, the Temple party, the Zealots, and fling yourself and your forces down against the might of the Roman army, courting disaster and annihilation, for what appears to be disaster is bound to be turned by God, according to His covenant with Israel, into triumph. And the answer is : " Thou shalt not bargain with the Lord thy God." He has really made no such promise, for the conditions of the promise on the side of Israel have not been kept. From the righteous laws of Moses and the social tradition of the prophets, the Jews had become apostate. God would therefore abandon them to their just fate.

Well, then, if this be so, there remains one other chance. Instead of trying to turn back and convert Israel to its ancient traditions, why not consider them as hopeless and turn to that other way ? He climbed to the mountain top, and there was shown to Him, as He saw the kingdoms subdued by the might of Rome, a picture of all the kingdoms of the world and the glory of them. All these could

be His—at a price. Other men were aiming at imperial
power with considerable chance of success. These other
aspirants, cunning and powerful, were no match for Jesus,
with His enormous powers and His great mind. His technique would far surpass theirs. The thing could have been
brought off ; but what was the price ? " If thou wilt fall
down and worship me." Accept for a while the cunning
crafty ways of the empire builders, turn a blind eye for a
while to the people's miseries, fall down into the mire of
bribery, corruption, compromise. Make friends with the
oppressors of mankind, or seem to be their ally. Once you
reach the summit, what good you can do ! All will be within your power, and, instead of using it for your own personal
ends, you can become a benevolent despot, a sort of Fascist
dictator, dictator over no narrow Jewish nation, but over
a world empire. And the answer came swiftly, " Thou shalt
worship the Lord thy God, and Him only shalt thou serve."

Once these suggestions had been clearly seen to be
Satanic and swept aside, Christ was able to begin His work
of social redemption. He would attempt to build up His
own nation, recalling them to repentance and to their
original mission as light-bearers to the nations, making
them the spear-head of God's own International, which
alone can sweep the empires of this world away.

III. THE SOCIAL GOSPEL OF THE
OLD TESTAMENT

The Convocation of Canterbury published a statement,
" The Moral Witness of the Church on Economic
Subjects." It insisted that we cannot discover the meaning
of Christ's " Kingdom of Heaven " without first considering
the social and economic teachings of the Law and the
prophets to which He Himself was perpetually referring
His hearers. " Christianity inherited from the Old Testament certain social principles, in part embodied in the Law
and in part enforced by the prophets and moralists. 'The

Lord will enter into judgment with the elders of His people and the princes thereof ; it is ye that have eaten up the vineyard ; and the spoil of the poor is in your houses ; What mean ye that ye crush My people and grind the faces of the poor?' . . . The tendency of the legislation was to raise the status of the Israelite slave to that of the hired workman who was to be treated as a brother. We find a prohibition of usury between Israelite and Israelite, and provision is taken against the permanent alienation of the land ; various enactments protect labour . . . the general well-being is a supreme consideration restricting the selfish acquisition of wealth. Manual labour is held in honour, it is the necessary basis of all society. . . . Christianity did not take over the formal legislation of the Old Testament, but it did inherit its moral principles which Jesus Christ deepened and universalised."

Dr. Gore, when Bishop of Oxford, wrote as follows : " Our Lord assumed all the Old Testament laid down. Do you see the meaning of that ? The Law and the prophets had been struggling and striving for the establishment of a great social system on a great moral basis. The Old Testament is full of all sorts of social and moral doctrine, social and individual righteousness. The Law is full of that. The prophets are full of it. Now do you see that every word our Lord said, He said to people who had got all that behind them . . . He could assume it all. . . . It is the point at which He starts. Till you have got there, you have not begun."

Moses has, with some justice, been described as the successful leader of a brickmakers' strike. And his mighty opposition to a mighty empire began with the killing of a taskmaster who was found bullying an Israelite. Our Lord is continually referring His hearers to the laws of Moses. By these laws the Pharisees meant one thing, our Lord another. They meant the washing of pots and pans ; He meant mercy and justice. He came, not to destroy Moses and the prophets, but to fulfil them.

What, then, did He mean by " the weightier matters of the law ? " There was the land question. In the Old

Testament, the ultimate landlord was God, who had given the earth to the children of men. This was no barren formula, for the land was in fact the common property of the various tribes, distributed in holdings among their families. Every seventh year, the land was to lie fallow, and its fruits to be common property. Every fiftieth year was a year of Jubilee (the " Acceptable Year ") when any family which had been forced through poverty to sell their plot, would regain it ; prisoners were freed, debtors were forgiven, and the law against usury more strictly enforced. A family which had been forced to sell was not allowed to sell the freehold, but only the usufruct, at prices varying with the number of years still to run till Jubilee. These provisions were designed to secure in perpetuity the land to the workers, and guard against the rise of a landlord class.

Land laws, unless coupled with laws against interest (usury), are useless. And so we find equally stringent provisions against lending at interest, a practice which leads the worker directly into debt, and ultimately eviction. These economic laws were again and again disregarded by the ruling classes.

Christ says little about land, because most of His ministry was in Galilee, where the people were still in possession of their holdings. In the south, He attacks with vehemence the Pharisees who have evicted the defenceless poor and are " full of extortion and excess," while for a pretence they make long prayers. But in Galilee, He roundly denounces usury, urging His hearers to lend expecting nothing in return, and not as sinners who hope for as much again.[1] Modern writers have expended much ingenuity in an attempt to prove that Jesus could not have been alluding to the practice of lending at interest, since it would be practically unknown among the simple country folk whom he was addressing. But the argument is worthless : the richer type of Galilean peasant would lend to the poorer, and, as in Russia in modern days, would charge considerable interest, and become a *kulak*. Again, we are

[1] Luke vi. 34–5.

expressly told that among Christ's audience were strangers from north and south, among whom usury was common.

In the life of the world to come (to use a phrase of the Nicene Creed, which in Dr. Gore's comment is " the life of the good time coming "), all will produce in common and share in equity. " This world and the next " in the Gospels is not a contrast between this life and the life beyond the grave, but between this epoch of usury and exploitation and the age to come. This was the interpretation of the phrase by the early Church, and by the apostles of the later New Testament.

It is a tragedy that the passage in Isaiah about their sins being as scarlet[1] is chiefly familiar to our generation through its misuse, wrenched from its social context, by revivalists and hot-gospellers. The sins described in it as " scarlet " are the sins of avaricious " religious " people who squeeze the last drop of blood out of the land and labours of the workers. As they lift up sanctimonious hands in prayer to God, their "hands are full of blood." [2] These words of the prophet are a warning to-day, alike to the Sabbath-loving Protestant and the incense-loving Catholic. For God hates their sacrifices and their prayer-meetings, their sabbaths, their incense, and their solemn assemblies. God is " fed up " with " the multitude of the sacrifices. . . . Your solemn feasts My soul abhorreth."[3] The prophets denounce the ruling classes, " for the spoil of the poor is in your houses." [4] They "grind the faces of the poor."[5] They "build up Sion with blood." [6] The message of Amos and Micah, country prophets, is one with that of the urban aristocrat, Isaiah. Micah made an attack on the lawcourts —one law for the rich, another for the poor.[7] He thunders against the sins of the urban nobility, with their town houses and their country estates, as " unscrupulous bloodsuckers and despoilers of the people."[8] It is the same with Deutero-Isaiah, with Jeremiah, with Ezekiel, and with the prophets

---

[1] Isa. i. 18.   [2] Isa. i. 15.   [3] Isa. i.   [4] Isa. iii. 14.
    [5] Isa. iii. 15.   [6] Mic. iii. 10.   [7] Mic. iii. 9 ff.
            [8] Cornill's paraphrase.

of the Restoration. Nehemiah is "furious" with the nobility and the new rich : he holds a mass meeting against them, demanding that they should cease their merciless money-lending, their mortgaging of cottages, and lands, and their evicting of the poor on the non-payment of their usurious demands. They must restore to the workers their holdings, and cease from usury and oppression. Their words seem in this instance to have been effective : they had the Jubilee law on their side. Either the nobles were conscience-stricken, or they were terrified at the strength of the workers under such powerful leadership.[1]

We now see what our Lord meant when He told the Pharisees that they tithed mint and cummin, neglected mercy and justice, and utterly ignored " the weightier matters of the law." They, the appointed guardians of the Law, "strained at the gnat while they swallowed the camel."[2]

We have now seen what the Kingdom meant for Jesus in the Law and the prophets to which He is constantly alluding. We are now in a position to understand His actual teaching of this New World Order in His Galilean ministry.

IV. THE GOSPEL OF THE KINGDOM

On the arrest of John the Baptist, Jesus came into Galilee teaching the Kingdom of God. After making a few disciples, who were to become the nucleus of the inner band of twelve, during a preliminary tour of Galilee, He came to His own town, Nazareth, and on the sabbath day He was allowed to read the " lesson " in the synagogue. He chose a Messianic passage from Isaiah, and says in comment that this very day the scripture is being fulfilled in their midst.

---

[1] Here, only the briefest summary of the message of the Jewish prophets is possible, but readers who want to study it at length are referred to George Adam Smith's book on Isaiah, and his *Minor Prophets* ; to Professor Cornill's *Prophets of Israel*, Open Court Pub. Co., Chicago, 1907 ; or, better still, to the books of the prophets themselves.

[2] Matt. xxiii. 24.

What, then, was this scripture ? " Good tidings to the poor. Release to the captives. Recovering of sight to the blind. To set at liberty them that are bruised. To proclaim the Acceptable Year of the Lord."[1] They are astonished at His words of grace, but He hardly dares hope they will accept Him, for " a prophet hath no honour in his own country." And He proceeds to alienate them by allusions friendly to foreigners : how God of old had sent Elijah not to Israelites, but to a widow, a foreigner ; how Elisha had been sent not to his own countrymen, but to Naaman the Syrian. His suggestion that the Good Time Coming would be for foreigners and might be rejected by Israel, aroused the jingo instincts of the crowd : they made a rush for Him and would have killed Him.

The people of Nazareth were hostile to His message of the good world to come, but He seems to have had considerable success in Galilee generally, for " the common people heard Him gladly."[2] The ruling classes were for the most part hostile, and later whole cities of Galilee were among those who rejected His message—Chorasim and Bethsaida, for whom the lot of Sodom and Gomorrah will be more tolerable in the day of judgment.[3] In spite of this, it was the Galilean pilgrim crowds who supported Him in His last adventure in Jerusalem, and who made it well-nigh impossible for the authorities to arrest Him.

That He should have had this popularity with the common people is natural enough when we consider His teaching as recorded in St. Luke's Gospel, and, indeed, in the so-called " Sermon on the Mount " of Matthew. In the beatitudes of Matthew, however, the corresponding " woes " are cut out ; but here in Luke the contrasts are given in full. (It is possible that sayings in Luke are another version of those found in Matthew, or they may have been given on a later occasion. It does not very much matter.) I prefer Luke, and I will paraphrase his version thus : " Blessed are ye poor, for yours is the New World Order." (This is not really in contradiction to Matthew's

[1] Luke iv. 16 ff.   [2] Mark xii. 37.   [3] Luke x. 13 ff.

"Blessed are the spirited poor."[1] "Woe to you who are rich, for you have received your consolation. . . . Blessed are ye which hunger now, for ye shall be filled. Woe to you who are full now, for ye shall hunger." Compare this with the Magnificat, our Lady's prophetic song, " He hath put down the mighty from their seats and hath exalted them of low degree. He hath filled the hungry with good things : and the rich he hath sent empty away."

" Blessed are ye that weep now (lamenting the present disorders) for ye shall laugh. Woe unto you that deride now, for ye shall mourn and weep." Does not this read like a forceful prophecy of the lot of the workers after a successful revolution as contrasted with the *émigrés*, outcast and bitter, mourning and lamenting, irreconcilable ?

" Blessed are ye when men shall hate you, ostracise you, reproach you, and vilify you for the Son of Man's sake (i.e. for the sake of mankind and the Kingdom as preached by Christ). Rejoice and be exceeding glad, for even so did they to the prophets which were before you." We have seen what kind of men those prophets were, and why they had been vilified, exiled and killed.

" Blessed are they who hunger and thirst after justice, for they shall be filled."

There is one passage almost always misunderstood ; it runs : " Blessed are the meek, for they shall inherit the earth." The word " meek " has unfortunately changed its meaning and become associated with " gentle Jesuism." Aristotle uses the term " meek " as the equivalent of reasonable and generous. Du Bose explains it as meaning good in team work with others. It is people who will co-operate in team work, who are reasonable and generous, who will inherit the earth. Moses is described as " the meekest of men," and it was this same Moses who led a successful strike of brickmakers and slew the Egyptian

[1] Which seems to be the meaning of " poor in spirit." It must be remembered that he was addressing a spirited crowd of Galilean peasants and fishermen.

tyrant. It is, then, in this sense, that Jesus pronounces a blessing upon the meek.

Of the golden commandment, "Do unto others as you would that they should do unto you," so much has already been written that I need not comment upon it. It is the basic law of the New World Order of which Jesus says : "Seek ye first the Kingdom of God and His justice and all these things shall be added unto you." "These things," it will be seen in the context, refer not to blessings in the sky, but to material things such as food, clothing and shelter.

Amongst Christians who do not deny what they lamely call the "social implications of the Gospels," there often exists an assumption that Jesus Christ gave certain persons their immense wealth, or their more modest incomes, to use in His service and for the advancement of His Kingdom. It is asserted not only of individuals, but of countries, with their God-given "civilising mission" to "lesser breeds without the law" (most often, not so much of countries in themselves, but of countries swollen into empires). A delightful, if somewhat blasphemous, example of this may be seen in a recent prayer published by the authority of the officials of the Church of England. It runs as follows : "Almighty God, who rulest in the kingdom of men, and hast given to our sovereign Lord, King George, a great dominion in all parts of the earth . . ." When we consider how our Empire has been obtained—by fraud, trickery and violence—the unctuous assumption that God has bestowed it upon His chosen Englishmen is almost British-Israelite in its pharisaic naïveté.

Wealth, according to these people, must be used as a sacred trust in the service of God and the ministry of men : but no questions are to be asked as to how it has been come by. The sin of Dives, according to them, is that he was callous, and did not give enough of the leavings in largesse to the poor, or did not put forward with his wealth large schemes for founding university chairs or Rhodes scholarships. In that case, he would have been called "benefactor"—as Jesus said these imperialist millionaires

loved to be called. All this is what I call the heresy of
stewardship. Christ is not only concerned with how you
spend your wealth, but with how you get it.

The point of the parable of Dives and Lazarus is not
that poor men because of their poverty will automatically
go to Heaven, and that rich men because they happen to
be rich will go to Hell. Dives was one of those who " trusted
in riches," i.e. who enjoyed and supported the economic
system which made him rich. He was clothed in purple
and fine linen, and fared sumptuously every day : he
probably argued that it was good for trade. He was not so
unkind, or blind, as to drive Lazarus from his door ; he fed
him on the leavings. But it came to pass that the rich man
died and was buried : he found himself, to his astonishment
and indignation, in Hell, the place of torment. The beggar
died and was taken to Abraham's bosom. The Lazarus
class has always been at the service of Dives & Co., so it was
natural for Dives to ask if Lazarus might come to serve
him, at least to give him a cup of water to assuage his
thirst. Abraham replied that it was impossible, for " between
us and you there is a great gulf fixed." It is implied that
this gulf had been dug by the rich in this life, who had
separated themselves off from the poor. But the sting of the
story is in its tail. Dives fears that his brethren, unless they
are warned, may come to the same torment. May someone
be sent to warn them ? Abraham replies that it would be
useless : they already have Moses and the prophets ; let
them hear them. If they have not listened to them " neither
will they be persuaded though one rose from the dead."
Dives had, very likely, been something like a churchwarden
in his synagogue, and read the lessons sabbath by sabbath :
his brethren had probably also been deeply " religious "
men. If they had really listened to what had been read, to
such passages, for instance, as have been quoted from the
land and usury laws, and the warnings of the prophets,
they could never have become inordinately rich.

It is, then, not merely a question of the sacred stewardship of riches, but of how you get your riches, of whether

CR

riches had been wrung by land grabbing, mortgages, and usury from the poor.

That this is the real point of the parable is seen in the sequel, where the question of the status of the rich man comes up for consideration. How hardly shall they that have riches enter into the coming Kingdom of God. They did then, and still do, find it well nigh impossible to enter into the spirit and comradeship of that New World Order which does away with their privileges. They can find relief only in the remark that " it won't come in our day." They say that the common people's desire for it is the work of " those damned agitators," who ought to be strung up as a danger to the State. They accused the " agitator " who told this story of being one who " stirreth up the people from Galilee unto this place."[1] The best thing to do with a seditious fellow of this sort is to hang him. " Crucify Him, Crucify Him."

This, in point of fact, is why Jesus, the working man of Galilee, was nailed upon a cross.

True, the Pharisees hated him for His theology, His sabbath breaking, His attack on their lifeless taboos ; but they could never have got Him out of the way on these counts alone. He had denounced them as lovers of money, as evictors of the poor, as being full of extortion and excess. It was on such counts, which hit not only them, but the Sadducees and Herodians, and ultimately the Roman exploiters, that they were able to combine forces to strangle His propaganda and to destroy Him.

It has been suggested that Jesus was an Essene. The similarities between His followers and this sect, although they exist, are superficial. The Essenes were Communist in practice : but they were vegetarian, which the Christians

---

[1] Luke xxiii. 5.

Note. If it be asked, How far did Christ and His followers practise a kind of interim Communism within the existing order of their day ? we may answer ; they had a common purse, and shared a common meal. On more than one occasion, He fed multitudes who were hungering for a New World Order of justice, and the distribution was made on Communist principles.

certainly were not : but the chief difference was that they had no interest in a New World Order, and it was the preaching of the New World Order which brought Jesus to His death.

V. JESUS, MILITANT

Albert Schweitzer[1] has shown that the catastrophic, apocalyptic, element in the Gospels is too much inwoven with the narrative, too much part of the very texture of Christ's teaching, to be disregarded. He has thus finally destroyed the picture of our Lord as a mild nineteenth-century humanitarian professor. But, in doing so, he has landed us in another impasse ; for he suggests that the alternative is a deluded dreamer who banked on the intervention of a *deus ex machina* from the skies, who would within a very few years set up the Kingdom ; and that the heavens failed to oblige Him. Jesus was a titanic figure, and His teaching was heroic, but He went down in defeat and delusion.[2]

The frank acknowledgement of the apocalyptic element in the gospel rightly gave the death-blow to the gradualists who saw in Christ's teaching a smooth programme of slow human progress, " broadening down from precedent to precedent." But it must not be allowed to kill, along with this, revolutionary Christianity. In point of fact, a Christianity in rebellion against the system of its day and of our own, with the fervent desire for a reconstructed world, alone is adequate. It is not only true to history : it alone can save the world from despair.

[1] Albert Schweitzer : *Quest of the Historic Jesus,* and *Mystery of the Kingdom of God.*

[2] Whether Schweitzer would write like that now is doubtful : his small book on Christianity compared with other World Religions suggests that he would revise this earlier judgment. Meanwhile it has done untold harm. It confused and broke Tyrrell's faith (*Christianity at the Crossroads*). The Schweitzer theory became a tool used by every reactionary historian and critic in the country to deride the picture of Jesus as announcing a New World Order, to be established on this earth with the co-operation of men.

It is often assumed that Jesus was a pacifist, in the extreme sense of the term. Certain sentences, such as, " They who take the sword shall perish by the sword," are quoted. Certain other sentences are wrenched from their context in the Sermon on the Mount. " The method of the Cross " is assumed to be the only method for the Christian, and so forth. Thus the picture is built up of a non-resistant Saviour, a Jesus meek and gentle, who never appealed to anything but persuasion for the attainment of His Kingdom. This " all-in " policy is put forward as the complete programme of the Messiah, and the Church down the ages, because it has consistently refused to endorse it, is condemned as apostate.

The Church has, it is true, tragically departed from the teaching of the Founder, and has often come very near to apostasy. But the pacifist gives a completely lop-sided view of the Christ, a view which we shall hope to show is unscientific, unhistorical, untenable.[1]

First of all, we must be on our guard against taking isolated sayings too literally. Jesus announced that he that hated not his father and his mother was not worthy of Him : yet He Himself showed His love for His mother in His last hour on the cross. Jesus said, " Resist not him that is evil " : yet He Himself resisted the evil Pharisees, and expelled with violence from the Temple courts those whom He branded as robbers.

Here, then, is a short summary of the evidence. The apparently pacifist passages which are well known, and which are all to be found in my longer study of the subject, will be taken as read. But they must be considered along with the following ; and readers must have in their minds this question : Whether or no extreme pacifism can be reconciled with these sayings and incidents ; whether they are reconcilable with the assertion that persuasion was the only method in His armoury, and non-resistance His sole practice. Does His saying, that it will be more tolerable

[1] A bare summary is given here, and readers are referred to my forthcoming *Life of Jesus* for the whole of the evidence.

for Sodom and Gomorrah in the day of judgment than for
Bethsaida and Chorasim, suggest an " all-in " policy ? Or,
" Many shall come from the east and the west, the north
and the south, and shall sit down in the Kingdom, but ye
yourselves shall be cast out " ? Then comes a picture of
the excluded *émigrés* weeping and gnashing their teeth
(a metaphor He constantly used).

How can the parable of the wheat and the tares, although
it counsels patience, be reconciled with an " all-in policy " ?
We are confronted with its conclusion—the wheat gathered
into the barn and the tares burned with fire unquenchable.[1]

How reconcile the story of Dives and Lazarus with the
view that the advent of the Kingdom must be postponed
until the conversion of the last obstinate rich man ?

Consider the woes in Luke's version of Christ's beatitudes.
" Woe unto you that are rich, for you have received your
consolation. Woe unto you that are full now, for ye shall
hunger." " It is easier for a camel to go through the eye of
a needle than for a rich man to enter into the Kingdom of
God."[2]

Or, take that parable which ends with the destruction
of " those murderers " and the burning up of their city.[3]
Or, again, the parable of the nations at the last judgment :
some will go away into eternal life, and others into eternal
damnation. We are not arguing that the word " eternal "
is the equivalent of " everlasting," but at least the parable
warns us that some nations will be excluded from the New
World Order whose merciful and just values they despised.
When He spoke of the disaster which fell upon certain
Galileans, He adds, " Except ye repent, ye shall all likewise perish."[4] Here, again, He is referring to their doom
in this world, not in the next.

The oft-quoted text, " The Kingdom of God is within
you,"[5] should probably be translated, " The Kingdom of
God is *among* you." It was said in answer to Pharisee
opponents, whom He described as snakes and whited

[1] Matt. xiii. 40.   [2] Matt. xix. 24.   [3] Luke xx. 17.
[4] Luke xiii. 3.   [5] Luke xvii. 21.

sepulchres. They jeeringly asked when this precious Kingdom of His was coming. They belonged to a party who
did not believe in hastening its coming : philosophically,
they were passive fatalists ; practically, the present system
suited them well enough. They were always demanding
signs of its coming, and anxiously straining their eyes for
those magic portents which should herald its arrival.

This is an attitude Christ repudiated. He said, in answer
to these critics : " The Kingdom of God cometh not with
observation."[1] The Kingdom was already among them, in
His presence, and in the shape of the communal group
which surrounded Him. It is like the wind before the storm,
the first sign of the coming order. He did not mean it would
come very secretly and silently, spreading, " without
observation," from heart to heart : this is clear from His
conclusion in the same passage—" for as the lightning
shines from one side of Heaven to the other, so shall the
coming of the Son of Man be." Then come the familiar
analogies of the crash and doom, referring to the fate of
Sodom, and the fate of Lot's wife, and the destruction of
the cities of the plain. As the Greek phrase can be translated
either " within you " or " among you," the sense and the
sequence of the whole passage compel us to adopt " among
you " as the only possible rendering.

How reconcile with a slow and " all-in " coming of God's
Kingdom the last great discourse of our Lord to His disciples
outside Jerusalem, the Parousian sermon ?[2] It will come
with the crash of the present corrupt system at Jerusalem.
It will come when few expect it, breaking in as a robber in
the night. It is likened to the rushing flood and sudden
disaster. The disciples must take heed lest their hearts be
overcharged with surfeiting and drunkenness and the cares
of this life, " lest that day come on you suddenly as a snare."

The Parousian discourse is too much of a piece with the
rest of His teaching to be considered a later addition. And,
if it were added later, how reconcile that addition with the

---

[1] " Intense watching " ;   cf. Young's *Analytical Concordance.*
[2] Luke xxi.

supposed pacifism of the early Christians ? Further, how reconcile " early Christian pacifism " with either the Acts of the Apostles, or the Epistles of Peter and Paul ? Does not St. Stephen, in the Acts, liken Christ to Moses, the revolutionary, who slew the Egyptian tyrant ? Does St. Peter use the method of persuasion with Ananias and Sapphira ? Compare with this the treatment meted out by St. Paul to Elymas, who is called the son of the devil, and full of all villainy ; he is not persuaded, but blinded, by the apostle. And we are told by St. Luke that in this very act St. Paul was " full of the Holy Ghost."[1]

Turn to the Pauline Epistles—to Thessalonians, the Colossians, and Ephesians.

" The day of the Lord will come as a robber in the night, and when they are saying, peace and safety, then sudden destruction cometh upon them."[2] The same note is struck in the other Pauline Epistles. Even more terrible are the warnings given by the author of the Epistle to the Hebrews. Readers should also study the Second Epistle of Peter, with its awful picture of the judgment day ; and St. James's epistle, with its " Go to now, ye rich men," and its threat to those despoilers of the poor who have " nourished their hearts as in a day of slaughter."

The Revelation of St. John (written by the apostle or by one of his school) abounds in allusions to the Christ as a terrible judge " with eyes like flaming fire " : and the message of Jesus to the unfaithful of one of the Churches is, " I will kill her children with death."[3] The Christians rejoice over the expected fall of Rome, and the ruin of her merchants : and the vision of the kings and the princes of the earth, and the chief captains, the rich and the strong, every bondman and freeman " hiding themselves in the caves and rocks." " And they say to the mountains, fall on us, and hide us from the face of Him that sitteth on the throne and from the wrath of the Lamb "

These passages are not consistent with the persuasionist interpretation of the gospel. They cannot be ignored, any

[1] Acts xii. 9.   [2] Thess. v. 2–3.   [3] Rev. ii. 23.

more than can those gentle passages which counsel love, sweet reasonableness, and infinite patience.

A true interpretation must take into account the flaming indignation of Christ against Pharisees ; His vituperative language against hypocrites ; His frontal attack upon the profiteers in the Temple courts who were exploiting His children : must reconcile all this with the Cross, with His mercy and loving kindness. I believe that they are not only reconcilable, but identical ; that these examples are a sufficient proof that God Himself is not regarded by Jesus as a pacifist, and that Jesus neither spoke nor always acted as one.

Much of the language which seems to say that the Kingdom would come through a *coup d'état* from the heavens is symbolic : it by no means implies that the workers have to wait with folded hands for the intervention of God from the skies. There is much in Christ's teaching to show that an act " from above " is by no means incompatible with the action of men. When Christ describes John the Baptist's movement as being " from above," He did not imply that John waited with folded hands for the movement of a *deus ex machina*. When the disciples, having converted many, return from a tour of Galilee, Jesus exclaims, " I saw Satan as lightning fall from Heaven." The response of men to the inspiration of God is often described as a coming of the Son of Man, or as God acting from the skies.

It is impossible in so compressed an account of the thought and teaching of Jesus, an account chiefly devoted to His revolutionary outlook, to keep the right proportions : but it would give a wrong impression to end on a note of fierce militancy. The catastrophic elements in His mission have been underlined because they are so often omitted altogether without them, the picture of Christ is falsified.

But He came, not to condemn, but to save the human race. He was meek and gentle with the broken and unfortunate : and He willed, if so as by fire and terror, that all men, including exploiters and tyrants, should be redeemed. He knew that it was " hard " for rich men to enter the Kingdom : and when the rich young ruler asked Him what he should do to be saved, " He looking on him loved him."

This love which was Christ's is foreign to many modern revolutionaries, and in this measure modern Communism falls short of the standard of Christ the Communist. The impression created in the ancient world was : " How these Christians love one another," and how, in thought and action, they were marked by a burning charity to all mankind. They remembered their Master's description of His heavenly Father, who makes " His sun to rise on the evil and the good," and who " sendeth rain on the just and on the unjust." So you must " love your enemies and pray for them that persecute you, that ye may be sons of your Father which is in Heaven."

This is part of the paradox of Jesus which we spoke of at the beginning of this essay, part of His apparent inconsistency. In this unique Man, burning anger and burning love are identical. There is eternal significance in that strange phrase, " the wrath of the Lamb."

III

THE JESUS OF HISTORY

by John Lewis

Lecturer in Social Philosophy under the
Cambridge Extra-Mural Board

*" The vision of Christ that thou dost see
Is my vision's greatest enemy. "*

BLAKE

I. JESUS OR CHRIST

TWENTY-FIVE YEARS AGO the *Hibbert Journal* symposium *Jesus or Christ* was published. Theologians of many nationalities and of the most divergent schools of thought debated the relation of the " Jesus of History " to the " Christ of Religion." The immense interest created by this discussion indicated that by the year 1909 a definite point in the development of religion had been reached. It had become clear that a Christ-cult might exist which had but the slenderest connection with the historical personality from which Christianity takes its name. Since that date this distinction has not only been reinforced by further anthropological and psychological studies, but the development of cultus has been related to the spiritual needs belonging to a particular stage in social development. The Christ-cult has been shown to be not a mere fancy or the product of inexplicable illusion, but a reflex of the particular mental condition created by the social environment in which the cult flourishes. In religion, as in other matters, we do not " read off " reality in a simple objective fashion, we " read in " to the object of our worship elements derived from our presuppositions, our needs, our *Weltanschauung*.

Every God is constituted as much by projection as by his own objective being and nature.

Let us glance at some of the attempts to recover the Jesus of history which followed the application of the higher criticism to the Gospels.

In the " Jesus or Christ " controversy it was the Liberal Protestantism which stripped the figure of Christ of its accretions in an endeavour to find the " real " Jesus that seemed at first to carry off the honours. To this period belong the *Encyclopædia Biblica* articles of Schmiedel and Bruce, Harnack's *What is Christianity?* and a host of modernist Lives of Jesus.

Bruce frankly acknowledges that Jesus was the child of His time and people, that His vision was limited, that into the traditions of His life legendary elements of a supernatural character have crept. " But His spiritual intuitions are pure truth, valid for all ages. God, man, and the moral ideal cannot be more truly or happily conceived. Far from having outgrown His thoughts on these themes, we are only beginning to perceive their true significance. How long will it be before full effect shall be given to His radical doctrine of the divinity of man ! . . . The apocalyptic presentation . . . is a matter of form."

The Rev. J. M. Thompson of Oxford, in his *Miracles in the New Testament*, made a clean sweep of the miraculous element in the Gospels, which he regarded either as mental healings or legends. Psycho-therapeutics, which developed rapidly in these years, gave sufficient scientific support to this position for most critical minds. Critics began to group the fictitious elements in the Gospels into " fish stories," " sea stories," and so on. Some went so far as to regard the Gospels as practically almost pure fiction with a negligible element of historicity.

One of the most typical of the modernist Lives of Jesus came from the German scholar Arno Neumann. He contended that the kernel of Christ's message was " the fatherhood of God." " It is this that imparts to His whole teaching its bright, kindly, gentle, large-hearted, character, genial gentleness, and deep-heartedness."[1] There is but one theme running through His teaching—God and the soul, the soul and its God ; one general idea of an exemplary, creative, piety. "Just as His religion and moral precepts were loyally followed, the Kingdom must gradually, but inevitably, in time become an accomplished fact."[2] Neumann is aware, however, that something must be said about the strange incidents which close the life of this gentle preacher and seem altogether out of harmony with His quiet enunciation of spiritual truth. Antagonism to His teaching, says Neumann, was due to His emphasis on the spirit rather than the letter of the law, on the superiority of the moral requirements of the Law to Sacrifice.

In thus endeavouring to correct formalism of religion, Jesus felt that He was fulfilling a Divine mission. This conviction in its most developed form is all that He meant by Messiahship. That He made no claim to be Messiah was due to the necessity of clearing away first of all the popular idea that the Divine hero would take warlike and violent action.

At first Jesus hoped for a gradual coming of the Kingdom by people simply following out His teaching, but, as the opposition waxed fiercer and fiercer, He came to believe in a miraculous interference of God. "It was His sheet anchor when He found the bark of life prematurely wrecked and finally sinking."[3]

Critical reconstructions of the life of Jesus have continued to appear from that day to this. In contrast to the mild moralism of Neumann we find the more challenging appeal of Tolstoi, who found in Jesus a spirit of renunciation, of repudiation of force and State authority, of utter self-giving love, which has made a wide appeal to idealists. Buck White, the American, in his *Call of the Carpenter*, wrote the first full-length Life of Jesus the Socialist, a startling re-interpretation which has found a more recent exponent in Father Conrad Noel. It was natural that just as the Liberal moralist should find

---

[1] Neumann, *Jesus*, p. 96.   [2] Ibid., p. 109.
[3] Ibid., p. 129.

a Jesus to his liking, so should the Christian Socialist; but
the Christian Socialist Jesus, while He could make no appeal to the conventionally moral theologian, and has therefore been treated with less than justice at his hands, is a far
more powerful figure than the Liberal Protestant Jesus, and
closer to history in that it is much easier to understand from
this point of view how He came to be hated and feared,
and how His Kingdom was apocalyptic in its character.

A gracious and moving portrait of Jesus was drawn by
Sir John Seeley in his *Ecce Homo*, which avoids the insipidity
of the Liberal Jesus. " No heart is pure that is not passionate ; no virtue is safe that is not enthusiastic." In the life of
Jesus we witness an enthusiasm for humanity which seeks to
build a Christian republic in the world—the Church is a
commonwealth, based upon the most comprehensive of all
blood-relationships, the kindred of every human being to
every other, demanding unlimited sacrifice on the part of
its members, and that the interest and safety of the whole
shall be set by each member above his own interest and
above all private interests whatever.

" The city of God, of which the Stoics doubtfully and
feebly spoke, was now set up before the eyes of men. It
was no unsubstantial city, such as we fancy in the clouds,
no invisible pattern such as Plato thought might be laid
up in Heaven, but a visible corporation whose members
met together to eat bread and drink wine, and into which
they were initiated by bodily immersion in water. Here
the Gentile met the Jew whom he had been accustomed
to regard as an enemy of the human race, the Roman
met the lying Greek sophist, the Syrian slave, the
gladiator born beside the Danube. In brotherhood they
met, the natural birth and kindred of each forgotten, the
baptism alone remembered in which they had been born
again to God and to each other."[1]

Seeley does not discuss the relation of this *imperium in
imperio* to existing political States, nor does he tell us whether

[1] Ibid., p. 109.

the Christian Church is to embody the ideals, which are so manifestly contradicted by the existing social order, in new social forms and political institutions.

Among our contemporaries, Bernard Shaw and Middleton Murry have given us interpretations of the life of Jesus of considerable interest and indubitable force. Here a profound disquiet with present social categories has sharpened the vision and awakened a somewhat surprising sympathy with the Galilean prophet.

Shaw's treatment,[1] in spite of inevitable defects in biblical scholarship, is powerful, suggestive, and sincerely moving. " I am ready to admit that after contemplating the world and human nature for nearly sixty years, I see no way out of the world's misery but the way which would have been found by Christ's will if He had undertaken the work of a modern practical statesman." Shaw finds in the Gospels, not an echo of conventional ethics, but ideas which are flatly contrary to common practice, common sense, and common belief, " and yet have, in the teeth of dogged incredulity and recalcitrance, produced an irresistible impression that Christ, though rejected by His posterity as an unpractical dreamer, and executed by His contemporaries as a dangerous anarchist and blasphemous madman, was greater than His judges."

Shaw finds that " Gentle Jesus, meek and mild," is a snivelling modern invention, with no warrant in the Gospels. His programme was Communism, an organic conception of society in which you are not an independent individual, but a member of society, your neighbour being another member, and each of you members one of another, the obvious conclusion being that, unless you love your neighbour as yourself, and he reciprocates, you will both be the worse for it. Jesus taught that the masters of the community should be its servants and not its oppressors and parasites ; that work should be dissociated from money payments ; that we must get rid of judges and punishments and revenge. Jesus comes to enrich the lives of ordinary people : " His

[1] Shaw, Preface to *Androcles*, p. x.

aim is not only that they should have life, but that they should have it ' more abundantly ' (a distinction much needed by people who think a man is either alive or dead, and never consider the important question how much alive he is)."[1]

Jesus is no longer the lifeless harmless image He has hitherto been, but a rallying centre for revolutionary influences which all established States and Churches fight. " A real person who meant what He said, a fact, a force like electricity, only needing the invention of suitable political machinery to be applied to the affairs of mankind with revolutionary effect."[2] Shaw ends on a mystical note. " Jesus also taught that the Kingdom of Heaven is within you. You are the Son of God ; and God is the Son of Man." Godhead, in other words, is something which incorporates itself in man. " Man walking humbly before an external God is an ineffective creature compared to Man exploring as the instrument and embodiment of God."[3]

Middleton Murry makes this the central fact of the life of Christ. Jesus expects a revolutionary change and an utterly new world, but the transition to it depends on that inward revolution which we call conversion. " Men were to become Sons of God ; if they would become Sons of God, they and all things would be changed. Not gently changed, in the sense that bad men would become good, but radically, catastrophically changed. A new kind of life, a new order of consciousness would begin, as different from that which men have now, as human life and human consciousness is different from animal life and animal consciousness. Between these two is an abyss. Such an abyss mankind would have leaped when they became Sons of God."[4]

II. LOSS AND GAIN

These critical attempts to recover the historical Jesus have resulted in real gain. Whatever the defects of Liberal

[1] Shaw, *Androcles*, p. xix.   [2] Ibid., p. vii.
[3] Shaw, *Black Girl*.   [4] Middleton Murry, *Life of Jesus*, p. 70.

scholarship we can never go back to the naïve beliefs of pre-critical days. Firstly, we know now that the Christ of theology was a development of the original picture of Jesus, and that the theories of His person which so profoundly modified that picture were explanations of the experience of Christians and not part of the primitive revelation. This view does not necessarily invalidate either that development or that explanation, but it requires that the secondary figure, the Christ of the Church, shall be justified on other grounds than His identity with the Jesus of history.

Secondly, we have been driven to a revaluation of the ethical teaching of Jesus, and a new emphasis on His unique moral attitude to society.

It is now contended by many that His Divinity was not something that belonged to Him alongside His human nature, giving Him, as it were, a certain " numinous " quality, but consisted in the ethical force of His character with its unconventionality and its transvaluation of all values. As Tyrrell puts it, there is a very great difference between the love of One who is believed to be God, because He is regarded as Divine, and the love of that which is Divine in Him—that is, His ethical and spiritual character.[1]

According to this view we recognise the Divine in Jesus only when we become vividly aware of, and respond to, certain new values, thrust down into the midst of our own values and preferences, to condemn them and to reorganise them according to a new pattern. In a recent volume by a group of Protestant theologians, devoted to the elaboration of this final development of Liberal Protestantism, Professor Miall Edwards says, " Christ's Divinity, then, means that the values incarnated in His character and the quality of His will are Divine, and reveal to us the nature of Ultimate Reality in so far as it is and can be revealed to man."[2] This is to lift the Christological discussion from the level of a dead metaphysics bound to the categories of a long

[1] Tyrrell, Lex Credendi, p. 27.   [2] The Lord of Life, p. 218.

outmoded philosophy, to the categories of ethical and personal values which are alive for our own day. The Jesus of history, however, has proved altogether too disconcerting for the Church. " The picture has come from its frame, the statue has descended from its pedestal, the story has become real, with all the incalculable consequences that may flow from this terrifying miracle."[1]

The sentences from the ancient Gospels, which have so long been recited in solemn and meaningless tones from Sunday to Sunday, move into more significant patterns. We hear in them, for the first time, stunning rebukes, daring simplifications, and passages of almost impenetrable darkness ! Whatever we find when we read the Gospels with open eyes, we do not find the platitudes of conventional Christian preaching.[2] There has been no violent rejection, no deliberate suppression, as was depicted in Dostoevsky's *Grand Inquisitor*, but simply an obtuseness and lack of interest in anything so unconventional and indeed unsafe as a live Jesus. It is little wonder that the Epilogue to Shaw's *St. Joan*[3] was not popular.

Joan : Shall I rise from the dead, and come back to you a living woman ? What ! Must I come again ? Are none of you ready to receive me ?

Cauchon : The heretic is always better dead. And mortal eyes cannot distinguish the saint from the heretic. Spare them.

Dunois : Forgive us, Joan, we are not yet good enough for you. I shall go back to bed.

Joan : O God that madest this beautiful earth, when will it be ready to receive Thy saints ? How long, O Lord, how long ?

III. THE APOCALYPTIC JESUS

This not inconsiderable achievement, however, lays itself open to severe criticism. If the Christ of the theologian was

---

[1] Shaw, *Androcles*, 1011. [2] Chesterton, *The Everlasting Man.*
[3] Shaw, *St. Joan*, pp. 112, 114.

but a lay figure decked in the constructions of medievalism,
perhaps the Jesus of History is only the reflection of a
Liberal Protestant face seen at the bottom of a deep well.
" A figure designed by rationalism endowed with life by
Liberalism, and clothed by modern theology in historical
garb."

Johannes Weiss and Schweitzer on the Continent,
Crawford Burkitt in England, and Benjamin Bacon in the
United States have carried New Testament criticism to a
stage which leaves Liberal modernism in a condition of
complete collapse.

The oncoming of this assault was foreshadowed in the
" mythological " critics who came forward after each fresh
advance of Liberalism. The Liberals did not see that the
more the Gospels were proved to be overlaid by legendary
and theological accretions, the more likely it would appear
that they were purely fictitious documents. The more the
modernists rationalised and moralised Jesus, the more did
complete scepticism grow. Hence the " Jesus Myth "
theories of Drews[1] and Kalthoff.[2]

Kalthoff, for example, endeavours to show that Jesus is
a fictitious character projected by a new socio-religious
movement formed by a combination of the plebeian Communists of Rome and Jewish believers in a Messianic
Kingdom.

Von Hartmann, while not accepting the myth theory,
rejected the modernised Jesus entirely, and declared that
the real Jesus was a plebeian anarchist with a pessimistic
outlook. This appears shocking, but it turned out to be
nearer the truth than the emasculated portraits of the
Liberalisers.

But there is another alternative. A school of criticism
arose which argued that the accretions stripped from the
figure of Jesus are not later additions on the one hand, or the
original catholicism of Christ on the other, but represent
an original element in the life and teaching of Jesus which
is known as " apocalyptic." According to this view, Jesus

[1] Drews, *Christusmythe*.   [2] Kalthoff, *Christus-problem*.

fully accepted the expectations of the Jews as to the imminent end of the world, and believed that He was ordained of God to play the Messianic rôle in the final events.

Some members of their school concluded that Jesus was a fanatic, but others felt that an apocalyptic world view is not to be judged by its fantastic form, but is an imaginative statement of the true world outlook. Social optimism is vanity. The world is always on the brink of eternity. Social cataclysm is unavoidable. We can but live by the rule of renunciation and self-giving while we await the inevitable end. Such is the view of Albert Schweitzer.

In his *Quest of the Historical Jesus* Schweitzer showed that the more honest our attempt to recover the actual Jesus of history the more His figure refused to be set in the midst of our age as Teacher and Saviour. Brought to life, He would not stay with us, but passed our age by, and returned again to His own as the freed pendulum swings back to its original position.

And what is the apocalyptic Jesus ? We know now that the century before Christ was for Judaism a period of bitter disappointment and increasingly eager expectation. The Roman occupation and Greek permeation were destructive of the national purity and dignity which belonged to the people of God. A considerable literature of fantastic expectation of supernatural deliverance and the dawn of a new age indicates the widespread feeling of the time. Jesus not only shared these hopes, but believed it was His task to bring about their fulfilment. His gospel was not good advice, but good news. It was the authoritative pronouncement of the end of the age and the intervention of God to overthrow pagan powers, to rid the world of evil and inaugurate the golden age. Jesus is to be explained in relation to this Messianic movement. His great influence rested on more than His moral appeal. No prophet who failed to capture this expectancy could have won the people's heart.

That Jesus was listened to, was not because He preached

" paternalistic theism," but because He proclaimed " the good time coming." The gospel, the good news, is that it is at hand, it is here. The Kingdom is not a slowly developing reality ; on the contrary, it has no real continuity with human history, it is a catastrophic invasion from the transcendental world. But its coming requires a period of rapid and intensive preparation and purification ; that is His appointed Messianic task. This does not mean that Jesus regarded Himself as Messiah from the first, but that He had a definite function to fulfil in relation to the coming of Messiah. As Burkitt puts it, Jesus was not a sage, He was a man lighting a fire, an incendiary. He came not to argue and convince, but to flash forth His message as a herald of God.[1]

All the parables proclaim this message. The mustard seed and the leaven are not types of slow growth, but of rapid transformation and violent upheaval. His ethical teaching is not a code of morals for all time, but a policy for the transition. The existing organisation of society is not indefinitely continuing, therefore concern for storing up riches, for security, for the gratification of ambition, is foolish ; but so is passionate railing against Rome, against all oppressors, against the rich. The sands are running out, their days are numbered. Law, world power, nationalism will soon pass away, meanwhile they may be suffered. The famous Mission of the Twelve is not educational and religious propaganda, nor the promulgation of a new morality, but the broadcasting of the announcement of the imminence of the End.

The moral demand accompanying this message is for repentance ; admission to the coming Kingdom requires an appropriate moral disposition. The Kingdom itself will be super-moral for, all evil being overcome, morality becomes unnecessary. The saint, therefore, is neither conforming to the present world nor trying to alter it ; he is qualifying for another world altogether. This spiritual discipline is of crucial importance, for it has an actual

Burkitt, *Jesus Christ : An Historical Outline*, p. 59.

effect on the development of events, *it hastens the Coming, it is like a powerful prayer*. Without it the Kingdom cannot come.

This describes the first period in the life of Jesus, but, with the delay in the fulfilment of His expectations, a change takes place. The Kingdom tarries, and it is borne in upon Him that He must go forth and raise the powers of darkness, which obstruct its coming, against Himself, and thus bring events to an issue. His death thus becomes a necessary and redemptive act. Jesus was persuaded that, unless He did of His own initiative court failure and a violent death, the new state of things so ardently expected and longed for would not arrive.

The deliberate challenge to the powers of evil is made by the entry into Jerusalem, the cleansing of the Temple, and the open conflict with the Jewish authorities ; it was the spirit of Jerusalem *versus* the spirit of the Kingdom. For days the issue hung in the balance. Jesus knew what to expect. " Wily priests, jealous for their wealth and position, would stealthily hint to the Roman Governor that the movement had a dangerous political aspect. The Sadducean priesthood and the Roman power, these were the new foes, and the deadliest. The high-priestly nobility in Jerusalem, who owed their place and power to Roman patronage, would not lightly yield control of the Temple, *the strongest fortress and the richest bank in Syria*."[1] What will such people say to the preaching of a new era in which Law and Temple will be superseded, especially if the disciples of the Messianic prophet show the fresh power already working, and manifest a sharp break between the new man and the old man, the new society and the old ?

Jesus is so convinced of ultimate victory that, when His defeat seems inevitable, He declares that a supernatural manifestation will immediately follow, in which He will not only be vindicated, but exalted from the Servant of the Kingdom to the Messianic Son of Man, the supernatural figure who is to rule as vicegerent of God. In that faith He

[1] Bacon, *The Story of Jesus*, p. 229.

died ; His secret, kept to the last, finally unveiled and bringing down on Him the charge of blasphemy which secured His condemnation.

IV. MARXISM AND APOCALYPTIC

At first sight this disturbing picture of Jesus reduces our minds to confusion and paralysis. Was Jesus, then, a deluded fanatic ? Is His gospel one of hopeless despair ? If so, is He not alien in spirit to all our progressive social ideals ?

The reply is that it is the Liberal who is deluded when he regards the revolutionist as a fanatic. The revolutionist, however, is often historically right, while the Liberal has failed to discern the signs of the time. It is, indeed, a gospel of despair—but it is despair of gradualism. It is, indeed, alien to progressive social ideals, because it is more akin to revolutionary social action. It was Von Hugel who first noted the remarkable parallel between apocalyptic and Marxist catastrophism.[1] The differences are also great, but it is an illuminating comparison.

The two faiths share the following beliefs :

(1) Historical advance is by a conflict of civilisations, not by persuasion. The world-to-be is at death grips with the world-that-is ; the new age rises amidst the destruction of the existing world order in a final catastrophe.

(2) There is an immanent teleology in history making for social progress. Man must co-operate, but he serves a destiny greater than himself. The pattern is woven in part unconsciously, and the evil world fashions the instruments of its own destruction.

(3) There is an enemy—unscrupulous and pitiless. There can be no truce, no reconciliation of the mutually incompatible, only the drawn sword and war to the end.

[1] Von Hugel, *Essays and Addresses* (Second Series), p. 273.

(4) Death and defeat are steps on the road to ultimate victory. Apocalyptic faith is a " citadel of hope built on the edge of despair."[1] Out of war, revolution, poverty, an oppressed proletariat, crucifixion, comes the new people, the new world. We die to live. " Fear not, little flock ; for it is your Father's good pleasure to give you the Kingdom."

The fundamental difference is that the Jew left almost all to God, because actually there was nothing at that time for man to do, whereas the modern Socialist faces a fully developed social situation in which everything is possible to the enlightened and the courageous.

The apocalyptic faith is not so pessimistic as belief in progressive amelioration. For this requires a big dose of resignation, since the far-off Divine event will never be in our time ; having no hope in immediate relief, it requires the doctrine of immortality, which is no less credulous a hope than that which expects a Divine intervention. That is why the gospel was good news for those who despaired of the world. The world is done for. Well for the hopeless— woe to the optimistic.

But, if the modernist Jesus reflects our nineteenth-century Liberalism, is there not also a subjective element in Schweitzer's Apocalypticism ? The truth is that this radical pessimism is a characteristic of the more penetrating minds of every dying era. Jesus and Schweitzer have much in common both in outlook and in situation. Schweitzer contends that the fact that the hopes of Jesus were fantastic does not invalidate His philosophy. His apocalyptic faith lifted Him above all hopes in social amelioration, and beyond all obligations to the world's false standards. Since all history is in God's hands, nothing is left to us but to be true to the inner call ; His will for us is the will to pity, not trust in the scheme of things. There is no ethic in nature or history, only in a force which will break in upon the universe,

<hr />

[1] Niebuhr, *Reflections on the End of an Era.*

and in our own yearning. With Bertrand Russell,[1] Schweitzer sets the human ideal and the world process in final opposition. Apocalyptic is only the wish-fulfilment fantasy of an ultimate harmonisation ; there can be no certain hope of the future. Yet the world is not denied or abandoned ; it is the arena of a hopeless but not unsatisfying conflict with pain and evil ; a field of infinite opportunity and possibility in succouring man, in giving ourselves, in coming out of our aloofness and security to do all that can be done and that needs to be done. The only authoritative element in the gospel, then, is this Divine will, " intent upon the ethical consummation of the world."

The sayings of Jesus reflect the direction of this will, not a knowledge of fact ; as such they are of eternal worth, the crystallisation of the only true religion, " Master, to whom shall we go ? Thou hast the words of eternal life." If we are unimpressed it is because we lack an inward tuning of the heart to the same pitch of will and hope and desire. " Many of these sayings," says Schweitzer, " are found in a corner, like explosive shells from which the charges have been removed ; behold what they have made of the imperial words of our Lord, what a weak and ambiguous sense they have put upon His peremptory, other-wordly requisitions, in order that He might not clash with our ideals of civilisation, and His other-worldliness might be brought into terms with our this-worldliness."[2]

This is a philosophy which is as weak in constructive effort and historical understanding as it is strong in criticism of facile progressivism, and bourgeois standards of morality. It is the Tolstoianism which Lenin saw as reflecting both the strength and the weakness of the blind pity surging up against the cruelty and corruption of Tsarist Russia. But he would be even more superficial than the Liberal optimist who did not see in this desperate realism something very far in advance of " the easy speeches which comfort cruel men," for it means at least destruction of most of the

[1] Bertrand Russell, *The Free Man's Worship.*   [2] Schweitzer, *Quest.*

religious and ethical illusions which hold men back from the exacting demands of the historical situation.

The profound pessimism of this view is not world denying. Rooted as it is in the Hebrew conception of life, it avoids altogether the radical dualism which separates spirit and matter and exalts the former over the latter. If this form of Christianity condemns the world, it is because it wishes to pass beyond a lower and transitory form of earthly life to a higher and more permanent one—a proximate pessimism, but an ultimate optimism.

What is of worth is the world of men ; redemption is not deliverance from the flesh, but transformation. Faith is allied with hope, not with hopelessness ; hope in the final accomplishments of God's Will *on* Earth as in Heaven. " I had fainted unless I had believed to see the goodness of the Lord in the land of the living." But optimism apparently can only have two grounds—the unaided powers of man or supernatural intervention. When experience has shed the illusions of Liberal idealism, and has discovered the follies of utopianism and preaching, what is left ? The despair that follows is an improvement on a shallow optimism ; it is shared by five hundred million Buddhists and three hundred million Hindus.

There are only two answers. An apocalyptic hope that is now impossible to all who are not suffering from arrested mental development, and a scientific Socialism that itself has discarded the illusions of utopianism and gradualism.[1]

Schweitzer's personal bias leads him to overlook a considerable ethical content in the teaching of Jesus, and to overstress the purely fantastic elements of His faith. But the grim struggle with corrupt religion and with the inhumanity of His times is real and moving. Why should the moral insight of Jesus, if He was as great a man as Schweitzer thinks, be less than that of Isaiah or Socrates ? We should expect to find the same grip of perennial moral situations that we find in the prophetic tradition wherever we strike it.

[1] *See* Engels, *Socialism, Utopian and Scientific.*

It is true that we cannot disentangle the eschatological from the permanent to leave a clear residuum of eternal moral truth. To strip the life of Jesus of its contemporary features is like peeling an onion or evacuating the rich content of a Shakespearean play to arrive at certain abstract doctrines. Form and content are indissolubly welded. Nevertheless, even while keeping closely to the historic situation, certain elements of great moral and social interest emerge.

Kautsky was correct when he argued that there was more of the rebel in Jesus than orthodoxy has been able to see.[1] The suffering of the masses created a social situation comparable to that which led to the great slave revolts under Spartacus (73 B.C.), Eurius and Kleon (134 B.C.). Christianity was not merely the result of the individual influence of a great man, it was a social movement set on foot when the time was ripe by a genuine leader of the masses. Jesus was very like Gandhi in His power of speaking for the disinherited, making them conscious of their claims, strengthening their aspirations, and arousing fear and panic in their oppressors. That His apocalyptic hopes deflected this proletarian fervour from the channels of actual revolt does not lessen His credit as a popular agitator, for, after all, He was right. Revolt would have been premature, and the Roman world contained within it the seeds of its own destruction. Jesus proclaimed a coming of judgment on the rich and powerful. This aroused enthusiasm on the one hand, and intense hostility on the other. But it did not come to pass, and Jesus was silenced. It is therefore surprising that it continued as a living hope. What gave it staying power so that it withstood His execution, and carried conviction and hope to the supine and demoralised proletariat of the empire, was the apocalyptic faith in the second coming of Jesus as Messiah which Judaism gave to the movement. The definite assertion and claim to this effect on the part of Jesus could alone account for the certainty of all His followers in His second coming. Two things

[1] Kautsky, *Foundations of Christianity*.

converged—the need of the masses for a deliverer, and the great, elevating idea of a Messianic renewal of the world. They converged in a powerful personality playing a definite historical rôle. Schweitzer's figure has not the power which philosophers and poets think it has. " Posterity has no laurels for dramatic performers."[1] Prophets must answer the concrete historic requirements of the times in which they live if they are to found religions and influence society. The fantastic element in the apocalyptic of Jesus must therefore be subordinated to the actualities of the social situation and His real achievements within it. What are these ?

(1) The old order is corrupt and morally unsound. Its standards are false. It is falling to pieces. When it is gone the people will come into their own—the oppressed, the humble, the poor.

(2) The great common meal of the five thousand by the lakeside foreshadows the " holy communion " which is to come ; the fellowship of an equalitarian society. Jesus was not merely waiting for a coming Kingdom, but founding an Order of practising " Sons of the Kingdom," among whom the new standards were accepted and the power and character of the new society were manifest.

(3) The Kingdom abhors all rank and privilege ; it calls the strong and wise to use their gifts, not to exploit, but to serve the weak and foolish. It values the personalities of the humblest. Its attitude to crime is that the sinner needs recovery, not punishment.

(4) In Jesus there was that intensity of compassion, of identification with every form of suffering, physical or spiritual, that marks the great humanitarians of the race. His pity not only saw need that must be alleviated at any sacrifice, but passed over into indignant protest and vehement challenge to callous privilege and wealthy indifference. It blazed forth in the anger that consigns

[1] Kautsky, *Foundations of Christianity.*

Dives to Hell, and declares of him who would inflict injustice and pain on a little one that it would be better for him that a millstone were hanged about his neck and that he were drowned in the depths of the sea. This is the quality of love that characterises the Kingdom of Christ. We see it in the impulse which drove Damien to the leper island of Molokai and Schweitzer to the Congo. It is no tepid, or even warm, compassion. It puts to shame the paltry charity and amiable humanitarianism that too often passes for Christianity. It is the white heat of love.

The gospel is rich in social-morality, in equalitarianism and revolutionary ethics. It is amazing with what obtuseness scholars and preachers move unheeding through its pages, or, with heavy insensitiveness, busy themselves with taking the edge off the Sermon on the Mount.

Historically it was regarded by the authorities as of real danger, because it was preached as the authoritative Word of God, enunciated by an accredited messenger sent to herald the actual and immediate end of the existing order.

It is the Messianic hope which like tinder awaited the spark, the Messianic framework of the whole life and teaching of Jesus, that gave point and force to what might so easily have been mere moral talk or harmless idealism.

V. JESUS' QUARREL WITH THE CHURCH

This social gospel, however, is only half of His message. What completed it, and, at the same time, aggravated His offence to an intolerable degree, was an attack on religion as devastating as that upon the social order.

Religion had become a cultus, which surrounded with a halo of reverence a wealthy priestly caste and a host of harsh moralists, whose twisted standards tolerated social inhumanity but thundered anathemas against the low vices of the poor and the irresponsibilities of the worldly. Punctiliousness in unessentials cloaked complete moral blindness. For Jesus this religion was an insuperable barrier to the coming of the Kingdom just because it claimed Divine authority and supernatural sanctity. His deliberate and devastating anti-religious campaign begins with the breaking of the sabbatical and ritual laws, and ends with the cleansing of the Temple and the prophecy of its destruction. What He clearly meant, in spite of the frantic contortions of Catholic commentators, is the end of ecclesiastical religion !

That Pilate and Caiaphas united to destroy Him, that over His cross was written, " The King of the Jews," indicates quite clearly that Jesus was equally a menace to society and to the religion which provided its sanctions.

Jesus was crucified because His Messianic movement definitely threatened their destruction. If He had not been suppressed by violence He would have carried to its completion His design for the new Kingdom. But such a prophet cannot escape a violent end.

VI. THE CHRIST OF THE MYSTERY CULTS

That the Jesus of history became transformed into the Christ of the Church is hardly to be wondered at. The failure of Christ to come again led naturally to the substitution of belief in a future life for belief in an immediate Second Coming. The Church became the substitute for the Kingdom, and its *Interimsethik*, modified by experience, became the Christian moral code. At the same time its existence as a society organised both locally and œcumenically compelled it to take on a more ecclesiastical and fully organised form. But the most potent influence for change was the religious atmosphere of the Mediterranean world, and the spiritual needs of thousands of converts who could not absorb the new religion without assimulating it to their own beliefs and needs. Yet when it was absorbed very little indeed of the Jesus of history was left. He had become the Divinity of a Mystery Cult.

It is frequently assumed that this implies an intrusion of alien elements into an existent Christianity of pristine purity, but this is to regard the development of Christianity in a very abstract and scholastic fashion. Religions are not the clear-cut things that theological experts make of them. They reach this purity and distinctness only in their loftiest exponents and rarest intellects. The primitive Church in Corinth must have been the queerest hotch-potch of people and beliefs, as different from Paulinism as Paulinism was different from the religion of the original Jerusalem *ecclesia*. It is not that pagan notions penetrate Christianity, but that a few (already modified) Christian ideas penetrate paganism, mingle with its beliefs, modifying them and modified by them, with the result that a new synthesis emerges which is certainly not the Messianism of Jesus. The best name for it is " Christianity," since it has changed very little in the course of the last 1,500 years. By Christianity is meant not the faith as theologically rationalised, but as believed and practised by the vast mass of its adherents. This faith is powerful and popular to-day. It persists and flourishes because it still answers an urgent psychological need. But that is no reason at all to claim truth for it. As Marx declared, it continues because " it is the sigh of the oppressed creature, it is the kindliness of a heartless world—the spirit of unspirited conditions." It is a topsyturvy world, and " religion is the general theory of this world ; its spiritual ' point of honour ' ; its energising enthusiasm, its solemn complement ; its general fund of consolation and justification."[1]

Kirsopp Lake says, " Not the men who had known Jesus, but those who had not, converted the Roman Empire. Catholic Christianity conquered because it was popular, not because it was true, and failed for the same reason."[2]

Marx, *Introduction to a Critique of Hegel's Philosophy of Law.*
[2] Kirsopp Lake, *Landmarks.*

The ancient world in the first century was alive with religious movements known as " mysteries," ecstatic cults of a God who had been slain and had been restored to life, Osiris, and Dionysos, and Attis and Thammuz.[1]

These cults no doubt had their origin in the dying vegetation and spring rejuvenation rites of primitive man, but it must be remembered that even these were never mere intellectual mistakes or foolish fancies, but a profound spiritual participation in the life–death–rebirth cycle which constitutes the basic fact of all experience. These cults centred round two rites : a baptism, which conferred supernatural life, and a communion, in which the God himself was consumed or communicated.

The closest parallel with early Christianity is the possession by the Holy Spirit which followed baptism, and which is practically the same as the rebirth in the mystery cult. If we compare Christianity in its earliest form with the mystery cult unaffected by Christianity (an almost impossible thing to do), it must be granted that there are important differences. The divinity of the cult has not the same historicity as Jesus, and lacks the solid content of His rich personality. The cultus deity does not come down and suffer the love of man in quite the Christian way. Christian salvation is incorporation into a communal life, not merely the achievement of individual immortality. And, finally, the Jewish notion of a real time process moving to an earthly goal is entirely different from the Greek notion of the unreality of time and history.[2]

But, on the other hand, Christian interest in the life of

---

[1] *See* Farnell, *The Evolution of Religion.* " The incarnation of the Godhead in human form was a familiar conception . . . and was attached equally to mythic personages as well as to actual men. That such a personality could serve as a mediator between man and the Supreme God was conceivable to the Hellenic imagination. More important still was the wide prevalence of the belief in the death and resurrection of the divinity," p. 59. The Eleusinian and Orphic Mysteries both taught that salvation after death depended on a religious act of faith and on a mystic communion with a divinity that might be attained on earth by a sacrament. *See also* Farnell, *Cults of the Greek States.*

[2] *See* Bevan, *Hellenism and Christianity*, chaps. iv., v.

Jesus rapidly faded until He became significant for what God had done for man through Him, not for what He Himself had stood for. Christianity passed from the religion of Jesus to the religion about Jesus. It is not denied that the theologian both sees and creates a great difference between Christ and the " gnostic redeemer " or mystery divinity, but did the ordinary Greek Christian of the first century ? Chesterton has argued that the only difference between the myth and the Christian story is that the latter is a *true* fairy-tale. In other words, he frankly recognises the myth-making as the reflection of a common need, and the Christian myth as satisfying that need. " Mythology," says Chesterton, " is a search."

That an immediate synthesis between Κύριος and Messiah took place is not in the least surprising.

Mr. N. P. Williams has very convincingly argued that parallelism between Christianity and the mysteries need not prove dependence. The connection may be collateral, both may be dependent products of the same psychological factor, since man everywhere tends to satisfy the same instincts in the same way.

" The basal human need which all alike claimed to satisfy was the craving of the sick soul for ' Salvation.' The ' failure of nerve,' which affected great masses of the population during the first century of our era, the widespread pessimism and world weariness which supervened upon the close of the Roman civil wars, appeared in the consciousness of the individual as a nameless and oppressive fear—a fear of the universe, of the ruthless power of Fate, of the malefic influences of the stars, of annihilation at death, or of the torments of Tartarus. It was from this fear that the ' Mystery Religions ' promised deliverance, bestowed by a philanthropic ' Lord ' (Kyrios) and ' Saviour ' (Soter), who himself had known the anguish of death, or at least of poignant sorrow and laborious toil, and, as it is alleged, promised to transfuse the virtue of his own divine life into the soul of his votary, assuring the latter thereby of pardon, inward peace, and a blessed immortality, through rites of a sacramental character. As the chief needs of the religious soul are purity and inward strength, it was natural, indeed inevitable, that these rites should have taken the forms of a cleansing bath and a sacred meal."[1]

We do not deny that Jewish Messianism introduced a virility and correctness into the mystery cultus which made " Christianity " a new species with a survival value beyond its competitors. Thus Christianity was certainly a more ethical, a more social, and a more world-affirming faith than the mysteries, and it rose to power as a political force deliberately aiming at the sanctification, not the abandonment, of the world order. Nevertheless, it became deeply impregnated with dualism, pessimism, and all the characteristic features of the world-denying mysticism of the East. Christianity has never been one thing ; it contains a radical inconsistency which cannot be explained away as complementary aspects. Its world-affirming, world-denying elements are incompatible.

To eliminate either from historic Christianity as it actually was, or from contemporary Christianity as actually practised to-day—all gnostic transcendentalism ; all Monophysitism[2] and Nestorianism[3] ; all Manichæan asceticism ; all conception of the essential evil of life being its materiality and transitoriness ; all fear of sensual passion as in itself evil ; all conception of the malignant power of mysterious spiritual " elements " or " forces "—would leave extraordinarily little pure and orthodox Christianity behind, a mere skeleton, " with all the outside taken off and all the inside taken out."

For countless Christians, Christ became a demi-God, His humanity quite unreal, or a curious compound of Divine

[1] N. P. Williams, " The Origin of the Sacraments," in *Essays Catholic and Critical*.

[2] Monophysitism : the heresy which consists of a mixture or confusion of the Divine and human attributes of Jesus in a third hybrid nature that is a blend of both.

[3] Nestorianism : the heresy that insists on the duality and separateness of the Divine and human creatures until a duality of persons is believed in.

DR

and human. For others more intellectual, Christ became, and is, the " enlightener." All men have " light " within them, but Christ does what the Light in men ought to do, but fails to do ; thus he sets free the redemptive Divine spark in men's souls.[1]

This is an heretical gnostic teaching, but is it not quite tolerable " Christianity " ?

There is little wonder that the early Christian Fathers, who apparently saw a much closer resemblance than modern theologians, declared that the mysteries were deliberate imitations of Christianity created by the Devil to lead men astray.

But it is clear that both religions provide a full satisfaction for the same spiritual needs—that is to say, for these cravings for purity and ghostly strength which had created them.

Christianity is thus seen to be " the supreme and ideal mystery religion "[2] ; and it need not derive these characteristics from outside—they arise within ; just as they arose within all the other mysteries. The culmination of the religious experience which every such mystery bestows on the worshipper is, says Rohde, " the feeling of its own divinity which in the ecstacy has revealed itself in a flash and develops into the abiding conviction that this soul is of a divine nature."[3]

This ineffable consolation is the water of life to him that thirsteth, the medicine of immortality to sick souls, " the general fund of consolation and justification." " It is the imaginary realisation of the human essence, necessary because the human essence has no true reality." In other words, this religion " is precisely the self-awareness and self-consciousness of man who has not achieved himself, or has lost himself again."[4]

The Christ of all existing religion of this type maintains

---

[1] The Fourth Gospel is rich in allusions to Christ as " Light."

[2] N. P. Williams, " The Origin of the Sacraments," in *Essays Catholic and Critical.*

[3] Rohde, *Psyche.*

[4] Marx, *Introduction to a Critique of Hegel's Philosophy of Law.*

His " reality " and appeal solely because a sick society cannot bear to live without the consolation He affords, and yet such consolation in the face of present opportunity is a narcotic and not a spur to action. This Christ bears no resemblance to the Jesus of history, and His worshippers move through the Gospels like men in the country of the blind.

When confronted with the Jesus who re-emerges as the result of modern scholarship, they are forced to admit that

> *The vision of Christ that thou dost see*
> *Is my vision's greatest enemy.*

As a man is so he sees. Is it likely that a conventional mind, saturated in middle-class ideas and values, as much as a member of that class as a typical business man or a shopkeeper, could feel any sympathy for the Messianic Jesus of the first century ? Class and political interests give a set and a rigidity to the mind which incapacitates it for revolutionary conceptions.

Samuel Butler, looking back on the Christians who had surrounded him in his childhood, said that they would have been equally shocked by Christianity being denied or taken seriously. There is no doubt that most congregations would resent the preaching of the religion of Jesus in their pulpits, and would share the sentiment of the Free Church deacon who affirmed that " a prophet is a nuisance in any Church."

Jesus was confronted with men of that type in the Pharisees and the scribes of His own day.[1] They were not deliberate hypocrites or evil men ; they were moral men, religious men, good citizens and husbands no doubt, charitable, honest according to their lights, upright ; yet it was impossible for them to regard Jesus otherwise than with repugnance and fear. Jesus, for His part, had nothing for them but bitter denunciation—vituperation is not too

[1]Abrahams, *Studies in Pharisaism and the Gospels.* Travers Herford, *The Pharisees.*

strong a word. Often He confronted them with a frozen silence that condemned more than anything He could have said. It must be the same to-day.

I'm sure this Jesus will not do
Either for Englishman or Jew.

In consequence scholars occupy themselves with a maze of comment, explanation, and theologising, astounding in its moral superficiality, its trivial pedantry, and its spiritual sterility,[1] while the more religious or ethically minded construct anæmic Christs, " hearty " Christs, gentlemanly Christs, pacifist Christs, or even Christian-Socialist Christs, according to taste. The one person they and their disciples do not want to have anything to do with is the Jesus of history. As Thoreau said, " It is necessary *not* to be a Christian to appreciate the beauty and significance of the life of Christ."

Some of these projections deserve consideration.

The Pacifist Christ not only reflects the usual " nonresistance " ethic of Eastern mystics, of Tolstoi and of Gandhi, but a rediscovery of the sacredness of personality to which orthodoxy was rendering but lip service. We should be grateful for this emphasis, for if it is held with real intensity, it must lead to the condemnation of our whole social system as intolerable. But does the pacifist value human life so dearly that he would not take the life of one man who intended to take the lives of a score of men, if that is the only way in which they could be saved ? Is he like Gandhi, who has forbidden the killing of plague rats no matter what the consequences in death-dealing disease ? Jesus believed in the reclamation of the enemy, not his vindictive punishment ; He believed that national " enemies " can be reconciled ; He considered a popular rising against Rome to be premature ; but there is nothing in all this to warrant us in assuming either that He did not

[1] I cannot forbear the mention of the *International Critical Commentaries* on the Gospels in this connection.

share the apocalyptic expectation of a final destruction of evil men and evil powers, such as is depicted in Revelation, or that He would not have taken all necessary preventive measures, had the contingency arisen, to protect the welfare of His little ones, and His humble ones, from criminal and callous invasion of their rights.

The Socialist Christ is a welcome recovery of the social challenge of the gospel and of the ideal of a regenerated society which is the theme of the Old Testament prophets, but it reads back into apocalyptic times the practicability of a political movement which only the passage of twenty centuries was to make possible, and the possibility of a *productive* Communism which could not be until the Capitalism epoch had been traversed. The Communism of the Gospels is distributive, and its politics a reliance on Divine intervention. This is not Socialism.

The Christ of Revolution is the theme of many books and sermons by advanced preachers of the type of " Dick " Sheppard and the late Studdert Kennedy. But there is an atmosphere about this preaching which suggests that it is meant to secure the maximum amount of moral enthusiasm with the minimum amount of serious action. Hence it eschews politics, is above party, and carefully avoids taking sides in all the real issues which confront the modern world.

Theirs is " a courage that challenges but does not challenge too much, which gives an opportunity for tempered revolt, feelings and words of revolt but calls for no great sacrifices, even provides warmth of feeling through companionship. With words and logic these men daily make gold from lead, make incompatibles compatible, lions and lambs lie down together. These men now try to show that there is no real conflict between labour and capital and that a spirit of co-operation can smooth away all difficulties, when as a matter of fact there is unending conflict to the death between these two."[1]

There is little wonder that the Christian preacher has

[1] Frankwood Williams, *How Soviet Russia Fights Neurosis.*

been described by a well-known psychologist as " the professional tragedy of this generation."

One cannot escape the impression that, even if Jesus is proclaimed as a great moral reformer, we are not meant to take Him very seriously, at any rate outside the Church.

.   .   .   .

We cannot expect any recovery of the Jesus of history in those who are reconciled to the social order and its moral values, or who flinch from class and party strife.

The apocalyptic crisis has descended upon our age, not prematurely as in the time of Jesus, but in the fullness of time. Opportunity as it confronts us is also the final sifting of chaff from wheat, the day of judgment.

The Church may try, but it cannot succeed to-day in crucifying the Christ. The new Christ is an insurgent Proletariat, the uprisen people of God, and the Church which fails to do Him reverence must be cast forth into the outer darkness.

The Day of the Lord is at hand.

IV

THE EARLY CHURCH

by Gilbert Clive Binyon

Vicar of Bilsdale, Yorkshire

I. THE CHURCH AND THE PAGAN WORLD

" Christianity is coming back to its pre-Constantinian situation, so to say ; that is the position in which the Russian Orthodox Church actually is already. It may well be that Christians are called to go further back yet, to the catacombs, and from thence to conquer the world anew."

Such is the opinion of Nicholas Berdyaer.

If, when, and where Christians are called to go back to something like the pre-Constantinian situation or the catacombs, it will be the early days of the Church rather than any later period of Church history to which they will naturally look for example and encouragement.

But history never really repeats itself, and, if some situation appears to repeat an earlier one, it is always with a difference created by the events of the intervening space of time ; in this case, many centuries of varied experience will render the Church far better equipped than it was in the time of Constantine to conquer the world.

Although no one can say what the future may have in store for Christians elsewhere, at present the Russian Orthodox Church is in a unique position ; and it might not unreasonably be argued that the circumstances of the Churches of Western Europe are so different from those of the pre-Constantinian era that they cannot learn anything of very much value from that period. And that view might be supported by the assertion that when, at the time of Constantine, the Early Church had a chance of showing what it could do, it threw its opportunity away—so that evidently there is not much to be learnt from it.

Such contentions deserve a moment's consideration.

In the first place, though it is true that the world got into the Church in the fourth century, that is not the whole truth. There is another side to the picture. There were not wanting those who wished to go further than was actually done ; their influence was, it is true, negligible, and their very names are little known to-day ; but they deserve honourable mention, especially Salvian, who, according to Dr. Bigg, ought to be counted the first Christian Socialist.

Nevertheless, of course, when all allowances have been made, it remains true that no adequate advantage was taken of the opportunity.

One fact to be born in mind is the Church's pre-occupation with theology. As to this, it is a great mistake to contrast the Sermon on the Mount with the Nicene Creed, and to say that the difference between them measures the Church's moral decline. It was entirely necessary that the Church should state its philosophy : metaphysical speculation without moral interest may be barren and un-profitable, but moral endeavour without the philosophical basis which religion can give it, is equally fruitless. " The Nicene Creed," it has been well said, "is a great triumph of Social Christianity. . . . Nicene Christianity has banished individualism from the inmost sanctuary of the Faith."

Again, it is very important to remember that at the time of Constantine the Church had been recruited for three centuries from the pagan world. This almost necessarily meant a certain watering-down of the Church. For the Jews were far ahead of the pagan world in their religious beliefs and moral and social ideals. They were indeed a Chosen People, chosen and called to be a model community, exhibiting the Divine Purpose for civilisation in the justice of their social life, and thus attracting the Gentiles by the missionary value of this model community.

The Jews were, of course, very far from realising this their vocation ; but it is none the less true that, through their possession of the Revelation which the Scriptures record, their whole thought was far ahead of that of the pagan world. Christianity is the crown of a long development, and Gentile converts had a long way to go before they could assimilate the wealth of Revelation ; it is only natural that they became somewhat of a drag upon the Church as a whole.

Further explanations could be given of the condition of the Church at the time of Constantine. But the subject will not be pursued here. It is clear that if the Early Church has lessons of value for to-day, it is to the Apostolic Age that attention may be most profitably directed.

The topic of the social theory and practice of the Early Church has been well worked over, and no attempt is made in these few pages to give anything like a complete summary of the subject. Two characteristics of the Early Church—those in which it differs most markedly from the Church of to-day—will be selected for treatment ; these are : (1) the expectation of the Coming of the Kingdom of Christ ; (2) the sharp distinction between the Church and the world. These characteristics, it will be maintained, when studied in the light of intervening history, suggest particularly sound doctrine for these our days.

The reader who desires full information about the Early Church should turn to Dr. C. J. Cadoux's book, *The Early Church and the World* ; as a short semi-popular study, the first volume of Mr. F. H. Stead's *Story of Social Christianity* is to be recommended ; while serious students will, of course, consult Dr. A. J. Carlyle's *History of Political Theory in the West*.

II. THE CREED-GOSPEL AND THE SOCIAL PROBLEM

In the contemporary Churches of Western Europe it is now widely seen that civilisation, nominally Christian, is

in a very bad way ; and some attention to " social problems "
is now common form.

Dr. Adolf Keller, whose experiences and contacts have
made him exceptionally well-qualified to speak, says that
the Churches have been no more successful than any other
bodies in their effort to combine forces against the evils
which have befallen humanity. He instances the scourge
of unemployment, the economic world crisis, the spirit of
hatred, and the exclusive nationalism which still menaces
mankind with disintegration and disaster ; and he calls
particular attention to the fact that " the collaboration of
the Churches in the field of these social problems leads back
to the study of the ultimate underlying theological concepts
on which the various Churches originally based their
activity."

The Christian Church—in the days before our unhappy
divisions—originally based its activities on the theological
belief or creed, which was also at the same time a gospel,
that " Jesus is the Christ (Messiah)."

An enquiry into the meaning of this creed-gospel may
explain the special characteristics of the Early Church and
its lessons for to-day.

III. CHRISTIANITY AND THE OLD TESTAMENT

This apostolic gospel shows how impossible it is to
detach Christianity from its roots in the Hebrew and Jewish
religion.

This is an important point nowadays ; for the literary
and critical study of the Old Testament, occupied with the
dates of documents and the search for original meanings,
has created an attitude to these documents which, though
supposed to be historical, might better be described as
antiquarian ; there is a disposition in some quarters to
regard the Old Testament as out of date and no essential
part of the Christian Bible. But a really historical study of

the Scriptures of the Old Covenant shows them to be not only the preparation for the gospel in temporal sequence, but its permanent presupposition in logical sequence, and brings out the fact that the moral principles and social ideals of Christianity are to be found in the Law and the Prophets read in the light of the gospel.

If the Social Revolution can claim the sanction of the Christian religion, it is on the ground of its affinity with the Law and the Prophets.

Israel was the recipient of a unique Revelation. The Prophets proclaimed the Kingship of God—God's judgments upon a people whose laws and practices were unrighteous—and called for repentance (a change of heart and mind) as a condition of entering God's Kingdom; Jewish history was written, not for national self-glorification, but for God's glory—as the background for prophetic teaching and the scene of its influence; the Law was framed, not for subjecting the people to the will of a governing class, but in order to carry out the will of the Lord who had heard the cry of Israel in Egypt.

The relations with their neighbour nations of a people with so distinctive a religio-social outlook as the Jews had, presented a problem. We find two lines of thought on this subject, side by side, opposite, yet complementary rather than mutually exclusive—the one dwelling on the difference between the Divine Revelation and the beliefs prevailing in the heathen world, on the holiness, the separateness of God's people; the other dwelling on the likeness of such approximations to Revelation as may be found outside the Chosen People, on the all-embracing, catholic nature of God's Self-disclosure.

According to the one type of thought, the heathen nations are necessarily the enemies of the People of God and the true faith, and " Babylon " becomes a symbol of the world and its oppressive Governments. This gives rise to such eschatological picturings as we find in Joel iii. 9 f., where the Lord is represented as appearing in judgment to mow down the enemy heathen nations.

In the other line of thought, there is a recognition that there may be some righteousness in the laws of non-Israelite Governments, that in their peace God's People may have peace (Jer. xxix. 7). In the Book of Wisdom it is assumed that the kings and judges of the earth receive their dominion from the Lord and their sovereignty from the Most High. By the beginning of the Christian era it had become a commonplace that the Gentile conception of the " Law of Nature " only differs from the Law of Moses by the absence of any proper theological basis.

Such are some of the presuppositions of the teaching of Jesus.

He continued the prophetic message, with the announcement of the imminence of the Kingdom, the Advent of which—in spite of all appearance to the contrary, the power of Rome, the unworthiness of the Jews, human sin and imperfection generally—was as sure and certain and as confidently to be counted on as crops in the fields. He gave no countenance to any idea of revolt from Rome ; and His command, " Render unto Cæsar the things that are Cæsar's," contains the idea of co-operation with the good work of Governments even of heathen nations ; but that does not exclude the possibility that Dr. Schweitzer may be right in speaking of the " irony " with which the words were uttered : what could be expected of worldly politicians like these ? if any nations were ripe for mowing down in the eschatological judgment, the Jews were among them ! Matt. xxv. 31–46 echoes Joel iii., but in such a way as to overthrow complacent confidence by warning and to turn pride into penitence.

If penitence, not merely in the sense of repentance for one's own sins, but in the sense of sorrow for all the sins of Israel that were delaying the Advent of the Kingdom, was a condition of entering it, He who announced that Advent was first in bearing that burden ; at the end, when His disciples forsook Him and fled, He bore it alone—at the last upon the cross—and so entered into His glory.

By His Resurrection, He was declared to be the Christ. So the apostles could preach, " Jesus is the Christ."

Did that mean, " God's Kingdom has now come, the Advent is over, no further expectation of a Divine intervention is to be entertained " ? The belief that Christians are in some sense already within the Kingdom of God finds expression in the New Testament ; but the Apostolic Age and the Early Church continued to expect and prepare itself for the Advent in glory at the End of the World ; and that belief is included in the Church's Creed—" from thence He shall come to judge the quick and the dead."

Here, then, we find the first of the two characteristics of the Early Church already mentioned : God's Kingdom is to come by supernatural intervention ; the motive for works of righteousness is preparation for the Advent ; hope is fixed upon what God will do, not upon what man may be able or even be enabled to do in future historical time.

The second characteristic goes with this : the Early Church was a religious community of believers clearly distinguished from the world around, conscious of themselves as the New Israel, or the Third Race (the other two being Jews and pagans).

The next two sections of this essay are devoted to these two subjects.

IV. THE HOPE OF
DIVINE INTERVENTION

The belief in a Divine Intervention and the near End of the World presents, during the hundred years following the Crucifixion and Resurrection of Jesus Christ, a remarkable and significant history.

The belief was of Jewish origin. It appears in the Gospels. For a time it was shared by Jews and Christians, with the difference that, for Christians, the Person of the Christ was already known. But by the middle of the second century the belief had disappeared from among the Jews, while it remained in full vigour among the Christians.

The explanation of this appears to be connected with the way in which the rôle of Israel in the eschatological drama is visualised. According to the true prophetic teaching, Israel was as much under the judgment of God as the heathen nations, and even more so, on account of its privileged position. But that was not the idea of all who believed in a Divine Intervention; for the less religious Jews (whether they were apocalyptists or not) the rôle of Israel was that of executant of God's judgments; in this tradition were the party of revolt—Judas of Galilee, the Zealots, all who brought upon the Jews the destruction of Jerusalem in A.D. 70 and the final disaster under Bar Cochbar in 135. The hopes of men such as these feed upon success; repeated failures create a disillusionment that crushes hope out; and after A.D. 135 it became clear that nothing was to be hoped for along these lines; apocalyptic expectations waned among the Jews; they settled down to the study of the Law, and abandoned this whole belief. They could not adopt the belief in its Christian form, identifying the Christ with Jesus, for (Prof. Nairne says) " they perceived no triumphant issue from His sufferings."

But for those who gave credence to the apostles' gospel, things were very different; the Resurrection of the Crucified Messiah was itself a " triumphant issue," and the sufferings of this present time were not worthy to be compared to the glory which should be revealed.

It was this mentality of tense, resolute, even joyous expectation that wrought wonders in moral renewal and in such social achievements as circumstances allowed. Disappointments and delays could not break this hope, for it was sustained not by visible success, but by faith in the God and Father of Jesus Christ; knowing the power of Christ's Resurrection, believers could bear to share in the fellowship of His sufferings.

It is true that complaint was made, " Where is the promise of His appearing?" It is true that Christian hopes sometimes assumed the fantastic form of Millenarianism (Chiliasm). But these were due to a literalness of interpretation. And the pagan mind found extreme difficulty in assimilating the true Christian eschatological doctrine. For outside the Hebrew-Jewish tradition, continued in Christianity, of Creation and Redemption, religious belief and philosophical thought tend towards an indiscriminate world-renunciation or life-affirmation ; and it is a long step from any such positions to belief in a cosmic transformation, a new heaven and a new earth. Because of the difficulty of assimilating this idea, eschatology became in course of time altered into something different—the doctrine becomes practically nothing but a doctrine about life after death, the End of the World being postponed to an indefinite future.

With this alteration, which only came about gradually, must be connected that social "defeatism" which Dr. R. Niebuhr finds to be the " besetting sin of both Catholic and Protestant orthodoxy."

But in the earlier part of the pre-Constantinian period of Church history, the belief was in full vigour—an expectation of, and preparation for, a glorious Advent.

V. THE ALOOFNESS OF THE CHURCH

It was only in an entirely subordinate way that the Christians of the Early Church thought of themselves as citizens or subjects of the Roman Empire ; primarily and essentially they considered themselves to be " the New Israel."

Perhaps there is no passage more worth quoting, to illustrate the position which they felt themselves to occupy in the world, than the following from the anonymous Epistle of Diognetus :

" Christians are not distinguished from the rest of mankind either in locality or in speech or in customs. For they dwell not somewhere in cities of their own, neither do they use some different language, nor practise an extraordinary kind of life. Nor again do they possess any invention discovered by any intelligence or study of ingenious men, nor are they masters of any human dogma as some are. But while they dwell in cities of Greeks and barbarians as the lot of each is cast, and follow the native customs in dress and food and the other arrangements of life, yet the constitution of their own citizenship, which they set forth, is marvellous and confessedly contradicts expectation. They dwell in their own countries, but only as sojourners ; they bear their share in all things as citizens, and they endure all hardships as strangers. Every foreign country is a fatherland to them, and every fatherland is foreign. . . . Their existence is on earth, but their citizenship is in heaven. They obey the established laws, and they surpass the laws in their own lives. . . .

" In a word, what the soul is in a body, this the Christians are in the world. The soul is spread through all the members of the body, and Christians through the divers cities of the world. The soul has its abode in the body, and yet it is not of the body. So Christians have their abode in the world, and yet they are not of the world. The soul which is invisible is guarded in the body which is visible : so Christians are recognised as being in the world, and yet their religion remains invisible. . . . The soul though itself immortal dwells in a mortal tabernacle ; so Christians sojourn amidst perishable things, while they look for the imperishability which is in the heavens."

This is a lucid and noteworthy statement of the position that, for Christians, the *real* " citizenship " is " in Heaven " —that the Christian community constitutes " a colony of the Divine Commonwealth " (as Professor Dodd has explained—Phil. iii. 20).

For the majority of Christians to-day, this is an unfamiliar thought ; and, when it is put forward for acceptance, is often resented when its implications are seen ; while thought

and action based on it are likely to be regarded, not as
Christian, but as unpatriotic. So far has whole conception
faded away. But a grasp of the idea that the Christian's
true citizenship is in Heaven is of primary importance for
understanding the social theory and practice of the Early
Church, or, indeed, of the Church at any period.

Seeing that the Jews had recognised some goodness in the
just laws of the Governments of the heathen nations, and
that Jesus Himself had given His command about rendering
unto Cæsar, while St. Paul continued this attitude to Rome,
there was, one might think, at least some chance of a happy
and useful collaboration in social action between the
Church and the pagan Græco-Roman world. And that
collaboration will appear to be a still more possible thing,
if the Stoic " Law of Nature " is recalled. This was a
religio-moral idealism of a Communistic nature, moral
rather than religious, but with some vague reference to God
or a pantheistic background. The affinity of this with the
Law and the Prophets has already been mentioned. It
might seem, then, there was a basis for common action.

Some such idea had a certain vogue in some circles in
the first two centuries. Some writers, known as the Apologists, speak of the benefits which the Church had to bestow
upon the Roman Empire. St. Luke might, though without
full justification, be regarded as the first of the Apologists ;
for in his Gospel and Acts he seems to wish to represent
Christianity in a manner likely to commend it to His
Excellency Theophilus. In these two New Testament books
the Christian ideal is, of course, undimmed ; but when we
come to the Apologists, that is not always the case. Melito
of Sardis found great significance in the fact that the beginning of the Christian Church synchronised with that of the
Roman Empire. There was, indeed, great significance in
that fact ; but not that which Melito found ; he thought
that the greatness, splendour, and glory of the Roman
Empire since the day when, with the Church, it began its
career were proofs of the usefulness of the Church to the
Empire. The persecutors had a better grasp of the situation

when they discerned in Christianity a power subversive of the Empire.

Yet we may well ask why this was so. When one reads the accounts of the last hours of the martyrs, one is struck by the great reluctance of the Roman officials to carry matters to extremes. They exhort the aged Polycarp to reverence his grey hair ; they call on the martyrs to " repent " ; to consider the philanthropy of Rome ; to cry, " Away with the atheists " ; where, then, lay the difficulty ? Why was Christianity rightly regarded as subversive of the Empire ?

In his essay on " The Two Empires," Bishop B. F. Westcott pointed out that Christianity could not fail to challenge persecution : it was *universal*, and therefore could not acquiesce in taking its place among, and as one of, the national religions which Rome was prepared to tolerate ; it was *absolute*, and therefore could not conform to the State worship ; it was *aggressive* or missionary, because it was universal and absolute. For these reasons conflict with the civil power was inevitable. These three characteristics, Westcott went on to say, were particular forms of one general characteristic : Christianity was spiritual.

In the pagan world there was some humanity, some sense of mutual obligation, some idea of service to the community ; it was reprehensible to despair of the republic ; it was admirable to serve the commonwealth ; and those who served it well were heroes. But this natural religion and morality lacked a supernatural basis ; as Westcott put it, the visible was the measure of hope and aspiration. That which may have been the worship of heroes degenerated into the worship of conquerors. The idolatry of service passed into the idolatry of success.

The best aspiration of the pagan world, because it never found anchorage in the supernatural world, drifted into becoming something very different from what it ought to have been ; its growth was perverted ; and this perversion culminated in the worship of the Emperor as divine.

Thus the issue was focused in the Cult of the Divine

Emperor. So long as participation in this cult was required as a test of loyal citizenship, resistance to it on the part of Christians, and persecution on the part of the Roman Empire were alike inevitable.

It is not the Apologists, at any rate as represented by Melito of Sardis, who take the correct view of the whole position, but other thinkers, as, for example, Origen, who says :

" God, who sent Jesus, brought about all over the world, for the conversion and amendment of mankind, the dominance of Jesus' gospel, and produced everywhere communities rivalling in the social field the political organisations of superstitious, licentious, and unjust men."

Christians, debarred from entering public life, could only, while the Empire remained pagan, oppose to the communities of superstitious, licentious, and unjust men that ideal and those principles which found a brief realisation in the quasi-communism of the Jerusalem Church and which continued to guide their own communities ; they could only oppose to the persecution of Rome the witness of the martyrs.

Thus we often find, from the Book of Revelation onwards, an indifference to the world outside the Church which may seem callous. But that is because it was seen to be in decay, in a hopeless condition. Christians, it has been said, kept themselves " gloriously aloof from the dead present."

VI. THE CHURCH OF TO-DAY

We have found, as outstanding characteristics of the Early Church, the expectation of the Advent and the idea of preparing for it (rather than that of building a new social order), and a sharp contrast between the Church and the contemporary civilisation (instead of the Church being in the midst of a civilisation nominally Christian).

These characteristics of the Early Church make it very different from that of to-day. But it is these very characteristics that may, perhaps, be most worth studying to-day.

It is not suggested that the aim of building a Christian social order has been a mistaken one. On the contrary, such is the manifest obligation of the Catholic Church, if its catholicity is to be what it should be—all-inclusive and world-dominating. But " catholic " is not the only title of the Church ; the Creed speaks of it as being also Holy. The title " Holy Catholic Church " is, it has been pointed out, of a paradoxical nature ; " for holiness in its original meaning of mysterious separation is precisely the negation of catholicity " ; the two words together indicate that the Church can only dominate the world if it is decisively distinguished from the world and all worldly policies. Everybody knows that there may be a false holiness, which leaves the world to manage its affairs without reference to God and His Will ; but perhaps the opposite error is not quite so well realised : anxious to claim the world for Christ's Kingdom, Christians may sometimes pay too little attention to the terms on which alone that can be rightly done.

What is suggested is that the special characteristics of the Early Church which have here been dwelt on may be valuable for the more effective accomplishing of what the Church has, since those days, more definitely learnt to attempt.

If our social conscience will not allow us to fall in with the " defeatism " of Catholic and Protestant orthodoxy, nor yet with what Dr. Niebuhr calls the besetting sin of Liberal Protestantism—a " sentimentality " which assumes that Christian principles " are influencing political life more profoundly than they really are "—it looks as if we ought to take up a more revolutionary attitude. And that is what eschatology gives us.

" Red " revolution might be regarded as practical eschatology—for those who regard themselves as executants of Divine Judgment ; and its " atheism " might be regarded as self-deification.

That the destruction of capitalist civilisation is God's judgment upon it, need not be doubted ; and that a consciousness of executing God's judgments has some place in Christianity cannot well be denied by believers in Church order and organisation : all Church government and discipline includes something of the kind ; but all this, if it is Christian, depends upon the consciousness of being already within the Kingdom of God and of already reigning with Christ, and it is very liable not to remain fully Christian, but to slide down either into an ecclesiastical imperialism or a political secularism, unless it is constantly corrected by the thought that God's judgment, like His mercy, is over all His works.

To the Christian consciousness, God the Creator of nature and human nature reigns eternally ; life, as we now know it on this planet as it is, can never finally satisfy man, who is not content to be imprisoned in time and space ; God, Himself beyond time and space, has entered into the world in the Person of His Son, and is ever seeking entrance into humanity—eternity impinges upon, presses on and into, time ; yet man, everywhere dependent upon God, asserts his independence ; the kingdoms of this world stand out in dark contrast to the Kingdom of God ; and from the sense of this contrast is born a shame and penitence for the sin of the world, and longing, expectation, and preparation for the Advent of the Kingdom.

The difficulty which most contemporary Christians feel about entertaining any eschatological expectations and a spirit of eager waiting and active preparation for the Coming of Christ's Kingdom can be explained, in large part, by a common inability to make a happy and natural use of language or ideas which it is felt must be taken not literally, but symbolically.

The result of this inability is that some take the New Testament word-pictures of the End of the World quite literally ; these sometimes (as Cranmer put it) " goe about

to renew the fable of the hereticks called Millenarii, and
cast themselves headlong into a Juishe dotage," announcing
that millions now living will never die ; while others
dissolve the symbolism into either a wholly next-world or
wholly this-world picturing of the future ; the former of
these is so far from being correct that it practically loses
sight of God's Kingdom *coming on earth* ; the latter is so
occupied with an earthly future that it is apt to forget
God's Kingdom.

Eschatological pictures of the End of the World have
no more to do with some event in a distant future than
the Story of Creation in Genesis has to do with some event
in the remote past. But, like the Story of Creation, these
picturings are inspired verbal symbols of a truth which
transcends finite minds.

When men, refusing to take literally the narrative of
Genesis, refuse also the doctrine which it enshrines, their
religious belief slides down into pantheism or beyond.
The truth which the word-pictures of Jesus enshrine must
also be retained.

An important point to be borne in mind here is that
the apostolic writers were not so particular as we are about
analysing ideas and drawing distinctions, about chrono-
logical sequence and dates of events, and a sharp distinction is not always made in the New Testament between the
Incarnation and a *second* Coming as two different events :
thus the same word *epiphany* is used to describe both, and
in 2 Tim. iv. 8 it might refer to either ; does it not here
refer to both ? It is probable that in this passage, which
might be paralleled with others in later Christian literature,
both ideas are brought together. In short, ever since the
Resurrection of Christ, which was in one sense the real
fulfilment of eschatological expectations, these word-
pictures of the Advent and the End of the World have
meant that the Incarnation has not exhausted God's Self-
giving energy ; they create and sustain that penitence and
renunciation of the world, that consciousness that an earthly
paradise is not enough to hope for, that awareness of the

urgent claims of suffering humanity, that responsibility and that care-free confidence in God's action (not man's) which should belong to Christian believers.

It is quite a mistake to suppose that an outlook which may be called eschatological makes attention to, and occupation with, earthly concerns " not worth while " ; the contrary is the case ; such an outlook means a release of energy, because it rejects the hampering search for support as a condition of doing things, and (still more decisively) the demoralising idea that if only a few will do the really right thing it is not worth while for any to do it.

If mankind remains so infatuated with exclusive national-ism and economic anarchy that, as it seems, it must " inevitably " bring upon itself their natural results— disintegration and disaster—that will mean, for Christians, greater detachment, renunciation, nearness to God, and *therefore* more vivid apprehension of His Self-giving and down-coming, and more vivid realisation of the insistent demands of the prophetic ethic ; and it is precisely these— rather than those who have screwed themselves up to a determination that " these things shall " not " be "—who are best fitted to resist, and even to reverse, the evil ten-dencies of the world.

So at least it was in the Apostolic Age.

And so it will be in this age, if Christians can bring themselves to allow a fellowship based on religious faith to take precedence over a fellowship based on the ties of neighbourhood, kinship, race, nation, class, party, and so on, and thus constitute themselves once more a " colony from Heaven " in the midst of a world which, refusing to have Christ rule over it, ever more surely draws upon itself its own destruction.

Group-consciousness based on race, nationality, family, class, area of government, political party, and so on, is not, by Christians, to be ignored, abjured, and repudiated out of hand ; any of these groupings may be a field for expres-sing, and so sustaining, a religio-moral social consciousness ;

but any of them may be hindrances to faith and the fellow-ship of the faithful, occasions of dragging-down to the level of the world ; so that what is here meant by giving pre-cedence to a fellowship based on religion is that the claims of these forms of group-consciousness should be scrutinised in the light of devotion to Christ Himself ; and by a fellow-ship based on religious faith is not meant an ecclesiastical group-consciousness (the claims of which need also to be scrutinised), but rather a consciousness that the Christian Church, however much it may at any time be infected by the worldliness of the world, yet as the Guardian of the Word and Sacraments contains the seeds of regeneration.

It is well recognised that at the time of Constantine " the world " got into the Church and has never since been got out of it. If the world is indifferent to the Church, it is because the Church is so little different from the world ; and the first step to attaining an effective influence over the world is a thorough dissociation from the assumptions and habits which prevail in the world.

One idea which stands in the way of any such thorough dissociation is that it would be throwing away oppor-tunities for influence or callously abandoning the world to its fate. But that idea is illusory ; it produces a result the reverse of that intended ; the world drags the Church down. And if the Church is not to be fatally involved in the troubles which the world brings upon itself, Christianity must get back to something more like the distinctive position of the Early Church.

V

COMMUNISM IN THE MIDDLE AGES AND REFORMATION

by R. Pascal

Lecturer in German, Cambridge University

I. ECONOMIC AND POLITICAL DETERMINANTS OF MEDIEVAL COMMUNISM

To give an account of medieval Communism, it is not sufficient to describe the various equalitarian beliefs of the period, with the religious systems in which the social aims were clothed. The history of Communism is not the history of an idea, but of a sociological process. Complicated ✓ as is the history of the primitive communistic beliefs so prevalent in the Middle Ages, their true history takes us not only into the labyrinths of human emotions and intellect, but also into the depths of human society. The Christian sects in particular—the womb of primitive Communist nostalgia—are essentially social groups, with their organisation and social code. Sustaining them we discover the whole structure of contemporary society—the social and ecclesiastical hierarchies, the relations between social classes, the constant, often turbulent, transformations in society caused by the emergence of new classes. Their history is profoundly affected by the rise of the new national groups, the strongest political development of the period.

The dominant form of medieval life was such as to nourish communistic tendencies. In strong contrast to the later individualism, medieval social organisation was essentially corporative. Each occupation and trade, each community, prescribed fixed rights and restrictions for each member.[1] This complex of corporations was, of course, never stable, but in the continual struggle of those times the claims of the community over the individual, over new social forms, were repeatedly asserted. Among the peasantry, especially up to the fourteenth century as long as there was no lack of land, communal possession of forest and meadow was usual. In the towns, and round them, " commons " existed for general utilisation by the burghers. Rites and festivals asserted every year the priority of the community over the individual, sometimes in the more general sense, as in the Festivals of Fools, sometimes in the more particular economic sense of the Rogation Processions, which asserted the proprietary rights which parishes had won from the feudal lords. The idea of owning in common, even though this applied only to certain aspects of property, distinguishes medieval from early capitalistic society ; that after the Reformation a lad was whipped at the Rogation Festival is a symbol of the change—is not the lad the community, grown propertyless and restive, scourged with contumely by the possessing ?

But the medieval system of corporative rights and ownership existed fundamentally to preserve the integrity of individual ownership. Ownership in town and country, in upper and lower classes, was dominantly individualistic. Only such movements as aimed at extending common ownership to further aspects of economic life, and replacing individual possession and enjoyment by communal, can be termed—and were recognised as—communistic. It is with these movements that we shall be concerned.

Communistic ideas are frequently met with in the early Christian Church. St. Paul describes, with approval, the sharing of goods practised in certain communities, and many of the early Fathers condemn the possession of wealth. The chief authority with which commentators wrestled was the command of Jesus to the young man (Matthew xix.

[1] *See* Gierke, *Das deutsche Genossenschaftsrecht.*

16 ff.) to give away his property for the good of his soul. This Communism differs from modern in two important aspects. It is based, in its justification, on entirely subjective considerations. The possession of worldly goods is harmful for the soul. And the method is only a Communism of distribution, and does not affect the problem of production, as Kautsky has pointed out.[1] To have carried out this command to the full would have meant a complete disorganisation of production, with no alternative mode proposed, and would have brought communities to starvation and misery. From the third century, indeed, the Church abandoned these communistic ideals, and entered fully into the system of property, becoming both a great land-owner and the moral sanction of the existing system of ownership and of government.

During the period of anarchy which set in with the break-up of the Carolingian empire, the Church, after many vicissitudes, established itself as the greatest organisation in Europe. From Gregory the Great to Innocent III (end of the eleventh century to the beginning of the thirteenth) it was able to play a leading part in European politics, to bend, in some measure, secular policy to its will. During this period countless ecclesiastical writers proclaimed the hegemony of ecclesiastical power, enunciated the doctrine of the subordination of secular lords to the pope. And this period sees the rise of the communistic heresies, a great wave of communistic aspirations within Christendom, their theory directed mainly against the pretensions of the leaders of the Church. Yet it is to be noted that the first steps taken against the heretics—the first hangings, burnings, torturing —were initiated by secular princes. In the eleventh and twelfth centuries princes not marked by any peculiar piety found it necessary to check the progress of heresy ; it is no great assumption to believe that they acted more on political grounds—against socially subversive bodies—than on religious. Only in the late twelfth century did an episcopal

---

[1] *See* Kautsky, *Foundations of Christianity,* and Troeltsch, *The Social Teaching of the Christian Churches.*

inquisition slowly form, and only in the thirteenth did the Church really advance against the heretics, with the Albigensian crusades. To understand the communistic movements of this period it is necessary to investigate the origins of the power of the Governments and the relations between papal and secular power.

From the eleventh century the age-old struggle of lords for military success and territorial expansion took on a new form, culminating in the creation of unified national States. The new factor which made this development possible, and stabilised the great nations (as a contrast to the instability of the Carolingian empire), was the growth of the towns. Forming round market-places, in the shadow of some powerful lord, the towns established themselves as centres of exchange, then as centres of production, striving always to widen the area of exchange, to create larger economic, and consequently political, units. The manors became less and less self-contained, more and more dependent on the manufactures of the towns, where specialisation produced goods of a higher quality. Their influence on agriculture was no less marked. The towns, though to some extent producing their own agricultural produce, provided a market for the land-owners—an expanding market. Land-owners in the neighbourhood of towns began to produce for profit, instead of for their own restricted needs, and consequently aimed at increasing production. It was many centuries before the land itself was made more fruitful by the application of new methods of cultivation—manures, scientific rotation of crops, etc. and the only method of meeting this increased demand was that of increasing the fruitfulness of labour. Thus, in areas round towns, the old conditions of villeinage became modified. Forced services were commuted into money-rents. The peasant was offered a freer and more profitable existence in return for increased production. Economic alliances were formed in larger and larger areas, as the nuclei of the national States. The basis of anarchy—the disparity between military strength and economic productiveness—was slowly undermined. The causes of the wars between powerful kings are to be found in the struggle for economic wealth—beneath the vagaries of the Hundred Years War lies the struggle for the fertile and productive districts of Southern France, for the trade-routes to the East. And though military prowess and strategic skill played its part in the course of the wars between king and vassal, between king and king, the ultimate political contours of the modern world were determined by the combination of the military strength of great princes and the military and economic power of the towns.

What part did the Church play in this development, which was to culminate in the Reformation, in the control, even, of the Church by the ruling princes ? No doubt the papacy profited by the hostility between the temporal lords, playing off one against another. Thus the emperors were humbled by a papacy allied to unruly vassals, to the hereditary foe in France ; thus Raymond of Toulouse was crushed by a papacy which appealed to the greed of rival lords. But the papacy was only a small territorial power, ruling only an insignificant land in Italy. And the cleverest strategy is futile without power. It would be false, too, to consider the papacy as merely a tool in the hands of the princes, even though the pretensions of the Decretalists regarding papal supremacy never corresponded to the facts. The interests of the Church itself made it follow a policy which ran parallel to that of the great princes.

In the tenth and eleventh centuries the Church was without moral or material authority, its leaders dissolute, swayed by local and transient influences. From the time of Gregory, who himself died a refugee, it built itself up as a political and moral force, instilling in men a respect for a law which was above expedience, enforcing, through a disciplined organisation, a unified will. To achieve this it had to overcome first and foremost the subservience of the local Churches, the bishoprics, the ecclesiastical princes, to the secular lords. The provincial ecclesiastics were in little different from feudal lords, participating in dynastic struggles, dealing in benefices, turning the lower clergy into servants and mercenaries.[1] Simony and pluralism in the Church were not merely morally reprehensible ; by such dealings feudal dignitaries built around them a power which could withstand all papal commands, refuse papal dues.

Against such Churchmen, heads of wealthy foundations, bishops, etc., the papacy proceeded ; and it was precisely the same feudal lords, though with secular titles, whom the great princes aimed at subjugating. And just as the princes were allied with the wealth and resources of the towns in their campaigns, so also the papacy built its strength on the towns. In order to break the simonistic ambitious priest-hood, Gregory called frequently on the masses to revolt and depose their impure clergy. The doctrine, later called heretical, that the sacraments were efficacious only if the administering priest was pure, was utilised to carry out the cleansing process.[2] The lay world, parishioners, were even granted the right of participating in the election of bishops —again a right later withdrawn. The theology of the Church, as formulated in its most authoritative form by St. Thomas, outlines a world-order giving to the worker his due place in the hierarchy of the world, assuring him his fragile rights in a law above force. The very form of this world-order, its definition and restriction of rights, seems based on the guild system. The Church, now far away from its old negation of the world, accepted the social order as part of the hierarchy leading to the Divine, and gave every estate its due part in this hierarchy. It was in the towns that the papacy found its support against feudal ecclesiastics, against the worldliness of a corrupt priesthood. And not only in politics was this alliance between papacy and townsmen productive. The cathedrals of the period bear witness to the creative faith of the guilds in the Church.

But the movement which purified the Church and

---

[1] See G. Volpe, *Movimenti religiosi e sette ereticali nella società medievale italiana*, 1922, p. 27.

[2] Cf. the decision of the Synod of Rome, 1059, forbidding anyone to be present at the mass of a priest known to keep a concubine or wife.

strengthened the papacy engendered currents of belief and politics which were its opposite. Though the economic bases and the policies of papacy and nations were at some periods coincident, they were bound to reveal themselves as warring forces. It has been observed, with some justice, that the chief social process of the Middle Ages was the formation of nations in their modern sense.[1] The hegemony of the Church was largely illusory, its doctrines merely tolerated or utilised by the great princes. Almost contemporaneously with St. Thomas, William of Occam was building a theological system which would, in the end, subordinate the Church to the earthly powers. A little later, Marsiglio of Padua formulated in even sharper terms the right of the secular arm to control the Church. Paris, where the doctrine of ecclesiastical absolutism was shaped, was also the home of the theoreticians of princely absolutism, and offered, in the fourteenth century, prolonged and bitter opposition to the papal Inquisition. These are the spiritual ancestors of Wyclif and Huss, who first organised conscious national movements against Rome.

These nationalistic movements were, of course, not communistic. Yet even they made an appeal to the tradition of ecclesiastical Communism. The chief aim of Wyclif, Huss, and Luther was to restore the Church as a spiritual force. In one aspect this meant the hegemony of the secular power, if necessary a purgation of the Church carried through by the secular arm. In another aspect it meant an insistence on the spiritual side of the Church. Priests should be devoted to the welfare of the soul, should scorn earthly wealth, be humble like Christ Himself. The principle of apostolic poverty is held up as the highest model. Rarely, however, is this ideal of blessed poverty suggested for the lay world. Wyclif, it is true, in an early work states that all property should be held in common, but his later writings do not envisage social reform of such a type. Huss and Luther were understood by some of their contemporaries to advocate economic equality, and gave

[1] Carlyle, *A History of Medieval Political Theory.*

an impetus to communistic movements, but in actual fact they attacked only ecclesiastical wealth. Yet it is indicative of the economic forces which shaped the nationalistic movements that they were never free of communistic elements. The national rising in Italy in 1375, led by Florence, had as its symbol a red standard with " Liberty " enscrolled upon it.[1] Wyclif's Poor Preachers advocated in certain districts an ideal of poverty for all, and were persecuted by the State. Philip the Fair of France had, in his propaganda against the pope, discovered the reserves of energy in the common people ; and, when the lower classes were called to political action, they were bound to discover doctrines suitable to their own pressing needs. Occasionally, even, such needs found idealistic expression in the cultured classes, as in Thomas More's *Utopia*.

Communistic yearnings existed frequently within the nationalist movements, nearly always in a confused form. Yet Communism was not a doctrine for any indiscriminate sections of the lower classes. Its emphasis on social responsibilities, on social discipline, imply its source in classes where a community of life and activity exists, and not in the riff-raff. In the Middle Ages, as nowadays, we find Communism strongest in classes with a clearly defined social function, though without corresponding social rights ; in classes which clustered together in their work, were conscious of their social value and aware of some measure of co-operative strength. And we find that communistic doctrines are strong not only among those classes, such as the peasants, which simply look back to a tradition of communal ownership, and strive at times to return to earlier social forms, but also among new semi-proletarian classes created by new economic processes. Medieval Communism was indeed strongest in the richest industrial districts, first in North Italy and South France, spreading to Flanders with the rise of Flemish trade. It is found, above all, in the largest and most profitable industry of those times—among the weavers of all countries.

[1] Pastor, *Geschichte der Päpste*, 1886, p. 79.

The weaving-trade in the Middle Ages differed from other types of production in two main characteristics—first, that it was organised for an export market, and, second, that it developed a modified form of capitalism on a large scale. The normal productive process of the Middle Ages envisaged a fixed market, with very small geographical limits—usually the town and the villages around it. On the basis of this fixed market a rigid control over production was effected by the guilds of masters, often supported by the princes. Maxima were established for the amount of production, for the numbers of apprentices and journeymen employed by any master ; the numbers of masters were strictly limited, prices were fixed. Individualistic competition and the expansion of production could exist only within certain limits. But this system broke down wherever production for export existed—above all in the weaving industry, later in the mining and metallurgical industries. The foreign market was undefined. It was capable of unlimited expansion. As a result individual enterprise could break through the restrictions of the guilds and develop production to unprecedented proportions. The carrying-trade, commerce, grew at the same time, often controlling the industry—hence the rise of the great class of merchants, the dominant type of early capitalist.

This new form of production for export effected deep changes in the structure of industry itself. Dependent on the merchants, the artisan weavers became more and more proletarianised. As the export grew they depended more and more on foreign raw material, on wool which came from distant parts, from overseas. Though the technique of production did not change essentially until the eighteenth century, and weaving remained a home-industry, the control of raw material, of markets, of prices fell into the hands of the few. The *Verlag* system became common whereby the merchant-capitalist provided the artisans with the wool, paid them for the work, and collected the finished goods for export. Thus the weavers became to some extent proletarians, owning their tools, it is true, but virtually

ER

working for a wage. The old guilds existed in a changed form, having the functions as much of a trade union as of a guild, attempting to guard the interests of workers against employers. And not only were the weavers a prey to the naked class-policy of proud capitalists,[1] but the dependence on an export market which could be closed by any of the various calamities of the medieval period—above all, by plagues and by wars—led to repeated crises which spread unemployment and famine among them. The political rivalries which led to the frequent closing of the English ports to the Flemish trade caused vast social unrest in the weaving area. The first strikes occurred in the weaving industry, and social upheavals were frequent in the cloth-making towns, especially during and after the fourteenth century.

These industrial struggles often, under the stress of circumstances, took on a political form, involving kings and princes. When the weavers of Bruges revolted, in 1302, against the patricians, a French expedition sent to restore the old powers was massacred by the insurgents. Sometimes these revolts of the lower classes were utilised by the great lords to enable them to establish a more complete domin-ance over the towns, for the patriciate would be forced to call on the military strength of the princes to subjugate the masses. Thus the dukes of Flanders often favoured insurgent movements in order to strengthen their own hold on the rich towns. But, even when the lower classes were able to assert their claim to a share at least in the town govern-ment, they remained far from power. In Liège in 1384, for instance, a coalition government was set up between the defeated patricians and the representatives of the weaving and other guilds. But even the great numerical superiority of the weavers, which made such a reform possible, was powerless to make this a permanent form of government. Always in such cases innumerable wrangles arose between the various types of artisans regarding their ancient and anachronistic privileges, indicative of their incompetence

R. H. Pirenne, *Les Périodes de l'histoire sociale du capitalisme.*

to create a constructive economic policy. Patricians and merchants could be overpowered and forced from time to time, but the rising capitalistic system of production could not be overthrown, and all the reforms left it practically intact.

Four great insurrections of the Middle Ages illustrate in particular this inability of the lower classes to replace capitalism and capitalistic government by anything more productive—in maritime Flanders, 1325–8 ; at Ghent, 1372–82 ; at Florence, 1378–82 ; and Paris, 1413. Some of these show no lack of revolutionary zeal and ability, the lower classes resisting with a grim energy attacks from within and without over a number of years. They were saluted by the lower classes in other parts of Europe with enthusiasm, being recognised as definite attempts at social reform, at the victory of the depossessed artisans over the powers of wealth. Practically always such revolts took place at a time of the eclipse of prosperity, when confusion reigned in the ranks of the ruling classes. But no efforts of the revolutionaries could bring back this prosperity. Nothing like a Socialist method of production was applied ; indeed, these revolutions, though directed against the ruling class, were not truly democratic. Each guild took advantage of the upheaval to strengthen its own monopoly ; not merely against the depredations of individualistic capitalists, but also against rival towns, against villages and peasantry. These were revolutions of a petty bourgeoisie, not of an organised proletariat, which did not then exist. Such Communism as, under certain circumstances, was effected, was a sharing of goods, and left untouched the whole question of the communisation of the means of production.

This was bound to be so from the very nature of contemporary capitalism. The merchants were the typical capitalist of those days, since capitalism existed primarily in distribution, and in the financing of commerce. Though the merchants held sway over thousands of small artisans, the methods of production were not capitalistic. Each small artisan owned his own tools, even though the raw material and the finished product was controlled by the merchant. The time was still far distant when the power-machine would be invented, to put the means of production completely into the possession of the capitalist, and to create a real proletariat—and to bring with it the idea of the communal ownership of the means of production. The aim of the revolutionary artisans was to recapture some of their former independence as a class from the patriciate and merchants. The economic measures they proposed were reactionary rather than progressive, for they could provide no commercial organisation to replace the capitalism of the merchants. The philosophy of these revolutionary movements indicates this weakness. Among the revolutionary groups flourished many varieties of ascetic doctrines, of mystical and ecstatic beliefs, all involving negation of the world. The Adamites, the most extreme ascetic Communists of Bohemia, find their origin in the Ghent revolution. Such doctrines are the counterpart of social impotence.

With this uncertainty of economic programme, medieval Communism was bound to be confused with regard to the complicated class-relationships of the Middle Ages, to the struggle for power between the various types of ownership. Even in the towns a constant war was going on between the more feudal patriciate, living on rents and hereditary office, and the rising, aggressive merchant class. The most complicated relationships existed between these classes and the great princes ; between princes and barons ; between the Church and all these. Alliance and hostility alternate in the great process of amalgamation and consolidation of the national States. In England and Germany the new nationalism affirmed itself in opposition to the papacy ; in France and Spain in alliance with it. Again, the Church which embodied in its doctrine the severest condemnation of usury, of capitalist enterprise, itself gave the greatest impetus to money-dealings. In this criss-cross of interests the lower classes were embroiled. Unable to construct a society on communistic principles, they gave their uncertain allegiance to other classes—sometimes turning back to earlier forms of production and to an alliance with barons ; sometimes proposing principles akin to those of the Puritans, the negation of feudalism ; sometimes the bitterest opponents of the Church, sometimes its most ardent defenders. Communist doctrines are prevalent in the Middle Ages, but never decisive and independent.

As a result the prevailing characteristic of Communism in the Middle Ages is, that it is personal, subjective, not social. Poverty is proclaimed as a blessed state of mind. Its expression is essentially religious, in that it begins and ends with pre-occupation concerning the soul ; and usually the Communists aim at forming small esoteric communities, shutting off the world instead of conquering it.[1] To a large extent, too, the focus of communistic thought is the Christian Church. The Church was the only organisation which appealed to the masses. Its ethical function was to link up the masses of the population with the social order. In it were united the worship of poverty of the Gospels and the affirmation of private ownership. The attack on the Church as the ethics of existing society was the first necessity of every social reformer ; that the medieval Communists aimed primarily at the organisation of a new kind of Church indicates their distance from a positive social policy. This confused relationship between social and religious aims must constitute the focus of our interest in medieval Communism.

II. RELIGIOUS COMMUNISM

THE ALBIGENSES

Nowhere is the intermixture of religious and social elements more subtle than in the greatest heretical movement

---

[1] This has led most historians to treat of the sects as essentially religious movements, and to treat of their social doctrines as mere adjuncts—e.g. C. Lea, *A History of the Inquisition in the Middle Ages*; I. Döllinger, *Beiträge zur Sektengeschichte des Mittelalters.*

of the Middle Ages, amongst the Cathari or, as they are usually called, the Albigenses. This heresy grew powerful first in North Italy, then in South France, during the twelfth century, in the most flourishing commercial and industrial districts of Europe, at a time when art and science were at a peak. Yet in this land of the troubadours a religion grew strong, tolerated if not favoured by princes, which turned in starkest abnegation from the world. The Cathari believed that this world was the realm of Satan, while God reigned only in Heaven ; Christ had not become an earthly man, but His body was made in Heaven ; He was conceived, not in Mary's womb, but through her ear. The task of the Perfect was to turn away from the world, to renounce all earthly possessions, all pleasures of the body, sexual inter-course, food, except the simplest. The highest achievement was the *Endura*, voluntary death by starvation. On the grounds of such beliefs the Cathari were persecuted first by princes (in the eleventh and twelfth centuries), then by the Church, being almost completely eradicated by the end of the thirteenth century.

The origins of the Catharan religion are obscure, and branched into various modifications. It has obvious connec-tions with the Manichæan belief, and types of the heresy lingered in Bosnia and Bulgaria till late Renaissance times. But its social origins and composition are clearer. In some districts of France the Cathari received the general name of weavers, in Italy they were often identified with the *Patarini*, a word which means rag-pickers. It is clear, then, that in the main the Cathari were poor and despised classes—the Inquisitor who was most active against them in Italy, Rainerio Sacconi, refers to them scornfully as " idiots and illiterates." In most of the Italian cities armed bands sup-ported the work of the Inquisitors, and these bands, *Crocesegnati* were composed of wealthy cavaliers. Again, though many of the Cathari were mere sympathisers, who did not carry out to the full the tenets of the heresy, yet the ideal perfection demanded an utter sacrifice of all worldly possessions, a return to absolute poverty.

It is doubtful whether the Cathari paid homage to Satan as the lord of this world. They themselves carried on bitter arguments as to the exact relationship between God, Christ, and Lucifer. Yet their harsh doctrines attracted proselytes. They offered small hope for humanity, and yet forces were working which swelled their numbers. The various formulations of their beliefs all express criticism of the established order, in particular a hatred for the Roman Church which gave its ethics to this order. The Cathari refused to take oaths, i.e. to participate in business, to accept the discipline of the law. They established in many places communities which lived apart (cf. that at Monteforte near Asti[1]), establishing a rule of life and conduct equalitarian, communistic. In the earlier stages they were known to foment public disorders, for Cathari were burned and hanged in 1022 and 1051 by the King of France and the Emperor, in 1076 by the burghers of Cambrai, long before the papacy acceded to the request of the Emperor Barbarossa to co-operate in the extermination of the heretics (1154). Their religious doctrines seem, however, to have been formed as a direct counterblast to the Roman Church. In the period when the latter was building up its existence as a powerful worldly institution, and was shaping its doctrine of the merit of earthly activity and society, the Cathari formulated the resistance to this. The Church, they said, should remain poor and persecuted. Its ministers should be servants. All the paraphernalia of the Church, which build it out into a concrete edifice, were opposed. Works of penance, the sacraments, the worship of images, everything that affirms the power of the Church over the believer, were repudiated. The Cathari emphasised the fundamental criticism of ecclesiasticism—the inefficacy of sacraments unless the ministrant be himself pure.

In its ethics Catharism proposed an ideal of self-abnegation to which, it was recognised, only a few, the " Perfect," could aspire. In its theology it built up a complex dogmatic structure, the acceptance of which was as

1 *See* Volpe, op. cit., pp. 16–19.

important as, if not more important than, living according
to the moral precepts of the sect. In this it followed the
example of the orthodox Christian Church, for which dogmatic belief had become more important than the " Imita-
tion " of Christ. And the same social complexity is evident
in the sect as in the Christian Church. Members of all
classes came to belong to the Cathari, rich and poor, noble
and commoner, merchant and labourer. The gloomy
asceticism of the moral tenets of the sect were reserved for
the few. The many adopted it as a religion opposed to
Catholicism, as an ethic opposed to the ethic of the empire,
and hence justifying a political rupture with the highest
authorities. The Catharan teaching on poverty, however
inadequately realised, attacked the Church in its weakest
spot, where it ran counter to the direct commands of Christ.
But it remained an ideal, restricted to the few ; and the
communistic trends in Catharism never came to any positive social formulation. Wherever temporal powers favoured
the sect, it established institutions similar to those of the
Roman Church—a hierarchy, monasteries, seminaries, even
convents for the education of girls of noble birth. While the
religious *élan* of Catharism seems to have come from the
poor, particularly the new, semi-proletarianised classes produced by the development of industry and commerce, its
general form as a religion, and its wide acceptance, seem to
have been the result of the attempt of particularist lords to
break away from the central control of empire and papacy.
And this revolt against the highest authority was bound to
be strongest in districts where new principles of trade were
being applied, and where the feudal order was most irk-
some for populace and lord.

The history of the heresy illustrates this, and shows how
a subjective belief in equality and poverty is not at all
equivalent to a movement for social reform. In Italy
Catharism was rife, during the twelfth century, among
patrician and noble families in the cities—lists of persons
convicted of the heresy show this. It was frequently adopted
by classes who were at war with the papacy as a secular

power, used as the philosophy of their antagonism. In some districts the Cathari were commonly dubbed Ghibellines. Above all, the history of the movement in South France, in the lands of the Counts of Toulouse, shows the equivocal nature of Catharan belief. Under the tolerance of the Counts, the heresy found thousands of adherents here, towards the end of the twelfth century. Situated in the midst of the rivalries of the Kings of France and England and the lords of Aragon, the Counts of Toulouse won a great measure of independence. They saw the detachment of their prosperous land from the allegiance to Rome as a further strengthening of their own wealth and power. Among the Court-singers a free criticism of the Church and papal manners was regarded with approval, and the libertinism of the Court was transmuted into Catharism among the burghers. The heretical religion was celebrated openly, despite papal emissaries; its bishops and priests were honoured.

But in Toulouse the limitations of the subjective belief in poverty are shown most clearly. In the persecutions which followed we find that wealthy burghers belonged to the sect, in spite of the formal belief in poverty. Catharism did not deny the existing social order, or attempt to replace it by another; it became, indeed, a bulwark of the Counts' particularist ambitions. And as such it was dealt with by the papacy. The papal legates sent to Toulouse in 1204 were treated with derision, one being slain. When the pope appealed for support from the secular arm against the heresy, he received no answer from a lethargic Christendom. But when the Albigensian crusades were organised, their success was conditional on the expeditions being directed against the temporal lord of Toulouse, and only secondarily against the heresy. The great barons of North France, envious of the independence and prosperity of Raymond of Toulouse, moved against him a great army of knights and men anxious for plunder. All Raymond's anxious submission to the Holy Father in Rome availed him nothing. His castles were subdued, his lands laid waste, and made over to a vassal of the King of France, later to devolve into the latter's own

possession. Only the cities put up a strong resistance, especially Toulouse ; and they were ultimately laid waste and
their inhabitants slaughtered without distinction of religion.
The success of the campaign against the Cathari was
identical with that of the campaign against the lords of
Toulouse. The heresy had grown strong under the stimulus
of the particularist ambitions of the Counts ; it failed with
them.

The Catharan faith, which polemically maintained the
blessedness of poverty, almost became the philosophy of a
national State. Its patrons and defenders were crushed, but
there still remained the masses of its believers—those who
strove to keep its tenets pure. Rulers may be wiped out, but
the lower classes, the conditions which produce yearnings
for release, cannot so be exterminated. Till the end of the
thirteenth century small fearful communities of Cathari
were still to be found all over Western Europe, continually
ferreted out by the Inquisition. But the method of force
alone could not avail. Within the orthodox Church itself a
means was found to satisfy these primitive desires for poverty
and equality, to canalise them within the margins of existing society. The Orders of St. Dominic and St. Francis,
particularly the latter, are, as much as the heresies, characteristic types of medieval communistic movements.

DOMINICANS AND FRANCISCANS

The earliest type of organised Communism in the Christian Church is the monastery, where, within the boundaries
of the settlement, work and possession are common. By the
twelfth century, monasteries in general, far from their early
form, were centres of wealth, envied by secular poor and
rich alike. Similar foundations occur frequently in the
medieval period, with the pure intentions of the early
orders. Such are the Umiliati, a group of austere men who
lived ascetically, preaching that only work could justify
life. These were confirmed as a semi-monastic order in the
middle of the twelfth century, though, characteristically

enough, the popes forbade them to preach publicly, to spread their doctrines abroad. By enclosing them within monastic walls Innocent III not only rendered their criticism of the social order harmless, but also gave them a constitution which made of them a sort of capitalistic group.

The Dominicans owe their importance to the needs of the times. St. Dominic himself, a Spanish dignitary, became involved more or less by chance in combating the Catharan heresy in Toulouse. He saw the necessity of winning over the common people to the Church, and set himself this task. Abandoning all his ecclesiastical dignities, he organised around him a small band of devoted preachers, who ventured amongst the heretical population, preaching adherence to the Church. His group renounced the splendours and possessions of this world, and gave a shining example of self-abnegation in themselves. Their work was widely successful, turning the heretics to believe in a Church which held such treasures of humility and self-sacrifice. But St. Dominic taught also rigorous subservience to the papacy—in the seminaries of the order was fashioned the ultimate theology of the papal Church. Difficult as it was to inculcate in the masses a trust in the wealthy papal organisation, yet the restriction of abuses among the provincial clergy was bound to find favour with the populace. Through the medium of the Inquisition, most of whose officers were Dominicans, the papacy was able to extend its authority over the provincial clergy of Western Europe.

Even more effective in the papal cause than the Dominicans were the Franciscans. Their emotionalism was nearer the lower classes than was the austere discipline of the Dominicans, and their history shows the reality of the social impetus in the religious movements of the Middle Ages. St. Francis's conversion was a purely personal revulsion against wealth and social privilege. With his band of twelve disciples he at first aimed merely at living again as Christ had done, in humility and poverty. When he organised his order he disdained theological study. The rule of the order made it necessary for all members to renounce property ; their aim was simply to teach the morality of the Gospels, especially the virtue of poverty and unworldliness. The Franciscans were to be " strangers and pilgrims in the world " ; their poverty was the source of their blessedness, as their rule has it : " this perfection of Poverty which has made you, dearest brethren, heirs and kings of the Kingdom of Heaven." This religion of poverty found hearts attuned to it, and the order expanded at an enormous rate. At the end of fifty years it is reckoned that more than 1,100 monasteries of the Grey Friars existed, comprising between 20,000 and 30,000 members. It was the example of the success of the Franciscans which led the Dominicans to adopt the rule of personal poverty. The two orders were important not only in social influence. The greatest thinkers of the thirteenth century belong to their orders—Albertus Magnus, Thomas Aquinas, Roger Bacon, Bonaventura, Duns Scotus. Around the orders were grouped large bands of " sympathisers," who adopted some of the rules, pledged in particular not to bear arms except in defence of the Church. This type of organisation was common to nearly all contemporary religious movements, heretical and orthodox.

In the praise of poverty the Order of St. Francis had much in common with the Cathari, more still with other heretical bodies such as the Waldenses. But the policy of Innocent III and following popes was to shackle this vague communistic feeling to the existing social order, to the Church. Thus the desire for poverty, the belief in the blessedness of poverty, was not condemned. It was even encouraged, and the order granted special papal privileges. But discipline was brought into the order, and absolute obedience to the Holy Father enjoined. In spite of the rule that its members were to be " strangers and pilgrims," the Franciscans were organised in provincial and local groups, monasteries were founded, endowments received. Very soon after the death of St. Francis this process unleashed a violent struggle in the order, which reflects a profound social conflict.

Elias of Cortona, who succeeded Francis in the general-ship of the order, actively encouraged the foundation of monasteries for the members, as only in such establish-ments could discipline be maintained—as long as the brethren wandered as beggars their doctrines and behaviour were removed from oversight. With the existence of monas-teries the order acquired property, and though the in-dividual members were still free of the taint of ownership, the order itself became wealthy. This led to a fundamental schism in the order. Those brethren following Elias, the Conventuals, endorsed the acquisition of poverty and became a bulwark of the papacy. Their opponents, the Spirituals, calling themselves the true heirs of St. Francis, advocated absolute abnegation of the world, and the ideal of mendicancy. While the Conventuals followed practical political tasks, being utilised in the Inquisitorial Courts both against heretics and against the provincial clergy, the Spirituals were a prey to visions of a new world, chiliastic dreams which reflect a tortured society. The prophecies attributed to Joachim of Flora, the Everlasting Gospel of 1254, appealed to such men and gave them a fanatical hope, foretelling a Kingdom of the Holy Spirit where selflessness and love will rule, charging the Church with failure. The Franciscans are indicated as the harbingers of this coming realm. The growing wealth and power of the Franciscans made the struggle between the two parties more and more bitter towards the end of the thirteenth century. Even a general of the order such as Bonaventura, or a saint like Birgitta, complained of the greed for wealth among the brethren, not to speak of the attacks of the secular clergy, William of St. Amour, and many others.

The popes, who used Franciscans as their emissaries, defended them against the attacks of the secular clergy, and attempted to heal the breach within the order. Nicholas III compromised by saying that while Christ Himself had completely renounced property, yet the property of the Franciscans was not theirs, but was invested in the Church. Since the order only enjoyed the usufruct of the property, and did not possess the capital, the Franciscans were not owners, and therefore did not break their rule of poverty. This interpretation—a fundamental principle of the Roman ethics—could not, however, stay the rising tide of conflict. Boniface VIII (1294–1303) was forced to persecute the mendicant friars as lawless heretics who fomented social discontent. The Spirituals declared their opposition, forming themselves into a separate group without papal approval. Around them they rallied other groups of visionary mendicants, chief among them the Fraticelli, who lived according to the example of St. Francis. The struggle came to its height during the papacy of John XXII, a worldly pope who, residing at Avignon, was much influenced by the French throne. The Fraticelli and Joachimites were persecuted zealously, and John went so far as to issue a decretal to the effect that Christ actually exercised the right of ownership. So absolute a denial of the ideal of poverty failed of its object, and brought Conventuals and Spirituals into joint opposition to the papacy. The Franciscans fled to the Court of the Emperor Louis the Bavarian. One of their number was made antipope by Ludwig, and invested in 1328 in Rome. After John's death the quarrel lost its virulence. Later popes admitted the poverty of Christ, and the Conventuals built up again the discipline of the order, which accepted papal authority. The Fraticelli and other small groups were forced into obscurity, subsisting as heretical communities in remote places.

The history of the Franciscans provides a picture of the contending forces which racked medieval society. It reveals the widespread longing for a world where distinctions of privilege and wealth would be abolished, with the conflict between this longing and the agents of earthly law and power. Amid the criss-cross of interests which strove to turn this conflict to political advantage—kings and emperors who encouraged the love of poverty, at various times, in order to have an effective instrument of propaganda against the papacy—the main process is its relation with the papacy, the Church. Either the Church was to condemn and excommunicate the communistic idealists, or it was to transform them, and make them into its defenders. Under the lead of Innocent III the latter course was pursued, with minor deviations, so that the worshippers of poverty became, by a strange paradox, the upholders of the Church, of the largest land-owner of the times, of the theological system which justified private property as being ordained by God. The more ardent spirits among the Franciscans remained in revolt, of course ; but the Church, by this policy, was able to isolate the more fanatical Communists from the rest, and proceed slowly to their eradication by force. It was rewarded by the loyalty of the most sincere and powerful thinkers of the period, who, while paying homage to the Franciscan and Dominican ideal, saw in the Church the only guarantee of this ideal.

What made this transformation of the ascetic, communistic beliefs of St. Francis possible ? That these beliefs were sociologically unstable can be seen from the use made of them by the temporal powers. They were common among the lower classes, and summed up a vast social energy. But however much they united the lower classes in belief, they did not unite them in social action. This " Communism " was entirely subjective. Poverty was a subjective ideal, brought salvation to the individual. Its most ambitious aim was the conversion of the world, not the overthrow of the existing system of ownership. Thus any overlord was served who granted the individual the right of confessing this ideal. In particular the Church was able to win the allegiance of these subjective Communists by giving them a social form in which to exist—their order, and the monastic system. Here their Communism could be both practised and preached. And at the same time, it was prevented even more from becoming a sociological doctrine, became more and more an individual refuge from society. The idea still lived, and continually threw up shoots— even in the early sixteenth century we find it inspiring a Franciscan like Thomas Murner to bitter satire of the wealth of the Church and the materialism of society. But as a movement it was harmless for the ruling classes, or, rather, provided a safety-valve for them, converting men from more dangerous subversive doctrines.

WALDENSES AND ANABAPTISTS

How uncertain the allegiance of the early Franciscans to the Church was is shown by the history of the heresies of Waldenses and Anabaptists, whose outlook resembles in many points that of the Franciscan Spirituals. In these centuries many local leaders rose who were adjudged to be heretics and persecuted. Some, like Tanchelm in Antwerp (*c.* 1108) and Eon de l'Etoile in Brittany a little later, tried to resurrect the customs of Christ's times, calling themselves prophets, even Messiahs, plundering the wealth of the Church and dividing the spoils among the poor. Others, like Henry of Toulouse, preached simplicity and poverty. Others, like Arnold of Brescia, tried to establish in place of the existing order a commonwealth of Poor Men, evoking the memory of the Roman Republic. Common to all these is a fierce attack on the secularised and wealthy Church. The remnants of the sects they founded, together with the few scattered communities of Cathari, joined, in the thirteenth and fourteenth centuries, with the vast movement of the Waldenses, of which the Anabaptists were a local modification.

Peter Waldo himself was a character very similar to St. Francis. A rich merchant of Lyons, a flourishing city, in which class distinctions were necessarily marked, he renounced his goods and family, and devoted himself to the preaching of poverty in his native town. He did not, however, organise his disciples in the manner of Francis, with an authoritarian head, but established a number of loose groups, led by deacons. Still his aims were expressly approved by popes. While making the New Testament his chief guide, he accepted the authority of Rome where there was no contradiction between the decretals and Christ's commands.

Such a movement as the Poor Men of Lyons was bound

to turn to attacking the Church, unless it was strictly organised. The deacons of the groups were, however, not controlled, and in spite of the later established bishops the movement never achieved the unity even of the Cathari. Very soon groups were established in Italy, under the name of the Poor Men of Lombardy, with different tenets and a more radical social outlook. While the Poor Men of Lyons despised labour, and freed their deacons from the earth-bound necessity of toil, the Lombard movement made labour the cornerstone of their ethics. Their doctrine of poverty was not like that of the Cathari, a violent revulsion against all earthly activity, against life itself; it was, in certain respects, much more positive, heralding an era when the world would belong to those who toil. Thus their movement flourished among the poor artisans and trades-folk—for by labour they meant manual labour, of course. And their belief in the value of labour expressed at the same time a fundamental criticism of the rich and powerful, of merchants, bankers, and land-owners, especially of the Church.

Differently from the Cathari, the Waldenses turned against all theology, opposing to the dogmas of the Church the simple gospel of Christ. Poor and illiterate, they yet outdid learned Inquisitors in their knowledge of the sacred texts, and were responsible for translating and distributing the New Testament in many tongues. Although we can call them, in the first stage, primarily an inner mission, yet this trust in an authority superior to the pope's made them soon into a sect and social movement.

At the Council of Verona of 1184, Lucius III excommunicated the Waldenses—it was this very council which gave the Umiliati their constitution and brought them under the control of the Church. The first persecutions of Waldenses occurred in Aragon, where Alonso II undertook their suppression on his own initiative. In the Albigensian crusades we hear now and again of Waldenses who are persecuted. At the Councils of Toulouse (1229) and Tarragona (1234) the possession of sacred books translated into the vernacular was forbidden, and the translations condemned to the fire, and these measures were directed at the literature of the Waldenses. In this period the social aims of the Waldenses were formulated : they attacked the Church as an institution, refused to recognise the efficacy of sacraments, prayers for the dead, the cult of the saints. They opposed the use of force in conversion, the shedding of blood for any reason. They repudiated the two arms of the earthly powers—war and justice. Like the Cathari they claimed a due social position for women, raising them from the position of servants to that of equals, giving them a position in their Church equivalent to their social value as workers and mothers.

During the course of the thirteenth century their simple evangelism, the purity of their lives—to which Inquisitors attest—attracted to them many remnants of other heretical subversive beliefs. In spite of persecutions the Waldenses grew, as a vast brotherhood of the poor. Their organisation was loose ; maintained often only by wandering journeymen, who spread their doctrines in their search for work. Where secular and papal authority combined, they were exterminated ruthlessly ; but survivors carried their doctrines into more remote lands, into the fastnesses of the Alps, of Bohemia and Moravia. We have seen how the secular power.was able to exterminate Catharan belief in France, a country where secular power early became centralised. Later, in a unified Spain, Catharan and Waldensian opinions could be crushed by a lasting Inquisition. But it is important evidence of the structure of medieval Europe that the Waldenses maintained themselves in Northern and Middle Europe, in the Netherlands, along the Rhine, in Saxony, Austria, Bohemia, Bavaria, Moravia. With the growth of the trade of these districts, the rise of the weaving industry along the Rhine and in the Netherlands, the development of German mining—Germany was the chief source of precious metals until the discovery of America—the Waldensian faith embedded itself in the working population. The weakness, lack of centralisation of the temporal power in these areas, together with the rivalry between temporal and ecclesiastical lords, formed the framework for the growth of the Waldenses. Above all they profited by the schisms within the Church, themselves the result of the conflicts among the growing nations. When the Avignon popes put themselves at the service of the French kings, when rival popes fought for the allegiance and taxes of Christendom, the Waldenses flourished and multiplied.

Yet what has been said above of the Franciscans applies essentially to the Waldenses. Their doctrines took a subjective form, expressing the belief in poverty and sharing as a method to personal blessedness. They gave an impulse to revolt against the established order, but did not organise social revolution, give it direction. Thus we find among revolting weavers in Flanders, revolting peasants all over Europe, the germination of Waldensian seeds ; but no new organic structure resulted, and the revolts were necessarily abortive. As with Franciscans, Joachimites, etc., the revulsion against social oppression only too readily took on purely subjective forms. The oppressed turned away from the world, forming small communities of " saints " ; frequently the individual turned to mystical speculation, to dreams of a different universe, such as were rife in Germany in the fourteenth and fifteenth centuries—so abstract and remote an attack on the secular Church that the popes did not even need to condemn it. Thus insurgent feelings were dissipated. The reasons for this process are profound. These burning passions for an egalitarian realm did not fail for lack of will. They remained individualistic, and failed to attain a social objective, because the economic basis of Communism did not exist. Where revolts took place, the reforms introduced were mainly of an economically reactionary character, consisting generally in a modified redistribution of goods, and the assertion of old guild rights against the encroachments of the capitalistic merchants, against the pretensions of financiers. No idea of socialistic production could exist among lower classes which still possessed their own tools, were still split socially and technically by numerous, jealously guarded privileges. Hence, although the lower classes frequently revolted against their rulers, they were never able to effect a social revolution.

The Taborite movement in Bohemia, though sharing most of the Waldensian tenets, especially those concerning wealth, grew strong only as part of a national movement. In France the king had harnessed the papacy to the nation. In England, after the temporary popularity of Wyclif's teachings, kings and popes had entered into an alliance against barons and unruly subjects. Nationalistic movements had broken out sporadically all over Europe, without success, in the fourteenth century. Under peculiar political and social conditions a revolt broke out in Bohemia, in the second decade of the fifteenth century, which was of vast portent in the history of Europe.

Under the influence of the Wyclifites, Huss and his associates preached a return to the religion of the Gospels, the purification of the morals of Churchmen, the spiritual rights of the secular world. In spite of the safe-conduct granted to Huss, the Council of Constance condemned his doctrines and burned him, setting fire to a national conflagration. The Bohemian nobles, peasantry, city-patricians and lower classes, united to overthrow their ruler, the emperor, and to establish a Church of their own in place of the papacy. Emperor and papal Church had united to condemn Huss ; and only the particular circumstances made it possible for this national revolt to be successful. The emperor's control over Bohemia was insecure. The barons had never been curbed, and possessed great military strength. The papacy had never established a strong centralised control over the Church in Bohemia, which had even withstood the reforms of the great popes of the twelfth and thirteenth centuries ; and during the Great Schism (1378–1417) the authority of the Church had become further weakened. Together with this, the middle class in Bohemia had become wealthy and strong, chiefly owing to the mines. The general political situation was not unlike that which determined the success of Luther's reformation, a hundred years later.

At first the leadership of the revolt was in the hands of the lower townsfolk, with beliefs similar to those of the Waldenses. Unable to carry through a thorough social reform in Prague, these " extremists " established their centre at Mount Tabor, forming a community where certain communistic measures were carried out. This " Communism," however, was confined to distribution. Deacons were charged with the collection and distribution of goods, thus establishing greater equality of consumption between rich and poor. Luxury was forbidden, the morality of the Taborites frowning on worldly enjoyment. It is clear that this " Communism " was only partial, for who would think of making common property of the spinning-wheels, the lasts, the anvils of the artisans ? But its practical effect should not be minimised. Apart from the feeling of equality which the distribution of surplus wealth engendered, a very real levelling of wealth was attained, since such ownership as there was, was extremely modest—necessarily so in any community where no commercial or landed patriciate existed, where financial practices were unknown. Above all, Taborite Communism was a " war-Communism," the community was the centre of an army, liable at any moment to sudden levies of men and material, never settling down to the peaceful accumulation of wealth. After the destruction of the movement, Tabor still retained, as a poor isolated settlement, many of the communistic ideals and practices of its great days.

The confusion between nationalistic and communistic aims in the Bohemian rebellion was evident from the start. To replace the deposed emperor, a king, a scion of the feudal house of Lorraine, was elected. While the Taborites under Ziska's leadership were successful in repelling imperial invasions, their discipline and devotion spreading the terror of their name far and wide, soon the great nobles and the upper bourgeoisie of Prague began intriguing with the enemy, trying to throw off the yoke of the Communists.

Even though the Taborites were successful in conquering their internal enemies in 1427, and in winning Prague, they did not introduce a complete social reform, leaving the upper classes in the possession of their property. Their economic measures resulted only in excessive taxation, and in the decline of trade and production. Thus their position became undermined, and in 1434, thirteen years after they had won power, the Taborites were overthrown and forced from the political stage. This most spectacular communistic movement of the Middle Ages illustrates, in sharp relief, the lack of an objective basis for Communism in that period. Communism is always interpreted as distribution of the superfluous wealth of the rich among the poor ; the source of this wealth is left untouched. Thus the root of class distinction is not removed. Political divisions between the various sections of the ruling classes, in particular the stalemate between barons and emperor, made a transitory victory for the lower classes possible in Bohemia. But the latter were unable to construct a new society, and the advantage slipped through their fingers.

The Taborites were a militant community, aiming at the reformation of all Bohemia, if not of the world—they maintained connection with Waldensian groups in other parts of Europe. Their defeat gave the chief power in Bohemia into the hands of the great barons and the patriciate of the towns, who for the two following centuries fought a losing battle against the pretensions of the emperors. Under cover of this struggle for power the lower classes maintained their beliefs, though in a different form. In the communities of the Bohemian Brethren a heresy was nursed, teaching negation of the world, hatred of theology and the Church, complete sharing of goods within the community. Turning away from social reform, stress came to be laid more and more on subjective blessedness, on purity of heart. The nobility began to join, and in conflicts between radical and conciliatory elements the radicals lost and were often persecuted. The communities became famous for the integrity of character of their members. They enjoyed the protection of the nobility both as a protest against Rome and the emperor, and also because of the prosperity the communities brought to the land. They formed in some sort capitalistic enterprises, chiefly in the weaving industry, having wide trade connections. Since personal luxury was strictly condemned, the profits were devoted to the community, to the development of trade. That antinomy noted later by Wesley existed here in all clarity : it is God's law to work, though not for personal gain ; but work brings gain willynilly, and the result is accumulation of wealth. These communities illustrate, despite the austerity of individual morality, many of the characteristics of capitalistic enterprise. Grimmelshausen, the German novelist, writing of such a community in so backward a region as Hungary in the seventeenth century, notes how rationally the division of labour is carried out, what wealth the community owns.

In certain districts the Bohemian Brethren became known in the sixteenth century as Anabaptists. Re-baptism had been common among Cathari and Waldenses, as a sign of membership of the community of the elect. In the sixteenth century it became the distinctive sign of that body of belief which wished to remodel social life in accordance with the communistic statements of the New Testament. Such belief spread widely as a part of the general attack on the papacy and emperor, as a section of the reformation of Luther and Zwingli. The political chaos in Germany, resulting from the rivalries between princes and emperor, made the insurgence of the lower classes a political possibility. The general economic crisis, the increase in prices, the restriction of traditional liberties, gave the impulse to social convulsions of vast extent. Riots and revolts of journeymen and peasants were frequent from the end of the fifteenth century. In the Anabaptist movement they find their most comprehensive theoretical form.

Like the Waldensian movement, of which the Anabaptists were the successors, this new movement was widespread. It first threw out a strong challenge in the centres where the Reformation was strongest, in Saxony and Switzerland.

Zittau weavers, after a vain attempt at levelling social distinctions in their native town, spread the hope for social reform over Middle Germany, even in Wittenberg, where they troubled even Melanchthon's respect for established authority. Luther's lieutenant, Carlstadt, was brought by the uneducated Zittau weavers to abandon his learned colleagues and to live as a peasant. Thomas Münzer, the great revolutionary figure of the time, carried out levelling reforms in his successive parishes, preaching the evil of worldly possession. Chased from Saxony, with the imprecations of Luther following them over Germany, many of these men found a refuge in the cities of the Upper Rhine, in the centres of Zwinglianism. Here Anabaptists like Grebel and Stülzer had tried to break down the established Church altogether, and replace it by free spiritual communities. Their attack on the tithe had, however, aroused Zwingli's resentment, and from 1523 they were persecuted. It is characteristic that one of the Swiss Anabaptist leaders, Hubmeier, had earlier (1516–19) led anti-Semitic agitation in Regensburg—i.e. an attack on usury. From 1525, when Münzer was executed and the peasant rising crushed, the Anabaptists were persecuted everywhere in Germany, and forced into obscurity, finding a refuge among the mining and weaving population of Tyrol and Moravia.

Persecuted like wild beasts by Catholic and Protestant lords and town governments, the Anabaptists were able to form fairly permanent communities, with clear social characteristics, only in Bohemia and Moravia. A famous community existed at Austerlitz, founded by Jacob Huter, for almost a hundred years, and gives us an example of the social aspirations of the heretics. In a hostile world, where power was clearly in the hands of the wealthy, the Anabaptist doctrine was pacific, defensive, in strong contrast to the Taborite. The general civil laws were obeyed, except for the war-tax and the special tax for provision of a wage for the executioner. Each man gave the surplus of his production to the spiritual directors of the community, who distributed it among the poor. When the community had more than it needed, the surplus was sold. Since personal luxury of all kinds was abhorred, the wealth of the community grew, to the envy of other towns in the neighbourhood. The great disorder in the economic organisation of Renaissance cities was overcome through a far-reaching division of labour, and through the stress laid on the moral value of labour. Children were removed from the immediate control of their parents, and brought up in pedagogic establishments, where they early learned social responsibility. As with the Calvinists, the community was conceived of primarily as religious, governed by a stern morality. But the priesthood did not crystallise out into a caste, and was controlled by the community. In 1622 imperialistic ambitions broke up the Austerlitz community, as it did the settlements of the Bohemian Brethren.

Anabaptism in its most militant form flared up for a few short days at Münster in Lower Germany in 1534. A weaving town, Münster was a place of refuge for the persecuted radical weavers of the neighbouring towns of the Low Countries. An ecclesiastical see under the rule of the archbishopric of Cologne, its government was undermined by the Reformation, and the policy of its bishops wavered between a papal and a particularist policy. Where Luther had control the Reformation had taken place under the direction, or with the approval, of the temporal powers. Church property had been put into their hands, or into the hands of town patriciates. In the see of Münster, however, while the bishop hesitated and the town authorities waited on the will of their lord, the lower classes took matters into their own hands, threw out the old government, and instituted one of their own. Their revolt against constituted authority was expressed in their adopting Anabaptism as their creed—all their members were baptised into a *new* community ; secular society, which Luther maintained, was cast off like an old garment.

The revolutionary government in the town was soon besieged, and soon, after a heroic resistance, overthrown by forces from without. It existed only in conditions of war.

Yet, even under these conditions, characteristic features of semi-communistic organisation are evident—a harsh repugnance to moral and material luxury, insistence on the division of surplus wealth among the poor, a stern corporate discipline.[1] The legends concerning the communisation of women we can treat as lightly as those spread after 1917 concerning Soviet Russia. At the same time, the usual restrictions to this " Communism " are observed. The means of production, weaving-looms, the tools of the artisans, etc., remained the property of each artisan ; the source of wealth was not communised, the old classes left intact. Traitors were left within the armed camp, and contributed to its downfall. Though the political situation made it possible for the Münster levellers momentarily to win power, economically their movement shows all the characteristics of medieval Communism. The wisest and bravest of the rebels against inequality could not establish, could not imagine, a Socialist commonwealth. The forms of production were still necessarily individual, their development could take place only through capitalism.

III. THE PEASANT RISINGS

In the towns medieval Communism comes to its clearest expression and most incisive action, as an accompaniment of the growth of capitalism. Economically the towns play a decisive rôle in the transformation of feudal society, in the formation of the modern national States. In spite of this, only a small proportion of the medieval population dwelt in towns, the overwhelming mass of the people lived on the land. A number of causes—economic, geographical, political—imposed a passive rôle on the European peasantry in this period, but under certain circumstances peasant risings took place of gigantic proportions, sweeping across the

[1] *See* Bernhard Rottmann, *Restitution rechter und gesunder christlicher Lehre, Münster, 1534*—the work of a contemporary.

countryside with the strength of a plague. In these risings, as in those of urban populations, we can discern characteristic features of medieval Communism, of communistic doctrines which struggled to give a direction to the unrest of the workers on the land.

The development of the towns as centres of industry and trade had a twofold effect on the countryside. On the one hand the towns established, more or less completely, monopolies of industry for themselves. Village-industry was often suppressed, the villages becoming a sort of colonial area for the towns, having to accept commodities at the prices fixed by the guilds. The development of trade brought with it the general development of a metal currency with a continual rise of price, from which the peasants suffered together with all land-owners. Under such circumstances land-owners intensified their exploitation of land-workers, increasing feudal dues, enclosing common land, meadows, and forests, appropriating fishing and hunting rights, etc. On the other hand, while this process went on in areas fairly distant from towns, in their neighbourhood changes were of a different nature. Here land-owners were within reach of an increasing market for agricultural produce. In order to increase the productivity of the land, the feudal dues of the peasantry were progressively remitted, commuted for money rents. The peasantry profited by this in many cases, whence come those constant complaints of town moralists concerning the wealth and luxury of the peasantry. But under certain circumstances this process caused the peasantry great distress. In a country such as England, where the greatest trade was the export of wool, the land-owners began to change from plough to meadow. Common lands were enclosed on a large scale, and the consequent distress was increased by the fact that the rearing of flocks and herds needed far less human labour than the production of crops. Sir Thomas More gives in his *Utopia* (1516) a graphic picture of the devastation caused among the peasantry by sheep-farming ; and the aims of the Governments were merely directed at preserving this misery. By the Statute of Labourers (1349–51) the Government tried to keep wages at the traditional rate, and the merchants of London continually strove, with more or less success, to prevent the price of wool from rising.

As the outcome of these conditions, the peasantry frequently joined in the revolts of the lower classes in the towns. In the revolt in Flanders 1323–8, peasants joined with the revolting artisans of Ypres and Bruges, refusing to pay the tithe and forcing abbeys to distribute their stocks of produce. But there were also more specific peasant risings, in which the peasantry pursued their own aims. The least important of these peasant revolts took the form of the Jacqueries in France (1358). Here the peasantry, oppressed by a long-continued anarchy and heavy taxation from feudal lords, rose in a wild fury, and revenged themselves on their oppressors. Isolated castles were sacked, their noble occupants subjected to tortures and cruelly slain. After a few weeks, a few organised bands of horsemen imposed peace on the rebels, slaughtering thousands. The rising was a terrible and vain revenge. It was characterised by no proposals for reform, by no moral beliefs, an act of helpless rage.

The great events of 1381 in England show a different complexion. In England more than elsewhere the countryside had been transformed from arable to grazing land, to serve the interests of the wool-trade. The peasantry was being deprived of its old rights and possessions, the lords enclosing common lands ruthlessly. The Black Death, decreasing the labour-power, had given an opportunity to the land workers to demand better wages, shaking the hold of traditional social relationships between lord and serf. Forbidden by the Statute of Labourers to receive more than the traditional wage, the labourers wandered over the land seeking employers who would grant them better conditions despite the law, and these migrations gave the peasants' movement unity and extent. As a final and immediate cause, the failure of the commercial policy of the last years of Edward III, the unavailing military expeditions to France, the consequent economic distress, bore down on the lower classes in the form of increased taxation. Under these conditions the great Peasants' Rising was born.

It cannot be said that the Peasants' Rising in England was predominantly communistic. In general the rebels, strongest in West and South England, made precise demands, which centred in the demand for liberation from manorial control and for lightening of taxation. It was with these demands that Wat Tyler approached Richard II. It was the chief object in the burning of abbeys and castles to destroy the manorial rolls, the symbol of servage. Because of this the rebels met with considerable sympathy in London itself, among nobles and middle class who considered their demands justified and economically desirable. But among the peasants there flourished at the same time communistic aims, preached in particular by John Ball. It was a characteristic peasant Communism, summed up in the rhyme :

> *When Adam delved and Eve span,*
> *Who was then the gentleman ?—*

a Communism which hoped for the restoration of society as an agricultural community of workers. Such a belief prospered in small sections of the peasantry. After the failure of the rebellion it spread wider, being absorbed in the more powerful movement emanating from Wyclif's Poor Preachers. During the rebellion itself the communistic trend remained in the background, repressed by the definite hope of positive concessions.

It was otherwise in the Peasants' Risings in Germany in the fifteenth and sixteenth centuries. The peasantry here did not in the main participate, as in England, in the advantages of the general economic development. The growth of the wealth of the towns resulted for them in an increase of feudal dues, in a deepened exploitation from their lords, themselves hard hit by the economic changes. Everywhere the risings arose out of attacks by lords on established rights. And while, as a rule, the rebellious peasantry demanded restitution of these rights, they were prone to desperate aspirations for a total reorganisation of society. Their backward condition made them a prey to emotions which, once their immediate hopes were frustrated, bore them on in the service of a visionary ideal.

For a variety of reasons the Peasants' Rising of 1524–5 bore a different character from those preceding it in Germany. It took place soon after Luther's defiant action at Worms, when the highest authorities of the land showed themselves to be at loggerheads. It absorbed in its service many of the radicals whom Luther in the north and Zwingli in the south suppressed and persecuted. It spread all over Germany, from the Tyrol to the Lower Rhine and Saxony. The numerous petitions and manifestos of the peasants show in general a protest·against encroachments on communal rights. In a few places, such as the Allgäu, where these petitions were received by the lords, and the peasants' demands granted, the rebels quietly dispersed. In the majority of cases, however, any reform was refused, and the movement of protest swelled into a revolutionary organisation. Attempts at a revolution of the social order had been made in the years following 1521, in Saxony by Münzer and his colleagues, in South Germany and Switzerland by the Anabaptists. These men, continually fleeing from authority, brought a measure of organisation into the peasants' movement, keeping up correspondence with circles of unrest in many parts. At the same time they strove to give the rising a clear social aim, the establishment of a " peasants' Communism "—a return to an equalitarian agricultural community, attacking commerce and finance, and all temporal powers. They proclaimed the kinship of their ideals with those of the prophets of the Old Testament ; their method of agitation, too, was prophetic, visionary.

The anarchical state of Germany favoured the rising. In districts not governed by the greater princes the insurgents were successful, even being able to press the smaller knights into their service. Small towns fell before them, though the large towns withstood the attack. In the end, however, the great princes organised their forces, and their practised and well-armed troops overcame the undisciplined peasants. This last and greatest of the Peasants' Risings was utterly crushed, its claims trampled underfoot. The progress of the world lay in another direction ; the aims of the peasants, if realised, would have laid the dead hand of immobility on economic and cultural life. Economically they would have put a stop to commerce, to financial operations, lending at interest, dealing in " futures," etc., through which the wealth of the Western world has progressed. As a substitute for this new economic order they proposed only a return to earlier forms, to restricted individual ownership. As with the weavers and lower classes in the towns, the idea of social ownership of the land is entirely absent from their minds. Given the primitive agricultural tools of the times, the restricted markets, the peasants could conceive of reform only in terms of the relative sharing of the product of labour. Thus they demanded at first moderation of taxation, later, as the extreme, the abolition of the landlords who lived on the sweat of their serfs.

It can be seen that the aims of the peasants, like those of the Anabaptists, in the last resort strengthen the claims of the individual to private ownership of the means of production, basing this right on the moral principle of work ; and, as such, they are part of the revolt of the bourgeois order, of capitalism, against feudalism. The similarity of their aims with those of the peasants in the French Revolution of 1789, even with those of the Peasants' Party in pre-revolutionary Russia, would seem to prove this. Their history, however, disproves such a formulation of their historical significance. On the one hand the contemporary middle class of Europe abhorred the peasants' demands, and contributed to their downfall. On the other, the ideals of the peasants were avowedly communistic. The explanation of this fundamental confusion is to be found in the complications of society of the time. Capitalism in the sixteenth century was essentially, in its most progressive form, a capitalism of commerce. Only in commerce were the essential forms of capitalism highly developed—large-scale distribution, ships which, though small, needed concentration of capital, capitalistic control of raw material and of markets. The essential struggle with the feudal powers centred in the struggle over the conditions of commerce. And in this struggle the peasants, like the Anabaptists, pursued aims opposed to the middle class.

The Communism of distribution of the lower classes was the antithesis of capitalistic development, and was an economically retrogressive policy. With it went their cultural backwardness. Opposing wealth, and supporting ideas which would not have increased wealth, they tended to oppose all worldly enjoyments, all worldly ambitions, including all that we understand by culture. Advocating an economy which was based on repression of the individual, the peasant Communists would have subjected society to the rigorous control of moralists, who drew their inspiration from religion. Society would have been—as it was in Anabaptist communities—dominated by religious observance, perversely repressing social needs and demands. Culturally, as economically, the peasants' Communism was reactionary—the product of desperate circumstances merely, and not leading to a positive reorganisation of productive forces.

IV. CONCLUSION

It can be seen from this survey that medieval Communism is extremely, even fundamentally, dissimilar from modern. There is a common origin in oppressed classes who revolt against the possessing ; but in economic basis and aim, and in theory, the two differ profoundly. Modern Communism grows out of highly developed capitalist society, is based on the proletariat, the organised masses of wage-workers. It replaces capitalism by a higher economic form, in which calamities such as crises, restriction of production, and wars are eliminated. Medieval Communism, on the other hand, praised poverty, the restriction of wealth, and disjointed the economic process. Modern Communism is profoundly unmystical, materialistic, seeing in the prevailing idealisms and religions only shackles to the action of the masses. Medieval Communism, on the other hand, is permeated with religion, replacing practical politics by personal inspiration. Mirrored in these two great differences we see the essential fragility of medieval communistic movements—that they were not constructed on a solid social class, clearly opposed, in theory and practice, to the fact of private ownership and the possessing class, but flickered and flared in classes half-owners, half-proletariat, with aims half-communistic, half-individualistic.

This lack of a proletariat is, of course, indicative of the whole nature of possession in the period under review. Feudalism was still dominant, and the success of the merchants, of capitalism in general, was only possible through the temporary strengthening of the absolutist, feudal rights of the great princes, at the expense of the lesser barons. Round this great political and economic struggle for hegemony all the movements of the times circled, including those of the lower classes. Without clear social objectives of their own, the lower classes, the semi-proletarianised artisans, the oppressed peasants, contributed now to one side, now to the other. Their energies could now be utilised by Philip the Fair against the popes, now by the popes against feudal barons ; now by the town governments against their feudal lords, now by lords or Church against the municipal governments. Various ties and various advantages drew them many ways ; their own helplessness made them unstable. And the whole process submerged them lower and lower in the social scale, making them into proletarians, serfs.

It would be wrong to look on this instability and lack of success in the medieval communistic movements as the result of their religious approach to their social problems. But their subjectivism, their religious doctrines, are the

F R

result, like their instability, of their economic situation. Suffering deeply from social injustice, what social remedy could they propose ? Their satisfaction, the remedy for their wrongs, they sought within themselves ; and gave others this " inward revelation," this consolation and substitute for material happiness. And this is the nature of religious Communism at all times. Even when advocating social revolution, the struggle of the proletariat against the possessing class, it cannot work out a stable politics of Communism. It may follow and support a Communist movement, it cannot create one. Its insistence on subjective values lays it open to abuse by opponents ; its idealism may become a substitute for practical attainment. Particularly in times of temporary defeat, it leads to the formation of esoteric communities, like Waldenses or Bohemian Brethren, renouncing the world for the sake of their soul ; a help, not a hindrance, to its opponents.

VI

LAUD, THE LEVELLERS, AND THE VIRTUOSI

by Joseph Needham
Fellow of Caius College, Cambridge

I. SEVENTEENTH-CENTURY ENGLAND

In SEVENTEENTH-CENTURY ENGLAND, we have the fascinating picture of a balance trembling on a poise of equal weights—Western religion having lost little of its ancient power, Western science having gained its first magnificent victories. Even within religion there was a moment of equal poise between the antagonists, before the medieval tradition, in the form of the Church of England, ceded the power to the Protestant and Puritan bodies. This contrast, like the former, was perhaps but an aspect of what was a more deep-seated one, namely, the passing of power from the feudal aristocratic and monastic system to the middle or bourgeois class arising out of the medieval town merchants. The civil war and the Commonwealth were the outward and visible signs of the victory of this new order. The abolition of the laws against usury ; the " freeing " of trade from galling restrictions ; the beginning of large-scale industrial " ventures " ; the great advances in technology backed by science ; the complete removal, in a word, of mercantile and economic life from theological control—all signified the triumph of the middle class.

II. THE LAUDIAN DIVINES

Of all the ages of the Church's history after the first two centuries there are few which can compare in brightness with the Church of England in the seventeenth century. Poets like George Herbert, Richard Crashaw, Henry Vaughan, and, we might add, Sir Thomas Browne and Jeremy Taylor ; saints like Nicholas Ferrar and Thomas Ken ; careful restorers of what was destroyed, like John Hacket, John Cosin, and Matthew Wren ; scholars like the Cambridge Platonists and Lancelot Andrewes ; statesmen like Laud—all combined to give the period a charm and depth which can never be forgotten by those who have studied it.[1] But while we usually think of these men in connection with their importance in the history of theology or philosophy, or with regard to the literary beauty, we forget that there was a significant economic aspect to their existence. This may be summarised by saying that they were the representatives of the old conceptions of social justice in economic affairs, and were opposed to the new aims of capitalist freedom in commerce.

William Laud, Archbishop of Canterbury, usually appears in history as the instrument of monarchical oppression, and not as the champion of popular agrarian rights. Yet there is no doubt that among the economic causes of the civil war and of Laud's own fall was the opposition which he aroused among land-owners by his agrarian policy.[2] The problem of enclosures was by no means new in English economic life in the days of the Stuarts ; it runs, indeed, like a connecting thread through all the economic life of the country from the Middle Ages to the nineteenth century. Pasture was more of a business proposition than tillage ; it was capitalist in its methods, and offered a better

[1] Cf. Grierson, H. J. C., *Crosscurrents in English Literature of the Seventeenth Century*, Chatto & Windus, London, 1929 ; and Willey, B., *The Seventeenth-Century Background*, Chatto & Windus, London, 1934.
[2] See Cole, G. D. H., *Church Socialist*, 1915 ; and Hancock, T., *The Pulpit and the Press, and other Sermons preached at St. Nicholas, Cole Abbey*, Brown & Langham, London, 1904.

chance of big profits. Thus the social obligations of the feudal land-owner were forgotten ; the peasant became a landless and insecure wage-worker, and the land came to be looked upon solely as a source of profit.

To whom were the peasants to turn for redress ? Not to the justices of the peace, for these were of the land-owning class ; not to Parliament, where the same interests reigned. They most commonly appealed to the King's Ministers, the Privy Council, and the Church. Laud strove by every means in his power to prevent such enclosures as de-populated the countryside, and, by heading the Commis-sion on Depopulation, infuriated the capitalistic land-owners whose interests were aligning themselves with the industrial capitalists of the towns. Laud had no respect for persons, and would allow no man, however powerful, to transgress the common law of Christ, binding upon man as man. Peter Heylyn,[1] his chaplain and biographer, seems to have thought that Laud could have kept his place and saved his life if he had paid adulation to the great enclosers, but " he failed in so many necessary civilities to the nobility and gentry " that it was clear he was their enemy and the peasants' friend. His visitation articles, in particular, questioned the churchwardens closely concerning enclo-sures, detentions, inversions, and so on. To put such questions to common men—as a writer complained a few months before Laud's death, when the Archbishop was safely in the Tower—was a " vassaldrie to the gentry of England," who, from the time of the Tudors, had been impropriating wholesale the common property of the people in their common Church, their common lands, and their common free schools. " Many nobles and worthy gentle-men," said the complainant, " are curbed and tyrannised over by some base clergy of mean parentage." As Clarendon says,[2] " The shame, which they called an insolent triumph over their degree and quality, and a *levelling* them with the

---

[1] Heylyn, P., *Cyprianus Anglicus ; or the History of the Life and Death of William, Archbishop of Canterbury*, London, 1668.
[2] Clarendon, *History of the Rebellion*.

common people, was never forgotten, and they watched for revenge."

A final instance : from among his injunctions to the Dean and Chapter of Chichester—" Use some means with Mr. Peter Cox [a land-grabbing alderman of that city] that the piece of ground called *Campus* now in his possession be laid open again, that the scholars of your free school may have liberty to play there, as formerly they had. And if he shall refuse, give us notice, or our vicar-general, upon what reason and ground he does it."

But if some bishops were fighting on the agrarian front, others were leading the struggle against usury.[1] Lancelot Andrewes, the admirable diocesan of Winchester, preached incessantly against it. He made short work of the settlement of 1571, which had legalised the taking of 10 per cent. Joseph Hall, Bishop of Norwich, John Jewel, Bishop of Salisbury, and George Downam (" the hammer of the usurers "), Bishop of Derry, were all prominent in this work.[2] But the merchants persisted ever that " it is not in simple divines to saye what contract is lawfull, and what is not."

In the end these controversies were not settled except by force of arms. In the civil war, the industrial and commercial cities were on the parliamentary side ; the agricultural parts of the country, except the Eastern Counties, where puritanism was so strongly entrenched, were royalist. It was no coincidence that the chaplains of the volunteer regiments of London were Presbyterian, as opposed to the Anglican influence on the other side. The golden age of seventeenth-century Anglicanism stood, in fact, on its economic side, for a scarcely altered version of medieval collectivism. The bishops were " medieval clerks," determined to control the market-place. The victories of Cromwell opened the door for the era of capitalist

[1] *See* the classical *Religion and the Rise of Capitalism*, by R. H. Tawney, Murray, London, 1926 ; and also H. M. Robertson's *Aspects of the Rise of Economic Individualism*, Camb. Univ. Press, 1933.

[2] Cf. Blaxton, *The English Usurer*, 1634.

enterprise, and, when the Church of England regained its possessions at the Restoration, it was at the price of most of its militant spirit. In 1692, when one David Jones was so indiscreet as to preach at St. Mary Woolnoth, in Lombard Street, a sermon against usury, his career in London was brought to an abrupt conclusion.

III. THE LEVELLERS

Let us now cross over to the other side in the civil war in order to trace another movement of great interest—that of the Levellers. If we regard, as we must, the civil war as England's " bourgeois revolution," we should expect to find a certain number of true Socialists on the left wing of the revolutionary party—men who would not be content with the political equality which the Cromwellian system would give, but would demand economic equality as well. This is indeed exactly what happened, and from 1684 onwards the parliamentary side was split into two portions, the main body quite satisfied with the defeat of everything that the royalist and Anglican forces had stood for, and a smaller body desirous of pushing on towards what we should now call a Socialist State.[1] The fortunes of this smaller portion, the Levellers, varied considerably ; at one time they were sufficiently strong to take the field against Cromwell's own forces in a short campaign which receives little or no mention in orthodox history books,[2] while towards the end of the Commonwealth they were mostly in exile, reduced to plotting in company with the exiled royalists.

They first appear about the year 1646, at which time the victorious army was dividing into the two sections above mentioned, the "gentlemen-independents" or " Grandees"

[1] For the Levellers, see the work of E. Bernstein, *Cromwell and Communism ; Socialism and Democracy in the Great English Revolution*, Allen & Unwin, London, 1930 ; also, *English Democratic Ideas in the Seventeenth Century*, by G. P. Gooch, 2nd edn., ed. H. J. Laski, Camb. Univ. Press, 1927 ; also, T. C. Pease, *The Levellers' Movement*, Washington, 1916.

[2] Contrast the excellent *History of Feudalism*, by A. Gukovsky and O. Trachtenburg, Moscow, 1934.

being opposed to the " honest substantive soldiers " and their elected " Agitators " or leaders. In the following year appeared one of the numerous pamphlets of the time, *The Agreement of the People*, in which a programme of reforms " to take away all known and burdensome grievances " was set forth. One of the authors was the indefatigable Lieut.-Col. John Lilburne (" freeborn John ").[1] At this time, the Levellers numbered among them many interesting and important pioneers, such as Richard Overton and William Walwyn, from whose writings it is impossible not to quote : " the world will never be well till all things be common." It would not by any means be " such difficulty as men make it to be to alter the course of the world in this thing ; a very few diligent and valiant spirits may turn the world upside down if they observe the seasons and shall with life and courage engage accordingly." To the objection that this would upset all and every Government, he answered that " there would then be less need of government, for then there would be no thieves, no covetous persons, no deceiving and abuse of one another, and so no need of government. If any difference do fall out, take a cobbler from his seat, or any other tradesman that is an honest and just man, and let him hear the case and determine the same, and then betake himself to his work again." There is a remarkably modern ring about these sentiments. They form a contrast indeed to the attitude of Cromwell, who was always protesting that he was a " gentleman born."

Perhaps the most remarkable pamphlet of the Levellers was *The Light Shining in Buckinghamshire*, which laid down what " honest people desire :—(1) a just portion for each man to live, so that none need to beg or steal for want, but everyone may live comfortable ; (2) a just rule for each man to go by, which rule is to be found in Scripture " ; (3) equal rights ; (4) government judges elected by all the people ; (5) a commonwealth " after the pattern of the Bible." Here the land was expressly stated to be the

---

[1] Cf. J. Clayton's biography of him in *Leaders of the People*, Secker, London, 1910.

property of the whole people, and, as we should say, its "nationalisation" asked for.

In April 1649, while Lilburne and other Levellers were confined in the Tower, there suddenly appeared at Cobham in Surrey a number of men, armed with spades, who commenced to dig up uncultivated land at the side of St. George's Hill, with the intention of growing corn and other produce.[1] They proposed to prove that "it was an indeniable equity that the common people ought to dig, plow, plant, and dwell upon the commons without hiring them or paying rent to any." A fortnight later they were arrested by two troops of horse, sent down by Cromwell, and their leaders, William Everard and Gerrard Winstanley, brought before him. The examination showed that these "true Levellers," as they called themselves, were in reality trying to found what we should now call a "collective farm," and their conviction was that, when men began to see the success of their venture, they would join it, and so establish in course of time a widespread co-operative system. The beginning was to be on common-land, for which they asked no permission, since from of old it had been the common property of the English people.

Of course, these beginnings were not allowed to proceed and the "true Levellers" gradually joined other later movements, such as the Quakers, which were not (or not so strongly) persecuted. Winstanley produced a pamphlet, however (*The Law of Freedom on a Platform, or True Magistracy Restored*, 1651), which unfolded the real principles of the agitation without any concealment, and propounded a complete social system based on Communist principles. Particularly interesting here is his treatment of social prestige in a classless society : " As a man goes through offices he rises to titles of Honour, till he comes to the highest Nobility, to be a faithful commonwealth man in a Parliament House. Likewise he who finds out any secret in Nature,

[1] *See* Berens, L. H., *The Digger Movement under the Commonwealth*, Simpkin Marshall, London, 1906 ; and Davidson, M., *The Wisdom of Winstanley the Digger*, Henderson, London, 1904.

shall have a title of Honour given him, though he be a young man. But no man shall have any title of Honour till he win it by industry or come to it by age or office-bearing. Every man that is above 60 years of age shall have respect as a man of Honour by all others that are younger, as is shewed hereafter."

Winstanley is irresistible. Here is one of his most arresting passages from *A New Year's Gift for the Parliament and the Army*, 1654 : " At this very day poor people are forced to work for 4*d*. a day, and corn is dear. And the tithing-priest stops their mouth, and tells them that ' inward satisfaction of mind ' was meant by the declaration, ' The poor shall inherit the earth.' I tell you, the scripture is to be really and materially fulfilled. You jeer at the name ' Leveller ' ; I tell you, Jesus Christ is the head Leveller." Or take this example from another of his writings : " This Divining Doctrine, which you call ' spiritual and heavenly things ' is the thief and robber that comes to spoil the vineyard of a man's peace, and does not enter at the door, but climbs up another way. They who preach this divining doctrine are the murderers of many a poor heart, who is bashful and simple, and cannot speak for himself, but keeps his thoughts to himself. This divining spiritual doctrine is a cheat ; for while men are gazing up to heaven, imagining after a happiness or fearing a hell after they are dead, their eyes are put out, and they see not what is their birthright, and what is to be done by them here on earth while they are living. This is the filthy dreamer and the cloud without rain. And indeed the subtle clergy do know that if they can but charm the people by their divining doctrine to look after heavenly riches and glory after they are dead, then they shall easily be the inheritors of the earth, and have the deceived people to be their servants."

The Levellers' crisis came in 1649. In January the King was executed, in February the Council of State deliberated measures for the suppression of " disturbers of peace " in the army. Soldiers who attempted to incite the army to mutiny were to be hanged. Lilburne immediately published a pamphlet, *England's New Chains Discover'd*, against the Council of State. In March the army itself, stationed at Newmarket, protested, in a "Letter to General Fairfax and his officers," signed by eight soldiers, who demanded the acceptance of the Levellers' "Agreement," and who were a few days later, after a short trial, expelled from the army. Twenty days later, the army Levellers published a pamphlet with perhaps the most remarkable title of all, *The Hunting of the Foxes from Newmarket and Thriplow Heath to Whitehall by five small beagles late of the Armie ; or, The Grandee Deceivers Unmasked.* The "foxes," of course, were Cromwell, Ireton, and the rest ; and their ambitious subterfuges were here exposed. A few days later there was a mutiny in London in Colonel Whalley's cavalry regiment, and, though quickly suppressed, it gave rise to a unique manifestation of popular feeling at the funeral of one of the Levellers, Robert Lockyer. I quote the account from Whitelocke's *Memorials*[1] :

"*Apr. 29-th, 1649.*

"Mr. Lockier a trooper who was shot to death by Sentence of the Court Martial, was buried in this manner.

"About one thousand went before the Corps, and five or six in a File, the Corps was then brought, with six Trumpets sounding a Soldier's Knell, then the Troopers horse came clothed all over in mourning and led by a foot man.

"The Corps was adorned with Bundles of Rosemary, one half stained in Blood, and the Sword of the deceased with them.

"Some thousands followed in Ranks and Files, all had Seagreen and black Ribbon tied on their Hats (the Levellers colours), and the Women brought up the Rear.

"At the new Church-Yard in Westminster some thousands of the better sort met them, who thought not fit to march through the City. Many looked on this funeral as an affront to the Parliament and Army ; others called them Levellers ; but they took no notice of any of them."

[1]Whitelock, B., *Memorials of the English Affairs*, London 1732, p. 379.

Ten days afterwards the struggle began in earnest. News came that the troops at Banbury, Wantage, Salisbury, etc., had cast off allegiance to Cromwell, and were preparing to enforce the Levellers' principles. After a good deal of marching and counter-marching by the Levellers and the Cromwellians, the former were surprised at Burford in Oxfordshire, and a fight in the streets of that town ended the chances of a second revolution. Early in June the great merchants of the City of London, who had often enough execrated Cromwell, and held tight the purse-strings in the face of the financial requirements of the parliamentary army, celebrated the overthrow of the Levellers by a splendid banquet given at Grocers' Hall in honour of Cromwell and Fairfax, the saviours of sacred property.

IV. THE VIRTUOSI

Lastly, in this rapid survey of some aspects of the seventeenth century, we must give our attention to the scientific movement proceeding in quiet, far removed from these excursions and alarms, but destined to be of the greatest economic importance. Out of all the events which make the seventeenth century one of the cardinal periods in the history of science, I would like to draw attention to the grouping together of scientific workers of the time into societies for the furtherance of experiment and observation.[1] These societies, of which the Royal Society in England was one of the earliest, were generally under the close protection of some prince or monarch. This royal patronage, we may believe, was dictated not so much by a purely disinterested passion for abstract truth, as by the desire to profit as much as possible by the new techniques which the decay of anti-usury doctrine, the urge of the rising middle class to industrial ventures, and the far-ranging thought of the scientists, was combining to produce.

[1] *See* Ornstein, M., *The Rôle of Scientific Societies in the Seventeenth Century*, Univ. Chicago Press, 1928.

The Royal Society began as a group of scientists meeting both in Oxford and in London, who called themselves the " Invisible College." The first mention of them occurs in 1646, but their incorporation under the present name did not occur till 1663. The pre-occupation of the early Fellows with the " improvement of trade and husbandry " is patent to anyone acquainted with its early history. Thus the great Robert Boyle wrote to a friend, Marcombes[1] : " The other humane studies I apply myself to are natural philosophy, the mechanics, and husbandry, according to the principles of our new philosophical colledge, that values no knowledge, but as it hath a tendency to use. And therefore I shall make it one of my suits to you, that you would take the pains to enquire a little more thoroughly into the ways of husbandry, etc., practised in your parts ; and when you intend for England, to bring along with you what good receipts or choice books of any of these subjects you can procure ; which will make you extremely welcome to our invisible colledge, which I had now designed to give you a description of." Among Robert Hooke's papers in the British Museum, Weld[2] records a statement, dated 1663—" The business and design of the Royal Society is to improve the knowledge of naturall things and all usefull Arts, Manufactures, Mechanick practises, Engynes and Inventions by Experiments." Or if we look through the account and defence of the Royal Society published by Thomas Sprat, Bishop of Rochester, some years later,[3] we find that he gives a series of thirteen sample papers from the reports of the society to show what good it has done. Of these thirteen, five are purely technical (wine, guns, saltpetre, dyeing, oysters), two are to do with exploration, and three with meteorology and astronomy, important for navigation, making a total of ten which would be " for the improvement of husbandry." The remaining three we should now call " pure science,"

---

[1] Quoted by Fulton, J. F., *Isis*, 1932, *18*, 84.
[2] Weld, C. R., *History of the Royal Society*, Parker, London, 1848.
[3] Sprat, T., *The History of the Royal Society of London*, Knapton, etc., London, 1722.

and were devoted two to chemistry and one to physiology. It is clear, then, that seventeenth-century science was expanding in the closest relationship with industrial enterprise. The scientific men took, indeed, little or no part in politics, but they definitely depended for their support on the party diametrically opposed to the two groups described above, namely, the Laudian Churchmen and the Levellers. The former were representatives of a dying pre-scientific collectivism, the latter were pioneers of a collectivism to which even yet we have not attained. It was inevitable that the scientists should be on the other side, since only capitalism, with its encouragement of technology, would afford science with the means for its development.

V. THE RISE OF MECHANISTIC ECONOMICS

Drawing these many threads together now a little, we may refer to one of the most fascinating aspects of the seventeenth century, namely, the rise of " mechanistic economics." In pure science the concept of mechanical causation, or, to be more accurate, the concentration of interest on the Aristotelian efficient cause, to the exclusion of the other Aristotelian causes, was of enormous importance. No advance beyond pure descriptive biology, for instance, could be made without it. And it was just at this time that such advances were made. Thus in 1644 Sir Kenelm Digby,[1] discussing embryology, in his " Treatise on Bodies," took the example of a germinating bean : " Take a bean," he wrote, " or any other seed, and put it in the earth ; can it then choose but that the bean must swell ? The bean swelling, can it choose but break the skin ? The skin broken, can it choose (by reason of the heat that is in it) but push out more matter, and do that action which

---

[1] Digby, Sir K., *Two Treatises, in the one of which the Nature of Bodies, in the other the nature of Man's Soule, is look'd into, in way of discovery of the Immortality of Reasonable Soules*, Williams, London, 1664.

we call germinating ? Can these germs choose but pierce
the earth in small strings, as they are able to make their
way ? Thus by drawing the thrid carefully through your
fingers and staying at every knot to see how it is tyed, you
see that this difficult progresse of the generation of living
creatures is obvious enough to be comprehended and the
steps of it set down ; if one would but take the paines and
afford the time that is necessary to note diligently all the
circumstances in every change of it." This was almost the
first declaration of belief in the comprehensibility of the
mechanism of generation. It was fundamental for the future
of biology. But, side by side with this, there went a similar
application of mechanical causation to economics, equally
fundamental for the future, but not of such happy augury.
In 1622 Gervase Malynes, in his *Lex Mercatoria*, wrote[1] :
" We see how one thing driveth or enforceth another, like
as in a clock where there are many wheels, the first wheel
being stirred driveth the next and that the third and so
forth, till the last that moveth the instrument striketh
the clock ; or like as in a press going in a strait, where the
foremost is driven by him that is next to him, and the next
by him that followeth him." So men were to be thought of
as selfish monads or corpuscles, like the atoms of natural
science, with the price-mechanism taking the place of the
Newtonian laws of motion.

Thus the theocratically legislative state of the medieval
clerk was dying, and could no longer attempt to control
the great merchants of London, Antwerp, or Venice, who
looked after themselves, and expected others to do the
same. Thenceforward, there was to be no interference with
the free play of capitalist interests. All that was lacking
was the supreme piece of cant elaborated by the eighteenth
century, the opinion that when the " natural economic
appetites " of men are allowed to take their course to the

---

[1] Malynes, G., *Consuetudo, vel Lex Mercatoria, or the Antient Law-Merchant*,
London, 1629. Malynes defends usury, and describes (p. 263) certain
silver mines which the owner will not allow to be worked. " Howsoever
I thought good to remember this for our posteritie, for there may come
a time when industrious men shall be more regarded."

end, a society results which does, by a strange but beneficent dispensation of Providence, provide the maximum of attainable happiness for all classes.

Mechanical causation was one concept taken over by seventeenth-century economics from science ; atomism was another. It is questionable whether the social connections of these changes have been sufficiently realised. Does not the shift of emphasis from the medieval State, carrying out in practice the detailed instructions of theology, *Regina Scientiarum*, to the seventeenth-century capitalists, men like Sir Thomas Gresham, pressing for the removal of every inhibiting influence on financial transactions—does not this shift of emphasis mirror in the economic sphere the transition from the four elements of the Aristotelians and the three primary substances of the Alchemists to the " *corpuscularian or mechanical philosophy* " of Gassendi and Boyle ? " No one can deny," wrote the foreign merchants of Antwerp, about 1590, to Philip II, in a protest against an attempt to interfere with the liberty of exchange transactions, " that the cause of the prosperity of this city is the freedom granted to those who trade here." And the unrestricted competitiveness of later capitalism, the continual cry that the activities of the State should be restricted to the bare minimum necessary to safeguard property, has something so obviously atomistic about it that the nineteenth century seems surprisingly late for the appearance of the codifier of atomic interpretation, John Dalton. To-day we are living in the time of the dissolution of this atomic form of society.

The fundamental drawback of atomistic capitalism[1] is that its parts have no organic connection with the whole. The sole concern of the industrial monads is, not that cost and price should balance, but that the latter should outweigh the former by as much as they can make it. Hence a condition of universal war.

It is interesting that the deficiencies of an atomistic society as well as the tremendous changes which applied

[1] *See* Wootton, B., *Plan or No Plan*, Gollancz, London. 1934, p. 159.

science was to bring, were realised, if dimly, by some contemporaries. Thus in 1641 Samuel Hartlib published his
Utopia, in which it was laid down that the State alone
should control and manage production as an economic
institution.[1]

In 1659 Cornelius Plockboy came forward with his
proposal[2] for a co-operative society, and described all the
advantages which would accrue from the combination
of agriculture with industry. " Whereas the Traders in the
World do oppress their workmen, with heavy labour and
small wages, instead thereof with us, the gain of the Tradesmen will redound to the benefit and refreshment of the
Workmen."

A rather similar co-operative association was later proposed by John Bellers in 1695.[3] No practical outcome of
these schemes is recorded.

VI. CONCLUSION

It is my profound conviction that we are standing
to-day at the turning-point between two civilisations, one
of those turning-points in history not unlike the first or
second Christian century, the Renaissance, or the seventeenth century in England. The transition from an individualist to a collectivist State of society is at hand. In
scientific words, the time has come for the atomistic, in-
organic, chaotic community to give to the organised, living,
planned community.

[1] Hartlib, S., *A description of the famous kingdom of Macaria ; shewing
its excellent Government, wherein the inhabitants live in great Prosperity, Health
and Happiness ; the King obeyed, the Nobles honoured, and all good men respected.
An example to other Nations. In a dialogue between a Scholar and a Traveller*,
London, 1641.

[2] Plockboy, P. C., *A Way propounded to make the poor in these and other
nations happy by bringing together a fit, suitable and well qualified people unto
one Household government or little Commonwealth, etc.*, London, 1659.

[3] Bellers, J., *Proposals for raising a Colledge of Industry of all usefull Trades
and Husbandry, etc.*, London, 1695.

In religious terminology,

> *hora novissima, tempora pessima sunt, vigilemus*
> *ecce minaciter, imminet arbiter, ille supremus,*

the times are very evil, the judge is at the gate[1] ; it is the duty of the Christian to join his forces with all who are seeking to bring in the new world order, the Kingdom on earth, *regnum dei.* As for the scientific worker, he can acquiesce no longer in the frustration of science, and must work with the rest for the overthrow of the capitalist system.

This change is hardly more likely to be achieved without tumult and civil commotion than it was likely that the middle class could peacefully overthrow the paternal-feudal system existing in 1600. But the harshness of the days that lie before us is somewhat mitigated for the reflective mind by a clear picture of the course that history has taken. These troubles did not begin in our time ; others before us have perished that the Kingdom might come. In the foregoing series of short pictures of seventeenth-century England, I have tried to show some of the forces at work.

Firstly, the Laudian Churchmen, quite apart from their brilliant scholarship and writings, were economically representative of the collectivism of the past. In the *Preces Privatæ* of Lancelot Andrewes, Bishop of Winchester in 1618, there are the following words, where he prays in the manner of the orthodox litanies for the people of England, that they may be " subject unto rule, not only for wrath, but also for conscience' sake ; to husbandmen and graziers, good seasons ; to the fleet and fishermen, fair weather ; to mechanics, to work lawfully at their occupations ; to tradesmen, *not to over-reach one another.*" And in another place, where he is rehearsing the attributes of God, he writes, under the heading " Munificent " : " Opening the eyes of the blind, clothing the naked, upholding such as fall, gathering together the outcasts, giving food to the hungry, bringing down the

[1] From the *De Contemptu Mundi* of Bernard of Cluny, 1145, ed. Hoskier H. C., London, 1929.

haughty, delivering the captives, loosing the prisoners, lifting up those that are down, healing the sick, sustaining the living, quickening the dead, lifting up the lowly, helping in time of trouble." Does not this catalogue of the divine actions curiously resemble the communist programme ? In the person of Lancelot Andrewes we link up the theocratic collectivism of the past with the proletarian socialism of the future.

Secondly, it is in the seventeenth century that we can study the beginnings of the great scientific movement, destined so to transform the nature of civilised life in subsequent years. It was in the nature of the case that science was associated with, and patronised by, the rising middle class. And from contemporary scientific theory, indispensable for progress within science itself, bourgeois economics took its canons. But inner contradictions, given time, always come to the surface. The individualism of capitalist production was congruent enough with science in its early days, but in our time scientific effort needs a co-operative atmosphere which capitalism cannot provide. Conversely, although the bourgeois class raised itself to power partly by means of science, its need for science is now much less, and its primary subconscious wish is to stabilise the existing condition of affairs. Fascism and Militarism are the result.

Thirdly, the Levellers, the extreme left wing of the revolutionary forces, were really envisaging the classless State. They were far too weak, however, to make the jump across three centuries of bourgeois domination, and the external conditions were not propitious. But is it not of some value to English Socialists, tired of hearing Communism identified with foreign-sounding names and doctrines, to know that the Communists of the seventeenth century had names that run like English villages—John Lilburne, William Walwyn, Gerrard Winstanley, Robert Lockyer, Giles Calvert, Anthony Sedley ? So it will be again, and not for failure.

VII

CHRISTIAN SOCIALISM IN ENGLAND IN THE NINETEENTH AND TWENTIETH CENTURIES

by Gilbert Clive Binyon
Vicar of Bilsdale, Yorkshire

I. SOCIALISM'S NEED OF THE CHRISTIAN PHILOSOPHY

S OM EONE who was lecturing on the history of the Christian Socialist Movement in this country remarked that " Christian Socialism reached the bishops, but it never reached the working man." In discussion, it was objected that this was the exact opposite of the truth.

The lecturer was referring to the Christian Socialism initiated by Maurice, and to Bishop Westcott and Bishop Gore ; and his statement was quite correct : the objector had in mind the Socialism, assumed to be Christian and therefore to be Christian Socialism, of Keir Hardie and the Independent Labour Party ; and it is, of course, quite true that that reached the working man but not the bishops.

The former type of Christian Socialism may have politics and economics in its purview, but it is primarily religio-moral ; the latter may be religious, but it is primarily ethico-political. The two types may, of course, fuse into one ; but it is worth while to emphasise the distinction. Anyone who wishes to trace the history of, or to estimate, " Christian Socialism " should first be clear as to whether he is primarily interested in the Workers' Movement and in the reform or revolutionising of society at large, and desirous of finding out what the Churches have done about it (and then get clear as to whether he wants to find this out in order to show up the Churches—in which case his hyper-Christian criticism easily shades off into anti-Christian sentiments—or in order to welcome anything they may have done), or whether, alternatively, he is primarily interested in the Church's teaching, and, while admitting its faults in past and present, is anxious that Christianity should be truly taught. One who is devoted to the Social Revolution may not unnaturally think well or ill of Christians in proportion as they share his devotion, without reference to their theology ; while one who is interested first in Christian Faith and Morals may be inclined to do less than justice to the Christian spirit and self-sacrificing labours of any Socialists whose expressed opinions about religion seem somewhat vague or heretical. The little incident described in the first paragraph shows that it is well to know just what one is talking about ; otherwise there may be unnecessary irritation and misplaced criticism.

From the time of Robert Owen, with his " New Moral World," the British Labour and Socialist Movement has had a moral base. But that is not necessarily the same thing as a Christian ethic ; and, where Socialism has definitely a moral base, we are in the presence, rather, of the ethic of Natural or Rational Religion—of what used to be called " The Law of Nature," which was recognised by the Church for at least sixteen centuries as man's natural righteousness.

In so far as the British Labour Movement has been religious, it has been so, almost without exception, according to the religion of Liberal Protestantism, which very easily blends with, and gives a Christian colouring to, the ethic of Natural Religion.

A quotation from a tract which at one time circulated by the thousand among Labour men—*The Christ that is to be*, by Philip Snowden—will be here in place :

" Admitting every count in the indictment which the anti-Christian can bring against the Church, against its creeds, against the infidelity of much of the present practice of Christianity, there still remains the great and potent fact that Christ has been the greatest influence in the world's history, and that such an institution as Christianity could not have survived to receive even the nominal adhesion of men if it had not been something which appealed to the eternal needs of humanity, if it had not in some way satisfied the cravings of the human heart. . . . But the recognition of the fact that there are in Christian teaching certain vital and eternal truths in no way involves acceptance of everything which Christ taught or is said to have taught. The rejection even of the belief in the personal Christ does not diminish, indeed to the highly cultured mind, it increases, the value of the teaching attributed to Christ, because it is probable that much of the teaching attributed to Christ represents rather the highest collective moral ideas of His time.

" In degree but not in kind does Christ differ from all great teachers ; from men who have more clearly than the average seen some great truth, a knowledge of which could make man wise unto salvation. But in the life of Christ we find these principles more fully illustrated, and in the teaching of Christ we find these truths more fully stated than in the life and teachings of any other master. There is, therefore, a sense in which all—Christian, agnostic, and atheist —in which they can all believe in Christ and all fervently accept Him as a teacher able to make us wise unto salvation. But these truths are not the laws of Christ, any more than gravitation is the law of Sir Isaac Newton, or evolution the law of Darwin. . . .

" This law of sacrifice, this law of love, of association, of co-operation, is not only the foundation of Christian teaching, but it is the basis of all the great ethical religions of the world and of all schools of morality."

The last pages of the tract contain a glowing description of the earthly paradise of the writer's vision : " but the only way to regain the earthly paradise is by the old, hard road to Calvary—through persecution, through poverty, through temptation, by the agony and bloody sweat, by the crown of thorns, by the agonising death. And then the resurrection to the New Humanity—purified by suffering, triumphant through Sacrifice."

The " Social Gospel " has often been presented in a much more definitely Christian way, notably by the two great outstanding figures of the movement, Keir Hardie and George Lansbury ; but always, even in the case of these, whom one cannot name without expressing profound admiration for them, there is present that excessive immanentism which characterises Liberal Protestantism.

To this type of Christian thought, those who are to-day both Catholic-minded and socially-minded are much indebted (though they do not always think so) for creating, by its influence on more orthodox forms of thought, the standpoint which they now occupy. At its best—during, say, the latter half of the nineteenth century and the first decade of the twentieth—it was a valuable corrective of the errors of unsocial Christianity, both Catholic and Protestant. It linked Christianity with the best secular aspiration of the time ; it emphasised the influence of environment, and brought in a certain determinist element which is a healthy antidote to a naïve and childish Utopianism ; it helped to restore to the Church the prophetic office ; it established a forward-looking outlook, concerned with the future of man ; it had an evolutionary progressive outlook, which made possible the idea of changes in the forms of truth and righteousness.

Any account of Christian Socialism ought to recognise this ; and any history of the movement ought to do full justice to the work of the ex-local-preacher Labour leaders, and numberless men of all denominations who have been active in the movement.

The purpose of this essay, however, is not to deal with the history of Socialism and see how Christians have come into it, but rather to sketch and comment on the history, during the past one hundred and thirty years, of the Social Teaching of the Church.

From this point of view, however fully and sincerely one may recognise the services rendered by religious men in the Labour Movement, however humbly one may admire the character of these men and acknowledge the faults of organised religion, one cannot help being aware that the very qualities of this type of religion, which have had such valuable results when they have been assimilated by historical, institutional Christianity, have had unfortunate results when Christianity has valued neither its historic heritage nor its traditional institutions.

For this type of religion has so emphasised Original Righteousness that it has forgotten the Fall and Sin and Forgiveness ; it has so emphasised the " building of Jerusalem " by human ethical effort that it has forgotten Redemption and the down-coming of the New Jerusalem from Heaven ; it has so assimilated the ideas of evolution and progress that it has found Judgment to Come unintelligible ; it has so emphasised Divine Immanence that it has approached Pantheism. This theological weakness carries with it an ethical weakness. Its disregard of the Transcendent creates a too great dependence on the spirit of revolt against hardship and oppression, on the comradeship of others, or on that kind of hope which requires for its existence the prospect of success. And thus, when a boom in capitalist industry has brought prosperity to the workers, or when election has brought promotion, this religion is liable to fade. Faced by heavy resistance to their programme, those who profess this creed may " put gradualness into reverse gear "—to use Mr. John Strachey's expression—or may even come to seek the glittering prizes which capitalism offers but does not always award ; if their religion does not wilt, it is likely—in some cases—to develop further its inherent monism and to produce something like the semi-Hindu mysticism of Edward Carpenter or some kind of theosophy, or else to shed off the remnants of its transcendent religion and turn to revolution and atheism.

Every excessively immanentist theology is on the down-grade to Pantheism or worse.

What is Pantheism ? It may mean " All is God " ; in that case, finding God everywhere, it ends by finding Him nowhere, and thus slides down insensibly into denial of God —Atheism. Or it may mean " God is All " ; in that case, finding no real existence, even of a dependent kind, in any-thing, it slides down into denial of the world—Acosmism. These two denials—of God, or of the world—are poles asunder, but they are as much alike as the Poles, North and South ; they easily pass over into one another. At neither pole can there be any real ethic ; sheer undis-criminating world-renunciation, and sheer undiscriminat-ing life-affirmation, can afford no basis for any rational or moral social order ; and if any social theory is associated with this Monism that can only be due to the unacknow-ledged presence of a remnant of ethic derived from else-where ; the Socialism which professes that philosophy occupies a precarious position on a slope that leads uphill to historical and institutional Christianity and downhill to some non-ethical Acosmism or Atheism. That does not mean, of course, that this whole type of thought, in spite of its ultimate tendencies, may not now, as in the past, have valuable contributions to make to the full understanding of Christian belief and practice ; and in the last section of this essay we will come back to that point. But, when all due acknowledgments have been made, it remains true that the ethic of the Law of Nature can only remain secure when it is taken up into the Historic Faith, with its doctrines of Divine Transcendence as well as Immanence, of Crea-tion, the Fall, Incarnation and Redemption, and the Hope of the World (or Age) to Come.

II. CHRISTIAN SOCIALISTS

That the political and economic ordering of society comes within the purview of the Historic Faith is plain to every student of that Self-revelation of God which is recorded in the Bible, as also to students of Church history from the beginning to somewhere about the middle of the seventeenth century.

About that time, any control—and then even any claim to control—these provinces became lost. How that came about has been told by Mr. R. H. Tawney, who shows that the social doctrines of the Church in their traditional form offered little guidance in an age of impersonal finance, world-markets, and a capitalist organisation of industry ; " they were merely repeated, when, in order to be effective, they should have been thought out again from the beginning and formulated in new and living terms. . . . Their practical ineffectiveness prepared the way for their theoretical abandonment. They were abandoned because, on the whole, they deserved to be abandoned. The social teaching of the Church had ceased to count, because the Church itself had ceased to think " (*Religion and the Rise of Capitalism*, pp. 184–5).

Thus Dr. Temple, in his introduction to *Christian Social Reformers of the Nineteenth Century*, can speak of the " long contraction of the scope of religious interest which reached its limit in the eighteenth century," and which made anything like Christian Socialism seem to be a " novel and paradoxical intrusion of an alien element into the spiritual concerns of the Christian religion," whereas in reality the whole Christian Social Movement should be regarded as the " history of the recovery of a forgotten part of Christian belief and practice."

It will be from this point of view that our subject will be treated here ; and emphasis will be laid quite as much on the recovery of forgotten Christian belief as the recovery of forgotten Christian practice. For there can be no recovery of Christian control over the lost provinces of politics and economics without a recovery of lost social ·traditions and their reformulation afresh, and without the theology and philosophy that go with that.

The first step has often an awakening of conscience,

prompting to compassion for, and alleviation of, suffering. Utterly inadequate as this seems to-day, it really was a step forward in the days when it was believed that " economic laws " must grind out fortunes for the few and misery for the many as unalterably as the stars move in their courses.

But this soon leads to another step—that of some modification of the capitalist form of industrialism, some correction of abuses of a system believed to be in itself tolerable if worked properly. Thus we have the great name of Shaftesbury, who taught Christianity " to speak with the voice of law " (*Christian Social Reformers*, p. 106).

The position reached by those who have taken these steps has been represented by a vast amount of activity throughout the whole period under review. And, in spite of profession to the contrary, this position has scarcely been passed by many trade unionists, Labour leaders, and Co-operators. But all this does not really come under the heading of Christian Socialism, which only begins when there is a repudiation of the whole ideology of capitalism.

This repudiation of the principles of capitalist civilisation begins, in the Church, with the Christian Owenites, notably William King, who was a true forerunner of Christian Socialism.

Another path that has led up to this repudiation is the exploration of Christianity itself. Here Samuel Taylor Coleridge is " the first voice of Christian Socialism." He pointed out that a classical education leads the governing classes to get their political theories from Greek and Roman history ; whereas Christians should find " The Statesman's Manual " in the Bible.

Here the Oxford Movement should be mentioned, of which " the social implications " have recently been expounded by the Rev. W. G. Peck.

It is, of course, with Frederick Denison Maurice that Christian Socialism really gets started. For in his teaching we find expressed, for the first time with adequate learning, the simultaneous claiming of new, or rather lost, territory for Christian influence, and the recovery of lost

Christian social ideals and principles. While Robert Owen acclaimed Communism as the principle of the *New* Moral World, Maurice recognised in it a principle of the " old moral world " of more fully Christian centuries.

Since the time of Maurice, Ludlow, and Kingsley—later joined by Hughes and Vansittart Neale—the voice of Christian Socialism has never been silent ; a repudiation of capitalist society and an assertion of Christian social ideals and principles have never been wanting.

An important point in the teaching of Maurice is the distinction, amounting to a definite antagonism, which he perceived between what he called " God's Order " and " man's system." He also distinguished between " digging " and " building " ; by " digging," he meant laying bare the foundations of the City of God, investigating the Bible and history generally for the purpose of discovering God's ways with man—" God's Order " ; by " system," he meant " the organisation of evil powers for the sake of producing good effects." Thus Maurice was at the furthest possible remove from those who put unlimited faith in some projected re-arrangement, such as an extension of the franchise or collectivism or social credit, or whatever may be the nostrum of the moment. He declared that his vocation was for " digging " ; and he dug the foundations of all later Christian Socialism well and truly.

And in this work he was not alone. Ludlow and Kingsley also took part in this " digging," in laying bare the foundations of God's eternal order, in proclaiming co-operation to be a truer principle of action in God's universe than competition, in preaching the Kingship of Christ as a fact, in the presence of which all tyranny and oppression of the poor must hide itself and disappear—or be ground to powder.

But all this raises a multitude of questions—easier to ask than answer—about the ends, and the means to those ends, of Christian Socialists.

" Digging " may discover the foundations of the City of God ; but, expressed in political terms, what are these ?

Can they be so expressed at all ? Does the Reign of Christ require some particular form of government ? If so, what ? Or can it operate through any ? Or does it spell the nega- tion of all *human* government ? And similarly about the industrial order. And, having raised these questions, where are Christians to turn for a solution of them ?

And is the Christian's only work that of preaching repent- ance, proclaiming principles, and converting people ? Or should he also take part in political and industrial move- ments ? If so, should Christians identify themselves with one political party ? Or should they form a Christian party ?

These are, of course, but a few examples of the questions raised by Maurice's distinction between " God's Order " and " man's system."

To some minds, the course to be pursued has seemed fairly clear ; answers to these questions have been assumed to be found ready made, or, if not, to be easily discoverable by experiment and experience, within the contemporary phases of the Workers' Movement, which has thus presented itself to these persons as an opportunity for good works prepared for them to walk in. Guided, of course, by their Christian principles, and always reserving the right, on the ground of these principles, to make criticisms if required, Christian Socialists of this school have thrown themselves into the movements they have found around them.

Thus, even before Maurice, William King and others became active workers in Co-operation ; in Co-operation Maurice himself, Ludlow, Kingsley, Hughes, and, above all, Vansittart Neale, recognised a Christian principle, and in various ways helped on the movement ; indeed, present- day Co-operation, with its immense ramifications, is, as Co-operators themselves declare, Neale's monument. These early Christian Socialists were also concerned with trade unionism, to which they rendered valuable service. And this line of Christian Socialist activity has been continued ever since, though there have been, naturally, variations in the forms which this activity has assumed. Ludlow in his later years became prominent in Co-Partnership ; the trade unionism of the eighteen-seventies, and the revived Socialism of the following decade, enlisted the support of the Rev. Stewart Headlam and his Guild of St. Matthew ; when a revolutionary spirit appeared, H. H. Champion was to the fore ; when the Fabian Society was established, Stewart Headlam became a member ; when the Independent Labour Party began its career, it received the vigorous support of a number of Socialist priests, who, in 1906, formed the Church Socialist League.

It must not be supposed that all the Christian Socialists here mentioned or alluded to shared the same beliefs either in theology or in politics and economics ; they did not. Still less must it be supposed that they simply merged themselves in the contemporary movements they found to hand ; they were concerned, not only with supporting, as Christians, these movements, but also with reforming, as Socialists, the teaching of the Church. But this current of Christian Socialism is somewhat open to the criticism that it is liable to be too much entangled with the fluctuating fortunes of the political and industrial movements with which it has at the moment identified itself—and that both in the region of theory and of practice.

Other Christian Socialists have been careful to avoid any such unfortunate entanglement. Among these have been some whose names have been best known and most revered, such as Westcott, Gore, and Scott Holland, of the Christian Social Union (founded 1888).

Westcott's Socialism must first be described : in his use of the word, Socialism meant a theory of life which is the opposite of Individualism, and which regards humanity as an organic whole (a vital unity formed by the combination of contributory members mutually interdependent), and adopts the method of co-operation, having as its aim the fulfilment of service, and seeking such an organisation of life as shall secure for everyone the most complete development of his powers. Westcott definitely declared wage-labour to be as little fitted to represent finally or adequately the connection of man with man in the production of wealth as at earlier times slavery or serfdom. He recognised the place of experience (experiment) in the solution of problems. But he never proclaimed a well-defined programme, such as is demanded in the Labour Movement.

These leaders of Christian Socialism did indeed give recognition to the Christian character of the ideals and principles at the back of the Workers' Movement : two quotations from Gore will illustrate this :

" We have our chance of letting men know that the ideas which are stirring in democracy, the ideas which constitute its divine justification, are the very same ideas which lie at the heart of the Christian religion. That with God is no respect of persons ; that all men should, as far as possible, have an equal opportunity of making the best of themselves ; that wealth is a trust rather than a right : that we are our brothers' keepers ; that a man who will not work should not eat ; these are democratic cries and they are also Christian principles. The Church, again, according to its original constitution, was the embodiment of that ideal of properly representative government under equal Divine law, which is astir in the popular movement " (from a sermon, 1894). " We must identify ourselves with the great impeachment of our present industrial system. We must refuse to acquiesce in it. But, more than this, we must identify ourselves, because we are Christians, with the positive ethical ideal of Socialist thought " (from a paper on Socialism, prepared for the Pan-Anglican Conference of 1908).

Gore also said :

" In thus claiming that the Christian should, because he is a Christian, co-operate with the ideal which men like Dr. Westcott have called Socialist, it is not, of course, intended that Christians or Churchmen should tie themselves to any one political party, or should behave as partisans of any one economic doctrine. Nor is it intended to deny that men may hold the Socialist ideal, in the general sense, as Dr. Westcott held it, and still differ among themselves as to how far, or on what lines, the legislative power of the

State can be invoked without impairing the sense of individual initiative and individual responsibility." Years before, he had confessed himself to be among those who would somewhat jealously set limits to the paternal supervision of the democratic State.

Thus these men held somewhat aloof from the political and industrial movements, refusing to identify themselves irrevocably with one political party or economic theory or programme. They concentrated rather on the work of calling to repentance and conversion—and that, be it noted, not only in a moral sense, but in a mental sense, a change of mind as well as change of heart—and of establishing principles and ideals. In an important passage in his *Bampton Lectures* (1891), Gore declared : " What I am complaining of, what I want you to complain of, with a persistence and a conviction which shall make our complaint fruitful of reform, is—not that commercial and social selfishness exists in the world, or even that it appears to dominate in society : but that its profound antagonism to the spirit of Christ is not recognised, that there is not amongst us anything that can be called an adequate conception of what Christian morality means " (p. 210).

The reason, or at least one reason, why the Christian Socialism which reached the bishops never reached the working man, is that the latter has been more ready to complain that commercial and social selfishness exists in the world and appears to dominate in society, than to deplore its profound antagonism to the spirit of Christ. Not unnaturally. Again it must be repeated that the Social Revolution is one thing and the recovery by the Church of its own social teaching is another thing ; and that men who have devoted themselves to one of these causes should not be judged according to their work in promoting the other.

Thus, within English Christian Socialism we can find traces of a distinction which, in a much more exaggerated form, has been described (by Mr. Laun, in his *Social Christianity in England*, pp. 39–40) as existing between Calvinism and Lutheranism. Calvinism, it is said, " sets its ideal of the Kingdom in the midst of present-day problems, and seeks through it a solution of social and international questions. But thereby it exposes itself to the opposite danger to that which threatens Lutheranism. Whereas the latter risks losing touch with progress by leaving the world to its fate and keeping pure the ' heritage of the Reformation,' the former almost sacrifices Christianity to the world out of fear of losing its influence over the latter. Similarly, with the two basic religious principles justification and sanctification ; while Lutheranism emphasises that there can be no new order in politics or economics without a change of heart, and in directing attention to this, never gets to any new order, Calvinism is in danger of simply assuming a change of heart, and going on to reform politics and economics before the new spirit is born, which alone can live up to the reforms."

The divergence within Christian Socialism in England has not been so pronounced as this ; but there has been something like it ; it was matter of complaint amongst the more ardent spirits, active as Christians in the Labour world, that these eminent Churchmen were nothing but " a warning voice," tiresomely reiterating the need for repentance and redemption and never getting beyond that to any new social order to be proclaimed and established ; while those who have uttered such complaint seemed, to the others, to be unduly occupied with politics, and to be putting their trust in a change of system rather than in a change of heart.

The whole movement has shown a wavering between generalities and an adoption of the Labour programme of the moment.

There can be little doubt that the thought which weighed most in creating a preference for the preaching of repentance and conversion, and the proclamation of principles and ideals rather than for any definite programme, was the profound conviction that only on the basis of conversion to, and loyalty to, Christ the Redeemer can any Christian social order be founded.

GR

An important question is here raised about the relation of the Church to the world ; are Christian social principles only applicable in a world of Christians ? Does a Christian social order require the conversion of positively everybody ?

One utterance of Gore's should here be quoted : " There is in Christianity a fundamental ideal of social life which has indeed its first application in the life of the Church, but has also its further application in the organisation of the State, so far as the nation can either be claimed as a Christian nation or shows itself ready to acknowledge the moral and social ideals of Christianity."

This whole question has been little discussed ; and the explanation of that is no doubt to be found in the fact that England is nominally and officially a Christian nation, and may therefore not unnaturally be expected to show itself ready to acknowledge the moral and social ideals of Christianity. That the nation should show itself ready to do so, was taken as a matter of course by most Christian Socialists in the nineteenth century ; thus the question did not, for most people, seem to arise in any very acute form. But in the twentieth century, especially since the war, that expectation cannot be so easily entertained ; and so this question has become now of more pressing importance ; and it was made a criticism of C.O.P.E.C. that it did not face the question " whether our sociology is to be designed primarily to create a distinctively Christian type of living among the faithful, or to act upon and dominate a society increasingly non-Christian in theory and practice " (*see* M. B. Reckitt's *Faith and Society*, p. 126).

Another factor which helps to account for this *holding-back from real Socialism*, as it seemed to some—or this *wise independence of Christians*, as it seemed to others—is the perception that, unless one is ready to attempt the revival of medievalism, the Christian social traditions of the past could not be simply repeated, nor could Christians find, without any reservations, a ready-made plan of action in programmes originating outside the Church ; that being so, what Gore called " an adequate conception of what

Christian morality really is " becomes as much a matter for enquiry and thought as for preaching and application. This consideration lies at the back of the present-day endeavour to formulate a Christian Sociology consonant with the needs of the age, about which more will be said in its place. But, until quite recently, little was attempted in this direction. The line to be pursued was, indeed, laid down by Westcott (in 1895) : " The Christian Law is the embodiment of the Truth for action in forms answering to the conditions of society from age to age. The embodiment takes place slowly, and it can never be complete. It is impossible for us to rest indolently in the conclusions of the past. In each generation the obligation is laid on Christians to bring new problems of conduct and duty into the Divine light, and to find their solution under the teaching of the Spirit." Westcott had already seen that what was needed was, as Mr. Tawney put it (in 1922), to think out again the traditional social doctrines from the beginning, and to formulate them in new and living terms. But in those days there were none whose vivid apprehension of the need for immediate action in word and deed would allow them to withdraw from the scene of action ; and it seemed that any investigation of social traditions of the past could only yield out-of-date results.

It thus came about that those who could not rest indolently in the conclusions of the past were limited to generalities, except in so far as they could adopt the Labour programme.

III. RECENT CHRISTIAN SOCIAL MOVEMENTS

But about 1910 a new situation began to come into being. The discussion which began then, or a little earlier, about Guild Socialism ; the Great Unrest of 1911 ; the Insurance Act ; discussion of Syndicalism ; the propaganda of Distributivism—all these tended to raise a certain amount of

misgiving and doubtfulness about any complete identification, on the part of Christians, with " Socialism " ; what,
precisely, did the word mean ? Those who felt such mis-
givings were thrown back upon their base, and led to
reconsider their standpoint.

The inter-National war of 1914–18, the Russian Revolution of 1917, and the sight of Capitalist Civilisation decaying visibly before their eyes in the post-war years, could
not fail to have their effects on men's minds.

Those who regarded participation in the war as a rising
up out of individualism into self-sacrifice to make the world
safe for democracy, and believed in the war to end war,
and hoped that the spirit of sacrifice and the comradeship
of the trenches, carried on into the post-war years, would
bring in a new social order, were destined to discover, before very long, a dissatisfaction with democracy and a fear
of another war stronger than ever before, and, instead of
a world fit for heroes, one starving in the midst of plenty.
While those who had thought of International Socialism
as being (in the words of Lowell's hymn) " God's new
Messiah," and regarded a summons to fight as the last
insult of the Capitalist State to the workers, were bitterly
disappointed at what seemed to them to be an almost complete capitulation, both of the Church and of Labour, to
the world. Meantime, " the heathen," regarding " Christian
Civilisation " from a distance, could ask, " Where is now
your God ? "

Thus for all Christians, new questions, or old questions in
new forms, presented themselves.

A " National Mission of Repentance and Hope " (1918)
was a beginning which led to the Archbishop's Commis-
sion, of which the Fifth Report became the mandate for the
propaganda of the Industrial Christian Fellowship. This
society, which received at first, from those who had been
in the Christian Socialist Movement for years, rather a tepid
welcome, has now, under its vigorous director, the Rev.
P. T. R. Kirk, acquired for itself a place as one of the really
live elements in the Christian Social Movement. But this

is to anticipate. The beginning made by the National Mission was followed by the much more important Conference on Christian Politics, Economics, and Citizenship (1924), known as C.O.P.E.C. This gathered up a number of threads, and really gave a new start to the Social Movement in the Church. Attended as it was by large numbers of distinguished persons, it could not be ignored ; and if, to the minds of some, it seemed that " they knew not what they asked " in claiming the world for the Kingdom of Christ, one can only say that it would never have been so widely influential as it actually was if it had not been open to some such comment. The chief outcome of C.O.P.E.C. has been the establishment of the Christian Social Council, of which the most important department is that for research, which is directed by the Rev. V. A. Demant.

Three other societies must be mentioned : the Catholic Crusade, under the leadership of the Rev. Conrad Noel ; the Socialist Christian League ; and the League of the Kingdom of God, which, in conjunction with the Christian Social Council just mentioned and with the annual Summer School of Christian Sociology held at Keble College, Oxford, is engaged on the task of formulating a Christian Sociology consonant with the needs of the age.

IV. CHRISTIAN SOCIOLOGY

What *is* Christian Sociology ?

One of the first to attempt an answer to that question was the Rev. N. E. Egerton Swann, who, in his *Is There a Catholic Sociology ?* (1922), explained what he regarded as " the Church's own programme." Other essays dealing with the topic are Fr. Thornton's in *Christendom* (Vol. I., No. 1), and Dr. A. E. Garvie's in *Stockholm* (1931, No. 1).[1]

[1] Reference should also be made to an essay by Mr. Christopher Dawson, in *Science To-day* ; to the volume of essays entitled, *The Return of Christendom* ; to an article by the Rev. V. A. Demant in *Christendom* (Vol. I., No. 4) ; to Mr. M. B. Reckitt's *Faith and Society*. The present

It seems clear that, whatever else or more Christian Sociology may be, it at least means or includes an attempt to reformulate the Church's traditional doctrines in a manner consonant with the needs of the present age.

Much work has already been done, and is being done, and more remains to be done, on these lines.

A notable example of results, so far, is to be found in a volume on *The Just Price*. The first two chapters deal with the Just Price in the Middle Ages ; then comes a statement of the theory behind it ; finally, we have the subject of Price in the modern world and the contemporary equivalent of the Just Price.

What could be better ? This is exactly what is required, surely, if ever the Church is to proclaim " its own programme."

But Christian Sociology is as yet in its infancy, and these essays were only put forward as a contribution towards an answer to the problem of the Just Price ; the question, it is definitely stated in the Preface, is " to be worked out by Christian thinkers and those practically involved in industrial and social affairs."

That collocation of Christian " thinkers " and " those practically involved in industrial and social affairs " is important. For these latter are not likely, in any large numbers, to be very much interested in the restoration and reformulation by the Church of its own lost social teaching (an enterprise which may seem to them somewhat academic, and remote from real life, and also to assume a non-existent readiness to acknowledge Christian moral and social ideals)—they are more likely to be occupied rather, according to their diverse natures, with considering what the next Labour Government will or might do, the possibility of using the machinery of democratic government for effecting swift and far-reaching social change ; the menace

writer may be allowed to mention two articles of his own, one in *The Pilgrim* (Vol. V., No. 2), the other in *Christendom* (Vol. V., No. 17). (The reader who consults Fr. Thornton's article mentioned in the text should note the correction of misprints which is given in the following number of the magazine.)

of Fascism, dictatorship, liberty ; revolutionary action, and the Russian Five Year Plans ; national sovereignty, inter-National relations, Internationalism, Open Conspiracy, world-peace ; agricultural wages, milk-marketing, slum clearance and ribbon-development ; the difference of standards of life in Asia and Europe ; and so on. Need Christians who are giving themselves to matters of this kind wait to come to any decision until the little band of thinkers has finally reformulated the traditional social teaching in new and living terms, and persuaded the bishops to utter them as the Church's own programme ? The Christian Sociologists in question do not think so ; they think that those who are practically involved in industrial and social affairs can, from their practical experience, contribute to what Westcott called " finding the solution of new problems under the teaching of the Spirit."

In an Introduction to this book on the Just Price, Fr. Tribe mentions " the difficult question of the enforcement of Christian principles, when their working is formulated. There are many living within the geographical area of Christendom for whom the Christian sanctions have no force. Christendom itself is divided, and a uniform Christian discipline is scarcely possible of enforcement. Moreover there is also the economic interdependence of Europe and a non-Christian world in Japan, India, and Africa." Not to mention China, the U.S.S.R., and the neo-paganism of the Nazis.

Once more the question comes before us, whether Christian Sociology should aim to set forth " a distinctively Christian type of living among the faithful " or to " act upon and dominate a society increasingly non-Christian in theory and practice."

In the circumstances of some times and places, the former of these courses may alone be possible ; and, at all times and places, the faithful ought, it would seem, to exhibit a distinctively Christian type of living. But an attempt to act upon, and as far as possible dominate, society in general may be more in accordance with the essential idea of

Christian Sociology. According to Maurice, " Christianity has been sound, because it has not been mine or yours, but has been a Gospel from Heaven concerning the relation in which God stands to His creatures, concerning the true law under which He has constituted them, and concerning the false, selfish tendency in you and me, which is ever rebelling against that law. . . . Christianity has become unsound just in proportion as it has become mine or yours, as men have ceased to connect it with the whole order of the world and of human life, and have made it a scheme or method for obtaining selfish prizes which men are to compete for, just as they do for the things of earth. . . . [If men] begin to look earnestly at the Bible history, at the creeds of the Christian Church, at the records of it from the Day of Pentecost to this time, I believe they will find more and more that they have the ground there, the only one upon which they can stand or work. They will not read in the Divine book of a great strife of individual competitors, but of a Divine family, expanding itself into a Divine nation, of a universal society growing out of that nation, recognising and preserving both the forms of human fellowship out of which it was unfolded." If Christian Sociology is something more and other than a statement, in terms adapted to each age, of the Church's social teaching, and is a scientific study of types of human association, it may, perhaps, have for its object the elucidation of what Maurice called the true law under which God has constituted His creatures. But a conclusion on this point must wait on the further development of the still-new subject of Christian Sociology.

V. CONCLUSION

The League of the Kingdom of God does not attempt, as a society, to take part in efforts directed towards actually establishing a Christian social order, though individually some of its members may do so.

The same is not the case with the Socialist Christian

League and the Catholic Crusade. Both these societies do, indeed, desire that Christians generally should share their beliefs ; but they appear to be more desirous of influencing the world at large in accordance with their principles— without caring very much what " the Churches " may think or do.

As explained above, this particular essay is written from the point of view of the Christian Social Movement as a recovery of forgotten Christian belief and practice. From this point of view these two societies are less important than the League of the Kingdom of God. But from the point of view of Christianity in the Labour-Socialist-Communist Movement, they are more important, or, at least, more in evidence. The possibilities of their effectiveness appear to depend upon the readiness of the world in general to acknowledge the moral and social ideals of Christianity. How far it is in harmony with the facts to assume any such readiness as at all widespread, and how far it is correct to say that society is increasingly non-Christian in theory and practice, is a question which different people are likely to answer differently, partly according to their personal contacts, and partly according to the way in which they construe Christianity and its social ideals : the question is not so simple as may appear at first sight ; for example, " A Just Distribution of the Means of Life " might be called a Christian social ideal, but it is one which is acknowledged by many who are non-Christian in theory and practice. In any case, participation in practical affairs—whether it take the form of administration of local government, activity within trade unionism or the Labour Party, or collaboration with more advanced Socialists or Communists, or whatever it may be—brings Christians into touch with those for whom Christianity means little or nothing or worse than nothing.

There is no reason why Christians should not engage in practical work alongside others who do not share their religion, and every reason why they should, so long as they can. And no doubt in England at the present time there are considerable opportunities of work along these lines. This is admitted by the League of the Kingdom of God, which has for one of its objects " co-operation with other bodies, religious or secular, on occasions when fundamental issues of social righteousness are at stake."

But it is inevitable that, sooner or later, a point will be reached when this co-operation becomes no longer possible.

Gore once spoke of the " false Socialism which ignores the fact of sin and the need for redemption." The ignoring of these is part of the excessively immanentist philosophy which is always sliding down, according as the world-renouncing or life-affirming element in ethics is emphasised, into pacifist Communist-anarchism or into Marxo-Leninist Dialectical Realism.

There are Christians who are ready, in practice, to join with Tolstoian anarchists in war-resistance, though their theory on the subject is different.

And there are Christians who are ready, in practice, to join with red-revolutionary Communists, and who see in the " atheism " and " anti-God propaganda " of Russian (and other) Communists something that is all a mistake, due to the misrepresentation of what Christianity really is ; according to this view, the hostility to religion is really an anti-*false*-god propaganda, which Christians can, at least to some extent, support rather than oppose ; and the " atheism " is really the service of the true God whom they ignorantly worship, and whom, once the misunderstandings have been cleared away, they will be ready to acknowledge. Christians who take this view would say, as Feuerbach did at one time, that " he alone is the true Atheist to whom the predicates of the Divine Being—e.g. love, wisdom, and justice—are nothing, not he to whom merely the subject of these predicates is nothing." Communists themselves, however, are not at all disposed to accept any such interpretation of their position ; and the later history of Feuerbach seems to show that if there is in Communism an unacknowledged remnant of Christian ethic, that is, unhappily, more probably in process of being lost rather than further developed, and that Marxo-Leninist Dialectical Realism is more likely to slide down into sheer undiscriminating life-affirmation (with complete world-renunciation for the disillusioned) than to climb uphill towards the Historic Faith of Christianity.

The appearance in history both of Tolstoian pacifism and of Red Revolutionism is due to a hopelessness and desperation caused by stubborn resistance to fundamental social changes on the lines of the Law of Nature and the Law and the Prophets. It is admitted on all hands that the normal Christian method is that of teaching, propaganda, persuasion, prayer, personal influence, and also constitutional laws. But if men will not hear the Law and the Prophets, though Christ be risen from the dead, what then? Are Quakers, Tolstoians, and other pacifists right in claiming the Sermon on the Mount and the story of the Cross as justifying their position? Or are Christian Communists right in thinking that Catholic Christianity recognises the use of force, and that it is justifiable, if necessary, to take up arms against the oppressors of the despised, rejected, and crucified poor in the Name of Him who has made their cause His own? Or is it neither the pacifists nor the revolutionists, but the Roman Catholic Newman who is right, when he said that if Christians can do nothing else—that is, in this context, if all their preaching and praying, their propaganda and efforts to use constitutional methods, produce no result—" at least they can suffer for the truth, and remind men of it, by inflicting on them the task of persecution "?

We are brought back to the question of the way in which Christianity and its social ideals are to be construed. And it is very significant that the League of the Kingdom of God declares itself for a theology in which the doctrine of the Kingdom of God is the regulative principle. Christian belief and practice cannot be sundered ; and practical action—unless it ends in an immersion in something less than Christian—leads to a fuller exploration of Christianity itself.

For it is the function of the Church, as Westcott put it, "not to rehearse a stereotyped tradition, but to unfold a growing message." As men gain new visions of truth and righteousness, and have a growing message to unfold, they become dissatisfied with the data of the tradition as it has been handed down to them. This dissatisfaction creates, in the case of prophets within the Church, a re-interpretation of the data ; through the ministry of the prophetic office, new perceptions of truth and righteousness become incorporated and digested into the living and growing tradition that is handed on from generation to generation. But these new visions, and this dissatisfaction, may also create, in other cases, an impatient casting-away of traditions and institutions, and a falling-back into mere law-of-nature ethic and what Gore described as false Socialism.

But a sympathetic understanding of the philosophy of the false Socialism which ignores the fact of sin and the need for redemption, may provide valuable suggestions for those who are dissatisfied with stereotyped tradition but do not wish to break with historical and institutional Christianity. For if it is true that Natural or Rational Religion with its law-of-nature ethic always declines into pantheism or worse, except in so far as it keeps within and under the Historic Faith of the Church—and the history of Holyoake's " Secularism " or " Practical Philosophy of the People " could be cited in evidence for that proposition—it is also true that historical, institutional Christianity can only keep sound and vigorous in so far as it includes and has as a background the religio-moral outlook of Natural Religion.

The pantheistic tendency of this philosophy diverges, it has been maintained, into Mysticism and Secularism, into pacifist anarchist-Communism of the Tolstoian type or red-revolutionary class-war and dictatorship. The contempt for history, and negation of property and government, that are found in the one form of this philosophy can open out the conception of man in God's universe, free from hampering traditions which human personality has outgrown ; while the class-war ideas of the other form can show that God's

Self-identification with the poor is not " a glorification of the pauper lot " (the phrase is Gore's), but a revelation that God declares His Will to the rulers of the kingdoms of this world through the needs of the poor. The world-renunciation of the one can foster a healthy detachment from the results of human effort, and a hope that does not depend upon the prospect of success ; while the life-affirmation of the other can emphasise the real value for God of secular skill and scientific discoveries and inventions.

Christianity has often been construed too much in terms of world-renunciation and passive waiting upon God ; or else, in reaction against this, too much in terms of life-affirmation and vigorous human action. If the one interpretation forgets the Resurrection and the Conquest of the world by the Risen Christ, and is thus liable to become " next-worldly," the other forgets the rejection of Jesus by the world and His willing submission to death, and is thus liable to seek only an " earthly paradise." In order to retain the truth that is in both these interpretations, it is necessary to go back to the eschatological background of the Gospels. A theology in which the doctrine of the Kingdom of God is regulative cannot fail to value the biblical symbolism of the End of the World. For this, as explained by Gore, " provides for men the sort of outlook on the ultimate future which is morally necessary for them, both to encourage them to feel that it is worth while doing their best without regard to the shortness of life ·and the seeming futility of human efforts after the highest ends, and also to prepare them for desperate struggle with the forces of evil within and without."

PART II

COMMUNISM AND RELIGION

I

THE EARLY DEVELOPMENT OF MARX'S THOUGHT

by John Macmurray

Grote Professor of Philosophy, London University

I. INTRODUCTION

THE PURPOSE of this essay is to give an account, as
objective as possible, of the development of the thought of
Karl Marx up to the date (1848) at which the *Communist
Manifesto* was written. There would have been some advantage in having such a contribution to this book written
by a Communist. There is, however, a counterbalancing
advantage in having it written by someone who, while not
a Communist, is willing to make the effort to achieve a
sympathetic understanding of how the final stage of Communist theory was reached by Marx himself. There is no
doubt some truth in the contention that only a person who
accepts the Communist position whole-heartedly, and who
is actively engaged in the effort to bring about the triumph
of the Communist Party is able to understand fully what
Communism in theory means. But it is not the whole truth,
and, in particular, it can hardly apply to the early writings
of Marx, which are themselves a record of how Marx ceased
to be a Hegelian of the Left and came to be the apostle of
Communism. Communists are rather liable to misinterpret
this early stage even if they do not entirely discount it. They
are naturally apt to read these early writings in order to
find in them the reflection of their own theory as it stands
to-day, and, therefore, to dismiss as youthful aberrations

those elements which do not square with the final outcome. This is, of course, highly undialectical. Marx was not born a full-blown Communist. His final view was reached through a dialectical process in his own thought. Communists sometimes speak as though this made it reasonable to disregard all but the final expression of Marx's view. But to anyone, whether Communist or not, who accepts dialectic, it is simply a mistake. The end of a dialectical process, the final synthesis, must be understood dialectically. If it is torn from its setting in the historical development through which it has come into being, it is necessarily misunderstood. It would equally be a misunderstanding of Marx to separate the early stages of his thought from their conclusion, though not to the same extent. For they *are* earlier stages, and though they can only be fully understood in terms of the theory which is their final outcome, they are historically earlier, and the conclusion was not explicitly in the mind of Marx when his earlier works were written.

The main difficulty which faces the sympathetic student who does not whole-heartedly accept the final conclusion lies in his tendency to produce a false emphasis through selection. This, however, is equally liable to happen with the Communist expounder. At most, the one and the other can only do their best to be conscious of the danger throughout and to correct and counteract it in themselves. This I have tried to do. I have endeavoured to exclude any effort at criticism from my exposition, and even to refrain from emphasising those passages which tell against the interpretation of Marx which is current among Communists at the present day. Unfortunately the severe limitations of space prevent me from using quotation in such a way as to vindicate my exposition from a charge of bias. Some bias there probably is, but not, I think, nearly so much as both Communists and anti-Communists are likely to suspect. I can only refer them to the collection of the early writings of Marx which is the basis of my own study, *Der Historische Materialismus*, by Landshut and Mayer. There is, unfortunately, no English translation of this work available at present.

II. THE TRANSITION FROM "IDEA" TO ACTUALITY

Any account of the development of Marx's thought starts naturally from the long letter to his father, dated 10th November, 1837. That letter reveals three things which are the roots of Marx's subsequent growth. He is deeply conscious of the time in which he lives as a climax and turning-point in world history, and he sees his own intellectual problem as a reflection of this universal crisis. He has to make a new departure in thought, and he sees this personal decision as if the whole previous history of humanity had to take a critical decision in and through himself. We find, in the second place, that this is bound up in his mind with the task of carrying philosophy beyond the point to which Hegel had brought it. He has made several attempts to do this, and is filled with chagrin to find that all his efforts end up where Hegel began. Hegel is already, half playfully, " the enemy," and, against his will, his thought delivers him like a traitor into the enemy's hands. Lastly, we see that he has already vaguely defined what it is in that philosophy from which he wishes to escape. He is determined to seek for the Idea in things themselves. Hegel produces the Idea like a conjurer bringing rabbits out of a hat. The young Marx wants to find the Idea for himself in the empirical reality which it offers to interpret, but he does not see how this is to be done. To Marx, as to other thinkers of the time who had come under the spell of Hegel's massive intellectual achievement, it seemed that Hegel had at last completed the development of speculative philosophy. The process could be carried no further. But history was not at an end. It was necessary for thought to find a new line of advance. The question that faces Marx, as it faced all other Hegelians of the time, is the question, " After Hegel—what ? "

To this question Marx devoted himself in the thesis which he wrote for his Doctorate in Philosophy. He saw that the problem was not a new one altogether in the history of philosophy. The same situation had arisen in Greek philosophy with its culmination as a speculative development in Aristotle. The clue which he was seeking might, therefore, be found by asking what happened to Greek philosophy after Aristotle. The answer is that with its completion as a speculative system, philosophy becomes practical. It seeks the realisation of philosophy in the lives of men and their societies. Philosophy, which has hitherto developed itself as idea, seeks its own embodiment in action. Of much that is interesting in the development of this analysis, and its application to his own time, there is one point which is determinative. Thinkers are not themselves men of action. Yet they are faced in such periods with the task of bringing theory and practice into relation. They can only do it, being philosophers, theoretically. Yet, philosophy, of which they are the vehicles, is seeking its further development, not in theory, but in action. The result is necessarily paradoxical. There are two lines between which the thinker must choose in this predicament. Philosophy, he sees, has reached the climax of its development in Idea. It is now the final expression of the historic reality of the world in thought ; and yet, when one turns from the truth which completely expresses the nature of the world to the actuality of the world itself, one finds that the two are contradictory. The world in its actual structure rejects the truth about itself. The dialectic which hitherto has set one incomplete idea in opposition to another, now sets the completed Idea over against its antithesis in the empirical actuality of history. It is these two, Idea and Fact, which have to find their synthesis. Since the antithesis is no longer an opposition of ideas, the synthesis can no longer be a synthesis in Idea. It must be a synthesis in History, and History is action. Reality, which has completed itself in idea, in the philosophy of Hegel, and the actual world in which we act and live, which is incomplete, must move from opposition into unity. Now, for the thinker, this may mean one of two things. It may mean that he stands on the completion of his philosophy and seeks to alter the world by action in terms of the philosophy. The philosophy becomes for him an ideal to which the world must be made, by his action, to conform. On the other hand, he may turn to the empirical study of the world, and from an empirical investigation may seek to develop another theory which will express the actual nature of the world as it is, in opposition to the ideal philosophy which the world contradicts. The practical philosophy which follows the completion of the speculative task will thus find itself divided into two opposing schools which have chosen one or other of these lines. From the purely theoretical side these two schools (they are, in fact, the Idealist and Realist schools in post-Hegelian philosophy), will seem to be the defenders and the opponents of the system of speculative idealism. But their debate really refers to the practical issue which underlies it. As a result, says Marx, each of the two schools succeeds in doing what its opponent set out to do, and fails to fulfil its own intention. The Liberals, as Marx calls them, who set out to maintain the Idea while transforming the world in its likeness, make no difference to the world, but they *do* destroy the Idea of which they are the professed defenders. Their opponents, in their attack upon the Idea, do not succeed in changing the Idea, but they do initiate changes in the world. They get at least so far as to set up tendencies and movements which have a practical significance for the transformation of society. This paradox is an inevitable outcome of the effort after the synthesis of Idea and Fact—of Theory and Action. For it is the Idea itself which is seeking to pass into action, and the thinkers in whom this tendency expresses itself will feel at once the tension between the Idea as they apprehend it in idea, and the pressure of the Idea in themselves towards action. The Idea itself will be felt by them as " the enemy " precisely because it is merely idea, and as such antithetical to action.

The defence of the Idea as Idea by a group of philosophers will merely signify their resistance to the Idea's own tendency towards self-realisation. The resolution of the paradox lies simply in the fact that the thinkers are thinkers, while their objective is action. The effort to unite idea and actuality, to fuse theory and practice, appears as the antithesis of the effort to maintain the purity of the Idea in its ideal isolation from the world.

III. DEVELOPMENT OF A DIALECTICAL SOCIOLOGY

This is a critical point for the understanding of Marx's intellectual development. His conflict with Hegelian idealism does not imply dissatisfaction with Hegelianism as theory. Hegelianism remains for Marx, and always did remain, the final and necessary culmination of philosophical theory as such. His opposition to it is a dialectical opposition. It does not mean that Hegel's philosophy is untrue, but that truth is not everything. Truth must complete itself by creating its own antithesis. It cannot develop any further as truth. It must enter into some synthetic relation with that over against which it stands, the reality to which it refers. It is impossible, therefore, for Marx to turn away from one theory to another theory. It is equally impossihle to turn away from theory to any activity in which theory is not a necessary element. Equally, as a convinced Hegelian in theory, it is impossible for him to turn from philosophy to empirical science. The scientific point of view is itself an abstract point of view, which has been overcome and transcended in the philosophical synthesis of Hegelianism. What, then, was he to do? His answer was that he must develop a new kind of thinking, which he called " Historical Critical Activity." This consisted in examining the historical facts in the light of the philosophical idea, and it led straight to a critique of the Hegelian philosophy of the State. Before touching upon this, we must consider why it is

that it is the sociological field which Marx enters, armed
for the purpose with the Hegelian Idea. The reason should
be obvious to any student of Hegel. The development of
the Absolute Idea first comes to self-consciousness in man.
The development of the self-conscious Idea in man reaches
its culmination in the Hegelian philosophy, as idea. The
Hegelian philosophy culminates in the philosophy of the
State. It is, therefore, in relation to the Hegelian philosophy
of the State, in which the purely ideal development reaches
concreteness, that the return to the world of historical
actuality must be made. In no sense is there a transition
from speculative philosophy to empirical science. No
Hegelian could be guilty of such a blunder. It is the further
development of philosophy that is in question, and, as we
have seen, that further development can only lie in the
future of human development. The antithesis on which the
further development rests is the antithesis between the
completed Idea (the Hegelian Theory of Society) and the
actual structure of the society, still in historical process,
to which the idea of society refers. Hegel has produced
the final ideal embodiment of the nature of human society.
But what produced Hegel? An actual, very imperfect,
very transitory Prussian State, at the end of the eighteenth
century. If we then turn to examine the actual Prussian
State which has produced the idea of itself through one of
its functionaries, a Professor of Philosophy in its University
of Berlin, we can see whether or not it is an actual embodiment of its own idea of itself, and, if it is not, we can ask
what Prussia proposes to do about it. The rest lies in the
future. Theoretically what is necessary is now a dialectical
sociology which will explain the discrepancy between
Prussia and Prussia's idea of Prussia. Practically it is the
conflict between the truth of the Idea and its own actual
constitution, which must force the development of Prussia
by revealing its failure to realise its own essential nature.
This, however, is only a particular way of putting it. The
Hegelian philosophy of society is the culmination in Idea
of world history. It applies to society as such. What is

required in general is a correct account of the stage which the development of human society has actually reached in the contemporary world. It is this that has to be brought into opposition with the completed development of the idea of human society which is the culmination of Hegel's thought. And this account, though in a sense it must be empirical, must itself be dialectical. In other words, the stage of development which has actually been reached in human society must be understood dynamically in terms of the historical process which has brought it into being, and which is not yet complete. Obviously no empirical scientist is in a position to give such an account. A dialectical sociology could only be developed in the light of a dialectical philosophy, and for Hegel science is necessarily undialectical. The process of historical-critical activity is, therefore, primarily the process of creating a dialectical sociology.

The development of Marx's sociology—that is to say, of his theory of the development of man in history—starts from the recognition of a contradiction between the idea of man and the historical fact of man. Human life contradicts man's own idea of human life, which has developed to its completion in Hegel. This is the problem which has to be resolved by an understanding of the historical process. Now, this means something quite definite for Marx which is apt to be overlooked. It means that in reality, though not in actual fact, man is free, and his freedom is his self-determination. Self-determination is the " essence " and " truth " of human nature. But an examination of human life in society, as it actually appears in history, shows man as determined by forces which are extraneous to himself. This is the situation so well expressed by Rousseau in the phrase with which the *Social Contract* opens : " Man is born free, but everywhere he is in chains." Marx asserts the same antithesis. But whereas Rousseau goes on to say, " How this came about, I cannot tell," Marx demands an account of how it came about. It is precisely this that his interpretation of history has to provide. If we may anticipate the economic interpretation which is the final outcome of the enquiry, we may frame the question as it presented itself to Marx at this stage of his development in the following words : " How does it come about that man, who is in the essence of his nature free and self-determined, becomes in the process of his history unfree and determined by the material forces of his environment ? How does it come about that a being whose nature it is to determine the social relations which express his real essence, is actually found to be determined in his life by those social relations ? " Marx uses two conceptions as correlatives to express this paradox. They are the conceptions of " self-estrangement " (*Selbst-Entfremdung*) and " appropriation " or " coming to one's own " (*Aneignung*). In history we find first the process by which man becomes estranged from himself, through which man reaches the negation of his own essential nature. The opposite of this is the process by which he comes to the appropriation of his own nature and enters into the possession of his freedom in self-determination. These are not merely two processes. It is not merely that up to the completion of the capitalist stage of human development man is becoming more and more the slave of extraneous forces, and then breaks into the freedom of self-determination through the establishment of Communism. This is part of the truth. But, seen more deeply, the two processes are one process which is maintained by the tension between its opposite moments. Idealists have often described the process of historical development as the development of freedom. Marx added to this that the same process could just as well be interpreted as the development of slavery. Thus a material interpretation is set over against the ideal interpretation. The completion of the ideal development has been achieved. Hegel has expressed the real nature of humanity in idea, and that development in idea is just as much a real fact of history as is the enslavement of humanity through the development of economic organisation. Thus Marx is led to examine contemporary society to discover the corresponding completion of the enslavement of humanity which is its antithesis. He finds this in the creation of the proletariat—that is to say, of a class of men who are completely deprived of their essence as human beings, who are completely without freedom or self-determination, and who have nothing to lose but their chains. We find, indeed, in a very interesting passage, at the beginning of his essay on " National Economy and Philosophy " (1844), that he conceives the necessity of a complete proletarianisation of society as a whole, as the necessary culmination of the process of human self-estrangement. It is the point at which the proletariat, by socialising all private property, reduces every class to its own level of complete and unmitigated determination by economic forces. But this, he goes on, cannot be the end of the historical process, seeing that it " involves the complete negation of human personality." Yet again, that very culmination of the process by which humanity becomes the opposite of itself is the beginning of its own realisation, in activity, of its true nature as free and self-determining. It is the point at which man the prodigal, feeding the swine in the far country, realises that he is starving in the midst of plenty, and says, " I will arise and go to my father."

My reference to the parable of the prodigal son, indicating as it does a relation between the development of Marx's thought and historic Christianity, is completely justified. For Marx was in this phase of his development very much concerned with religion, and with Christianity in particular. It could not well be otherwise. After Hegel's death, in 1831, the Hegelian school split into two parties, the right and the left, on the question whether Hegel's philosophy was indeed consistent with Christian theism. The left decided that it was not, and began the process of humanising religion. The landmark of this decision was the publication of Strauss's *Life of Jesus*. But the philosopher in whom the consequences of the left position were worked out most clearly was Ludwig Feuerbach. Feuerbach described the full trajectory from idealistic theism to humanistic materialism, and the core of the process was the re-interpretation of Christianity in purely human terms. If we remember that Marx recognised in Feuerbach a necessary stage in the development from idealism to his own communistic materialism, and that the final stage of Marx's development is ushered in by his criticism of Feuerbach, we cannot be surprised to find an extremely important, even if indirect, relation between Christianity and Marxism. Nor shall we be surprised to find Marx himself maintaining that " the criticism of religion is the beginning of all criticism." By criticism, in this phrase, we must be careful to understand what Marx understood by it, not the blank denial of religion, but the historical understanding of its necessity and function in society, which leads to its dialectical negation when its function is completed. Marx meant that the understanding of religion was the key to the understanding of social history, and he would have agreed, I feel certain, that the correctness of his final position stands or falls by the correctness of his interpretation of religion.

But we must leave the question of Marx's attitude to religion until a later stage. The immediate point at which the antithesis of Idea and Fact is worked out in detail is in relation to Hegel's theory of the State. At that point the Hegelian philosophy professes to pass into concreteness, and to exhibit the contemporary State as the embodiment of the Idea. It is hardly an overstatement to say that, in effect, Hegel identifies the completed idea of human society with the actual organisation of the Prussian State in his own time. Accepting the truth of the Hegelian Idea, Marx proceeds to show that this identification is false. He does this by means of a detailed and penetrating criticism of Hegel's philosophy of the State from this point of view. The gist of this criticism has been made again and again by a large number of critics belonging to different schools of thought, but never with such accuracy of analysis or in such detail as by Marx. It is that Hegel was really not concerned primarily with the facts of history at all, but with the systematic development of his idea of organic interconnection. He used history to suit his own purposes, without too much regard to the empirical facts of historical development. He made history a commentary upon the truth of the Idea, instead of making the Idea a commentary on the facts. When, therefore, he reached the point at which the Idea in its development must complete itself by becoming real in the objective world, he looked to the organisation of his own society to provide him with the necessary material. Instead of turning to examine realistically the structure of Prussia in order to discover whether it corresponded to the idea of true human life in society, his primary interest in abstractions led him to assume that the facts must square with his theoretical analysis, and proceeded, with all the subtlety and ingenuity of his philosophical genius, to fit the facts into the framework which he had devised. It is important to understand Marx's attitude to Hegel here. An historian might have examined the structure of the Prussian State and shown that it did not exhibit the particular form of organic interconnection which the Hegelian theory demanded. He might have concluded from this that Hegel's theory was a bad one. But that is not Marx's conclusion. Marx maintains instead that Hegel's idea of society is proper, that it represents in its formal structure a true understanding of the essence of human life in society. The fact that Prussia is not an embodiment of this idea, as Hegel had pretended, merely proves, therefore, that the social development of mankind in history is not yet complete, and that the Idea has still to embody itself in human society through a continuation of the historical process which will transform Prussia (and with it human society as a whole) into a form of actual social life which will be the expression of the Idea. The essence of humanity has yet to find its self-expression in history.

Marx's devastating exposition of Hegel's failure to exhibit the contemporary State as the embodiment of his ideal conception of the State has more in it, however, than a merely negative result. For though Idea and contemporary fact are not identical, they are not unrelated. The Idea is obviously itself part of the historical process whose present expression is Prussia, and Prussia is equally part of the historical process by which the Idea is realised. The Idea and the Fact, even in their antithesis, are parts of one historical process, and the driving force of the process is, indeed, expressed in the tension between them. From this point of view, Marx is able to define the relation between Prussia and its companion States, which together make up the contemporary stage of the social process, and the Idea which anticipates their future development. He does this through the idea of democracy, which he takes as the proper expression of the essence of human life. " Democracy," he writes, " is related to all other forms of State, as Christianity is to all other forms of religion. Christianity is Religion κατ' ἐξοχὴν, the essence of Religion. . . . Democracy is the essence of all forms of constitution." With this clue we can restate in more general and familiar terms Marx's position in relation to the Hegelian theory of society. Hegel, in effect, he would maintain at this stage of his thought, has expressed formally the nature of a democratic society. He has gone on to identify democracy with the political structure of the most advanced forms of contemporary society. These States, particularly the republican ones, do as Hegel has done. They identify themselves with the idea of democracy, and think themselves its embodiment. But they are in error. A comparison of the idea of democracy with the actual life of such societies shows that they are not *really*, but only *formally*, democratic. At best they represent a temporary stage in the process from " the democracy of un-freedom " of medieval society, to the democracy of freedom which is yet to be realised.

The formality of the so-called democratic States of modern times consists for Marx in the fact that the State is essentially a bureaucracy which identifies its ends with the common good of the community which it governs. Yet these ends are purely formal or political ends. The State, which is, in fact, the organisation of government, is a special part of the activity of society with purposes of its own which it lives to realise. Formally, these particular purposes are identified with the general purpose of society. In fact, they are separated from, and antithetical to, the actual life of the society itself. For society is really a group of persons entering into relations with one another for the ordinary purposes of human life. The form of their society is the form of their actual relations. If a society is to be really democratic, the form of co-operation between its members in their ordinary life must be democratic. The form of their relations as co-operating for the provision of their material needs, for example, is a real form of social relationship. Indeed, it is obviously the most fundamental form of social relationship, if only because the provision of the means of livelihood is a condition of all other forms of social relationship. Unless this form of co-operation is democratic, no formal organisation in the political field for political purposes can produce a democratic society. Modern democracies are not democratic societies in this sense, even if their political form is democratic. To think that they are is in fact to think that the political organisation of the society *is* the form of the society. It is to imagine that, apart from the relationships imposed by law upon its members, the society is completely without structure— that there are, in fact, no relations binding men together in society except those imposed by the State. Such a theory of society presupposes, as Marx points out, the *bellum omnium contra omnes* of Hobbes's State of Nature. To think that a society is made democratic by the formal organisation of its political machinery implies that the society is in reality composed of competitive units engaged in continual struggle with one another. Only so can the ends which are served by the organisation of the bureaucratic hierarchy be identified with the common end of society as a whole, and even then only formally, since there is, in fact, on this view, no other common end except the particular end which is pursued by the State.

IV. BOURGEOIS DEMOCRACY

This is not, of course, the empirical truth about modern democracies. In fact, they have a complex social structure which is not political, and which, indeed, determines the actual course and outcome of their political life. This actual structure is the essential content of the social life. It is this which constitutes the community. But it is certainly not a democratic structure. Yet these societies have a democratic idea of themselves which is reflected in the formal structure of their political organisation. There is, thus, a contradiction within them, between the real complex of human relations, purposes and activities which constitute the actual life of the society and its formal representation in the legal and political structure of the State. Here again we find, therefore, the antithesis of Idea and Fact, involving, as it must, the pressure of the formal Idea towards its own self-realisation in the reality of social life, and the resistance of the actual organisation of society to the transformation of social life that this would involve. The bourgeois State is formally democratic, and, therefore, expresses formally in its constitution the ideas of equality and freedom. But bourgeois *society* is not equalitarian, nor are its social relationships free. Yet these two contradictory structures are both real expressions of the nature of the community. The life of the community expresses itself in idea and in formal organisation in a way that contradicts and fights against the expression of its own nature in action. This contradiction at the roots of modern democracy is dialectical. It expresses the tendency towards the social synthesis of Idea and Fact, of Thought and Action. It involves the development of the society towards the embodiment of its own Idea in the structure of its social life. When these modern societies assert democracy, when they enunciate the principles of freedom and equality as the basis of human society, when they write these principles into their political constitutions, they are expressing the truth, they are apprehending their own essence as human societies.

Democracy is, in fact, the essence and truth of all forms of human society. But this truth contradicts the living structure of the societies which have discovered it. Their assertion of democracy is the recognition of their destiny, not of their present actuality. It is the realisation in idea of what they are to become in fact.

There is, therefore, in bourgeois democracy a severance of society and State. This shows itself most clearly in the conception of the " private life." Every person in such a society is, as it were, reduplicated. In his *private* life he appears as a member of society with a particular way of earning his livelihood ; with a particular social standing determined mainly by the way he earns his livelihood ; with a wife and children, let us say, to support and educate ; with certain interests with which he fills his leisure, in the form of religion or sport or stamp-collecting, or any of a hundred other activities which depend upon his private whims and his possession of the means to gratify them. In this private life the differences between individuals are enormous. The inequality of their incomes and opportunities determines to a very large extent the different kinds of private life which they are able to lead. In their private lives they are by no means in possession of equality, even equality of opportunity for self-development. Neither are they free in their private lives. The relation between what they can do and what they desire to do is largely determined by the way in which they are compelled to earn their livelihood, and by the responsibilities which their status in society forces upon them. On the other hand, each member of bourgeois society is *also* a citizen—that is to say, a member of the democratic *State*. All citizens are, in their capacity as members of the State, free and equal. They are equal before the law. They are free in the sense that the State will not interfere in their private lives so long as they obey the law. And this freedom and equal citizenship has as its peculiar symbol the possession of a vote in the election of the legislative assembly. The ideal of this democratic State is expressed in the formula, " One man, one vote."

That is its symbol of freedom and equality. In other words, the man appears in the State organisation as an *individual,* abstracted from the empirical reality of his private life as a member of society. In this abstract and formal sense each man is one individual, and, therefore, all men are equal. The equality, however, is a purely formal, almost a numerical, equality, which is only achieved by separating his legal existence from his social existence as this particular person leading this particular kind of life in society. In the same way his freedom belongs to his political, not to his social, existence. He possesses certain formal rights before the law, which all citizens equally possess. So long as he keeps within the law, he will be defended by the power of the State against any *illegal* interference by others. If he breaks the law, he will be tried by the same courts and by the same procedure and on the same legal principles as any other citizen. He has free access to the courts, and equal treatment in the courts, for the settlement of his disputes with other citizens. The fact that he may be unable to take advantage of this freedom, owing to poverty, or the conditions under which he earns his living, has nothing to do with the matter, because it belongs to the sphere of his *private* life.

We see here what Marx means by maintaining that bourgeois democracy is formal and abstract, and that it rests upon a separation of the political and the social existence of its members ; that it rests, indeed, upon the exclusion of the private life of the individual from political recognition. For the private life of individuals in society is their real life, and the interrelated private lives of all the members of a society is the real life of the society. It is the substance, the empirical content, the historical actuality of that society at that period in world history. No man can *exist* as a mere individual, though he can be *thought* as an individual. He can only exist as this particular person, carrying on these particular and special activities in relation to other particular persons, and their activities. His legal existence as a free and equal citizen of a democratic State is, therefore,

HR

only *ideal*. It exists only in thought, because it is thought, by himself and all the other members of the society. And the practical effect of this is that the *real* existence of the *State* consists in the private lives of a certain number of the members of the society, who are political officials, administrative, legislative, or judicial. The State exists in reality only as the hierarchy of the bureaucracy. The lives of its officials have a political significance. Their purposes are political purposes. But because the political life of such a society is formal and ideal these political ends are themselves only formally, not really, public. They are, that is to say, dictated by the organisation of the political machinery, not by the concrete and therefore private needs of the human life of the society itself. Marx would allow, of course, that in many particular points the real life of society forces itself upon the State-life and compels politicians to deal with reality in real ways. Any society is in process, and bourgeois society, just because of this separation of political and private life, is peculiarly unstable. Indeed, as it develops, the occasions on which it is compelled to allow an intrusion of the private life of society into the political lives of its official Government will necessarily multiply, and ultimately must destroy its abstract and ideal aloofness. But such exceptions only prove the rule, and the Olympian world of the officials will only allow its " office ends " to become real human ends when the pressure of public opinion becomes too strong to be resisted.

V. THE "EARTHLY" AND THE "HEAVENLY" CITIZENSHIP

We must notice that this contrast between the abstract, ideal life of the State and the actual life of society is itself a reflection of the general contrast between Idea and Actuality with which Marx's thought began. In philosophy we found it in its most general form as the contrast between the completed Idea which expresses the essence and truth of Reality and the actual nature of that Reality as it appears from the empirical point of view by the light of the knowledge of its own essential nature. Now we find it in the political field as the contrast of the abstract and formal —that is to say, the legal—nature of bourgeois democracy, and the undemocratic structure of the real life of bourgeois society. But now, just as we had to turn from the Idea to the empirical nature of human history in order to find the Idea realising itself in Action, we have to turn from the ideal life of democracy, from that self-realisation of the nature of society in idea, which the abstract forms of democracy express, to the empirical life of these bourgeois societies, in order to discover the democratic idea realising itself in the actual existence of bourgeois society in the concrete. Just as before, we have to re-interpret this empirical life of society in the light of the abstract legal form which is its separated State-life. Again we find that the first result is to bring out clearly their antithetical character. Democracy, having completed itself formally, turns to seek its formal nature embodied in the social life whose truth and essence it expresses, and it finds its own opposite. Again the two contrasted lines of development appear ; either to hold on to the formal structure and transform the actual life of society into its likeness, or to attack the form—that is to say, the actual structure of the political State—and to determine the form of organisation of the life of society which expresses the actual structure of that life. The first line is that of Liberalism, which is thus in the political field the analogue of Idealism in the philosophical ; the second leads to the effort to substitute for the democratic State a form of political organisation which expresses the actual, contemporary structure of the real life of society. As we have seen in dealing with the philosophical aspect of this, neither of these parties can succeed in doing what it sets out to do. Each of them succeeds, in fact, in doing what the other intends. Marx had a good deal to say about the first of these alternatives—that is to say, the effect of Liberalism in politics. Its intention is to maintain the legal forms of the

democratic State, and to use these to transform the actual
life of society into concrete democratic life. But it must
always fail, and, in fact, produce the opposite result, since
the maintenance of the legal structure implies the maintenance of the antithesis between State and society. Only
the synthesis of the two could produce what Liberalism
intends. About the other alternative, Marx has less to say,
and tends perhaps to identify it, rather loosely, with the
Communist effort. It is, therefore, worth while to point out,
in the light of contemporary experience, the reality of this
second alternative, in contrast with the course which Marx
actually followed. The undialectical effort to negate the
formal democracy of the bourgeois State must deny the
truth of democracy as Idea. It therefore sees merely the
empirical antithesis and seeks to create a political structure
which reflects the actual inequality and lack of freedom in
the contemporary structure of the private life of society.
Such an effort produces the Fascist society, which takes the
form of an effort to stabilise the existing social order, and so
to bring the dialectical process of the self-realisation of
democracy to a stop. The Fascist State is the contradictory
of the Liberal State. As the latter is purely ideal, so the
former is purely empirical. But the reality is both at once
in their antithesis and opposition. Therefore, the Fascist no
more than the Liberal can achieve his intentions, and must
achieve, against his will, the professed intention of the
Liberal. The simple reason for this is that democracy is
the essence and truth of all political constitutions, and that
humanity, whether we like it or not, is developing towards
the realisation of its own essence. The Fascist could only
realise his intention if he could put a stop to the process of
human evolution. In fact, he can only produce a particular
stage in that evolution.

But we must return from this digression to our exposition.
In speaking of the relation between the actual life of the
member of a bourgeois society and his formal existence as
the citizen of a bourgeois State, Marx makes use of an
illuminating phrase. He speaks of his material life as a

human being in society, as his *earthly* existence, and his citizenship of the democratic State as his *heavenly* existence. There is more here than a mere metaphor. It reveals how the antithesis between the actual and the ideal breaks out afresh when we leave the political forms out of account to concentrate upon the concrete life of society. It appears there in the religious form, which is the most fundamental form of all. It is the most fundamental because it is universal, and it is universal because it expresses the antithesis which maintains the process of human development in its most concrete and dialectical form. So long as that process is incomplete, so long there must exist in the real life of every human being a tension between his essential nature and the actual nature of his daily life. Since his essence cannot be realised in his actual existence, it must seek its realisation in Idea. For Marx, religion is the primary field in which man's real essence (as freedom or self-determination) finds expression for itself as Idea. Thus man comes to have a double existence—an actual, or earthly, existence, and an ideal, or heavenly, existence. The development of religion is the primary social development of man's essence in Idea, and the further it develops the more the contrast between what man essentially is and what he actually is increases. The more man's slavery to material conditions grows in the process of history, the more his recognition of his own essential freedom grows as its antithesis. Marx's statement that " Christianity is the essence of all Religion " must mean that he recognised in Christianity the completion of the ideal development in its religious form. Nor is this surprising when we remember that Hegel considered that his philosophy expressed abstractly the essence of Christian theology. So complete does this religious separation of idea and fact become that it expresses itself in a complete severance between the earthly life and the heavenly, between this world and another world, between the present life and another life beyond the grave. The historical-critical analysis of religion must start by re-establishing the unity of these two worlds. It must recognise that religion is part of the actual life of humanity, and that the other life, the spiritual life, arises in and from the actual material experience of this life. Man is not made by religion ; religion is made by man. It must go on to understand the antithesis between the spiritual and the material, the Divine and the human, as an antithesis within the reality of human life, and so proceed to interpret it dialectically. Again we must insist that the negation of religion must be dialectical, and that any denial which represents religion as a mere mistake cannot be dialectical. Religion must have a real function in the life of humanity. This is, of course, Marx's view. The development of religion is the development of truth, though in an illusory form. Its function is to preserve and maintain in human life, over against the actual denial of it, man's recognition of his own true essence and destiny. It is an ideal solace for the denial of his own nature in the miseries and frustrations to which social conditions subject him. Of course, it can be used, and has been used, by ruling classes as a means for maintaining among the oppressed classes an attitude of passive submission to their lot. But that is a secondary and derivative use to which it is put. It is not its real nature, and, indeed, religion can only be used in this fashion because it has a necessity of its own which maintains it. But its real function depends upon the necessity of the separation between essence and actuality. So long as the process of history is still at a stage in which man's essential nature is necessarily negated by the material conditions of his life, so long religion is a necessary feature of human society, and so long it will continue. The maintenance of the antithesis between man's idea of himself and his actual life is essential to the dialectical process. At such a stage the attempt to destroy religion is an attempt to destroy the essence of humanity in favour of the *status quo*, and must necessarily be unsuccessful.

When, however, the ideal development is complete, and seeks its realisation in actuality, the pressure in human life to the realisation of religion necessarily takes the form of an attack upon religion. It is impossible at once to maintain the separation of the two worlds, and to unify them. To realise the Kingdom of Heaven on earth necessarily involves the disappearance of the idea of Heaven as another world in which the wrongs of this world are righted. Just as the realisation of democracy as a reality of social relationships necessarily involves the destruction of that purely formal democracy which exists in ideal separation from the private lives of its citizens, so the realisation of religion involves the destruction of that ideal world of spiritual blessedness which exists in the mind of the believer in virtue of its separation from, and contrast to, his earthly life. Even if religion contains in its own way the essence and truth of humanity, still the *essence* of religion lies in the separation of this truth from its embodiment in concrete experience. Since the realisation of this truth in human life means the disappearance of the distinction between essence and actuality, it must needs destroy the essence of religion. The embodiment of the Christian idea in human community here and now as the brotherhood of men must mean the disappearance of Christianity as a religion. Its necessity has gone. " For what a man seeth," as St. Paul put it, " why doth he yet hope for ? " The man who turns from the realisation of the truth in religion, to the creation of the form of human life which that truth expresses, will surely find that he is engaged in a struggle with the inertia of religion. For religion not merely expresses, but also sustains and perpetuates, that dualistic habit of mind which wishes to maintain the purity of the heavenly world from contamination by the earthly. To maintain opposites in separation is to refuse their synthesis. To make the effort of synthesis is to seek the destruction of the isolated existence of the elements which are to be fused.

This, it seems to me, is the underlying structure of Marx's attitude to religion. To complete it we must add one other point. Ideas can exist only in minds—that is to say, in men. If an idea is to have a social existence, it must express itself in the structure of society through institutions. Thus, formal democracy, Marx maintains, is only the idea of democracy, yet it exists as the actual political structure of modern States. This is only possible through the separation from society of a set of individuals, a social group, who are, as it were, the functionaries of the Idea. That is why Marx identifies the modern democratic State with the bureaucracy —that is to say, with the group of officials of all sorts whose function it is to carry on, in and for society, a State life which is separated from the real life of society. Similarly religion, which is also only idea, can exist as a social fact only through its embodiment in organised institutions ; and these institutions only through a group of persons in society who are set apart or dedicated to the religious idea. The realisation of the religious idea in the actual structure of social life, and not merely as a separated institutional form within society, means not merely the disappearance of the idea of the heavenly world, but the disappearance of those institutions which are at present set apart for its service. When humanity " comes to itself " and negates its own self-estrangement, there can no longer be any *raison d'être* for the existence of organised religious institutions. " When that which is perfect is come, then that which is in part shall be done away." The effort to establish the true human society necessarily implies the destruction of the Churches. The Churches, however, as a religious bureaucracy, will naturally resist their own supersession. And to do this they must maintain that ideal separation between the ideal world of religion and the real world of earthly life upon which their function in society and their mode of life as private individuals depends.

VI. THE ECONOMIC FACTOR

This essay has been concerned with the philosophical and sociological aspects of Marx's thought, and not primarily with economics. This is partly justified by the fact that the detailed working out of the economic theory belongs to the last phase of his development. But this does not mean that Marx was not conscious, from a very early stage, of the fundamental *rôle* played in the process of social development by economic pressure. In conclusion, therefore, I must say a word about the relation of the economic aspect of social life to the philosophical and sociological analysis with which we have been concerned. The first point that requires to be stressed is that Marx's economic theory will be completely misunderstood unless it is interpreted in the light of his philosophical analysis. It seems to me hardly too much to say that if the theory expounded in *Das Kapital* is interpreted as an empirical economic theory amongst other such theories, then we should have to conclude, as most empirical economists do, that it is pretty bad economics. It is, in fact, something quite new—a dialectical theory of economics, and, as we have seen, no empirical science can be dialectical. Just as Marx transformed sociology by interpreting the empirical facts of history in the light of the Hegelian account of the development of the Idea which is antithetical to them, so he transformed economics by interpreting the empirical facts in the light of their dialectical opposition with the development of the economic idea. This means, in general, that he wrote his economics as a part of his sociology. But it means also, in particular, that he was concerned with the facts of economic development in dialectical relation to the development of economic theory. For Marx the ideal aspect of any social process is a part—and an essential part—of that process. In a sense which, though inadequate, is illuminating, we might say that Marx's economics involves the acceptance of Ricardo as the completion of economic development in idea, just as his sociology depends upon his acceptance of Hegel as the completion of the development of humanity in idea. But such a discussion lies beyond the proper scope of this essay.

Where, it might be asked, does Marx's materialism come in, in the account which we have given? The question would arise from the belief that Marx's economic theory is the essence of his materialism, and that, therefore, his materialism

could not be expounded except through his economic
theory. Now this is not the case. Marx's economics is a
corollary, though a very important corollary, of his
materialism. His particular materialism appears the
moment he recognises that the development of human
thought is part of the development of human life. Thought
is in its nature ideal and abstract ; as part of the development of human life it is the formal aspect of human development. The substance of human development does not lie
in thought, but in practical activity—in the living of human
life. Now action is essentially material. Thought can only
arise in a being whose existence is a complex of substantial
or material activities. It is only by positing a dualism
in the essence of human life that thought can be dissociated
from material activity, or that mind can be separated from
matter. And, as Marx says, " there can be no actual
dualism of essence." It is only within the complex of
material activities which constitutes human life that the
opposition of mind and matter, of formal nature and substantial nature, can arise. And it can only arise as a
dialectical opposition within a single substantial reality.
So far as ideas are true, they must represent the formal
aspect of a concrete reality. The thought of human development is at once the reflection of human development in
human beings, and a part of that development. As a formal
reflection, it constitutes a superstructure built upon, and
sustained by, the activities in which real life consists. As
part of the development it stands in contrast with these
practical activities, and interacts with them. Thus the
idea and the fact of human life form a single whole ; and
their dialectical opposition within the whole is no evidence
that they constitute two different natures, but merely that
the one nature which their tension constitutes is a living
and developing nature. The whole that they constitute is
also a *material* whole, because the substantial activities in
which human life consists are material activities. The idea
of them could not exist apart from them. They could exist,
though not in a *human* form, without their idea. This is

Marx's materialism, and it is a materialism which involves an important modification in the traditional conception of matter. For matter can no longer be defined as incompatible in its nature with mind and idea. On the contrary, material existence can be human existence, and, therefore, can include thought and the development of thought in itself.

The concentration upon the economic aspect of human activity arises in the effort to understand how the synthesis of idea and actuality must be accomplished. When the idea of human nature and the actual fact of human nature have been separated out as completely antithetical, when the knowledge of the essence of humanity as free and self-determining faces the fact of a humanity completely enslaved, and the process of self-estrangement is complete, what is it that compels the two into synthesis in the development of history ? Why must the essence of human nature realise itself in human existence ? The general answer to that question is that it is nonsensical. It is to ask, Why must an acorn grow into an oak ? But it hides a real question, which is the question about how the process takes place, and what are the forces which keep the growing organism moving and changing until its growth has reached maturity. In the case of human society the answer that Marx gives is that any society, if it is to exist at all, even in a form which denies its own essence as a human society, must at least provide for the material needs of its members as animal organisms. It may, by its form, deny their human needs, and still exist, though in a state of unstable equilibrium. But it cannot deny their needs as animal organisms without bringing its own existence to an end. If a society keeps a large section of its members in slavery, it must still keep them alive to be able to do so. It is even possible to imagine a society which was completely enslaved, and it would be a society which existed purely to supply the animal needs of all its members—a society, that is to say, which was completely determined by its economic structure, and is therefore completely non-human. But it could not remain in that condition, because it could only provide for its animal needs in a human way. It would have to use reason for ends which exclude the essential nature of the rational being who uses it. So long as a class in society remains relatively self-determining, this class can use the remainder in a way that treats them as slaves. But if the whole society were enslaved that possibility would be gone. Thus the complete proletarianisation of society would, by its very negation of the human nature of human society, be forced to base its organisation of human relationships for the supply of economic needs on universal human principles. There would no longer be any reason, or any motive, for behaving otherwise. It is this simple fact which leads Marx to concentrate, both from the point of view of social theory and of social practice, upon the economic forces in human society, as those that are ultimately decisive. It is the animal basis of human life which makes it impossible for human beings to cease from the struggle to realise their own *human* nature in the actual forms of their social life. The dialectical understanding of the economic development of mankind is the understanding of the necessity which determines that humanity must realise freedom.

II

WHAT COMMUNISM STANDS FOR

by John Cornford

Trinity College, Cambridge

I. PRIMITIVE AND CONTEMPORARY COMMUNISM CONTRASTED

To BEGIN WITH, a distinction must be made between Communism in the sense that the word is used by the Communist Parties now, and between primitive communism, the communism of an order of society which has not yet developed to the stage of the private ownership of the means of production. Whereas primitive communism is essentially based on a low level of productive forces, on a very simple form of pastoral or agricultural production, Communism in the modern sense is based on the collective ownership of large-scale means of production. There is no ethical " idea " of Communism in the abstract that applies to both forms. The same word covers two distinct types of social organisation. It is to the latter form that I propose to confine myself.

This distinction is simple and elementary. Nevertheless, it is necessary to make it ; because hundreds of the more ignorant opponents of Communism have not even found out this elementary fact. In the same way a sharp distinction must be made between Communism in the Marxist sense and between the various communist experiments of earlier periods—early Christian communism, the Taborites, the Social Levellers of the seventeenth century. These were certainly closer to Marxist Communism than was primitive communism, because they arose as a revolt against class

exploitation. But they are still sharply distinguished by the
fact that they are based essentially on small-scale individual
production which puts its products into a common pool,
whereas Communism now is based on the collective
ownership of socialised industry.

II. WHY CAPITALISM DECLINES

It is clear, therefore, that the precondition for the rise
of Communism is the development of industrial capitalism.
The essential features of capitalism are threefold :

(1) The monopoly of the means of production is concentrated in the hands of a small ruling class of industrialists,
financiers, and landlords.

(2) Goods are produced not for consumption by the individual producer, but as commodities for sale on a market.

(3) The driving force of society, the motive for production,
is not the satisfaction of the needs of society, but the
hunt for profits of the capitalist class itself. Production is
not for use, but for profit. Every crisis reveals that as soon
as production becomes unprofitable, however great may be
the needs of society, it is at once discontinued.

To make such a system of production possible, there are
two necessary preconditions ; at one pole the accumulation
of a vast capital in relatively few hands, at the other pole
the formation of a propertyless class that has nothing but
its labour-power to sell, so that it is forced to continually
hire out its labour-power to maintain its existence, and to
hire it out in such conditions that the capitalist class
invariably has the whip hand in the bargaining.

Both classes can be found in an embryonic form in the
medieval city—within the guilds the formation at opposite
poles of a patriciate of merchant-monopolists and a semi-
proletariat of propertyless journeymen ; although for their
most rapid development it was necessary for capitalist
property relations to smash through the narrow guild restrictions. The principal sources of capital accumulation were

the profits of merchant capital, the slave trade, etc. The proletariat was recruited in the main from the countryside. The development of a commodity economy, the development of a market, smashing through the limits of the old feudal self-sufficing economy, giving birth to capitalist relations in the countryside, the simultaneous break up of the bands of feudal retainers, " set free " a new class. They freed it in a double sense. They freed it from the old feudal services. And, by dispossessing it, they freed it from any personal property in the means of production that it once ·possessed.

The profit of capital comes from the unpaid labour of the workers, from the new values produced by the workers over and above that necessary for the renewal of the means of production and their own maintenance, and appropriated by the capitalists in virtue of their ownership of the means of production. Consequently, for capital to attain its full profitability, it must find some way of disposing of the surplus of goods that remains over after the payment of wages and maintenance costs. It finds this in three ways. First of all, in its own luxury consumption ; but, however much it spends on itself, this can only constitute a small fraction of the total surplus. Secondly, and more important, a big proportion of the surplus is reinvested in an extension of production. What is then left over—often the most important section of all—is disposed of in foreign·markets.

Consequently, capitalism must always expand at an increasingly rapid rate. This necessity for continual expansion forcibly extends capitalist property relations all over the world with fantastic speed. The old feudal self-sufficing economy, and the more or less stable Asiatic system of production, are swept away by the flood of cheap commodities. In the political sphere, the feudal land-owners and the absolute monarchy (which represented a temporary balance of power between decaying feudalism and the rising bourgeoisie) are violently swept from power, as in the revolution of 1789–93, or, as in England, forced to an unfavourable compromise.

III. THE PERIOD OF PERMANENT CRISIS
AND WAR

But even in the periods of its most rapid expansion, capitalism carried with it the seeds of its own decay. Its historic function was to develop at an unprecedented rate the means of production and technical advance in general ; and, whilst it was still engaged in spreading this development all over the world, for all its barbarity, it was the historically appropriate form of social organisation. Capitalism is the system of production appropriate to the period of uncontrolled aggressive outward expansion. But at a very early period it shows itself incapable of organising the productive forces which it has itself brought into being.

Capitalism is only capable of systematic organised production within the limits of a single concern. The scramble for profits between rival producers, and even between different branches of production, makes the organisation of production as a whole an impossibility. The competition between the capitalists forces each of them to continually reinvest his surplus in an extension and improvement of the means of production, which, as the sums spent on more complicated and expensive machinery increases, is accompanied by a continual *relative* diminution of exploitable labour-power. And, since profit can arise only from the direct exploitation of living labour-power, there is a continual tendency for the rate of profit to fall to a limit which makes production no longer profitable. An immense and ever-increasing flow of goods is poured into a market which is *relatively* contracting, owing to the continued relative impoverishment of the mass of the people. There follows a crisis of overproduction.

E. Varga describes the mechanics of such a crisis in these terms[1] :

" To put it more simply : prosperity continues so long as

[1] Varga, E., *The Great Crisis and Its Political Consequences*, Martin Lawrence, 1935.

the process of real accumulation is in full swing, as long as new factories, harbours and railways are built, and old machines are replaced by new ones. But as soon as this process reaches a certain conclusion after a considerable number of new production plants have been completed, the demand for the commodities of Division 1 (means of production) diminishes, entailing a drop in the demand for consumers goods as well, since the workers in Division 1 are becoming unemployed. At the same time, the supply of commodities increases, since the new and reconstructed factories begin to pour goods into the market. Overproduction already exists, but the open outbreak of the crisis is delayed since the capitalists (who never believe that a prosperity phase will come to an end) are producing for inventory. But production exceeds consumption to an ever greater extent, until the crisis bursts into the open."

At the time at which Marx wrote, the crises of capitalism were still crises of a period of expansion, which, in spite of their temporarily devastating effects, could still be overcome within the framework of the system by means of the expansion to new markets and the more extensive exploitation of old. But within capitalism there were forces at work, noticeable in an embryonic form even at the time when Marx wrote, whose development has meant that this solution is no longer open to capitalism. The fierce competition between rival capitalists has led continually to the growing concentration of capital, the squeezing out or incorporation of the smaller and less efficient concerns, the division of the markets amongst an ever-diminishing number of industrialists and financiers. This process towards monopoly is inextricably linked to the development of the colonies as closed markets, as a closed source of cheap raw materials, as a closed sphere for the export of capital. It was for this reason that Lenin described this stage in the development of capitalism as the imperialist epoch.

The consequences of this development are twofold. It is

no longer possible for capitalism to overcome its internal crises by outward expansion, since the whole of the world has already been divided up by four or five major powers into colonies, markets, and " spheres of influence." Consequently, the nature of the conflicts that are carried on is changed. From 1871 to 1914, the period of imperialist expansion, there was a continual series of wars of expansion, wars of colonisation of the big imperialist powers against small and backward nations ; 1914 saw the end of that process. With the development of German capitalism, and its famous struggle for a " place in the sun," the world was no longer big enough to serve as a market for the rival imperialisms. The epoch of imperialist wars, of wars between the great powers for a redivision of the world, is introduced. Capitalism can no longer solve its problems peacefully ; each successive crisis in the imperialist epoch is a prelude to a more desperate world war.

Of course there have been, and, for all I know, there still may be, theories that the growth of monopoly capital, the concentration of capital in fewer and fewer hands, will lead to a planned capitalism, a peaceful division of the world market between a handful of trusts, which will eliminate the need for war. This is not so. The concentration of power in the hands of a few big trusts simplifies the basic antagonisms ; it does not eliminate them. The fate of the International Steel Cartel is the fate of all attempts at international capitalist organisation. But there is no need to prove this point theoretically. History has already proved it.

IV. THE LIMITATION OF PRODUCTION UNDER CAPITALISM

It is not simply because it is unjust that Communists work for the overthrow of capitalism. They do not judge anything by abstract ethical standards. During the period of its rise to power, capitalism was as barbarous as it is to-day. The early history of the Industrial Revolution, of the old colonial system, of the slave trade, is proof of this. Nevertheless, for all its brutality, it was historically a progressive force. But to-day that is no longer true. Capitalism cannot organise the productive forces that it has called into being. On the contrary, the capitalist property relations have become a check on the development of production. Once the stimulus of a higher rate of profit drove capitalism to expand its production at a colossal rate ; now factories are idle, and the market is glutted with unsalable goods, not because there is no consumer for these goods, but because they cannot be sold at a profit. Even in its boom period, capitalism is immensely wasteful of the productive forces of society. Stuart Chase estimated that in America in 1925, in the clothing trade and in the shoe industry, 30 per cent of the working year was lost ; that productive waste was 50 per cent in textiles, 81 per cent in the metal industry ; that the ratio of workers engaged in production to workers engaged in distribution had fallen from 80 : 20 in 1850 to 50 : 50 in 1920—in other words, that, owing to the cost of marketing, competitive advertising, etc., it cost as much to sell articles as to produce them. And British capitalism, quite apart from incidental waste, is burdened with an immense weight of obsolete exactions, which no force in capitalism has the power to shake off, but which utterly cripple the economic life of the country, and condemn it to a chronic crisis, with a chronic surplus of unemployable labour.

Even in its boom periods, capitalism cannot organise production. And the consequences in the period of crisis are therefore hardly imaginable. According to the economist E. Schultz, the economic loss caused by the world war works out at somewhere around 744 and 833 milliard gold marks, whilst the loss caused by the crisis in U.S.A. and Germany alone between 1929 and 1932 came to 500 milliard gold marks. Capitalism cannot organise production. And the consequence is not only a wanton destruction of productive forces. It is a destruction of human lives. The deaths from starvation, from premature exhaustion, from preventible accidents, from preventible disease, yearly mount up to a more colossal total. And the process reaches its logical culmination in the limitless destruction of imperialist war.

As R. P. Dutt writes[1] :

" The more obvious and glaring expression of this process, the burning of foodstuffs, the dismantling of machinery that is still in good condition, strike the imagination of all. But all do not yet see the full significance of these symptoms ; first, the expression through these symptoms of the extreme stage of decay of the whole capitalist order ; second, the inseparable connection of this process of decay with the social and political phenomena of decay which find their expression in Fascism ; and third, the necessary completion and working out of this process in war. For war is only the most complete and most systematic working out of the process of destruction. To-day, they are burning wheat and grain, the means of human life. To-morrow they will be burning living human bodies."

The continuance of capitalist property relations not only stops any further advance of the productive forces, it endangers life itself. Society must be reorganised, or humanity wiped out. There is only one force capable of this reorganisation—the working class.

V. THE HISTORIC MISSION OF THE WORKING CLASS

In 1847 Marx and Engels wrote[2] :

" But the bourgeoisie has not only forged the weapons that will slay it ; it has also engendered the men who will use these weapons—the modern workers, the PROLETARIANS."

As capitalism develops, so it develops the working class. From the very beginning of the formation of the capitalist

[1] Dutt, R. P., *Fascism and Social Revolution*, Martin Lawrence, 1934.
[2] *Manifesto of the Communist Party.*

class there have been revolts of the oppressed semi-proletarian classes, starting with the weavers and metal-workers of thirteenth- and fourteenth-century Flanders. These risings were always defeated. And in many instances these risings put forward demands that were basically reactionary—demands for the return to the sheltered conditions of feudalism and guild production. Thus in the early period in England some of the first working-class organisations had as their specific object the enforcement of sixteenth-century legislation against the introduction of machinery. In the conditions of scattered small-scale production, when the proletariat has not yet been properly constituted as a class, when the most exploited of journeymen has some sort of a chance, albeit a diminishing chance, of becoming a master himself, then, in spite of the intolerable conditions under which he is forced to work, there is no sort of hope of working-class victory, nor even of stable working-class organisation.

But with the concentration of capital the workers also are drawn together. They learn very quickly that organisation is the only weapon of a propertyless class. The conditions of industrial capitalism teach that no advance can be gained without a bitter struggle. And because of the decisive part they play in the productive process ; because the very conditions of their life teach them the necessity of organisation and solidarity ; because their lack of property means that they have nothing to lose, and consequently they can dare to advance where the middle classes shrink back—for all these reasons the working class is the only class that has the power to overthrow capitalism.

Throughout the whole of history there have been peasant revolts against feudalism and against capitalism. They have always been beaten. And the reason for this is, that although in periods of extreme oppression they may be forced into a defensive alliance, yet peasants remain property owners, often with conflicting interests on the market, their experience teaching them how to compete with one another and not how to organise together ; and, consequently, the only fairly stable revolutionary organisations that have been formed in the countryside have been amongst the very poor peasants and the landless labourers. It is not through any ethical subjective superiority, but simply through the daily repeated experience of their living conditions, that the working class is the only consistently revolutionary force in modern society. For the middle classes, the professional classes, the trading classes, the peasants, the students, though they may suffer as badly as the workers during the crisis, are yet not brought face to face with their main enemy—capital. They see the crisis in the form of rising food prices and rising rents, of debts they cannot meet, of competition with the chain stores, and not in the form of speed-up, wage cuts, and dismissals. That is why they are so much more easily swayed to Fascism, to Douglas Credit, to religion, to hysteria, to anything that promises an easy way out without facing realities. And in periods of prosperity they do not get along so badly, they altogether cease to be anti-capitalist. Whereas the working class in the period of the crisis is attacked in the factories and at the Labour Exchanges, and comes directly face to face with its main enemies—the capitalist class and its State machine. And even in periods of "prosperity" the working class relatively loses ground. Pre-war England and pre-crisis U.S.A. were often quoted as examples disproving the Marxist theory of class struggle, and proving the identity of interests of workers and capitalists. But here are the figures. In England between 1893 and 1909 the wealth of the capitalist and landlord classes increased by £336 millions (Inland Revenue statistics), whereas the income of the working class increased by—at a maximum estimate—£30 millions[1]; and in America between 1900 and 1924, while the real wealth of the nation increased by 96 per cent, wages increased by—at a maximum estimate—25 per cent (the British Mission estimates 14 per cent). Thus in the two classic periods of class collaboration the share of the working

[1] The Department of Labour, whose statistics covered more than 50 per cent of the working class, estimated £14½ millions.

class in the national income actually declined. Always, and at all times, the interests of the vast majority of the working class are opposed to capitalism. That is what makes the working class the only force capable of the reorganisation of society, and that is why Communism, if it is to accomplish anything, must be rooted in the working-class movement.

VI. THE RISE OF SCIENTIFIC SOCIALISM

But it was a long time before the working class was able to give a scientific formulation of its aims in the struggle against capital. In the early history of the working-class movement there are to be found three main tendencies.

First, there is the anarchic revolt that cannot distinguish between the progressive rôle of the rising heavy industry and the reactionary exploitation of capitalism, and finds its expression in machine wrecking, the fight to re-enact legislation against machinery, etc.

Second, there is the Utopian Socialism, which, though it is founded on ideas of absolute truth, reason, and justice, nevertheless recognises the necessity of a Socialism that will be based on some form of social ownership of large-scale means of production.

Third, there is the revolutionary democracy, which, without having a clear or developed social programme, yet recognises the conquest of State power by the working class as a precondition of any possible transformation of society.

The first of these finds its classic expression in the Luddite movement, the second in Owenism, the third in Chartism, and, more particularly, in the writings of Bronterre O'Brien.

On the basis of these gropings towards Socialism, and on the basis of similar tendencies in European politics, arose scientific Socialism—Marxism—which was able to select what was true and revolutionary from these half-formed theories and reject what was false and irrelevant. These are the essential characteristics of revolutionary Socialism.

(1) Socialism is not seen as an abstract ethical system, but as the culmination of a period of historical development. It is based not on what seems to Marx to be just or true or reasonable in an absolute sense, but on a prolonged and scientific study of the laws of movement of capitalist society.

(2) Socialism is seen as the collective ownership and administration by the working class of large-scale industrial means of production.

(3) The view that capitalism can grow into Socialism is explicitly rejected. The means of production must be wrested by the working class from the hands of the capitalist class.

(4) Socialism that faces reality must base itself on the capture of State power, on the destruction of the old State machine, and its replacement by a new State of a higher type.

(5) The class struggle is not completed by the victory of the working class. For a certain period the repressive machinery of the State must be kept in existence to put down the remnants of the old exploiting classes. That is what is meant by the dictatorship of the proletariat. Only after this resistance has been utterly crushed will the State be enabled to disappear, to " wither away."

(6) It will not be possible immediately after the revolution to operate the full Communist programme " from each according to his abilities, to each according to his need." For a long time after power has been taken it will be necessary to continue paying wages, etc., not according to need, but according to the amount and quality of work done, according to formal bourgeois ideas of justice. Only when all scarcity problems have been solved, will it be possible to go over to the complete classless society. Until then, equality means simply the abolition of class exploitation.

VII. THE CHARACTER OF A REORGANISED SOCIETY

An analysis of the growth and development of capitalism, of the chief results of capitalism in the economic, political, and cultural spheres, of the main forms of exploitation to which the workers are at present subjected, indicates clearly enough the main lines along which society must be reorganised if it is to survive. The salient characteristics of this reorganisation are :

(1) The abolition of classes. It can no longer be tolerated that the whole motive of production should be the profit of a handful of capitalists, so that the world is subject to continual useless waste and periodic devastating crises when production becomes unprofitable for this handful. The first task is the abolition of this monopoly of the means of production, the collective ownership and control by society as a whole of the means of production.

(2) Planned production. The waste, the anarchy, the disorganisation of capitalist competition and capitalist crisis must be brought to an end. At the present level of development of the productive forces, it is absolutely impossible to continue further without the systematic planning of production in the interests of society as a whole.

(3) The mainspring of production must be the satisfaction of the needs of society as a whole, not the profit of a few individuals. To end the present chaos and misery of a society with vastly developed productive forces in which the great majority of the people are still somewhere around, or even far below, the subsistence level, it is necessary to introduce a form of society in which the property relations are no restriction on the extension of production, in which the productive classes are guaranteed the full product of their labour (of course, minus a fund for the replacement and extension of production, for social services, etc.).

(4) It is necessary to put an end to the virtual educational and cultural monopoly of the capitalist classes, by which higher education is restricted within very narrow class limits. It is possible and necessary to extend educational and cultural facilities to a vastly greater extent than the economic and political needs of capitalism make possible.

(5) It is necessary to put an end to the intolerable position in which the whole world is exploited by five or six " advanced " imperialist powers. It is necessary and possible immediately to liberate the colonial peoples. It is not any defect in the structure of the economy of Europe and America that makes colonial exploitation a necessity. Once again it is simply the needs of a ruling minority.

(6) It is necessary finally to end the inequality of the sexes, expressed in difference of social position, difference of wage rates, etc., which exists in capitalist society. This inequality is simply a survival of an obsolete epoch. It is perfectly possible to put an end to it. In fact the conditions of modern society demand that it should be ended. But it will never be ended under capitalism.

These are a few of the characteristics of the necessary reorganisation of society. These are the essential features of Communist society. There is no inherent stupidity of human nature which makes these sensible and necessary measures impossible. The only obstacles are the capitalist property relations, which the capitalist class will fight tooth and nail to defend. For there is one class which stands to lose from the revolution in society which will benefit humanity as a whole.

VIII. THE CAPITALIST STATE AND THE DICTATORSHIP OF THE PROLETARIAT

If proof of what Communism can do is wanted, it is not necessary to look further than the U.S.S.R. The construction of Socialism in Russia started in a country whose economy had been utterly shattered by the world war and the civil wars and wars of intervention that followed. The 1920 index of production was 18 per cent of the 1913 figure. Starting from complete ruin, Russia has been converted from a backward country, dependent on Anglo-French loan capital, into a powerful independent industrial State. Industrial production has increased fourfold as compared with the 1913 figure. In spite of immense difficulties, Socialist reorganisation of agriculture has produced a far higher yield than was ever possible before. Unemployment has been wiped out. Wage rates have been increased three and four times. A cultural revolution has been carried out. From a country that was predominantly illiterate, Russia has been transformed into a country where the most advanced literary and scientific works, which are lucky very often to sell a few hundred copies in those capitalist countries where they are allowed to be sold at all, are sold in hundreds of thousands. All the reactionary medievalist tendencies of Italy and Germany find their polar opposite, not in the decaying " democracies " of England, France, and the U.S.A., but in the rising power of the U.S.S.R.

Eighteen years of Soviet power have shown that, to any-one who can face realities, all the material pre-requisites for a complete transformation of society are already in existence. It is not human wickedness in the abstract that prevents this transformation. It is the political power of the one class that stands to lose. Never in the whole of history has an obsolete order gone down without a violent struggle. And there is nothing in the least surprising about this, for a privileged class has its economists to show it that any other system of production is contemptibly inferior ; it has its priests to show that any other system of morality is sinful ; it has its critics and writers to show that any other system will mean the destruction of culture. It is true that in the period of crisis its theories are no longer self-consistent, no longer show the least connections with realities. But that does not matter very much. No class minds being inconsistent when the alternative is the realisation of the necessity of its own extinction. So naturally enough the capitalist class fights like fury against its own overthrow, which is not only unprofitable, but also barbarous, sinful, and a guarantee of material and spiritual disaster.

The machinery by which capitalism maintains its rule is the State. The modern capitalist State machine is an instrument designed solely for the maintenance of existing property relations. It is obvious that where one class is oppressing another, any machinery which aims at the maintenance of " law and order " is in fact a machinery for putting down the revolts of the oppressed, since the ruling class has no possible reason for disturbing the peace. It is only when two sections of the ruling class are at war with one another that one section will use the State against the other. And, even there, it handles the offenders with kid gloves. Compare the treatment of Clarence Hatry with that of an unemployed miner who " steals " 6d. worth of coal. It is only necessary to look through any day's file of court cases to see that the present machinery of " law and order " exists not to defend justice in the abstract, but a certain system of property relations. For instance, it is perfectly legal to starve, but for a starving person to help himself to a farthingsworth of a millionaire's property is a criminal offence.

If any proof is needed of the class character of the modern capitalist State, it is only necessary to refer to its activities during the General Strike. Looked at from a formal point of view, the General Strike was in its origin a sympathetic strike of the heavy industries in support of the struggle of the miners for a living wage, which the coal-owners could perfectly well have paid, if they had been prepared to surrender a fraction of their royalties and profits. However, they were not prepared to. The whole machinery of the State was mobilised to crush the strike. The strike was declared illegal. The police and the army were mobilised to protect the strike-breakers. Strikers were arrested, beaten up, imprisoned. On the fifth day a special ordinance was issued to the troops in action at the time, excusing them in advance for anyone whom they might happen to kill in the defence of order. Bourgeois members of Fascist and semi-Fascist organisations were armed against the workers. The capitalists gave the workers an excellent lesson in class war. They showed that, in the event of a serious attack on the sacred rights of private property, the whole State apparatus, king, lords, commons, judges, civil service, police, army, and navy, will be mobilised against the workers for any step, including civil war, that the profits of the ruling class require.

But it may be objected : all this took place because the General Strike was " unconstitutional " ; it is possible, provided you are very tactful, to take over control and make all necessary reforms by parliamentary democratic means. That is still the line of argument of the majority of the British working class. It is therefore necessary to examine more closely the nature of capitalist democracy.

It is perfectly true that at the time of its rise to power, at the time of its fight against the relics of feudalism, the bourgeoisie stood for an extension of democracy. At the time of the first Reform Bill, when the industrialists needed the support of the workers to wrest from the landed aristocracy a proportionate share in the control of the State, they developed a whole ideology of democracy. It is not so often remembered that the first Reform Bill was a purely bourgeois reform within very strict property limits, that, in the Chartist period that followed, the bourgeoisie were prepared to resort to civil war to resist universal suffrage, and that the subsequent Reform Bills were only enacted under very heavy pressure. Nevertheless, in the period of its expansion, capitalism stood for a certain limited democracy ; in the first place, because after 1848 its power was never seriously challenged ; in the second place, because it provided a safety-valve for working-class politics.

But all the time it kept in hand certain very strong safeguards, in case this limited democracy should ever touch its class rule. In the first place, the very possession of wealth gives it a powerful advantage. In any election campaign it has at its disposal the cinema and the Press on a scale with which a working-class party cannot compete. At a time of " national emergency," as in 1926 or 1931, it will also have the radio. A capitalist candidate can pay with ease the £150 deposit which is a serious burden for a worker candidate. He has at his disposal a fleet of cars and sums of propaganda money, with which, again, a worker candidate is unable to compete. And similarly on all questions such as the halls for propaganda meetings. In London the Conservatives or the Fascists can take the Albert Hall any time it amuses them. The largest hall in London available for the Communist Party is the Shoreditch Town Hall, and that it cannot afford very often.

Thus the whole machinery of parliamentary democracy, quite apart from the way in which the scales are weighted in favour of the backward county constituencies (more than three-quarters of the industrial workers' votes in less than half the seats) is built up in the interests of the party that has money to finance lavish propaganda. But apart from this there are very strong checks on the activities of Parliament. First of all there is the House of Lords, an unassailable stronghold of the reactionary property-holders. Secondly there is the judiciary, at the present composed almost entirely of men who were previously notoriously reactionary in politics, who are scarcely able to fit the existence of trade unions into their legal theory at all, and who, right from the time of the Criminal Law Amendment Act, *vià* the Taff Vale judgment and the Osborne judgment, to the decision that made the General Strike illegal, have shown a powerful anti-working-class bias. Thirdly, there is the Crown. Constitutional historians argue that, as the royal veto has not been used since the reign of Queen Anne, it is obsolete as an instrument to block the will of the people. That argument would hold water better if we had not seen the National Government so recently reviving legislation of the reign of Edward the Third against the leaders of the unemployed. Fourthly, there are the higher officials of the army, navy, police, and civil service, all of whom have very strong reasons for supporting the present order of society, and would not hesitate to use their position to thwart a legal attempt at Socialism. The army and navy officers take their oath of allegiance direct to the Crown. Fifthly, there is the whole machinery by which the rank and file of the military and civil services are separated from working-class politics. Recent articles by military authors show that officers of the army can use their position to do Fascist propaganda and get away with it every time. For a rank-and-file soldier to take part in revolutionary politics is a very serious offence. Sixth, there is the whole machinery of emergency legislation, by which, if it pleases His Majesty to declare that a " state of emergency " exists, every single democratic right can be at once suspended.

Thus the whole machinery of parliamentary democracy ensures that this democracy will only work in one direction. But, even though it is quite impossible to take power within this framework, the very restricted rights of capitalist democracy—right to hold meetings, right to a legal Press— sometimes become a check on the full development of the capitalist offensive. So in that case open Fascism is introduced. The propagandists of the British Union of Fascists are never tired of pointing out that Mussolini formed a constitutional Government at the request of the king (though they do not emphasise so much the fact that Fascism's rise to power would have been impossible without the active support of the army command, and that the march to Rome was made in a sleeping-car). They are never tired of pointing out that Hitler assumed the chancellorship at the constitutional request of President Hindenburg, through the one loophole in the otherwise perfect Weimar Constitution. And they are right. Every capitalist constitution admits of the " democratic " introduction of Fascism when necessary. In England the machinery already exists. If there is not yet an open rule of violence against the working class, it is solely because the capitalist class can manœuvre well enough to maintain its power without it. As soon as its power is seriously threatened, the Emergency

Powers Act and the Incitement to Disaffection Act will make short work of the remaining liberties of the English people.

Thus the whole structure of capitalist rule eliminates the possibility of the peaceful conquest of power by the working class. If the working class ever wishes to take power, it must prepare for civil war. R. P. Dutt writes[1] :

" Once you are in a fight, the choice of weapons depends on circumstances and your adversary. Civil war is simply the final most extreme form of the class struggle. Civil war is not a question of subjective choice ; if it could be avoided every Socialist and Communist would make heavy sacrifices to avoid it, short of the sacrifice which cannot be accepted under any conditions, the sacrifice of the working-class cause itself (which is the real meaning and inevitable result of the ' rejection ' of civil war). In the words of the *First Manifesto of the Communist International*, ' Civil war is forced upon the working masses by their arch enemies.' "

It is not from any love of violence for its own sake that the Communists declare that it is necessary to prepare for civil war. The choice of weapons does not lie with them. The capitalist class repeatedly shows that it is prepared to adopt any form of violence rather than surrender its power and privilege. The fate of the dozens of constitutional " Socialist " Governments—in Germany, Austria, Australia, Great Britain, Scandinavia, Spain, etc., not one of which has been able to introduce an atom of lasting Socialism, is the fate of the Socialists who " reject " civil war. In the only country where the majority of the workers followed the line of the Communists, the result has been very different. The rule of the Hungarian Soviets is the only example in history where the working class was able, owing to the utter collapse of a war-defeated bourgeoisie, to come to power for a short time without a bloody struggle. But they only assumed power because the Communists had already

[1] Dutt, R. P., *Socialism and the Living Wage*, 1927.

made systematic preparations for civil war. And immediately after their victory they were forced into civil and
international war to hold their power against the counter-
revolution of the land-owners and industrialists backed with
the armies and money of the Entente.

For the working class to take power by the existing
machinery is impossible. And even if one were, like the
Socialist League, the left of the English Labour Party, to
make an assumption of this impossibility, even then it would
still be necessary for the working class to shatter this machine and replace it by its own State form, for the whole
structure of the capitalist State means that it is possible for
it to work in only one direction, and for the construction of
Socialism it would be both useless and dangerous. The
savage repression which the working class has met, will
meet, and is everywhere meeting to-day in its fight for
power means that it is quite impossible for the workers,
immediately on the assumption of power, to abolish the
State, as the anarchists would like to see. If the working
class is to maintain its power it will need a very powerful
State machine in the early years of its rule. But right from
the beginning it will be a higher type than the capitalist
State.

The example of the Paris Commune is useful to show
that the proletarian dictatorship is not a Russian phenomenon, that, in fact, it first originated in one of the Western
" democracies."

These were the principal measures of the Commune :

(1) Army. The army for the first time became a genuine
people's army. The standing army and conscription were
abolished, and all citizens capable of bearing arms were
free to enlist in the National Guard. (In the U.S.S.R.
the continual threat of invasion has made it necessary to
maintain a big standing army. But this army is distinguished from every other army in the world by the fact
that its rank and file take an active part in politics, and
no barriers are placed between the soldiers and the

IR

working classes. Moreover it is not the only armed force. A high proportion of the factory workers also are armed.)

(2) Bureaucracy. The wages of all officials were restricted to the same rates as the averagely well paid worker. In this way the danger of the bureaucracy coming to have a separate and distinct class interest is guaranteed against. Every post was made elective, and every individual subject to instant recall.

(3) Judiciary. In the same way the judiciary was made elective, responsible, and subject to instant recall.

(4) Education. Every administrative post in the department of education was made elective. Education was removed from clerical control.

Thus in every sphere the Commune stood for an expansion of democracy, and the drawing of the greatest possible number of rank-and-file workers into the task of administration, the breaking down of the obsolete barrier between executive and legislative.

An examination of the Constitution of the U.S.S.R. shows a systematisation and an extension of these principles. The great historic contribution of the Russian revolutions of 1905 and 1917 was the development of the Soviet as the specific form of the working-class State. The Soviets (workers' councils, elected directly from factory and district units) combine in a single form all the advances made by the Paris Commune. The universality of the Soviet form was shown clearly in the revolutionary wave of 1917–21, when Soviets were formed not only in Russia, but in Finland, the Baltic States, Bavaria, Hungary, Canada (Winnipeg), etc. The Soviet revolution, led by the Communist Party, is now proving in China, even according to the admission of the London *Times*, the only form of government which can end the agrarian crisis and introduce stable government. The Soviet is not only the universal State form of the working class, it is also the highest form of democracy yet seen.

IX. THE PRE-CONDITIONS OF REVOLUTION

But a revolution does not make itself. Capitalism does not break down of its own accord and allow the working class to sweep effortlessly to power. The Russian revolution is often presented as due solely to the breakdown of the corrupt and inefficient old order under the strain of the war. A very slight acquaintance with the facts shows that this was not the case. The war breakdown greatly facilitated the victory of the revolution ; but, unless the movement had been consciously planned, organised, and prepared in advance, it would not have had a more permanent success than the Austrian and German revolutions of 1918–19, or the Italian occupation of the factories. And the decisive factor in the preparation for a victorious revolution is the party. Lenin defines a revolutionary situation in the following terms [1] :

" One must make sure, first, that all the class forces hostile to us have fallen into complete confusion, are sufficiently at loggerheads with each other, have sufficiently weakened themselves in a struggle beyond their capacity, to give us a chance of victory ; secondly, one must ensure that all the vacillating, wavering, unstable, intermediate elements—the petty bourgeoisie, and petty bourgeois democracy, in contradistinction to the bourgeoisie— have sufficiently exposed themselves in the eyes of the people, and have disgraced themselves through their material bankruptcy ; thirdly, one must have the feeling of the masses in favour of the most determined, unselfishly resolute, revolutionary action against the bourgeoisie.

" Then, indeed, revolution is ripe ; then, indeed, if we have correctly gauged all the conditions outlined above, and if we have chosen the moment rightly, our victory is assured."

Lenin, V. I., *Left-Wing Communism.*

Thus, under all circumstances, a disciplined revolutionary party, possessing complete confidence of wide masses of the working classes, with the ability to analyse clearly and react rapidly to every change in the situation, is a pre-condition of successful revolution. Chatterers like Wells who, without having studied Communist theory or practice, are fond of declaiming against Communists for their " obsolete " propaganda of armed insurrection, would do well to stop talking for a bit and study very carefully this and other passages from Lenin.

Not only the example of Germany and Austria, but the defeat of the revolution of European countries—Finland, Hungary, Italy, the Baltic States—immediately after the war, and the recent defeats in Austria and Spain, show that, however good the objective possibilities are, without a powerful and experienced revolutionary party victory will be lost. In England in 1926, in Spain in 1931, in America during the early days of the Roosevelt administration, crises arose which, had the Communist Parties been as strong as were the Bolsheviks, or even as strong as the Communist Party of France to-day, could have been trans-formed into revolutionary crises. But the Communists were not strong enough and the opportunities passed.

Stalin defines clearly the objectives which the Com-munist Parties set themselves.[1]

" In order to be an effective vanguard, the party must be armed with a revolutionary theory, with a knowledge of the laws of the movement, of the laws of revolution. Lacking this, the party is not really fit to rally the pro-letariat for the fight, or to take over the function of leadership. The party is no true party if it limits its activities to a mere registration of the sufferings and thoughts of the toiling masses, if it is content to be dragged along in the wake of the ' spontaneous movement ' of the masses, if it cannot overcome the inertia and political indifference of the masses, if it cannot rise superior to

[1] Stalin, J., *Leninism*, Vol. I.

the transient interests of the proletariat, if it is incapable of inspiring the masses with a proletarian class consciousness. The party should march at the head of the working class ; it should see further than the working class ; it should lead the proletariat and not drag in the rear.

Without such a party the Russian revolution would have been impossible. Without such a party the revolution in the other countries will be impossible. To-day it is perhaps only true to say of the Communist Parties of France and China that they have reached this standard. But it is also possible to say that the Communist Parties of Germany, Japan, Austria, Poland, Bulgaria, Spain, Hungary, Czechoslovakia, Cuba, and Greece are on the way. Superficial observers in Great Britain are often misled by the relative weakness of the Communist Parties of Great Britain and the U.S.A. into believing that the Communist International is a negligible force (*see* the *Manchester Guardian* leader on the Stalin-Laval *communiqué*). There is no need here to produce arguments against these gentlemen. History itself will give them a very rude surprise.

  . . . .

I have attempted in this essay to outline a few salient points of Communist theory and Communist policy. It has been necessary to devote what may seem a disproportionate amount of space to the analysis of capitalist economic development and the capitalist State, because without such an analysis the Communist programme becomes unreal and unintelligible. For Communism is not a scheme of social revolution according to an abstract scheme of what seems desirable, but according to existing realities, which are the realities of capitalism. If there are certain assertions without sufficient factual material behind them, that is not because Communists in general are dogmatic, but because there is not space here for a comprehensive study.

III

COMMUNISM AND RELIGION

by Ivan Levisky

"REVOLUTION has always been anti-religious and anti-Christian," says Berdyaev. On the Continent such a statement would meet with general acceptance, but in England and America there have always been those who sought a reconciliation between Socialism and Religion. It is possible for an American Socialist to say, " I am a Marxist. I, also, am a Catholic Christian."[1] On the other hand, members of the Third International are quite unambiguous. " Atheism is a natural and inseparable part of Marxism."

> " The fight against religion, the opium of the people, occupies an important position among the tasks of the cultural revolution. This fight must be carried on persistently and systematically. The proletarian power . . . uses all the means at its disposal to conduct anti-religious propaganda."[2]

We propose to set forth this criticism of religion in the clearest and most uncompromising terms, and without any attempt to mitigate the severity of the orthodox Communist criticism of religion, and more especially of contemporary Christianity.

Religion is false—that is to say, it inculcates belief in what does not exist. Nevertheless religion exists, and is of

[1] Francis Henson, member of the Revolutionary Policies Committee of the Socialist Party, in *Christianity and Marxism.*
[2] The *Programme of the Communist International.*

the greatest social and political importance. No revolutionist can afford to ignore its existence. Religion is not merely an intellectual error, it serves a definite class interest in dulling the social emotions of the workers and binding the oppressed classes, by faith in the Divine, to submission to their oppressors.

This is not to say that it is a deliberate fabrication of the governing class to serve as an instrument of exploitation. Religion is a product of society ; a form of the organisation and thinking of society ; one of the categories of human thought. It is impossible for it not to exist. This implies that it serves some necessary function, for without survival value it could not persist.

That function is twofold. It fills the gaps of human knowledge, and is a method of grappling with the unknown and partially known. It gives a supernatural sanction to tribal regulations.

" On the one hand, men have imperatively required some assurance that they are not altogether helpless and alone in the face of the gigantic and perilous indifference of the natural forces which surround them. Such assurance religion supplied by personifying these forces so that, at least, they might be invoked, cajoled, and propitiated. On the other hand, it was imperative to the stability of the human communities of the past that the strongest possible prohibitions should be placed upon some of men's strongest instincts. This need religion also supplied, by providing that these very natural forces of which men were principally afraid should, in their personified form, as the gods, or as God, forbid the ' anti-social ' acts. Thus a sanction far more awful than any that could be provided by a human tribunal was secured for the tabus necessary to the main forms of civilisation, which have hitherto existed. For it was necessary to convince the great majority of men, by means of a partly conscious act of deception on the part of their rulers, that they would in their own persons be certainly, dreadfully, and eternally punished, if they committed acts which tended to make the then existing type of community life impossible."[1]

As society changes, so its needs become different, and religion changes to meet them. Religion does not change because seekers after truth achieve a greater measure of illumination, but because the character of society changes and law, art, religion, morals change with it.

I. COMPARATIVE RELIGION

Animist conceptions and primitive magic arose on the basis of the low economic conditions of primitive society. They appear to be a reflection of the impotence of man before nature, and a reflection of the social control to which all members of the primitive clan in those dangerous and difficult times were forced to submit. The system of taboos in particular is a powerful means of repression whereby the established order of things is maintained unchanged. A very wholesome fear preserves the food supplies from wantonness by sacralising abundance and security and establishing the attitude of reverence towards the beneficent forces without. Religious faith, says Malinowski, " establishes, fixes, and enhances all valuable mental attitudes, such as reverence for tradition, harmony with environment, courage and confidence in the struggle with difficulties and at the prospect of death. This belief, embodied and maintained by cult and ceremonial, has an immense biological value."[2]

As a settled agricultural life developed, the peasantry created a whole staff of spirits to serve as specialists in agriculture and the protection of cattle. The helpless position of the peasant, exploited for centuries, facing nature with a primitive technique, found its reflection in the belief in the existence of various supernatural beings.

[1] John Strachey, *Coming Struggle for Power*, p. 159.
[2] Malinowski, B., in *Science, Religion, and Reality*.

Finally the merging of tribes into a State organisation under the leadership of some conquering tribe is also reflected in a readjustment in the world of spirits. The gods of the conquering tribes become the chief gods. The gods of the subject tribes take the place of secondary gods, or are reduced to the position of demons. Finally, with despotic monarchy we see the full development of monotheism.

The rise of the great religions marks the growing necessity for Divine sanction behind the demands of the government machine and the class inequalities of society. Both medieval Christianity and Hinduism supported a rigidly stratified and hierarchical social system in which each section fulfilled its allotted function and no other. Feudalism was reflected in the theology of such works as Anselm's *Cur Deus Homo*, in which the relations of God to man are strictly those of a lord to his vassals. The Indian caste system sanctifies and perpetuates the class domination of the Brahmins, while Buddhism, with its rejection of struggle and its teaching that life and all desire are the source of disappointment and suffering, is characteristic of a social order in which the masses have been reduced to hopeless despair. Impotence and submission are encouraged, non-resistance is preached, and religion thus becomes the most powerful buttress of the privileged.

Islam also preaches resignation to the Divine will. Dr. Leitner, defending it, is quite frank about its social function.

" There would be no Socialists in Europe were Western Society constituted on the basis of Muhammadanism ; for in it a man is not taught to be dissatisfied, as is the great effort, aim, and result of our civilisation."[1]

Christianity itself was, as Engels says, " basically the religion of the disintegrating slave economy."

" The history of early Christianity has many characteristic points of contact with the present labour movement. Like the latter, Christianity was at first a movement of the

[1] Dr. G. W. Leitner, *Muhammadanism*. Islam=surrender, resignation (Arabic).

oppressed ; it began as a religion of the slaves and the freed, the poor and outlawed, of the peoples defeated and crushed by the force of Rome. Both Christianity and Proletarian Socialism preach the coming deliverance from slavery and poverty. . . . Both teachings suffered repressions and persecutions, their followers were driven out, were brought under exceptional laws, the one as the enemies of mankind, the others as the enemies of the State, of religion, the family and the social order. Nevertheless in spite of all these persecutions and even as a result of them both forged ahead victoriously."[1]

Engels adds that Christianity transferred this deliverance to Heaven, but this is incorrect. Kautsky, quite correctly, sees that Christianity was not always a purely reactionary force. " The liberation from poverty which Christianity declared was at first thought of quite realistically. It was to take place in the world and not in Heaven." According to Kautsky, Christianity passed through a dialectical process.

" Christianity became victorious only after it had been transformed into its opposite ; not the proletariat was victorious in Christianity but the exploiters who monopolised the clergy. Christianity became victorious not as a destructive force, but as a conserving power, as a new reinforcement of exploitation and oppression."[2]

The urgency of the immediate task of combating religious prejudices in Russia is probably responsible for a considerable deviation from the strictly Marxian line to be noticed first in Lenin, and to an even greater extent in Lukachevsky and Yaroslavsky.

In his letters to Gorki, Lenin declared that " the idea of God *always* dulled the social emotions ; replacing the vital by the deadening ; it has *always* been an idea of slavery— the worst inescapable slavery. Never has the idea of God

[1] Engels, *History of Primitive Christianity.*
[2] Kautsky, *Foundations of Christianity.* Lukachevsky rejects Kautsky's position, and holds that Christianity was always reactionary.

bound the individual to society."[1] But in the same letter
Lenin flatly contradicts himself, saying, " There was a time
in history when, in spite of the origin, and this the real
meaning of the idea of God, the democratic and proletarian
struggle took the form of a struggle of one religious idea
against another." This is the correct Marxian position.
Marx never denied that class struggles have often been
fought as religious wars, " when the ruling class within a
country identifies itself with one form of religion so that
an attack upon its religion is an attack upon the whole
complex of social institutions of which its religious practices
are a part."[2] The struggle of bourgeois democracy with
feudalism, which called forth the critique of feudal religion,
was conducted in the form of a religious struggle.

" There have been phases in history," admits Lukachevsky, " when the proletariat fought its class struggle for
emancipation under the banner of religion."

At the period of the Reformation, Calvin " put the bourgeois character of the reformation in the forefront, repub-
licanised and democratised the Church . . . the Calvinist
reformation served as a banner for the republicans in
Geneva, in Holland and in Scotland, freed Holland from
Spain, and from the German Empire and provided the
ideological costume for the second act of the bourgeois
revolution which took place in England. Here Calvinism
justified itself as the true religious disguise of the interests
of the bourgeoisie of that time."[3]

Cromwell's Ironsides, charging the Cavaliers, roaring
imprecatory Psalms, do not seem to be deadened, devita-
lised, and paralysed by their religion !

Ruling classes are often extremely religious and maintain
for themselves elaborate ceremonial and sacramental cults
which establish their sense of superiority and maintain their
social confidence. This is not opium for the poor, but a
stimulant for the rich.

---

[1] Lenin, *Religion* (italics are Lenin's).
[2] Hook, *Towards the Understanding of Karl Marx.*
[3] Engels, *Ludwig Feuerbach.*

While Mohammedanism has certainly preached acquiescence to the " unfortunate," it has also been a fighting religion, and the faith of the dominant military caste after conquest.

II. RELIGION AND SCIENCE

But with the growth of scientific understanding religion is pressed back into those areas which are still beyond the reach of scientific analysis. Physics, chemistry, and medicine no longer fall within the province of the supernatural, but, on the other hand, economic and social events still seem to be incalculable and uncontrollable, with the result that man becomes the sport of forces which destroy his hopes and happiness. Man and society seem to be under the dominance of destiny. Blind animal and racial passions force men into conflict ; nothing can be done about it.

The less men understand of economic crisis and its consequences the more will they be compelled to cling to a religious explanation of such things, and to seek some mystical consolation for the personal tragedies in which they are involved. Just in so far as it is not to the interests of certain classes to discover the scientific causes of social confusion and industrial decay will they prefer and maintain a religious explanation. Man cannot dispense with religious belief and practices until

" the relations between human beings in their practical everyday life have assumed the aspect of perfectly intelligible and reasonable relations as between man and man and as between man and nature. The life process of society, this meaning the material process of production, will not lose its veil of mystery until it becomes a process carried in by a free association of producers, under their conscious and purposive control."[1]

As the new social relations replace the old social forms the

[1] Marx, *Capital*, Vol. I., p. 54 (Everyman).

" religious " reflection of the world will disappear. Lenin concludes that so long as

" society is composed in such a manner that an insignificant minority has wealth and power at its disposal, whereas the masses continually suffer want and bear the burdens, then it is quite natural that the exploiters should sympathise with a religion, which teaches men to suffer human hell without grumbling for the sake of a possibly heavenly paradise."[1]

" To protect its rule, every exploiting class needs two social functions : the function of the public executioner and the function of the priest. The executioner must suppress the protest and the revolt of the oppressed, the priest must picture to them the perspectives . . . making the hardships of the victims palatable while maintaining the class rule and in so doing reconcile them to this rule, hold them back from revolutionary enthusiasm, and destroy their revolutionary authority."[2]

It is, however, probably more accurate to say that this is increasingly the function of religion in the present age, but that it also ministers in exactly the opposite way to the spiritual needs of the governing class and their mercenaries. However, the place religion once held it holds no longer, since it cannot serve any progressive class, as once it did, as the ideological garb of its aspirations. Therefore its whole character changes as it becomes " more and more the exclusive possession of the ruling classes, applied as a mere means of government to keep the lower classes within limits."[3]

III. THE METAPHYSICAL BASIS OF COMMUNISM

There is no metaphysical basis of Communism. So, at least, many Communists would own. But what is meant is

[1] Lenin, *Politics, Agitation, and the Class Point of View.*
[2] Lenin, *The Crash of the Second International.*
[3] Engels, *Ludwig Feuerbach.*

only that they are metaphysical " realists " and reject a transcendental spiritual reality lying behind the world as known to experience. But this is metaphysics.

The denial of the existence of a supernatural world carries with it the denial of the creation of the world in time. Matter is eternal, and its development from level to level is not due to a series of creative acts or to a " creative principle " at work within or beneath matter, but is due to the capacity of matter itself to change. Not only matter, but also movement, is eternal. Movement, which seems a simple thing at first sight, can neither be explained in terms of anything else nor denied. It is the principle from which all change is derived. Beginning with simple movement we pass to those patternings which give new chemical combinations, then to the new behaviour of these elements which we call metabolism, and finally to the highest form of movement known as thought. Let it at once be said that this is not to reduce metabolism and thought to a form of mechanical movement, but exactly the opposite ; it is to show that metabolic and mental movement are totally new forms of movement, that when matter moves in these ways its effects are unique. Thought is what it is, and not anything less. It is spiritual, it is self-consciousness, it is creative, but it is not the function of spiritual substance apart from matter, but a function of matter itself at a particular level.

Therefore matter is basic, and thought is a property of highly organised matter. It is emphatically denied that spirit precedes nature, or is the cause of change in matter, or adds new qualities or some new substance (soul, life energy) to matter. To attribute *separate* existence to anything in the nature of thought, mind, life, or even energy, is " idealism," and is closely akin to religion with its belief in a supernatural world. Therefore any kind of idealism, of dualism or parallelism, of spiritual monism or transcendentalism opens the door to religion—that is, to a superstitious belief in supernatural beings or forces.

Communist philosophy is not only materialistic and atheist, it also emphatically denies our inability to know the actual world. Every form of agnosticism or " fictionalism," by separating objective existence from the apprehending subject, attaches an independent existence to thought, and thus lapses into idealism. This is a particularly important epistemological position, because it resists the scepticism of Kantians and neo-Kantians, pragmatists, fictionalists, and symbolists, who are extremely popular to-day. It strongly opposes, for instance, the agnosticism of scientific philosophers like Eddington, since to affirm that the truth of what thought reveals can only be accepted by an act of faith is to open the door to any kind of superstition in the sphere of religion. " To destroy palpable superstition should be an easy matter if dualist confusion were not on the look-out for the gaps of science in order to lay its eggs there. Such gaps are to be found especially in the field of epistemology."[1] Agnosticism of various kinds, and also, it should be noted, any form of physiological materialism which regards the end effects of nerve action as purely mental processes, considers mind states as a succession of subjective experiences from which at best it is only possible to infer an objective cause. This is Berkeleyism, and leads inescapably to solipsism. Lenin is on perfectly sound ground in his rejection of subjective idealism, and rightly estimates the confusion which the prevalence of idealistic blunders of this sort are bound to spread. Do we perceive sense data or concrete things ? Are we conscious of mental processes or external objects ? Lenin is not taking a philistine or uninstructed view when he asserts that to be *conscious of* anything is to be aware of the thing outside us, and not of our own perceptions.[2]

Turning to the question of causality, the Communist affirms that scientific laws are not limited to those now known, since the potentialities of matter are infinite. New

[1] Lenin, *Materialism and Critico-Empiricism*, p. 295.
[2] Many philosophers have pointed out the egocentric fallacy on which solipsism is based. Because you cannot be conscious of the objective world without thinking, it does not follow that all you are conscious of is your thinking. *See* Perry, *Present Philosophical Tendencies* ; Hocking, *Types of Philosophy* ; Evans, *New Realism and Old Reality*.

combinations and patterns produce new effects. What these effects will be cannot be predicted, and therefore are really new. The emergence of novelty is characteristic of matter, and means that new laws are always being discovered. This conception of causality avoids a merely mechanistic theory, but at the same time completely rules out supernatural or mystical explanations.

Communist philosophy is severely critical of mechanistic materialism, not only because it is unscientific and abstract, but because, like idealism, it opens the door to superstition —a somewhat surprising statement. But the interaction of elements with known properties to give predictable effects, deducible resultants, cannot possibly explain development and change. Nature is remarkable for presenting us with the paradox of continuity *and* change, unity *and* difference. There is unbroken continuity between the egg and the chick, without the intrusion of any new element from without ; and yet a chick is not an egg, it is absolutely and entirely different. It cannot, therefore, be the mechanical resultant of the factors actually existent in the egg. How, then, does the mechanist explain the change ? He cannot do so without postulating an outside force. Therefore the obscurantist can find in the very arguments of the mechanists a most cogent case for postulating God, or some supernatural agent, as the cause of the emergence of novelty. Communist philosophy, with its doctrines of self-movement and re-patterning, sees the possibility of a jump to new entities, with new behaviour as the result of a new ordering of all the factors in the situation. Hence the explanation of real diversity and a real succession of levels in the universe as opposed to the levelling of everything down to changeless unity with all differences reduced to mere " appearance."

It is sometimes supposed that the materialist conception of history means that religions and philosophies are mere epiphenomena—almost meaningless reflections of determining social and economic causes. A consideration of the attitude of Communists to philosophical deviations will clear this point up.

Mechanistic materialism is a philosophical error. It is untrue because it does not correspond to the facts ; it can be refuted by scientific evidence and reason. Nevertheless it is not unrelated to politics. A theory which denies sharp breaks and insists on continuity without real changes from level to level will tend to be popular among social reactionaries. It will spread an atmosphere congenial to conservatism. If it is widely developed and popularised, it will, in its turn, create a mentality disposed to resist evolutionary jumps in social development. To take a perfectly concrete example, a mechanistic ideology goes with the political tendency to depreciate the ending of *kulak* farming in Russia and its replacement by collectives—an altogether new social form.

These mechanistic tendencies, and several others, have appeared in Russian Communist philosophy, and, though they have been severely criticised and have certainly lost ground to correct dialectical materialism, the existence of these philosophical controversies should dispose of the idea that differences and discussion are impossible in Soviet thought.

IV. BOURGEOIS RATIONALISM

Communist atheism must not be confused with the rationalist and atheist movements of Liberalism. From Voltaire to Bradlaugh there persisted a radical criticism of the supernaturalism which buttressed feudal privilege which was of assistance to the rising capitalist class. It was of limited influence because too much atheism might have weakened the authority of the capitalists over the masses, and because a chilly rationalism affords these no comfort in their sufferings. For the same reason it tended to substitute abstractions, such as Nature and Natural Law, for God, since these could also form the basis of an economic system which was inescapable and irresistible.

The fallacy of bourgeois rationalism is to suppose that

superstition is merely an intellectual error or a " pious
fraud," the cure for which is enlightenment and the
suppression of the priesthood. But, as Lenin has explained,
the basis of religion is social ; it arises from the apparent
helplessness of the masses before the blind economic forces
of the system, blind because its action cannot be foreseen,
forces which " at every step in life threaten the worker and
the small business man with ' sudden,' ' unexpected,'
' accidental ' destruction and ruin, bringing in their train
beggary, pauperism, prostitution, and deaths from starvation—this is THE *tap-root* of modern religion which, first of
all, and above all, the materialist must keep in mind, if
he does not wish to remain stuck for ever in the infant school
of materialism."[1]

Enlightenment is powerless so long as social injustice and
irrationalism continues. Repression can never destroy religion so long as its social roots remain. Therefore religious
belief will be destroyed, not primarily by anti-religious
propaganda, but by the conscious and deliberate planning
of social and economic activities.

V. RELIGION IN RUSSIA

We see now why anti-religious propaganda is regarded
as of the utmost importance in the Soviet Union. Hand in
hand with the reconstruction of the economy must go the
remoulding of the consciousness of the masses.

The success of the atheist movement is due, not to the
effectiveness of propaganda or the reactionary record of
the Church, still less to repressive measures on the part of
the Government, but primarily to the tremendous strides
in mastering the environment made since the revolution.

A summary of the steps taken by the authorities will make
this clear.

(1) The Church is formally separated from the State, which
withdraws its financial support, and grants to every person

[1] Lenin, *Religion.*

the right to choose any religion he pleases or to profess no religion at all.

(2) Registration of births, deaths, and marriages is performed exclusively by the civil authorities, although separate religious rites are also permissible.

(3) Religious instruction by the clergy in the elementary schools ceases. The educational system is secularised.

(4) Churches become the property of the community. Where they are of archæological or æsthetic interest, they are carefully preserved. Where a congregation desires to occupy and maintain a building, it is allowed to do so. Where is is no longer possible to provide for its upkeep, and the community no longer desires to use it for religious purposes, it may be given over to secular use. Collections on behalf of Churches still continue, and the buildings and their officiating priests are thus maintained.

In the early days of the revolution processions and demonstrations were arranged to propagate anti-religious views and expose superstition. This has now ceased, and the official programme instructs Communists " carefully to avoid giving offence to the religious sentiments of believers, which only leads to the strengthening of religious fanaticism." There was never any persecution of religion as such, but counter-revolutionary activities on the part of the Church were dealt with severely.

Effective propaganda is conducted through exhibitions or anti-religious museums, which demonstrate scientific explanations of natural events, expose the faked incorruption of the bodies of so-called saints, and, by photographs, statistics, and documentary evidence, show the support given by the Church to despotism in its ugliest forms, to pogroms and to war.

In addition the Communists expose the class basis of religion—that is, " they lay bare the class motives of those who are interested in upholding and spreading religious beliefs," while at the same time propagating science and general education—through books, newspapers, lectures, moving pictures, and posters—with the object of overcoming religious prejudices and beliefs.

Propaganda is directed not only against the Church, but also against Nonconformist sects and groups of fanatics. The Baptists, under the new Communist decrees, were for the first time set free to expand, and they did so to an extraordinary extent. So much so that the authorities became alarmed, and put numerous obstacles in the way of their social work and denominational organisation. The fanatics, some of whom practised self-mutilation, were suppressed in all those cases in which they overstepped the bounds of decency or endangered public safety.

The Church is still an obstacle to Socialist advance in the rural areas. It persuades the peasants that the reconstruction of society is beyond human efforts, and that all the experiments of the Soviet power will be destroyed by God. " Anti-religious propaganda in the village must assume the character of exclusively materialistic explanations of the phenomena of nature and of social life, with which the peasants come in contact. The correct explanation of the origin of hail, rain, drought, the appearance of insect plagues, the properties of various soils and the action of fertilisers, is the best form of anti-religious propaganda."[1]

" The school and the village reading-room, under the guidance of the party organisation, must become the centre of such propaganda. Special care must be taken not to offend the religious sentiments of the believers, which can be overcome only by years and decades of systematic educational work."[2]

Thus the Communists regard " the struggle against religion as a delicate task, requiring gradual, patient explanation, teaching, enlightenment—the exposure of the lies and deceptions underlying religion, the elucidation of its origin, significance, and harmfulness without the use of

[1] Yaroslavsky, *Religion in the U.S.S.R.*
[2] Resolution of XIII in the Congress of the Party.

coercion against the believing population. It means laying bare the social basis of religion and taking an active part in the task confronting the Party, and the working class, of annihilating the bases of religion and creating a new, a Communist society where there will be no room for religion."[1]

Dying classes, such as the *kulaks* and the remains of the city bourgeoisie, are still clinging to religion as a lifebelt in the struggle with Socialism. The character and function of religion in Russia has thus changed. It is not only a reactionary force, but reactionary in a new and advancing society in which it is a part of the defeated and disintegrating capitalist and feudal order that has been superseded. As such, it attracts only the dregs of the population, and its whole atmosphere becomes increasingly one of corruption and neurosis.

As far as ordinary people are concerned, religion is thus a *private* affair in that the State in no way interferes with their beliefs. But this does not mean that the State is unconcerned with the prevalence of superstition. It means that it does not combat it by administrative measures. It means that it seeks to eradicate it by every possible means, except those which interfere with the liberty of conscience and would therefore drive its roots still deeper in. Nor is it permissible for a member of the Communist Party to accept religion. " A person cannot act correctly, cannot act in an organised manner as a Communist, if his brain is poisoned by religion. In order to overcome the tremendous difficulties which confront us ; in order to remould the world as the working class and the peasantry want it to be ; in order to subjugate all the forces of nature and compel them to work for the welfare of mankind ; in order to eradicate war between nations, to exterminate poverty from the face of the earth —it is necessary that every person, that every peasant and worker, sees things as they are, without the intervention of gods, and other spirits. Religion acts as a bandage over the eyes of man, preventing him from seeing the world as it

[1] Yaroslavsky, *Religion in the U.S.S.R.*

is. . . . It is not possible to be a Communist and at the same time to believe in devils or gods."[1]

VI. IS COMMUNISM A RELIGION?

It is sometimes declared that Communism itself is a religion on the grounds that it lifts the individual up into a cause and a purpose greater than himself ; that it believes in " a power not ourselves that makes for righteousness " ; that it uplifts and transforms its followers with an energising and purifying enthusiasm ; that its ideal is the classless society, the co-operative commonwealth and the brotherhood of man ; and, finally, that members of the Communist Party " scorn delights and live laborious days," devoting themselves in a spirit of renunciation to the cause in which they believe.

This is all true, but it is not religion. Religion involves belief in and dependence upon a supernatural order. Communism does not even base its hopes on an immanent power unfolding towards an inevitable goal, neither is its faith in some Vital Urge which carries history along on its crest. It believes rigidly that there is nothing but the universe in time and space ; that spiritual values are human values ; that there is no power but the power exercised by men who understand the laws of nature and of the development of society.

It is sometimes foolishly asserted that the body of Lenin has become a kind of mummified saint or god. This is grotesquely untrue, because for even the humblest Russian worker or child it is the ideas, the historical understanding of Lenin, that matter. Leninism is a working guide to daily action ; not even a body of doctrines, but rather a map of the very ground over which men are walking. No Russian is ever asked to venerate Lenin for himself alone, the whole force of Communism is directed to making the millions clearly self-conscious of their historical rôle. That and that alone is Leninism.

[1] Yaroslavsky, *Religion in the U.S.S.R.*, p. 29.

In the early days of the " Bolshevik " movement a number of leading Marxists, including Lunacharsky and Maxim Gorky, endeavoured to construct a Communist religion on the basis of a philosophical surrender to a form of neo-Kantianism which reduced reality to sensations, and truth to useful fictions.[1]

This was the theory of " god building " according to which it was incumbent on mankind to *build* itself a god according to its ideals. Lenin violently opposed this movement both in his important philosophical work, *Materialism and Empirio-Criticism*, and in his two letters to Gorky.[2] Lunacharsky was prepared to deify the highest potentialities of man, and to accept the class struggle not as explained and justified by social science, but as an act of faith. One can only *believe* in Socialism. It is surrender to an emotion. Lenin held that this would be to lose all objectivity, to substitute self-contemplation for deeds, to lapse into a " dull frail philistinism." " Rotten philistinism is disgusting always, but ' democratic philistinism,' engaged in its ideological corpse worship, is especially disgusting." Lenin looked upon religion as something obscene, as the vilest form of subjection of the human spirit. The gods are the symbol of man's subjection to man. " Religion is a kind of spiritual intoxicant, in which the slaves of capital drown their humanity and blunt their desire for a decent human existence."

There was a time when helpless humanity, impotent in its struggle on earth, sought comfort and reward in Heaven, or trusted in supernatural beings to do what it was powerless to do. But as the social and political relationships of men lose their obscurity and the relations between man and nature become intelligible, religion becomes unnecessary and obstructive. Marx says : " The demand that one reject illusions about one's situation, is a demand that one reject a situation which has need of illusions." In the decline of capitalism man has " more and not less need of that

---

[1] Cf. Vaihinger, *The Philosophy of " As If."*
[2] To be found in *Lenin on Religion*.

greatest, dearest, and most comfortable of all illusions : the illusion of religion."[1] But, as Socialism advances, the proletariat comes to know that neither God, nor Tsar, nor hero will deliver him, that he must do it with his own strength. Neither religion nor imaginary gods will help him in the class struggle.

VII. RELIGION IN THE WEST

The victory of Socialism in the East endangers the whole capitalist order in the West. The well-known financier Gibson Jarvie has declared that " Russia is going to be a very great danger to capitalist countries because of the tremendously high standard of living which is being established there for the workers. In the face of this," he argues, " our workers will not tolerate the steady lowering of their own standard."

Among the forces which are mobilised to defend capitalism against this impending working-class assault, the Church must be reckoned, and no small part of its defence of capitalism consists in a bitter attack of the Soviet Union. This takes three forms.

Firstly, the crusade against the alleged persecution of religion in Russia, in which dubious atrocities and a complete misrepresentation of the facts are utilised to awaken all the latent forces of religious fanaticism.

Secondly, the direct incitement of the invasion of Russia.

Thirdly, resistance to the menace of materialistic Communism in Western Europe.

This movement is in part blatant and explicit, in part subtle and disguised. Roman Catholicism is the head and front of the open " Crusade " against Russia and Communism. The Pope and his supporters give the full force of their authority to the usual campaign of slanders against the U.S.S.R., although it is difficult to believe that they are convinced of their truth. It is to be noted that the

[1] Strachey, *The Coming Struggle for Power*, p. 171.

Church is silent as to Fascist atrocities, and as to the never-ceasing atrocities of evil social conditions, unemployment, the colonial exploitation of Africans, Indians, and Chinese, and of the ruthless massacres of war ; nor can they possibly be concealing from themselves the consequences in death, torture, and bloody suppression which would inevitably accompany a successful intervention or counter-revolutionary movement in Soviet Russia.

On the basis of the hatred and fear which the Church has in this way fostered, there is a more direct incitement to military measures. The Pope calls upon " all the nations to unite their forces in a single front against the battalions of evil, for the peril threatens all and aims at overthrowing the very foundations of the social order and of all authority. In this combat all legitimate human means must be used."[1] The encyclical is followed by a leading article in the Pope's official paper suggesting that it is absurd to discuss disarmament before the Soviet Union is destroyed. In England the Archbishop of Canterbury has allied himself with various movements, mainly consisting of White Russians and their allies, who fill the Press with accounts of a famine in the Ukraine, for which there is no fraction of evidence, and prepare the way quite deliberately for a German-Polish campaign to " liberate " the Ukraine, where, it is suggested, a suffering population yearns for the advent of the invading armies of the West. Deep concern is expressed for " liberty," civil and religious. We may be sure that the Church would see to it that the highest motives were appealed to in the event of a war against the Soviet Union.

At the same time the permeation of Western society by Communism is not only deplored, but steps for its forcible eradication are urged in explicit terms. While the workers are urged " never to resort to violence in defending their own cause, nor to engage in riot or disorder ; and to have nothing to do with men of evil principles, who work upon the people with artful promises of great results, and excite foolish hopes," as far as the owning class is concerned. " The

[1] Papal encyclical, *Caritate Christi Compulsi*.

chief thing is the duty of safeguarding private property by legal enactment and protection. Most of all it is essential . . . to keep the people within the line of duty. . . . The Authority of the State should intervene to put restraint upon such firebrands, to save the working classes from being led astray by their manœuvres, and to protect lawful owners from spoliation."[1]

VIII. CATHOLICISM, COMMUNISM, AND THE MASSES

Communism accuses the Church of giving authoritative support to capitalism and using all its religious influence to weaken the working-class movement and encourage Fascism. That these charges are not exaggerated is clear from the many official statements of the Roman Church on social questions. Communism points out that every such statement naturally expresses pity for the poor, without which it would, of course, meet with no acceptance, and levels certain mild criticisms at individualism and the excesses of capitalism. This is intended to give the impression that Catholicism is impartially severe with the sins of both parties in the struggle. It is perfectly clear, however, that the Church is really saying to its friends, " You must excuse me shouting at you and pretending to be extremely angry with you ; you understand, of course, that I intend to do nothing about it ; but, if you will put up with it, it will enable me to carry off a much more effective attack on Socialism with a convincing air of impartiality."

Hence the rich receive admonitions, but the principle of private monopoly of the means of life is not attacked but defended. Employers are urged to give a living wage, but the wage system is declared to be fundamentally just. The Communist replies that, under the conditions of a fully developed capitalism, private monopoly makes the steady worsening of wages and conditions inevitable if business is

[1] Encyclical, *Rerum Novarum.*

to pay at all, in which case even if the capitalist desired to behave with the benevolence enjoined by the Pope he would be unable to do so.

On the other hand the principles of Socialism are both misrepresented and categorically condemned. All the fundamentals of a class society are endorsed and given Divine sanction, while anathemas are hurled against all attempts to subvert the existing order.

The only claim to the fruits of labour is the ownership of the means of production, not the exercise of Labour.[1] .

The wage contract is not essentially unjust.[2]

While the employer should aim at a living wage, it is unjust to demand wages so high that an employer cannot pay them without ruin.[3]

It is fundamentally false and unchristian principle to affirm that community life is intended for the advantages which it brings to mankind.[4]

Socialism " cannot be brought into harmony with the dogmas of the Catholic Church." "No one can be at the same time a sincere Catholic and a true Socialist."[5]

Finally, class distinctions are to be preserved, each is to labour, at his own post and in his own sphere, for the common good.[6]

" The pains and hardships of life will have no end or cessation on earth. . . . To suffer and to endure, therefore, is the lot of humanity . . . no strength and no artifice will ever succeed in banishing from human life the ills and troubles which beset it."[7]

" There are two means with which to cope with the increasing misery of the times, prayer and fasting. Let the rich carry out the fasting by almsgiving. And let the poor, and all those who at this time are facing the hard trial of want of work and security of food—let them in a like spirit of penance suffer with greater resignation the privations imposed upon them by these hard times

[1] Encyclical, *Quadragesimo Anno*, p. 24.   [2] Ibid., p. 34.
[3] Ibid., p. 33.   [4] Ibid., p. 53.   [5] Ibid., pp. 53, 54.
[6] Encyclical, *Rerum Novarum*.   [7] Ibid.

and the state of the society which Divine Providence, in an inscrutable but ever-loving plan, has assigned to them."[1]

This last extract bears out the words of Pope Benedict XV when he declared that force is not the only way to repress popular risings; the Church has another way, equally effective—it knows, he says, how to " repress the souls of men."[2]

The Church has given a considerable measure of support to Fascism in Germany and Italy, and has been careful not to pass any serious criticism on its violation of the principles of justice and humanity. It has intervened only where its own vested interests were threatened. In his latest pronouncements the Pope warmly commends Fascist corporations and the Fascist prohibition of strikes, and advances the usual arguments in favour of peace and unity within the class State and the wickedness of class war—a palpable sophistry where peace only means submission to a tyranny which cannot be relaxed so long as the wheels of capitalist industry are to continue to revolve. Conformity to the necessities of the business world means a steady worsening of conditions for the workers. Under such conditions it is impossible to satisfy at the same time even the barest demands of the workers and the requirements of the owners. It is not a case of a just settlement being possible if both sides will be reasonable. The utmost that even a generous capitalism could do would still necessitate the infliction of intolerable injustice on the workers. Under such conditions " peace in industry " can only mean the forcible suppression of working-class resistance to such injustice. Yet it is precisely peace of this sort of which the Church is the increasing advocate. The unity for which the Church pleads, and which Fascism achieves, is simply the dictatorship of the minority in their own interests. Any attempt to eliminate injustice is a disturbance of peace which is resented by these

[1] *Caritate Christi Compulsi.*
[2] *The Pope and the People* (Catholic Truth Society), p. 206.

who, profiting by that injustice, naturally desire the un-interrupted continuance of the *status quo*.

We have in the world-wide movement known as " Catholic Action " an anti-Socialist movement with great influence among the masses. Its purpose is to give political effect to the principles set forth in the encyclicals. In every conflict between Labour and the State it will call upon all good Catholics " to uphold and assist the Government, which is the lawfully constituted authority of the country and represents therefore, in its own appointed sphere, the authority of God Himself."[1]

It is already taking active steps to mobilise Catholic workers in defence of capitalism. It will undoubtedly prove an invaluable ally of Fascism and reaction as the struggle with the workers gains in intensity and moves towards its climax.

IX. REFORMISM IN THE CHURCH

Communism is not only opposed to the intransigent Christian Fascism of the Roman Church, but to the pseudo-Socialism of progressive Churchmen, and to the widespread movement to capture the more earnest and troubled con-sciences of our time for a spiritual attitude to life and social problems.

The Christian Sociologists have endeavoured to work out a framework for a Christian order of society which will supersede the materialism of a purely secular Socialism. They believe in the sanctity of private property, and ad-vocate a wider distribution of ownership. They resist collectivisation " not so much for the sake of defending the possessions of the rich, as in order to preserve for the disinherited that potential right of property which we must wish to see, as soon as may be, actualised for them."[2] They therefore advocate a transition from the wage system to a dividend system by encouraging the poor to invest their savings in future issues of capital in the industries in which

[1] Cardinal Bourne.   [2] Egerton Swann, *Is there a Catholic Sociology ?*

they are engaged. The largest section of this movement has landed in the Douglas Social Credit camp, which promises social distribution of the product of industry while retaining the full claims of private ownership to surplus value !

This pleasant *hope* of a wider distribution of property and incomes is merely a sop to the conscience. In actuality every known force in the world is operating in the opposite direction, and the Catholic Sociologist does not attempt to grapple with those forces. No idea can be anything more than a delusive dream that is not an analysis of the concrete situation with a view to controlling it.

There may be all the difference in the world between what a man intends to do, and thinks he is doing, and what he actually is doing. A movement is judged by its objective results. The effect of Christian Sociology is, firstly, to buttress the idea of private property, and thus to sanctify all existing property rights however anti-social their consequences ; secondly, to make it appear that Socialism is unnecessary, and to divert progressive energy and thought into the futile channels of impossible alternatives. To put it brutally, these alternatives were never meant to work ; their only purpose is to hold men back from Socialism. Whatever the intention, that is the objective result.

The result is a stream of quack remedies and palliatives to distract attention and absorb unrest. As a religious journal recently put it, if we cannot get our people into isolation camps from possible Communist infection, " *inoculation is the only remedy left.*"[1] Give the Christian a mild but harmless form of the disease, and he will never catch it seriously.

The social conscience which Christians are developing in these days is only a substitute for a social programme or a predisposition to fall for New Deals which turn out to be only a disguised form of "crisis-capitalism." More dangerous are the many spiritual revivals of our time, often expressing deep concern for the evils of capitalism, and speaking,

[1] *The Student Movement.*

somewhat vaguely, of a transformed and Christianised society. Nicholas Berdyaev is an influential leader of this school because of his frank acceptance of most of the Socialist criticism of capitalist civilisation. The Oxford Group Movement also deplores social evils, but tells us that

*Just the art of being kind
Is all this sad world needs.*

Widely respected theologians like Principal Micklem of Mansfield College, despairing of man-made schemes, endeavour to turn a discouraged and bewildered Church away from practical reforms. " Much has been lost," he says, " because our religious teachers confine their ideas to the present life alone. Our business in this world is not to establish a new order, or to aid in the progress of civilisation, but to prepare ourselves for the higher experiences which will be ours when this life's schooling is ended."[1]

Karl Barth persuades his followers to make a virtue of their helplessness and unwillingness to grapple analytically with the problem of evil by waiting for God to save them. The world is under a curse. God is waiting to break in. The new world will not be man's achievement, but God's gift. Berdyaev's solution is similar. The Church is not sufficiently spiritual to save the world. We must give our allegiance to an " ideal " Church and an " ideal " society which will never be realised here. Meanwhile our deepest spiritual experience must be to endure suffering. In the manner characteristic of spiritual decadence, at one and the same time he repudiates the evils of the world and accepts them. The one thing he cannot and will not do is to make the necessary effort to alter them. The attitude of such religious reformers is revealed in the closing words of a book by Seibert on Russia, " Let us fight with a full sense of revolutionary responsibility to bring into being that new commonwealth in which Socialism shall live not as a form, but as a spirit."[2]

---

[1] Sermon preached at King's Weigh House Church, London.
[2] Seibert, *Red Russia*.

Exactly. Those who fight for the spirit without the form are fighting for the shadow and throwing away the substance, are canalising their energies to divert them from the urgent claims of present opportunity and responsibility into futility and effortless dreaming. That is why, in Berdyaev's own words, " Socialism has always been antireligious."[1]

X. THE INCOMPATIBILITY OF MARXISM AND CHRISTIANITY

It would appear that both theoretically, historically, and practically Religion and Communism are sworn foes. Since the breaking-point of modern capitalism is in the Christian West, it is here that *all* the forces of reaction form their united front against the insurgent proletariat. Since Religion provides the ideological background and supernatural sanctions of the reaction, it is Christianity which here in the West is called upon to fulfil this rôle. As such, it is one of the most dangerous allies of capitalism *in extremis*.

In these circumstances Christianity itself undergoes rapid changes corresponding with the decay of institutions, the spiritual rottenness, the swinging into alignment and the hardening of opposing forces, which characterise the decadence of our civilisation and the dawn of the final stages of the class struggle.

" The greater the development of antagonism between the growing forces of production and the extant social order, the more does the ideology of the ruling class become permeated with hypocrisy. In addition the more effectively life unveils the mendacious character of this ideology, the more does the language used by the dominant class become sublime and virtuous."[2]

Of no department of thought is this truer than of religion, hence the new developments, the subtle evasions, the

[1] Berdyaev, *The Russian Revolution.*
[2] Plekhanov, *Fundamental Problems of Marxism*, p. 82.

pseudo-Socialist reform movements, the multiplication of new sects, new cults, new theologies, and the great revival of mysticism, mystification, and superstition in the field of contemporary religion.

Behind the confusion of the religious opposition to Communism certain determining differences may be discerned and should be brought into the foreground. Their plain enunciation should clear the air and put an end to all fruitless efforts to harmonise what are fundamentally incompatible.

I. AGAINST THE MARXIAN ECONOMIC INTERPRETATION OF HISTORY, CHRISTIANITY OPPOSES THE MORAL INTERPRETATION OF HISTORY

According to the religious view, history is moved by the purity and strength of ideals. Preaching is therefore the main instrument of reform. The backwardness of society and the social evils from which we suffer are due to sin, to wilful or careless blindness to the moral structure of reality.

Communism opposes this view. What is meant by the " moral structure of reality ? " It may mean that the world as we know it is " moral " ; or it may mean that there is something unreal about this world, and that the ideal is more real than the concrete. Only the latter view is conceivable. But, if this is the contention, it is difficult to escape the conclusion that however bad the world looks it is " really " quite perfect, so that whatever is is right. It would appear to be more comprehensible to say that reality to-day is not good at all, but bad. Reality has an *immoral* structure. But it is our job to change reality so that to-morrow reality, if not " good," is at any rate " better." Religion will assert that you cannot change reality. Communism asserts that the universe is not a " block universe," absolute and changeless, but that it is an evolving universe which changes itself. Nor will Communism accept an immanent teleology which makes evolution the mere

KR

unfolding or unrolling of what is " really " there already, " involved " or latent. For this is as bad as saying that the universe is " really " perfect, except that it adds the notion of a meaningless and mechanical process of folding up and then unfolding again.

Communism also criticises the view that social evil is due to sin. In America in 1929 things were prosperous, in 1932 there was poverty and social collapse. Were people more wicked in 1932 than in 1928 ? People are not much better at one time in history than at another, or in one country or another, and yet social disaster is present in some cases but not in others. Before modern medicine, plagues and epidemics came and went. Priests regarded them as due to sin, but we know it was nothing of the kind. The causes of plague were external to the moral qualities of men. But even supposing that avarice is *one* of the factors in the economic situation, why is it that avarice in the nineteenth century leads to the doubling of working-class incomes between 1850 and 1900, while it now leads to a catastrophic fall ? It would appear that something else is the *determining* factor of the situation. That this is so becomes clear when we ask what men would do to improve things if they ceased to be avaricious. They would have to change the economic mechanism, or its working, in some way to get different results. *In what way precisely ?* Surely the actual change in structure or method which produces the desired effect is the actual cause of that change, and not merely the will to find and operate that cause.

The capitalist is not a sinner who has brought disaster upon us by deliberately committing an offence. He did not know what he was doing. A Labour leader might easily make a similar mistake.

Communism seeks primarily for the economic causes of industrial collapse, and for the necessary steps which must be taken to escape from the situation. It believes that when men *know*, those whose interest it is to escape will take the necessary steps to do so just as they would bolt for the exits in a theatre fire.

II. AGAINST THE ROMANTIC MARXIST HOPE IN A
SOCIAL APOCALYPTIC, CHRISTIANITY HOLDS THAT
THE SINFULNESS OF MAN MAKES A HUMAN
UTOPIA IMPOSSIBLE

Religion claims to be more realistic than Communism √
and to have a deeper understanding of human nature.
This is in part a misreading of Marxism, but, at bottom,
it represents a fundamental divergence. Communism is not
Utopian, but scientific. It bases its hopes in the necessity
of economic reconstruction, upon the breakdown of all
forms of private ownership and the serious curtailment of
production thus involved, and in the ripeness of industry
for social ownership, and the possibility, by this means, of
releasing the powers of production. Faced by the necessity
of reconstructing his economic institutions or slowly starving,
man, like any other animal, will change in order to survive.

" By acting on the world and changing it, man changes
his own nature." It is not only true that man is to a great
extent made by his environment, it is also true that under
the compulsion of circumstances he refashions that environment, creates new institutions, re-educates himself to
educate the new generation on new lines. Communists
do not believe that man is inherently sinful. The sense of
sin is due to neurosis. It is a mechanism whereby we
absolve ourselves from social responsibility. " Sin " is something within us, and yet not ourselves, which we can condemn, but which will not allow us to behave as we should.
" It is not I but sin within me that makes it impossible for
me to co-operate for the common good." Extending the
argument from the individual to society, it is argued that,
however desirable reform may be, men are too corrupt for
the change. If religion adds that only supernatural grace
can effect their change, the optimism is purely verbal. It is
a camouflaged pessimism, for it is not seriously believed
that this miracle will happen. The objective result is
defeatism, since reform by human effort is believed to be
impossible. It is difficult to avoid the conclusion that there is

some insincerity about a position that so effectually paralyses effort and lends itself to the requirements of reaction.

The Communist does not believe that man is naturally good, or that in a reconstructed society he will be perfect. With Plato he believes that in a " plutocracy " we shall find " plutocratic men," and in a capitalist society capitalistic men. Modern society puts a premium on aggression and social irresponsibility, the comradely man does not survive. In a Socialist society it will be possible to behave socially ; there will be every inducement to do so, and it is believed that the opportunity for the first time offered as a genuine option will not be refused. Man has not a *fixed* nature, either good or bad. His nature depends upon the social organisation of which he is a part.

Communism, therefore, holds that the Christian view of the divided nature of man is a piece of dangerous and reactionary ideology.

III. AGAINST THE MARXIAN VIEW THAT COERCION IS LEGITIMATE, CHRISTIANITY BELIEVES IN PEACEFUL PERSUASION AND THE VICTORY WON BY LOVE ALONE

The Communist replies that Christianity believes nothing of the kind. Christianity for all its lip service to the Sermon on the Mount has upheld bloody wars and ruthless repression. The existence of pacifists in its midst is a convenience, since it suggests that all Christians should, and might, become pacifists, and that Christianity is to be judged by the " ideal " attained by the more saintly of its exponents. In the same way " good " capitalists act as a screen for the essential evils of capitalism, suggesting that all capitalists could behave benevolently. Both kinds of saint are parasitic on a system which is quite opposite in spirit to themselves. We can only be pacifists so long as most people are not. A handful of people can be cranks only so long as most people do the normal work of the world.

The plain historical fact is that Christians use force. " A

thing is what it does," not what it says it is. There is neither logic nor sense in saying Christianity is " really " pacifist, though for fifteen hundred years it has officially and enthusiastically supported and enjoined mass murder.

Communism also believes in violence. The only difference is that it reserves this violence exclusively for the suppression of the criminal classes when these endanger society, whereas the capitalist State uses it in predatory conflicts with neighbours for economic ends, and to suppress the legitimate grievances of the oppressed.

Communism will defend the achievements of Socialism against any minority attempt to set the will of the majority at naught and subject the masses once again to privilege. The bloodshed involved in this suppression of criminality is infinitely less than that involved in capitalist war, in intervention, and in the massacre of the revolting masses by the governing class.

Communism does not make a fetish of force. It uses it only in the last resort when the destruction of a hostile minority threatens to prevent the liberation of society and imperils the lives and happiness of millions. Such obstruction is always violent, and it must be met by violence just as a lunatic at large with a gun would have to be disarmed and pinioned, or, in the last resort, shot.

The near approach of the moment when the proletariat must assume power is naturally marked by a great outburst of pacifist preaching. For one person who timidly opposes war twenty will be found to preach non-resistance to the workers. Capitalism needs Christianity at this juncture as never before. A great religious revival is probably at hand.

IV. AGAINST THE MARXIST VIEW THAT SOCIAL CHANGE IS ECONOMICALLY AND HISTORICALLY DETERMINED, CHRISTIANITY BELIEVES THAT INDIVIDUALS ARE THE CREATIVE PRINCIPLE IN HISTORY

Communists, however, do not believe that history is made without leadership. Man makes his own history, but he

cannot make it as he will and without any relation to conditions. These conditions set out the chess-board and confront man with the problem, but man solves the problem.
Conditions present man with opportunity and possibilities,
even with necessities, but man must decide and respond.
It is a mistake to suppose that even necessity destroys freedom. It is the condition of freedom. To sail across the
Atlantic with the prevailing " trade winds " the sails *must*
be set in a particular way—only then are you free to make
your voyage. The correct understanding of the economic
and social situation makes it possible for men to take steps
which will lift civilisation on to a new level.

Blind social forces and mass movements of themselves do
nothing. Intelligent leadership is essential. Even the man of
exceptional genius may be necessary.

" A man specially endowed by nature, or entering the
political scene at a moment when the constellation of
social forces is rapidly shifting (e.g. Lenin's return to
Russia), will exercise an influence not uniquely deducible
from the normal operation of these social forces without
him."[1]

Stalin puts the matter clearly, and, since he is himself
a great man, he ought to know.

" It is men who make history. But, of course, men do not
make history according to their imagination, as pictured
by their minds. Every new generation encounters certain
conditions which existed in completed form already at
the moment this generation was born. And great men
are only of value in so far as they know how rightly to
grasp these conditions, to understand how they are to
be changed. If they do not understand these conditions,
and seek to change them according to their own imagination, then these people find themselves in the position of
Don Quixote. Therefore one must not oppose men to
conditions. It is men who make history, but only in so

1 Sidney Hook, *Is Marxism Compatible with Christianity ?*

far as they rightly understand the conditions which existed already in a complete form, and only in so far as they understand how these conditions are to be altered."[1]

The Christian who looks to Christ, as some heroic or saintly paragon, to set the world to right by the sheer force of His personality, purity of His character, and clarity of His vision of eternal truth, is looking for a spell-binder, not a revolutionary leader, and while he is looking and waiting, meanwhile submitting to domination, it is certain that he will neglect to understand the indispensable conditions of progress and miss the flood-tide of the proletarian movement. Such a belief, therefore, is a distraction, a will-o'-the-wisp, a delusion to keep men from effectiveness. In moments of social crisis it is definitely reactionary and counter-revolutionary, a weapon in the hands of the anti-social forces.

XI. CONCLUSION

The future will see a consolidation of all religious forces against Communism. A " United Front " of religion and reaction. The long prayed-for " Reunion of Christendom " will take place in the last ditch with the diehards. Christians will be compelled to choose between reaction or revolution. Every form of religion in one way or another, either openly or under the guise of qualified support for some better kind of Socialism than Communism, will aid the forces of reaction in the last fight.

The social principles of Christianity can never be adequate to profound social change. In essence Marx was right.

" The social principles of Christianity have had eighteen centuries in which to develop, and have no need to undergo further development at the hands of Prussian consistorial councillors. The principles of Christianity justified the slavery of classical days ; they glorified

[1] Stalin ; from a verbatim report of an interview.

medieval serfdom ; and they are able when needs be to defend the oppression of the proletariat, though with a somewhat crestfallen air. The social principles of Christianity proclaim the need for the existence of a ruling class and a subjugated class, being content to express the pious hope that the former will deal philanthropically with the latter. The social principles of Christianity assume that there will be compensation in Heaven for all the infamies committed on earth, and thereby justify the persistence of these infamies here below. The social principles of Christianity explain that the atrocities perpetrated by the oppressors on the oppressed are either just punishments for original and other sins, or else trials which the Lord in his wisdom ordains for the redeemed. The social principles of Christianity preach cowardice, self-contempt, abasement, submission, humility . . . and the proletariat, which will not allow itself to be treated as *canaille*, needs courage, self-confidence, pride, a sense of personal dignity and independence, even more than it needs daily bread. The social principles of Christianity are lick-spittle, whereas the proletariat is revolutionary. So much for the principles of Christianity ! "

IV

CHRISTIANITY AND COMMUNISM IN THE LIGHT OF THE RUSSIAN REVOLUTION

by Julius F. Hecker
Moscow University

I. THE APPROACH TO THE PROBLEM

" CHRISTIANITY is excellent, but it never has been tried," is a dictum frequently expressed by critics as well as apologists of Christianity. To my mind the same assertion may be made in regard to Communism. These are but rhetorical phrases, and are not true. As a matter of fact Christianity has been tried on an enormously large scale, and for as long a period as 1,900 years. In Russia it dominated the life and culture of a numerous people for one thousand years. If it has failed to retain its hegemony and is now rapidly disappearing from the scene of modern Russia, it is not because it had no chance ; it is because it was weighed in the balance of history and found wanting. The matter stands differently with Communism. While its so-called Utopian and Christian variety has been tried on a small scale, its scientific form is only now being introduced on a large scale in Russia.

In this essay I shall take Christianity such as it was, and still is, in the life of the Russian people, and not as it should have been according to the notion of some modern theologian or philosopher. The same method will be applied to Communism, with this disadvantage, however—that, since the time it had for being tried out has been so short, it is too early as yet to generalise about its success or failures. Communists in Russia are still working at the foundations of the new structure. They dig in deep and make a wide, solid base upon which the new social order is rising. While handicapped by enormous difficulties and survivals of the dying past, Communism is steadily forging ahead, and in its path is ruthlessly destroying every opposition ; among which organised religion is considered the most formidable.

The bitter struggle between the Christian Church and the revolutionary movement dates back much farther than the year 1917. Its association with atheist propaganda may be traced back to the impact of the encyclopædist enlightenment of the period of the great French revolution. The influence of Voltaire, of Holbach, of Diderot, and other French bourgeois revolutionary thinkers was greater in Russia than anywhere else outside of France. Nearly a century later the Marxian ideology was grafted on to the minds of Russian intellectuals and workers which to a large extent were influenced by French atheist thought. Lenin traced his Marxian philosophy to three sources : the English classic economists, the French Utopian Socialists, and the great German school of philosophy which culminated in Hegel and Feuerbach. We see, thus, that Lenin's system of thought had distinctly foreign sources, and yet Marx-Leninism as well as the Communist movement in Russia have developed into an indigenous system of thought and policy.

Russian Christianity had Byzantium for its home, but its development was unique, and the religion of the Russian people attained a quality quite of its own, in spite of pretended catholicity, orthodoxy, and a passionate adherence to the old cult. Whatever the sources of a philosophy of life might be, it cannot escape changes and adaptations corresponding to the social economic conditions and traditions of a people. Christianity and Communism are now world-wide rivalling movements. When two forces meet, the result is that one of these is either destroyed or absorbed

by the more powerful. In every case none retains its original
purity. This has been the story of Christianity. It soon lost
its original Jewish character, merging with Hellenic thought
and culture, and in later centuries was absorbing the *mores*
and beliefs of various barbarian people of Western and
Eastern Europe.

The conflict of Christianity and Communism which, in
the Soviet Union, will probably end by the destruction of
organised Christianity, may, in a country like England,
result in a more or less peaceful compromise. This is possible
because of certain peculiarities of the British economic and
social background into the description of which we cannot
now enter. The English people, while always ready to taste
a new wine, wherever it may have grown, somehow or other
are managing to pour it into the old skins, which so far
have proven remarkably tough and flexible to hold both
the old and the new. The Abbey of St. Albans may be taken
as a symbol of the syncretistic qualities of English thought
and culture. There, at St. Albans, we have under the same
roof a most amazing continuity of architectural style. Beginning with the crude old Saxon, it rapidly passes through
the later Saxon, the Norman, the old Gothic, and terminates
with the exquisite fine lines of the English Gothic.

For obvious reasons the Russian character and tradition
are different. Having had little or no property which he
could call his own, the Russian is not afraid to destroy—
he rather enjoys it. He often does it long before he has
decided what he is going to put up in place of the demolished
structure. When the huge Moscow Cathedral of the Saviour
was pulled down to provide a building site for the Palace
of the Soviets, there was hardly a word of protest on the
part of anybody. The same is true in respect to the closing
of many old sanctuaries, such as the Sergievo and Kiev
monasteries, and thousands of sacred shrines, which have
been turned into museums or put to other uses, and sometimes demolished to make room for new roads and buildings. In this manner more than half of the churches of
Russia have already been closed, and in large cities like

Moscow hardly 20 per cent of the original churches are still functioning. The skyline of the gilded domes and crosses is rapidly disappearing, and, while there are still many people who find their way to the shrines and churches, their number is daily decreasing.

Is this process of disintegration of Russian organised Christianity to continue? Are there no signs of its rejuvenation? Is it to be replaced by some new form of Christianity like the Nonconformist sects, or is Communism itself to become a religion? Finally, is a reconciliation of the old ecclesiastical with the new secular culture possible? These and similar questions press for an answer. Within the limitations of my knowledge and the space of this essay I shall attempt to reply to these queries.

II. THE DISINTEGRATION OF THE RUSSIAN ORTHODOX CHURCH

The process of disintegration of Russian Orthodoxy commenced long before the October Revolution. Asceticism, intellectual sterility, and servile submission to the interests of the autocratic State were the chief causes which made the Church unfit to adapt herself to changing conditions and brought her into an inevitable, bitter conflict with the developing revolutionary forces.

A thousand years ago Byzantine Christianity began to spread among the Southern Slavic tribes, particularly among the roving warriors. The political contacts of Prince Vladimir of Kiev with the Byzantine Court, and the development of feudalism in Russia, helped this type of Christianity to become the religion of the Russian people. In comparison with the old nature worship of the Slavs, Byzantine Christianity was æsthetically and culturally on a much higher level, but in its ascetic emphasis it betrayed the disintegration of Byzantine civilisation which at the time was overrun by the sword of Mohammed. The barbaric conditions of the Russian people favoured the interpretation of the ascetic ideal in anti-intellectual terms. Learning was considered hazardous to piety and a temptation which was to be fought against. It was likened to the eating from the tree of Good and Evil which led to the fall of man. Besides there was really nothing which needed to be discovered. During the first eight centuries of the Christian Church the learned Fathers of the Church had formulated the Divine doctrines, which were stereotyped by the decisions of the œcumenical councils of the Church, and the new converts from paganism were charged neither to add nor subtract an iota from this body of truth, but preserve it unchanged to the end of days.

Such doctrine could not encourage intellectual activity. It undoubtedly greatly contributed to establishing the anti-intellectual traditions of Russian Orthodoxy. Of all the great branches of Christendom the Russian Orthodox Church is unique in its indifference to learning and the lack of initiative in the establishment of higher education. The pursuit of knowledge by monastics and theological study was rare ; wherever it existed, as, for example, among some of the monks of Kiev, it developed under pressure of Roman Catholic, chiefly Jesuit, propaganda. Thus the establishment of Russian secular and theological education under Peter the Great was carried through by Theophan Prokopovitch, a Ukrainian trained in a Jesuit college in Rome. His educational reforms were possibly due to the ruthless disregard by Peter of the traditions of the Church and the wishes of the clergy. Peter's educational innovations never received any enthusiastic support on the part of the Church. Teaching and preaching remained an alien function till modern times. The rank and file of the clergy were not sorry, therefore, when the decree of 23rd January, 1918, prohibited the teaching of religious creeds in State, public, and private schools. Even the closing of the priests training schools, due to lack of support on the part of the Church, has not been greatly lamented. The Church seemed to get along quite well without them, and in my opinion it proved to be a good thing for the Church because of their low moral and intellectual standard.

The ascetic tradition and the intellectual sterility of the Church were chiefly responsible for alienating the rising intelligentsia from religion. According to the teachings of the Church the " flesh " is intrinsically evil and opposed to the spiritual man. The ascetic idea split man into two, and taught that in order to save the soul the body must be sacrificed. " Sinning," according to this doctrine, meant the abuse of the body in unrestrained lustful living. " Saving the soul " meant despising the flesh and mortifying the body in ascetic practices. Whichever way was chosen meant to hurt the body, and hence the mind. Christianity became a cult of death rather than the sanctification of life. " My kingdom is not of this world."

This low standard of morality and of scholarship of the orthodox seminary was generally recognised and lamented by those intellectuals who still remained within the Church. Most of these schools became hotbeds of radicalism to which the best elements among the students gravitated. Many outstanding revolutionaries were trained in theological seminaries, but left them in protest against the training they received and the corrupt atmosphere of the schools. The theological academies which rose to university standards produced a number of outstanding Church historians, but were not a dynamic force to revive the Church from its lethargy. " Christianity, particularly contemporary Christianity, is exclusively construed upon the idea of death, and, if there were no death, there would be no Christianity," wrote one of the modern Russian apologists on the eve of the world war.[1] From these premises he concluded : " The Church could not receive the intellectuals and unite with them, for this would have meant to pay tribute to the prince of this world."

This ascetic life-denying keynote of Russian orthodox Christianity also accounts for the uncompromising hostility

[1] Lakighevsky, *Religion*, 1913.

of the revolutionary movement towards religion. It was just the opposite to the revolutionary optimism and the belief in the possibility of the good, abundant, free life here on earth. The revolutionary considered the " religion of the beautiful sorrow," as Christianity was presented to the people, as an opiate which the Church administered to the poor that they might forget their miseries and facilitate their exploitation by the ruling classes. This distinctly psychological difference between the life-denying asceticism of the Church and the creative life-asserting impulse of the revolutionaries made co-operation impossible. The Church could not make the cause of the revolutionaries its own, for this would not only have meant to betray its " eternal traditions," but it would have required a different type of clergy to take the place of the existing " servants of the altar "—the priestly type, which the Church had trained for centuries, and which made it impossible to develop the much-needed prophetic type. The purpose of the theological education in tsarist Russia was to select the priestly type and drive out the prophetic, dynamic types, for there was no place for them in the tsarist Church. These prophetic types, as we have already mentioned, found their way into the revolutionary movement, and carried with them the conviction of the utter futility of the Church and of its servants for any creative activity. To them the Church was but an institution to eulogise and sanctify death and protect a dying social order.

In fairness to the case, it must be said that there rose from time to time men—usually laymen—who wanted to give the Church a different direction, and who interpreted its aims in terms of an abundant free life. Such a man was A. S. Khomyakov, who was active in the middle of last century, known as the brilliant exponent of the Slavophil nationalist philosophy. To him the Russian land was the bearer of the Christian truth, and the Christian truth was in the Orthodox Church, which he defined as a living organism, a unity of love and truth, " a faith impossible to rationalise."[1] Khomyakov denied to the Church any authority, since the Church knows only brotherhood, recognising no subjects. Its unity and strength being the result of voluntary agreement and mutual love analogous to the mystery of the voluntary unity of Christ with rational creation. This anarchistic interpretation of the Christian Church was considered dangerous doctrine by the ruling hierarchy of the Church and the State authorities. In consequence, Khomyakov's treatise on the Church was not permitted to be circulated in Russia, which in itself should have been a proof to the author that his idea about " Holy Russia " and its Church as an " organism of love and truth " was Utopian and had no reality at its base.

Vladimir Soloviev, another saintly Russian philosopher, aspired toward unity of the Western (Roman) and the Eastern Greek Orthodox Churches, under the hegemony of the tsarist State, which should realise the ideals of Christianity in the social and political life of humanity. Soloviev arrived at this conclusion proceeding from the premises which he layed down at the base of his system of thought—namely, that the individual and society are a development of three primary characteristics peculiar to the human species : the sense of piety, the sense of pity, and the sense of shame. Because of these psychic peculiarities man is more than a social animal. He is a socio-individual being, and his highest development he finds as a member of a Christian brotherhood ; thus the Catholic Church represents organised piety, the State, protecting society, is organised pity, and humanity's economic maintenance is secured by organised restraint, the third peculiar characteristic of man.[2] The pious ideas of Soloviev found no response, because they were deduced with utter disregard of the real situation in the Russian State. Church and class stratified society, and hence proved to be inapplicable to reality. Now his ideas are quite forgotten by

[1] Cf. Khomyakov, *Works*, Vol. II.

[2] Cf. Soloviev, *Works*, Vol. VII., Part I. Cf. Hecker's *Russian Sociology*, pp. 48–52, 1934 edn.

the people of his own country. There is, however, a group of White Russian political *émigré* intellectuals, living in foreign exile, who find much comfort in the teachings of both Khomyakov and Soloviev. The so-called Paris centres of Russian theological and philosophic thought, with Berdyaev and Arseniev as leaders, are continuing these philosophic traditions of the Slavophils.

Among the few prophets who hoped to rejuvenate the Russian Church and make it socially minded must be mentioned Father Gregory Petrov, an intellectual who entered the services of the Church. He preached a social gospel to the proletarians of St. Petersburg in the hope of arresting the disintegrating process which, cancer-like, was eating into the dying body of the Church, particularly into the upper strata of the hierarchy and the Court circles. Petrov's famous letter of protest, addressed to Metropolitan Antonius of Petersburg, reveals the hopeless condition of the Church as he saw it. There we read such passages :

" The ruling regular clergy, with its cold, heartless, bony fingers, has stifled the Russian Church, killed its creative spirit, chained the Gospel itself, and sold the Church to the Government. There is no outrage, no crime, no perfidy of the State authorities which the monks who rule the Church would not cover with the mantle of the Church, would not bless, would not seal with their own hands. . . . In the Church the creative power of truth has become withered, dried and anæmic ; separated from life, the thought of the Church was condemned to turn about in the world of abstract dogma and theological discussions. . . . God was reasoned about without being introduced into life itself. A sort of special Atheism was created, practical Atheism. Certainly in words and thoughts the existence of God was recognised, but life activity went forward as if it was not so, as if God was only an abstract word, a sound without meaning. . . ."

The unholy alliance of tsarism and the Church could not be severed by the initiative of the prophetic elements within the Church or the State. A third independent and more potent factor was needed, and this proved to be the social revolution led by the Communist Party.

The culmination of the disintegrating process in State and Church was the Rasputin scandal. This ghastly story is too well known to be told here once again. The personality of Rasputin—the " holy devil," as his rival, the not less maniacal Heliodor of Tsaritsin, had called him— was quite symbolic of the impotent and corrupt status of the Church and of the classes which ruled it. With uncanny premonition this beastly monster prophesied to the Tsarina that his downfall and death would also mean the end of the Romanoff régime. He was right. His foul death signalised the downfall of the Romanoffs and of the social order they represented. Wherever the leadership in State and Church depends on the will and blessing of such Rasputins, it is evident that their régime cannot long continue. It falls as an overripe worm-eaten apple falls from a tree.

III. EFFORTS AT REJUVENATING THE ORTHODOX CHURCH UNDER COMMUNISM

THE REVIVAL OF THE PATRIARCHATE

The abdication of the Tsar and the sweep of the revolution were received with alarm and fear on the part of the Orthodox Church. The upper hierarchy tried to stem the revolutionary tide even after the fall of tsarism. Shortly after the abdication of the Tsar.the Holy Synod, in despair of what had happened, issued an appeal to the Church in which it pleaded to turn the wheels of the revolution backward. The appeal concluded : " Stand as an impregnable wall around the Tsar's throne. Hasten, not out of fear, but for conscience' sake, to aid the representatives of the power of the autocrat. Let now the bell of catholicity assemble all

Russia under a united, great, holy banner upon which with flaming words will be written : For the Faith, the Tsar, and the Fatherland."[1] For a thousand years the Church and the throne had been bound in inseparable union. The Church sincerely believed that it could not live without its head—the Tsar and the throne did not feel secure without the Church. One can understand, therefore, that the Church fought to the last to save her head which the revolution had already severed from her body. To heal these wounds, if possible, the ruling hierarchy, together with the provisional Government, decided to call a council of the Church—the so-called Territorial Sobor which was to rally the vital forces of the Church and reorganise it to meet the emergencies of the situation. Meanwhile the revolution was deepening, and in desperate struggle the Bolsheviks captured power. There was little hope for an immediate restoration of the monarchy, and therefore the Sobor decided to re-establish the institution of the Patriarchate. The tradition of the Russian Orthodox Church was that when the throne was empty the Patriarch ruled interim.

On 8th November, 1917, while the struggle for the possession of the Kremlin was still raging between the Red and the White Guards, the shaking hand of the ninety-year-old blind monk Alexis drew the ballot which made the Metropolitan Tikhon Patriarch of the Orthodox Church of Russia. The rule of Tikhon was a continuous, bitter struggle of the Church with the Soviet State in which the Church had set its hope upon reaction and the victory of the White counter-revolutionary armies which it blessed and helped to organise. When the White armies and the foreign interventionists were defeated and driven out of the country, the Church continued to support every possible enemy of the Soviets, including the ghastly famine and pestilence of 1921–2. Here again it was defeated, and it cost the Patriarch his throne and the Church her unity. The clergy split on the issue of recognition of the Soviet régime.

[1] Published in the *Church News*, N. 8, 25th February, 1917.

The conflict ended in the humiliation of the Patriarch and of the Church. In the summer of 1923 Tikhon made his sensational " Confession " to the Soviet Government, pleading pardon, and promising loyalty to the State. The inglorious rule of the Patriarch came to an end by his death in April 1925, and with him passed away the hope to rejuvenate the Church by reviving the institution of the Patriarchate. There was no soil in which it could have taken root. Tikhon left the Church a broken reed, dismembered and cut into parts ; like a bleeding beheaded body the once proud Church apparently had not enough vitality to re-establish her unity and to reform herself.

THE LIVING CHURCH MOVEMENT

The heroic efforts of men like Gregory Petrov to appeal to the conscience of devoted Churchmen was never altogether forgotten in the Russian Orthodox Church. There were numbers of priests and laymen throughout the country who realised the need for thorough reform and rejuvenation of the life of the Church. There were others, particularly among the village clergy, who loathed the despotic rule of the bishops[1] and hoped for their downfall. These discontented elements finally revolted when in 1922 the ecclesiastical régime broke with the arrest of the Patriarch. Tikhon at that time was facing heavy charges for resisting the Government in its efforts to relieve the starving by making use of the surplus wealth of the Church.

The chief leaders of the revolt were the Leningrad priests Krasnitsky and Vedensky, who forced the retirement of the Patriarch. In Moscow they were joined by the insurgent Bishop Antonine, who was well known for his revolutionary sympathies, and had been retired from active service already during the Tsar's régime. These leaders called a conference, during the summer of 1922, of the progressive

[1] Bishops were monks and were called the *Black* clergy.

clergy, which became known as the Living Church Movement. At this conference, for the first time in the history of
Russian Orthodoxy the discontented elements of the Church
had come together to discuss their grievances. Most of these
men had never seen each other before, and their interests
were far from being the same.

There were those—probably the majority—who resented
the despotic rule of the monastic episcopacy. They were
chiefly village and poor parish priests, who could gain
nothing from the conflict of the Church with the State.
They wanted peace with the Soviet, and a leadership
which understood and appreciated their problems. At the
conference these ecclesiastical proletarians formed a group
which they called the Living Church Group, which stated
as its purpose : " To guarantee to the Orthodox parish
clergy liberty in carrying on their pastoral duties and freeing
them from dependence on the economic ruling elements of
society." To attain this purpose the group sought, by means
of organised action at the Sobor, the following rights for
the White clergy :

" (1) The right of occupying episcopal seats (i.e. becoming
bishops).

" (2) The right to participate in the administrative
activities of the Supreme Administrative Organ of the
Church and in diocesan administrations on a par with
the bishops.

" (3) The right to particpate in the distribution of the
funds of the Church which are to be united into a single
diocesan Church treasury.

" (4) The right to organise a union of the White parish
clergy for further realisation of their rights."[1]

The Leningrad priest Krasnitsky led this group, and his
idea of reform was along the line of improving the social
position of the clergy and of collaborating with the Soviets.
Later he accepted the whole Communist programme except

[1] *Living Church Journal*, N. 4–5, pp. 18–19.

the point on anti-religious propaganda. Another group which shaped itself at this conference was led by the priest Alexander Vedensky. It called itself the Old Apostolic Union ; it was not very clear in its demands ; it emphasised purity of faith in the spirit of the apostolic age ; it also showed modernist tendencies in the interpretation of Scripture, etc., and on the whole represented the liberal city clergy with their special intellectual interests and problems of which the village clergy were not conscious. One could compare the Vedensky group to the " Broad Church " of the Anglican Communion. A third group was led by Bishop Antonine, calling itself the Union of Regeneration, and emphasising purity of cult and morals. Besides these there were smaller groups who advocated evangelical reforms such as preaching, Bible study, conscious conversion, etc. There were also a few who favoured a Christian-Socialist programme and discussion of social problems. Their number, however, was surprisingly small, and shows how alien the social gospel was to the practices of the Orthodox Church. These various groups and interests covered by the name of the Living Church Movement agreed only in the necessity of making peace with the State and of bringing order into the Church by calling a council of the Church. Thus the second Territorial Sobor of the Church took place in Moscow in the early summer of 1923. It deposed the Patriarch, unfrocked him, and abolished the institution of the Patriarchate in the Russian Orthodox Church as a monarchist survival and gave the parish clergy the same rights as the monastic. These decisions of the Sobor were rejected by the Patriarch, who, shortly after the council had adjourned, succeeded in regaining his liberties by making peace with the Soviets. At once he undertook to organise an independent administration, and thus the split within the Orthodox Church became a fact. The death of the Patriarch in 1925 brought the incident to an end, but the division continues. Now, after a decade of separation and the disappearance of the main issue which led to the split, the Orthodox Church is still a divided, disintegrating body. It continues to function by sheer inertia ; while there are many bishops and two rival synods one can hardly speak of a leadership in the Church. The Living Church Movement failed to become a rejuvenating reform movement. It is true that 25 per cent of the functioning Churches nominally adhere to the so-called Reform Synod, but there is no practical difference between them and the so-called Old Church Synod, except that the former have a few widowed or married bishops whereas the bishops of the Old Church Synod are supposed to be monastics. Why has the Living Church Movement failed to carry through a real reform ? The answer is that the people who still attend and support the Church do not feel any need for reform ; on the contrary, they wish to have things go on in the same traditional manner. Previous to the split those of the laity who had evangelical leanings left the Church and united with the evangelical sects. Those who wanted social reforms joined the Communist Party, or worked in the trade unions, the labour clubs, or other educational centres which were much better equipped for this purpose than the Church could ever hope to be. In the Church remained the mystically inclined—those who loved the old traditional ways of worship, and those who by their former class position were alien or hostile to the revolution. This type of people was usually in control of local Church affairs, and would not support a priest with revolutionary or reform sympathies.

The reform movement in the Russian Church failed because it came at least a half a century too late. What is called a " reform " now is but a political expedience on the part of the clergy who seek co-operation and contact with the new régime. The professional independence of the clergy after the separation of the Church from the State seemed to them altogether abnormal. They were so accustomed to being part of the ruling class and the bureaucratic system, that they do not know what to make of their independence. The revolutionary Government, moreover, refuses to accept the services of the Church. In this respect it is probably the only Government anywhere which rejects the voluntary service of the Church to maintain the established order. The Communist Party considers organised religion an implement of the exploiting class, and it lays its plans to have it destroyed together with the remnants of the exploiting classes. In the Living Church Movement was a small number of men who showed the true ardour of reformers, but they were too few compared to the rank and file of priests and bishops who held to the old traditions. For a while the newly opened Moscow Theological Academy succeeded in attracting a faculty and students among whom there were men with a modern outlook. These spiritual and truly ethical elements proved a thorn in the flesh of the old ecclesiastics, and the reactionaries gradually drove out the progressives till at present hardly a trace of them is left.

If a rejuvenation of the Russian Church ever occurs it will have to begin at the bottom, among the people and clergy of the local congregations, for it cannot be expected in the ranks of the old upper hierarchy. These latter must die ; there is no way to reform them. Fortunately the process of disintegration of the Russian Church under pressure of the new régime acts also as a means of purging the ranks of the clergy and of the congregations themselves. The Russian Church of to-day is no longer an attraction to make a career or secure a leisure existence. Those congregations which have survived and continue to conduct public worship are gradually cleaning their ranks from priests and bishops who entered the service for selfish interests. In most congregations it is the laity which takes the lead. The influence of the hierarchy is growing less and less, and the functions of the priest are frequently supplied by men who have been set apart by the congregations from their own ranks. The significance of these amateur, theologically untrained priests and lay functionaries must not be underestimated ; while they do not possess much professional learning they have pious ardour and sincerity, and this the Russian Church needed far more than its obscure theology.

This lay piety alone can preserve the Church from complete disintegration and extinction. But there are no signs that a social consciousness is awakening among the Orthodox Russian Christians. While the social revolution hit the Church very hard, it also did more to purge it from hierarchical abuse and clerical corruption than anything the Church could have ever done for itself. If the Church has any vitality to survive the present crisis, it will be thanks to the purifying function of the social revolution and the Communist criticism of religion.

PRESENT STATUS OF ORTHODOX CHRISTIANITY

The casual visitor to the Orthodox Churches in Russia is impressed by the fervour and sincerity of the worshippers. Those who gather there apparently feel a profound desire to worship. Compared to the yawning, bored audiences of the respectable middle-class churchgoers of England, for example, the present Russian church audience consists of people who live in an apocalyptic expectation. They impress one like a person who knows that he soon must die and humbly has resigned himself to the inevitable. There are few young people and children in the audience. The old and middle-aged women predominate. In Moscow, which I know best from personal observation, most churches are still well attended, and some are even crowded. This may be accounted for by the fact that only one-fifth or one-sixth of the former churches is functioning. Some eighty or ninety churches suffice to accommodate the worshippers of a population from two to three million of formerly Orthodox adherents. The priests, too, are old or ageing ; few young men enter and remain in the service of the Church.

If one speaks to an older priest, and he is frank in his opinion, the best he can hope for is that the Church he serves will last his lifetime, and that he will not be forced into destitution at old age. Begging priests are not uncommon in the streets of Moscow. All this adds to the feeling that the Church is a dying institution which only a miracle can save. There are people who believe that this miracle will happen, that God will not permit His Church to perish and that the godless Bolsheviks will be swept away by a miraculous interference of the insulted Deity and His saints. These hopes are particularly strong among the White Russian counter-revolutionary *émigrés*, who, aided by the Churches of the West, are able to maintain a number of ecclesiastical centres. The Paris group especially has been training priests for the Orthodox Churches of the Russian *diaspora*. These ecclesiastics hope to take the lead some day in the re-establishment and rejuvenation of the Church in Russia. They are sure the Communist régime will be broken and disappear. These same hopes are cherished by some of the old Orthodox clergy still functioning in the Soviet Union. While they have little direct contact with the *émigré* clergy, their desire for co-operation with them is still evident. They are waiting for the miracle which is to destroy their Communist enemy. Meanwhile the disintegration process within the Church continues.

The young generation of the Soviet Union, and this means two-thirds of the population, numbering over one hundred million under twenty-five years of age, have practically lost interest in the religious faith of their fathers. Communist education and abundant opportunities for self-expression in the new social life occupy their minds. The former hostility to the Old Church has practically disappeared, and excesses against the clergy are exceedingly rare. On the contrary, there is frequently observed something resembling pity for the impoverished priestly class, but on the whole a widely spread indifference is the rule. And not only toward religion, but also towards atheist propaganda. Only 3 per cent of the young Communists are actually members of the anti-god movement. Its negative tenets have no attraction to them. They are in search of an ideology which asserts the new life and opens new horizons of interest before them. Let the dead bury their dead—this is the feeling of Soviet youth in respect to religion and the Church.

IV. NONCONFORMITY AND COMMUNISM

THE EARLY DISSENTERS

Russian nonconformity dates back to the great schism of the seventeenth century, the so-called Old Believers' dissent. In its theological setting it was a reactionary movement, a protest against innovations and changes of the established cult introduced by Patriarch Nikon and the Tsar Alexis ; but upon its social background it was a revolt of the exploited petty townsfolk and of the numerous serfs of the peasant population who rose against the unbearable conditions of Russian feudalism and the despotic autocracy.

The Old Believers soon differentiated into the so-called priestly and priestless branches. The former continued the old cult and the administration of sacraments with the aid of priests ordained in the Established Church, but they refused to accept the jurisdiction of the Patriarch. The latter, when the Patriarchate was abolished by Peter I, and since 1720 replaced by a synod with the Tsar himself as the head of the Church, rejected these reforms with even greater resentment. The priestly Old Believers were the more moderate and socially the more prosperous branch of the dissent. From their ranks developed the wealthy class of manufacturers, bankers and traders, many of which finally united with the established Church through the so-called " Edinovertsy " (united) Church.

The priestless Old Believers were the more radical and uncompromising branch of the dissent. By breaking the old traditions of the Church and by giving up the old books, they argued, the Nikonion forfeited all rights to the apostolic succession. The official clergy is no longer a Church, it is Satan's synagogue. All communion with these ministers of hell is sin ; consecration at the hands of these apostate bishops, pollution. The priestless Old Believers' movement became entirely a laymen's institution, and in consequence

it split into many sects. Some of these were extremely
fanatical and anarchistic, some ascetic, others mystical,
rationalistic, and occasionally communistic. Others, again,
after coming in touch with the German evangelicals who
settled in Russia in the eighteenth century, turned to the
Bible and to evangelical forms of worship.

Among the extremist anarchistic sects should be mentioned the " Wanderers " or " Runners." They followed
literally the text : " If any man come to Me and hate not
his father and mother . . . and whosoever doth not bear his
cross, and come after Me, cannot be My disciple." They
denounced city life, the private ownership of land, declar-
ing that " the land was, is, and ought to be God's ; man
should use it collectively, but never own it." Refusing to
submit to the laws and regulations of the State these
Wanderers spread all over the country, some settling in
remote parts of the huge territory of Russia, particularly
in the north, in East Siberia and the lower Volga. When
pursued by Government troops they again took to wandering ; when no escape was possible they gave themselves up
to " the baptism of fire," i.e. burned themselves, in their
homes and chapels, alive. It has been estimated that some
20,000 of these fanatics thus exterminated themselves during
their persecutions in the seventeenth and eighteenth centuries. Some of these Wanderers have survived to this day.
A few years ago some members of a scientific expedition to
Siberia discovered a settlement of these early wandering
nonconformists which had been cut off from the rest of the
country for at least two centuries, and their existence was
therefore not known. The leader of the expedition told these
settlers of the revolution which had occurred, and of the
execution of the hated antichrist, the Tsar. He promised to
come again and bring them teachers of the new enlightenment. On reporting about this numerous settlement of
the seventeenth-century Old Believers the Government
equipped an expedition of teachers and physicians with
cinemas and gramophones, etc. But, when the expedition
arrived, they discovered that the settlers had abandoned

their fields and houses, and disappeared into the primeval forest—probably to escape the advancing civilisation which, as they instinctively felt, was endangering their traditional beliefs. Compelled by circumstances, and by their doctrine of the " Divine ownership of land," some of these sects took to communistic forms of living. For these reasons the Soviet Government tolerated them and encouraged them to continue in their Communist traditions, hoping to utilise them for their great collectivisation schemes when the country will become ready to push Socialism on a larger scale into the rural area.

THE EVANGELICAL SECTS

The spreading of the evangelical sects was impossible in the early seventeenth- and eighteenth-century period of the dissent because of the almost total illiteracy of the people and the absence of Bibles in the vernacular Russian. This was made available through the patronage of evangelisation by the Tsar Alexander I and the work of the British and Foreign Bible Society, which distributed the Bible in many thousands of copies throughout the country.

The oldest of the evangelical sects are the pacifist Molokans (Milk Drinkers), so-called because they drank milk on fast days. While maintaining some of the Old Testament taboos as to the eating of pork, they interpreted the Bible " spiritually " and allegorically, rejecting the sacraments, and in many respects are similar to the Society of Friends. They were very active during the early nineteenth century, spreading from the province of Tambov to the south, the Caucasus and Siberia ; some, under pressure of persecution, also migrating to Turkey and the United States (California). Living in close communities they grew prosperous, and with it their evangelical ardour waned. New revivals under influence of German Baptist missionaries brought some of the Molokans into the Baptist community, which in turn split into what now is known as the movement of Evangelical Christians. These latter and the Baptists differ little from the fundamentalist evangelical sects of the West.

Like the earlier sectarians the Evangelicals were suppressed by the tsarist régime. The reason for their persecution was their alleged danger to the solidarity of the State, due to their divided loyalty and their hostility to the Established Church, whose head was the Tsar ; therefore anyone against the Church was equally against the State and the Tsar. Frequently the leaders of the Evangelicals were arrested and kept in the same gaols with the revolutionaries, and exiled to the same remote parts of the country. In this manner a certain personal contact was established between revolutionaries and the sectarians, and, while ideologically there was little in common between them, they were victims of the same enemy, and hence certain sympathies were inevitably developed.

When the revolution swept away the tsarist régime and the exiled revolutionaries and sectarians regained their freedom, it was natural that they supported each other against their common enemy—the Orthodox Church, which had survived the downfall of the tsarist State. The reasons for attacking the Church on the part of the atheist revolutionaries was quite different. These feared the Church as a bulwark of counter-revolutionary reaction, while the Evangelicals saw in it, above all, the corrupter of the gospel, obstructing the road to salvation. Nevertheless the atheist revolutionaries and the pious Evangelicals allied themselves in fighting the Church. As a result a turbulent revival swept the country. Some of the Churches formerly occupied by the Orthodox were turned over for the use of the Evangelicals, whose numbers increased rapidly. There were no limitations to their propaganda. Evangelical missionaries could be heard in the market-places, in the parks and squares and sometimes on the steps leading to the Orthodox churches and cathedrals.

THE CONFLICT OF THE SECTARIANS WITH
THE COMMUNISTS

For over a decade the evangelical movement spread and multiplied, and became a formidable organisation, rivalling in places the Communist Party, and capturing the leadership in trade unions and local Soviets. This alarmed the revolutionary anti-religion propagandists, who feared that a more formidable rival was taking the place of the Orthodox Church, which by that time had been badly broken up and weakened, and was no longer a dangerous competitor for the cultural and spiritual hegemony. As a result the agitation for the limitation of the religious propaganda and of social activities of religious organisations began, which found its expression in the Government decree of April 1929, which, while tolerating religious worship, permitted neither religious propaganda nor any social or educational activities within the religious societies. The Orthodox Church greatly welcomed this decree, for it hit only its rivals ; the evangelical sectarians by this time having developed all kinds of auxiliary, social and educational functions, whereas the Orthodox Church continued in its traditional worship. In practice this means that the preaching and proselyting of the evangelical sects are limited to their chapels and meeting-houses, and for this reason has somewhat arrested their growth. Nevertheless there are at present some 3,000 local societies composing the Baptist and Evangelical Unions, which are allowed to have their central administrative organs located in Moscow.

While the sectarians had developed a number of closed communes, and showed a great deal of co-operation among themselves in promoting co-operative enterprises, they refused to co-operate in the Soviet Government's scheme of the collectivisation of the farms. The sectarians as a rule represented the more prosperous section of the community, and it was not in their interest to pool their land and cattle with the poor peasants not belonging to their sect. As a result a bitter conflict was waged between the Government and the sectarians, including the Evangelicals. The latter excused their non-co-operation on biblical grounds, quoting as proof text the first Psalm, which they said prohibited them to " sit in the council of the ungodly," by which they meant the councils of the collective farms. The Government could, of course, not stop its collectivisation schemes, and crushed the resistance of the sectarians by counting them among the *kulaks*, and frequently removing them from their former communities to remote, unsettled parts of the country, chiefly in Central Asia and Siberia. This meant many hardships, but it also has taught the sectarians their lesson, and many since have learned to co-operate with their poorer and less fortunate neighbours.

There cannot be real co-operation between the Evangelicals and other sectarians on the one hand, and the Communists on the other, unless the former adjust their fundamentalist ideology and be willing to appreciate the Communist culture based on modern science rather than on tradition and the literal interpretation of the Bible. The children of the Evangelicals who are trained in Soviet schools with their emphasis on science and technique are in a particularly difficult position, and have to pass through the painful readjustment of their minds between school and home where they are taught in the fundamentalist evangelical faith of their fathers.

V. THE COMMUNIST POINT OF VIEW ON THE PROBLEM

The Communist takes Christianity as a system of thought, and organised religion as he finds it in history. The chief attribute of historical Christianity is the belief in God the Creator, existing previous to and independent of nature. Christianity without this is as meaningless as medieval alchemy without the philosophers' stone. The Communist rejects, therefore, the modernist attempt at a monistic interpretation of Christianity where the theistic idea is replaced by a veiled pantheism or agnosticism. This he justly brands as a falsification of Christianity. Communism insists that the chief attribute of the Christian religion is the belief in a supernatural world and the existence of God independent of human consciousness and nature. This he calls the mystic and animistic aspect of religion.

Another, and probably the more important, aspect of religion is its social or class content. Lenin particularly emphasised the importance of this phase of religion. Accordingly the origin of religion may be traced to man's impotence before the overwhelming forces of nature, and with the rise of classes it is associated with the fear of, and the dependence upon, the ruling class. Religion " tied the oppressed classes to a faith in divine oppressors," said Lenin, and his conclusion was that with the disappearance of class dependence, with the mastering of nature, and with economic and social security granted to all in a Communist society, religion will wither away.

Before the time of the natural and social sciences, national and class struggles were waged with the aid of religious ideologies. The oppressed rose in revolt, inspired by the revelation of some prophet, as the Jews repeatedly rose in the name of Jehovah against their many national oppressors. In time of defeat, religion offered an escape, comforting the oppressed and defeated with the hope in a future better world. Heaven and Paradise were awaiting the faithful, and Hell and damnation the evildoers. These beliefs in another better world gave support to many such institutions of oppression, as those of slavery, serfdom, and the exploitation of the proletarian class. For these reasons the governing classes lend their support to these obscure doctrines. To strengthen and maintain its power over the masses the master class uses organised religion to sanction the established social order. These are well-known facts of the history of every religion, including that of all branches of Christianity.

It may be said that, while this is true of the priestly religion, there also exists a prophetic tradition which fought

LR

against injustice and led the oppressed against their oppressors in the name of the God of justice and freedom. The Communist does not deny these historic facts, but he points out that this was inevitable and necessary before the age of the natural and social sciences. The English bourgeois revolution against feudalism led by Cromwell was the last of the European revolutions fought under religious slogans. Beginning with the great French revolution down to our days, progressive movements turned to the sciences to construct their theories of revolutionary progress. Religion is now almost exclusively monopolised by the reactionary forces, and by a few well-meaning, but deluded, philanthropists and reformers who for religious reasons reject the revolutionary logic of social development and seek, by petty reforms and compromise with the governing classes, to maintain and improve the established order. Or, like the Christian-Socialists, they believe that the old prophetic traditional of Christianity may be revived and Communism may be attained by stimulating co-operative living and by persuading the ruling classes voluntarily to surrender their power. England is the classic country of this Utopian Christian-Socialism. Its masses are probably the least alienated from religion because of the Cromwellian traditions and the close relation of the early trade-union movement to the Nonconformist chapel. But British Nonconformity, which during the days of Cromwell, Bunyan, George Fox, and the Wesleys was chiefly the religion of the poor, has long since grown respectable, and is now controlled by the middle classes, which have become the stronghold of bourgeois Liberal ideology and while active to improve life within the existing pattern are uncompromisingly hostile to a radical change of the pattern along Socialist and Communist lines. Nonconformity occasionally flirts with Christian-Socialism and Communism. Conforming to its Liberal traditions it permits the Socialists, and sometimes the Communists, to present their case. It does it chiefly as a safety device, fearing that repression may add to the revolutionary fervour of these movements. But the petty and large property-owning classes within the Nonconformist or the Anglican communions alike will never surrender their class privileges and their property rights voluntarily ; they will scrap their Liberal traditions, introduce some form of Fascist dictatorship, build more gaols and concentration camps, increase their army and police, probably try another imperialist war to decrease unemployment and recapture the waning world market—it will do anything and everything, but it will not accept Communism, which is the only alternative to the present class-stratified, competitive, profit-making system of economy. What will be the part of organised Christianity, which now is almost completely controlled by the governing classes, in this period of breakdown of the old social order ? It is impossible to expect that it will come out whole-heartedly in favour of revolutionary Communism. There are, and will be, a few noble types, like Conrad Noel and his Catholic Crusaders, who will stand by the Communists, and there are a few class-conscious revolutionary Christian Communists in almost all religious denominations, but they are only voices crying in the wilderness. Their bourgeois co-religionists as a class cannot understand them, and will not follow them. Therefore, like in the recent crisis in Germany, the religious people will in their great majority take the side against Communism and identify themselves with Fascism. This in spite of the fact that the teachings of Jesus, the prophets, and the Church Fathers are in harmony with the Communist aims of a classless society and justice to " the blessed poor." The Churches will go with the reactionaries, because as organisations they are controlled by the classes which are hostile to the Communists, and the Church will use the religious emotions and its pietistic traditions to paralyse the working classes and hold them back from action in favour of Communism. This is the real situation, and applies to all the Western countries, including England. It was even more so the case in Russia, where there was practically no Christian-Socialist movement, and religion was either an other-worldly escape for defeated spirits or it was superstition and a force of darkest reaction. These facts determine the actual relation of Christianity to Communism, and I see no hope that the Churches will change their attitude. This is not only my impression ; it is shared by many who know the Church well. An English clergyman wrote to me during the summer of 1933 : " The main aim of the Church, I am quite convinced, is to side-track idealism, and tie your hands with certain impossible conditions and qualifications which make your Socialism no Socialism when the testing-time comes. I have been an active worker in the Christian-Socialist movement in the Church for over twenty years, and I have watched the whole development of the movement up to the present crisis. It is an extraordinary story. What betrayals ! "

VI. WHAT IN PLACE OF RELIGION?

Christianity has become the weapon of the governing class to perpetuate the existing order. This charge is difficult to disprove, but is it not possible to free Christianity from its Babylonian captivity and make it serve the spiritual needs of mankind also in a Communist society ? The Marxian Communist rejects this idea not only for practical reasons, but on the basis of his philosophy, which he is sure will meet all the needs of man in the new social order. What, then, are the implications of this philosophy which claims to satisfy all of man's intellectual, ethical, and spiritual needs ?

The philosophy of Communism is *Dialectical Materialism*. It differs from the idealist metaphysics and from mechanistic materialism in respect to its doctrine of ultimate reality and in its laws of evolution.

The idealist denies objective reality independent and prior to consciousness. He knows only *quality* ; what we call matter or objective reality are to him but creations of his mind. The mechanistic materialist knows only *quantity* ; he denies quality as an intrinsic attribute of ultimate reality. The Dialectical Materialist accepts both quantity and quality, or extension and mind, as the attributes of ultimate reality. Thought and being are not quantitative differentiations of the *same* substance ; they are intrinsically different though always in inseparable unity. Nature is thus potentially endowed with the attribute of spirit, which merges into consciousness in the process of development. The universe has never been created. It is eternal, real, independent, and prior to human consciousness. This hypothesis leaves no room for God the Creator existing independent and antecedent to nature. It is therefore atheistic. It has no place for a personal God in the Christian theistic sense, nor for a " supernatural " world independent and prior to this world. Atheism in the Communist sense does not mean, therefore, the denial of spiritual quality with which highly organised matter is endowed, and therefore must be accepted as a part of reality ; it means the rejection of a supernatural world, and God or gods existing prior and independent of nature.

The potential spirituality of nature emerges into consciousness in man, and develops into a spiritual culture in correspondence with the development of the productive forces and social forms ; under Communism it will be free to find its natural expression unhampered by the perversions which characterise the historic religions. These have split reality, and opposed it as the natural and supernatural with no unity and harmony between the two.

According to the dialectic philosophy the world is not the result of chance. The universe is not a mere kaleidoscope which arbitrarily changes its design at every turn. There is law and order in the universe. Nature unfolds itself in a dialectic process of a continuous movement in the unity of interpenetrating opposites. That is what is meant by dialectics. The mechanist knows only continuity ; the dialectician accepts unity in multiplicity, a continuity with breaks, with jumps, or creative mutations. In the dialectic sense, therefore, revolutions are a part of evolution. It is the breaking of the unity of opposites and the beginning of a new systhesis upon a different plane. It is not true, therefore, that the Communist philosophy denies an eternal order ; it only denies a static metaphysical order which has no place for the creative or emergent process of evolution. The dialectical philosophy does not deny that the ultimate truth of the world is knowable, as the agnostics do. It only denies that the whole of the absolute truth in time is knowable. Truth unfolds itself to our consciousness in bits, like the unfolding of a film or the screen of our intellect.

The dialectical materialist philosophy differs from the dialectical naturalism of the mergent evolutionists in so far as it accepts the unity of nature and society. The same basic dialectic laws of becoming which govern the process of nature govern also personal and social relations and the workings of the human mind.[1] Because of this unity of man and nature, and because the same basic laws control the workings of the mind and of nature, it is possible for man to know objective reality. Thus the anarchy which characterises the departmental habit of thinking of bourgeois society disappears in the Communist social order. In place of it is offered an integral philosophy of life, permitting to co-ordinate all human interests, and directing society and the individual in all their doings. We may conclude, therefore, that in Communism the dialectical philosophy may replace the dualist ideology of historic Christianity, and of the idealistic philosophies which are given religious significance.

Organised religion conveys its ideas in symbols which appeal directly to the subconscious. In Orthodox Christianity this symbol was the cross. It conveyed the idea of the futility of this life and the hope of a better glorious future life in an afterworld. Psychologically the Christian symbols do not fit into the new life of Soviet Communist society. The new symbols of the sickle and the hammer upon the background of the Red flag stand for the toilers' creative

_____

This does not exclude that at every new stage of development of society a new set of laws peculiar to this stage also begins to function.

efforts in field and factory, and red is the symbol of international unity of the toilers, of the blood union of the proletarians of the world. Can there be an integration of the Christian symbols of the past and of the Communist symbols of the present ? The cross, it is said, symbolises victory by means of suffering and sacrifice, with rewards to be received in a future world ; Communism has nothing to promise in a future world. It offers its rewards in the present life, which, however, are not easily gotten. They mean sacrifice and hard work. Victory over nature and society and its unwanted social heritage is gained by " way of the cross." Hence there should be no logical objection to the cross as a symbol. However, the new wine does not hold; in the old skins. The new ideals do not readily fit into the old symbols. Therefore, as far as Soviet Communism is concerned, it can hardly be expected that the old Christian symbols will integrate with the new forms of life. In these matters the psychology of the Anglo-Saxon may be different. His profound respect for and appreciation of the past may permit a synthesis of the old Christian values with the new ideology. With a simultaneous integration of the old and new symbols, the new thought may merge with the old, just as the Cathedral of St. Albans continued its development undisturbed by its architectural past.

At present Soviet Communism is developing a flourishing spiritual culture. Its social and ethical standards, its art and letters, while permeated by a new scientific spirit, contain, of course, many rudiments of the past. The historian of culture will readily detect them. It is a syncretistic process resulting in a new synthesis. Historic Christianity absorbed many elements of antique culture ; therefore some say that there is nothing new in it. While its elements are old, they have reappeared with a new quality which cannot be reduced to the past without a residue. Therefore it may justly be called Christian, not Jewish, Roman, Greek, Persian, etc., even though elements of all these cultures are present. Such is the law of evolution. It is its dialectic process. The old reappearing with a new quality upon a different plane. This is happening now with the developing Communist culture. Its new quality is its scientific approach to reality and the elimination and the withering away of the supernatural which was dominating Christian culture. This does not mean that the new culture will not have any objects of reverence, and that the emotions of awe, love, and beauty will not find their channels of expression. In this transitional generation which had to do the grim fighting and the hard work these subtler qualities are somewhat submerged ; but they are not dead, and will reappear in later generations so much the more intensively.

If concrete examples are wanted, they may be observed at every step ; there is the profound reverence for Lenin and the martyrs and the heroes of the revolution ; there is the dynamic of an almost apocalyptic expectation of the decisive and final struggle with the resisting forces of dying capitalism ; there is a great creative activity in the development of the country's natural resources ; there is a flourishing art—particularly in the theatre, which is becoming the vehicle for the teaching of the new spiritual culture ; there is a deepening of the new ethical sense expressed in a profound loyalty to the communal life interests ; there is a wide sympathy expressed in service to the weak and suffering toilers of the world ; finally, there is an undaunted assertion of life which leaves little interest in the dead and dying past. This explains the rather striking fact that at present the negative aspect of the anti-god movement arouses so little interest among the young generation. The leaders of the atheist movement themselves calculate that their work is about done, and that their society will soon cease to exist unless it changes its tactics and takes up the task of teaching the young generation the correct way of life and its meaning. In other words, it has to cease to be negative and take upon itself positive functions.

All this corroborates that the old orthodox Christian culture is dying. It must die before it can find a new life in the ascending Communist spiritual culture. But will it then be called Christianity ? We hardly think so.

V

COMMUNISM AND MORALITY

by A. L. Morton

IN OCTOBER 1920, Lenin spoke to the Third All-Russian Congress of the Young Communist League. It was a time in which the whole question of morality was being hotly debated, and nowhere more hotly than among the boys and girls who had grown up in war and revolution.

" Is there such a thing as Communist morality ? " Lenin asked.

" Of course there is. It is frequently asserted that we have no ethics, and very frequently the bourgeoisie says that we Communists deny all morality. That is one of their methods of confusing the issue, of throwing dust into the eyes of the workers and peasants.

" In what sense do we deny ethics, morals ?

" In the sense in which they are preached by the bourgeoisie, a sense which deduces these morals from God's commandments. Of course we say that we do not believe in God. We know perfectly well that the clergy, the landlords, and the bourgeoisie all claimed to speak in the name of God in order to protect their interests as exploiters. Or, instead of deducing their ethics from the commandments of morality, from the commandments of God, they deduced them from idealistic or semi-idealistic phrases which in substance were always very similar to Divine commandments.

" We deny all morality taken from superhuman or non-class conceptions. We say that this is a deception, a swindle, a befogging of the minds of the workers and peasants in the interests of the landlords and capitalists.

" We say that our morality is wholly subordinated to the interests of the class struggle of the proletariat. We deduce our morality from the facts and needs of the class struggle of the proletariat."

In the phrase " our morality " is contained the germ of any scientific approach to the subject. The recognition that morality is not absolute or abstract, but is historically produced leads directly to the conception of morality in terms of class interests. At any given time that is moral for any class which strengthens the position of that class in society. In a broader sense, that is moral which serves the needs of the historically progressive class in any epoch.

The first necessity, therefore, is to discover what has been the historical evolution of morals, what kind of people, what kind of moral ideas, were characteristic of different stages of development, and how these ideas came into being. In doing this it will be possible, by implication, to discover the basis of the morality appropriate to the man of a Communist society.

I. MORALS AND HISTORY

Among the earliest men morality must have been almost entirely instinctive. In a society practising primitive Communism morality was the behaviour which made it possible for the group to maintain itself in existence. Under the precarious conditions in which it lived a group which did not observe these conditions simply ceased to exist. The basis of morality, the one absolutely essential virtue, was solidarity. Primitive man practised, without taking thought, the " golden rule " of doing to others as he would be done by. It is a curious reflection that this maxim, surviving into an age of competition in which it has no application whatever, is made the basis of most of those idealistic systems of morality to which Lenin refers. So remarkable has it seemed to later generations that they are forced to conclude that only a God could have thought of it, and it has become the last refuge of Christian apologists driven into a tight corner. Primitive man did not, of course, practise this virtue for any idealistic or abstract reasons : it was forced upon him by simple necessity. The basis of primitive Communism was solely the fact that the prevailing technique of production was so crude that no individual's labour could produce appreciably more than was necessary for his subsistence. And, since there was no surplus, there was no possibility of exploitation or indeed of the idea of exploitation. Slavery was obviously impossible when the slave could do no more than produce what he himself consumed. War was little known—the most recent evidence of archæology and of anthropology support this view—where there was little or no accumulation of property to fight for, and where population was too scattered to produce any territorial problems.

The attitude of mind so created has persisted among backward peoples to-day—even in cases where the technique of production and the cultural level is far higher than that which we have been discussing. Evidence of this was found by W. H. R. Rivers among the Polynesians, a relatively advanced people :

" When I was travelling in 1908 on a vessel with four Polynesians of the Niue or Savage Island, and took the opportunity of enquiring into their social organisation, they retaliated in a manner I am always glad to encourage by asking me about the social customs of my own country. Using my own concrete method, one of the first questions was directed to discover what I should do with a sovereign if I were so fortunate as to earn one. In response to my somewhat lame answers, they asked me the definitely leading question whether I should share it with my parents, brothers and sisters. When I replied that I might do so if I liked but that it was not the usual custom, they found my reply so ridiculous that it was long before they left off laughing. It was quite clear from their ejaculations that their amusement was due to the incongruity with their own attitude of my conduct with regard to

my earnings. Their attitude towards my individualism
. . . revealed the presence of a Communistic sentiment
of a deeply seated kind."[1]

The changes which were produced when an improved
technique afforded the possibility of a surplus, while of a
revolutionary nature, must have been slow to take decisive
effect. A process of simple accumulation would not at first
lead to the establishment of definite classes, and the case
of the Polynesians, or of those northern peoples whose life
is mirrored in the sagas which attracted Morris because
they depicted a relatively classless society, shows how wide
a gap had to be bridged. An intermediate stage, still
apparent in certain tribes, is that in which the largest
accumulations are in the hands of the oldest members of
the tribe. This leads to a changed attitude towards the old.
From being a burden, as they are among the most primitive
peoples who still kill off the old when they become helpless,
they become the most powerful and most feared members
of the community.

In time, however, and in certain areas, we can trace
the rise of a society divided into classes. At this point in
history the nature of morality changes. *For the first time the
interests of all cease to be identical, and the dominant class imposes
its interests upon those of society as a whole.* With the beginning
of classes the State begins, rudimentary in form at first, but
developing with the deepening of class divisions and class
struggles. And at this point, too, religion begins and gives
an external sanction to morality.

Religion in the proper sense—that is to say, as a cult with
a ritual, a system of offerings and sacrifices, and a regular
priesthood—is a costly affair which could not exist in a
society without a surplus considerable enough to allow the
withdrawal of some individuals from productive labour and
the setting aside of a proportion of the product of labour
for a non-productive purpose. The individuals so withdrawn
were from the first closely connected, and often identical,

[1] *Psychology and Politics*, pp. 36–7.

with the dominant class. It was their business to give support to a morality which no longer derived directly and obviously from the common needs. A double morality, for masters and for slaves, came into existence.

The virtues of a slave, as slave, were those which made him a ready and efficient instrument : patience, industry, obedience, reliability, meekness. From the point of view of the slave they were not slave virtues, but slave vices, since they made the subjection and exploitation of his class easier, and hampered it in its struggles against the masters. They could only become virtues when used deliberately by class-conscious revolutionaries in the interest of their own class. This was hardly possible at this time, and slave revolts in the ancient world were sporadic and usually quickly crushed. They lacked, also, any positive, historically progressive objective. The economy of the ancient world, using its slaves purely as instruments, made it impossible for the slaves to secure their emancipation as a class, or to gain the knowledge and cohesion necessary to transform the social order. At the same time the absence of machinery left men too much at the mercy of the natural forces around them to have allowed the transition to a classless society to take place even if this had been consciously desired. Slave revolts were, consequently, blind, desperate affairs. Even Spartacus had no conceptions beyond those of plunder and of leading his slave army out of Italy and back to their own homes to begin life anew as small independent producers. For the modern proletariat, however, the qualities of patience, industry, and discipline which make them efficient as workers under capitalism are capable of this dialectic transformation through revolutionary consciousness into weapons against their exploiters and for the building of a Socialist economy.

Over against the slave morality was the aristocratic morality of the masters. Here, whether the ruling class were slave holders or the feudal aristocracy of the medieval world, the supreme virtue was physical courage, the capacity for imposing their will by force upon the wills of others.

Largely divorced from the actual process of production the aristocrat was concerned mainly with extending his power through the number of slaves or serfs whom he could exploit, which meant, in practice, adding to the extent of land on which these could labour. And though fraud and bargaining and cunning played their part, the characteristic method of adding to territory was through wars of conquest.

If courage is the supreme virtue of an aristocracy, solvency is the supreme virtue of the bourgeoisie. In their struggles for power the bourgeoisie, while they were able with the help of the peasants and urban petty producers to defeat the aristocracy by force of arms, always depended largely upon their accumulated wealth, which enabled them to weaken their opponents before the actual armed struggle began. As a class the capitalists, whether merchants, money-lenders, or manufacturers, were strong just in so far as they were wealthy. Later their hold over the pro-letariat which the capitalist system created was of the same kind, and this wealth has enabled them to pay others to do their fighting for them while they remained at home adding to their possessions. To this class the attitude of the four-teenth-century Henry of Langenstein, who declared : " He who has enough to satisfy his wants and nevertheless ceaselessly labours to acquire riches, either in order to obtain a higher social position or that subsequently he may have enough to live without labour, or that his sons may become men of wealth and importance—all such are incited by a damnable avarice, sensuality or pride," seemed not only crazy, but positively wicked, since it was pre-cisely this labouring to acquire wealth that was the founda-tion of all virtue.

If this labour is the foremost virtue of the bourgeoisie it is the most deadly vice for the proletariat, and the measure in which it has penetrated their ranks is the exact measure of their weakness. For the supreme virtue of the proletariat is a militant and aggressive solidarity, which is totally different from the instinctive solidarity of men in a state of primitive Communism. Only when the proletarian has abandoned all hope and desire of acquiring wealth and becoming an exploiter, of entering as an individual into the bourgeoisie, will he begin to act as a proletarian— that is to say, to follow the interests of his own class, which are his interests also, since only an inconsiderable minority can ever emerge from their class as individuals. This virtue of the proletariat is totally incomprehensible to the bourgeoisie, since it contradicts absolutely their own ethic. They can never understand, for example, the hatred and contempt which workers have for blacklegs, and, to a slightly lesser degree, for all foremen and bosses' men. The morality of the proletariat is in many ways far closer to the aristocratic than to the bourgeois. This is natural, since the proletariat, being without property, is obliged to rely upon force to secure its ends. But, while among the aristocracy the emphasis lies upon individual violence to secure the ends of each individual member of the class, the emphasis here lies upon the social organisation of force to secure the ends of the class as a whole. In the first case the ends of the class are served through those of the individual, in the second the ends of the individual through those of the class. In this way, as is very frequently the case, an old moral form receives a new content, and is transformed from a reactionary to a progressive factor in history.

II. PROPERTY

In all periods morality has been inextricably bound up with the prevailing forms of property relations. So much is this the case that it often appears as an attitude to property relations, and the morality of any class can never be understood except in connection with the prevailing forms of property and the attitude of the specific class towards them. As Engels says, and as the preceding section has tried to demonstrate :

" When we see that the three classes of modern society, the feudal aristocracy, the bourgeoisie and the proletariat each have their special morality, we can only draw the conclusion that men, consciously or unconsciously, derive their moral ideas in the last resort from the practical relations on which their class position is based —from the economic relations in which they carry on their production and exchange."[1]

Upon the prevailing form of property in any age, and not upon any absolute or immutable moral laws, depend the prevailing attitudes toward such questions as the family, sex, theft, and, more broadly, the social relations of man to man.

In pastoral society the main form of property was flocks and herds. In such a society the basic unit was the enlarged family—that is to say, not only a man, his wife, and his children below the age at which they left home and themselves became heads of families, but a man with his sons, their wives and families, and often a number of more distant kinsmen as well as slaves or servants. And, since every man's wealth depended upon the number of his cattle, a large family was desired in order to tend and follow these herds. As a rule there was no acute shortage of a grazing land, and if there were, a large family was even more necessary to extend and defend these lands against surrounding family groups. Thus Abraham was able to muster three hundred and eighteen armed men for the rescue of his partner Lot, and Esau went out to meet Jacob with a company of four hundred. A large family was thus a source of strength, and especially a number of sons. Even daughters were welcome, since a girl could look after herds, and a marriageable daughter was a valuable commodity. In such a society those who were rich enough to do so, and especially the heads of families, practised polygamy, and the head of the family exercised a despotic power over the whole group. On the death of the patriarch, one of his sons, the eldest or strongest or most favoured, might take his place. Or there might be a division of the herds. Such a division was easily made, and in good

[1] *Anti-Dühring*, p. 108.

conditions the numbers of the herd would increase rapidly, with no limit other than the available grazing ground. Consequently there was no rigid rule about inheritance, a fact which has led to curious misinterpretations of the Book of Genesis by critics accustomed to a strict system of primogeniture. There seems to have been no strong moral reprobation of theft. The lifting of cattle from neighbouring groups was regarded as an act of merit, and within the family group itself the opportunity for theft must have been extremely limited.

With the development of agriculture a totally different situation arose. Agriculture was mainly practised in areas such as the Nile valley, Mesopotamia, or the narrow mountain-enclosed territories of the Greek city States, where the land available was strictly and absolutely limited. Land, the new basic form of property, differed from cattle in that it could not breed and was only divisible within limits. Even to-day in areas which depend almost entirely upon agriculture the pressure of population upon natural resources is a permanently critical problem. The infinitely expansive patriarchal family was replaced by a much smaller group, and the family was superseded by the village or city as the basic social unit. A large number of children, instead of being a source of wealth were a menace to the stability of the social organism.

All this led to revolutionary changes in the position of women in society. First, monogamy became the rule and polygamy a rare exception. Whether this was a gain is doubtful, since the married women, especially in Greece, were cut off almost completely from the outside world and became little more than slaves and breeding-machines. The second change, in any case, was clearly for the worse. A daughter, from being an asset marketable upon reaching a marriageable age, became a liability who could not be married at all unless a dowry was provided. Hence arose the moral practice of infanticide—moral because necessary for the well-being and possibly the survival of society, but nevertheless productive of an immense amount of suffering.

A third change was the institution of prostitution, a direct result of the monogamous marriage, because monogamy was merely a social necessity and did not correspond to the sexual desires of the individual. The large class of slaves and freedmen in the cities were outside the family relationships of the land-holders, and it was from among their women-folk that the prostitutes were drawn. At the same time, the exposure of a substantial proportion of girl children of the land-holding class meant that many of the young men could find no suitable partners within their own class, and many of these young men were themselves cut loose from the family owing to the limited area of land available. The exposure of girl children was common : that of boys less so, since the city needed soldiers, and, in any case, those sons for whom there was no land at home could engage in trade, which was now becoming considerable in extent, or could be sent to the colonies which were springing up all round the Mediterranean coast.

Similar in origin was the custom of ultimogeniture, the inheritance by the youngest son, a custom of an extremely widespread character, and of which traces survived in medieval England under the name of Borough English. Here, each son as he came to maturity left home to make his own way, until only the youngest was left at home to look after his parents in old age and to inherit.

As slavery extended throughout the ancient world, agriculture developed upon a wider basis, great estates and ranches cultivated by slaves superseding the smaller holdings of former times. Simultaneously merchant and usurers' capital became important. The absence of machinery and the difficulty of organising a centralised Government with the existing means of communication set very definite limits to these developments, and, under the strain of the barbarian invasions, they vanished almost without trace. A new society established itself, with land once more as the basic form of property and a feudal aristocracy as the ruling class. The basic form of exploitation was now no longer slavery, however, but serfdom—that is to say, the land was no longer the direct source of wealth for the ruling class, but was exploited indirectly through the serf, who was forced to surrender a proportion of his produce in return for the right to cultivate the soil.

Here, too, the family was based upon the inheritance by one son of the whole extent of the land held by his father. This applied both to the ruling class and to the serfs. For the ruling class a strict entail was a necessity, since any division of the land meant the weakening of power. And the lord insisted upon the holdings of the serfs remaining undivided, because each holding paid a fixed tribute for which a single individual must be held accountable.

Thus the family became a fixed institution not only for the ruling class, but for the subject class as well ; here differing from the ancient world in which the slaves had no family rights at all, and were only allowed to breed by the permission, and for the profit, of their masters. The monogamous character of marriage thus assumed a more universal character, both marriage and the family relationship turning entirely upon the tenure of land.

In the midst of this system a new system grew up in the towns, which were at first purely trading centres. Here a new form of property arose—namely, capital. This marked the death of the aristocracy, for whom property continued to mean land and land only. It is highly significant that the aristocracy, until the period in which it ceased to have any social function and became wholly decadent, while always extremely tenacious of its hereditary estates, never developed a sense of the value of any other form of property. While holding on to the land it became wildly extravagant in other ways, and the close of the Middle Ages was marked by an orgy of spendthrift display. This very recklessness helped to establish the position of the rising and more thrifty bourgeoisie, who were quick to seize any chance to secure a hold upon the nobles through loans and marriage into aristocratic, but impoverished, families. The close of the Middle Ages saw an immense growth of usurers' capital.

Thus capital, and first of all in the form of the precious

metals, established itself upon an equality with land as a form of property. Its greater fluidity quickly gave it a decisive advantage. Appropriately enough the discoverer of America, scene of the first great gold rush, was among the first to express clearly the new doctrine.

" Gold," wrote Colombus, " constitutes treasure, and he who possesses it has all he needs in this world, as also the means of rescuing souls from Purgatory and restoring them to the enjoyment of Paradise."

It was the first of these properties which had the greater and more lasting attraction for the bourgeoisie.

The effect of the bourgeois revolution upon the family was twofold. The bourgeoisie, especially at first when it was a revolutionary class with the world to win, concentrated all its efforts upon the amassing of capital. Any form of dissipation which stood in the way of this end was regarded as sinful, and sexual indulgence became the sin which was reprobated above all others. Consequently the bourgeois family took on a new rigidity. At the same time the greater divisibility and capacity for expansion possessed by capital as compared with land led to the abandonment of entail, and the bourgeois family developed striking points of resemblance to the patriarchal family of pastoral times. (The Old Testament was the revolutionists' handbook of the sixteenth and seventeenth centuries.) The wives and children of the bourgeoisie were regarded as property, and highly valued as such.

For the proletariat the position was different. The expropriation of the peasantry broke up the territorial basis of the family, and men, women, and children became isolated units flung into the labour market. The result was an increasing weakening of all family ties, and family solidarity of the feudal period gave place to a class solidarity based upon common exploitation. Marx, in the *Communist Manifesto*, launched a burning and magnificent diatribe against the bourgeoisie who talk of the sanctity of marriage while their whole system is making it a mockery.

" On what is the present family, the bourgeois family, based ? On capital, on private gain. In its fully developed form it exists only for the bourgeoisie, but finds its complement in the destruction of family life for the proletariat and in public prostitution.

" The bourgeois family vanishes naturally when its complement vanishes, and both disappear with the disappearance of capital. . . .

" The bourgeois declarations about the family and education, about the sacred relations between parents and children, become all the more disgusting as the development of Modern Industry tears asunder all family ties for the proletarians and transforms their children into mere commodities and instruments of labour. . . .

" The bourgeois sees in his wife a mere instrument of production. He learns that the instruments of production are to become common property, and naturally can only think that the lot of becoming common property will likewise fall to women.

" He never suspects that the real point aimed at is to do away with the position of women as mere instruments of production."

With the decline of capitalism further changes can be noticed. The cheapness of female labour forces more women into the labour market under peculiarly disadvantageous terms, and a visit to any of the " Distressed Areas " reveals clearly the continued disintegration of the family as well as the bitter resistance of the workers to this process. More recently Fascism uses an attempt to drive women back into complete domestic subjection (as the slave of a slave) as a means of attacking indirectly the wage standards of the whole working class.

Among the bourgeoisie, also, there is a general loosening of family ties. Having long ceased to be a revolutionary class, they have abandoned the puritanism which helped them to seize power. The growth of a huge *rentier* class with nothing to do but to draw its dividends and enjoy itself has accelerated this process, and the sexual morality of this section of the bourgeoisie is precisely similar to that of any other class which has power and wealth but neither function nor responsibility. While the form and pretence of monogamy is retained, it has little meaning except from the point of view of the inheritance of property.

The relation of the proletariat towards property in the present period depends upon the fact that it is at the same time a propertyless and a revolutionary class. The natural attitude of a merely propertyless man towards property is purely acquisitive. This is the attitude of the *lumpen*-proletarian to-day. The attitude of the proletarian is quite different. Instead of individual acquisition, he has as his objective the conquest of property in its present characteristic form of capital, and its revolutionary transformation to a social use. The thief is essentially bourgeois in outlook, and is as parasitic upon the ruling class as an archbishop, depending for his livelihood entirely upon their continued existence. The instinct of the Kentish rebels who sacked London in 1381 was entirely sound when they executed one of their number for looting, and a revolutionary working class would be forced to act in exactly the same manner to-day. While theft is no part of proletarian morality, it is likewise no business of the workers to assist the capitalist to accumulate wealth through the exploitation of their labour. On the contrary, it is their duty to see that the surplus value extracted from them is as small as possible, and to extract as large a wage as possible for the shortest possible working day.

With the seizure of power by the working class their relation to property changes once more. All property is now their own property as a class. This does not conflict in any way with the holding of personal property by individuals. On the contrary, the common ownership of the means of production is the greatest safeguard for the personal property of the individual. It is just because of the private ownership of the means of production that the amount of property available for the majority of individuals for consumption purposes is so limited. It is one of the objects of the common ownership of the means of production to raise the output to such a point that every individual will be able to possess enough consumption goods to satisfy all his needs. In these circumstances the common ownership of these means of production gives property a sacredness which it has never before possessed, and misuse or misappropriation of this property becomes the gravest crime against the community. At the same time, social work to increase the common property becomes the duty of all citizens, and the attitude of the proletariat is correspondingly transformed. Thus, we can see already in the Soviet Union an absolute hatred of exploitation and exploiters. The most dangerous criminals are now not workers driven to rob or kill by poverty or bad conditions, but the social enemies of the new society, former exploiting elements, counter-revolutionaries, and *saboteurs*. And since work is now directed towards social ends and shared by all, it is no longer something to be avoided. Whereas under capitalism the time-setter, the man who raises the standard of the work which the capitalist expects from his employees, is a menace to his class, in the Soviet Union the Shock Brigader is an asset to the workers' State and to his class, and is honoured accordingly.

With the ending of the transition period and the abolition of the wage system a further transformation takes place. The sum of production has now reached the point at which all can share in the product according to their needs. Hence the possibility of theft also disappears, and labour plays a relatively smaller part in the social life. Engels summarises this development :

" From the moment when private property in movable objects developed, in all societies in which this private property existed there must be this moral law in common : Thou shalt not steal. Does this law thereby become an eternal moral law ? By no means. In a society in which the motive for stealing has been done away with, in which therefore at the most only lunatics would steal, how the teacher of morals would be laughed at who tried solmenly to proclaim the eternal truth : Thou shalt not steal ! "[1]

III. SEX AND MARRIAGE
AFTER THE REVOLUTION

From what has already been said the attitude of the proletariat towards sex and the family can easily be deduced, and it is possible to make use of the developments in the Soviet Union since 1917 to see how closely theory coincides with actual fact. One of the first tasks of the victorious working class is to remove all traces of the subordination of women characteristic of all exploiting societies. An early step in this direction was the complete revolutionising of the laws relating to marriage. In capitalist society the current agitation for the revision of the divorce laws is not the result of the raising of the status of women, but merely of the general disintegration of the bourgeois family already referred to. At the same time the economic independence of women was ensured by enabling them to enter industry and the professions on absolutely equal terms with men. Just as the revolution destroyed the parasitism of the ruling class, it destroyed the parasitic dependence of one sex on another. For the first time men and women became equals, working for a common purpose. So that their sex relations could be normal—also for the first time—instead of being a reflection of the abnormal social conditions in which women are either drudges or the recreation of a leisure class, and are not infrequently both.

Soviet marriage law, on the other hand, is based upon the complete equality of the sexes. Marriage takes place by a simple act of registration, but any stable union is regarded as a *de facto* marriage. Divorce may take place at the request of either party, with due safeguards for the property of both husband and wife and for the proper care of the

[1] *Anti-Dühring*, p. 109.

children. No person can be party to more than one marriage at the same time. Provision is made for the establishing of paternity, and a man is held responsible for his children after divorce whether the marriage was registered or *de facto*. Some of these clauses, such as that relating to paternity and the maintenance of children, are clearly of a transitional character, and would have no application in a fully Communist society. Behind the whole code, however, lies the fact that women as well as men are now equally—allowing for biological differences—workers engaged in social production. It is recognised that no person can any longer have any property rights in another, and that the only sound basis for marriage is the mutual willingness of both parties.

In the first years after the Revolution sexual questions were the subject of fierce controversy, and the wildest theories were tried out experimentally. The first natural reaction, especially among the young, was to condemn all sexual restraint as bourgeois and reactionary, and to reduce each sexual contact to its simplest biological terms of physical satisfaction of a physiological need. The theory that each sexual contact was an isolated act, crystallised into the " glass-of-water theory," gained wide currency. Other theories advanced the view that some form of communal sex life was the only truly Marxist solution. Yaroslavsky commented caustically : " If there are even among class-conscious comrades those who call Karl Marx a philistine because he was faithful to his wife, we cannot be surprised that we should find others who are of the opinion that Communist family life must resemble the love of the worker bees."

It was left to Lenin, with his profoundly Marxist grip of reality and his never-failing common sense, to expose these theories, and especially the first, which was by far the most widely current, as an anarchistic, mechanical, and wholly undialectical reaction from the restraints and inequality of bourgeois society. Speaking to Clara Zetkin he said :

" Although I am far from being a sombre ascetic, the
so-called ' new sexual life ' of the young people—and
sometimes of the old—seems to me to be often enough
wholly bourgeois, an extension of the good bourgeois
brothel. . . .

" I consider the famous ' glass-of-water theory ' to be
wholly un-Marxian, and moreover, unsocial. It is not
only natural factors which operate in sexual life, but also
those which have become an element in civilisation,
whether high or low. Engels, in his *Origin of the Family*,
pointed out how significant it is that the universal sexual
impulse has been developed and purified into individual
sex love. After all, the relations between the sexes are
not simply an expression of the interplay between social
and economic conditions and a physical craving that is
isolated intellectually by regarding it from the physiological standpoint. Of course thirst cries out to be
quenched. But will a normal person under normal
conditions lie down in the dirt on the road and drink
from a puddle ? Or even from a glass with a rim greasy
from many lips ? But most important of all is the social
aspect. Love involves two, and a third, a new life, may
come into being. That implies an interest on the part of
society, a duty to the community."

Already it is clear that in practice as well as in theory
Communism does not involve or desire the abolition of
marriage and the family, but its transformation. The
bourgeois family was, and is, based upon property rights ;
upon inequality of class and inequality of sex ; upon the
subordination of the women and children. In the Soviet
Union a new form of the family is already coming into
existence, based upon equality, social, political, and
economic, upon common responsibility and common
partnership in the construction of a Socialist society. For
the first time in history marriage is based upon human,
and not upon property, relations.

IV. THE CLASS STRUGGLE

Cutting across all systems of morality, whatever claims they may make to an absolute and immutable validity, is the fact of the class struggle. At every stage in history men have had their standards of conduct, of right or wrong behaviour, but these standards have always been applied within the class, and never to dealings of that class with individuals outside its ranks. This is the double standard of morality which has made relations between members of different classes impossible from the time when classes began. This double standard covers the whole field of behaviour, from the most trivial questions of manners to the most serious crimes in the moral code.

No " gentleman " will raise his hat except to a " lady " —that is, to a member of his own class. And a letter published recently in a Liberal paper records the embarrassment of a refined household when a small boy visitor, who came from abroad and had not yet mastered the intricacies of polite manners, rose to open the door for a servant whose hands were filled with a tray loaded with dishes. On a higher plane, but still outside the scope of morality in the narrower sense, is the whole code of honour and sportsmanship which, it is claimed, is the distinguishing mark of an English gentleman. This whole code quickly reveals its class basis upon analysis. Thus, the most gentlemanly of all British kings, Charles I, never even dreamed that it was necessary to keep his word to his Commons. This was not in the least because Charles was peculiarly dishonest, but because it never entered his head that questions of honour ran except between equals.

Even more illuminating is the conception of " fair play." This conception serves two ends ; first, to ensure easy and pleasant relations between equals, and, second, to prevent the combination of the inferior class. The maxim, " Two to one is not fair play," for example, serves admirably the interests of a small, highly armed ruling class surrounded with a class whose one advantage is the power to mass in decisive numbers at a critical point. In terms of the class struggle, the maxim should read : " One armed man to one unarmed man is fair play." The acceptance of such ideas by the proletariat is an obvious gain to the bourgeoisie, especially since there appears to be nothing in it to prevent a score of policemen beating a single demonstrator into unconsciousness, or to prevent the whole capitalist world attacking the Soviet Union as it did in 1919.

The prohibition of theft has exactly the same character. " Thou shalt not steal " does not mean what it appears to mean, but merely : " Thou shalt not steal from a member of thy class, or in such a way as to damage the interests of thy class." It is no hardship for the rich to be prohibited from housebreaking or picking pockets, and a general prohibition of this kind of theft is obviously in their own interests. There is no prohibition, however, of the daily robbery of the workers through high rents, profiteering in food, cornering the necessities of life, or, above all, through the extraction of surplus value in the form of profits. On an international scale, the great European Powers have cheerfully stolen millions of square miles of land from the peoples of Asia, Africa, and America, and have made saints and heroes of the men through whom this, the greatest robbery in all history, was accomplished.

Even the command, " Thou shalt not kill," does not mean just what it appears to mean. The question of wars can be set aside as too big to be dealt with here. But it must be noted that the killing of a slave has never been regarded as murder by any slave-holding class. Even Socrates, most humane and just man of the ancient world, was shown in the *Euthyphro* as being quite unconcerned by the death of a slave, and in law a man had the right to dispose of his slaves as he thought fit. In England after the Conquest murder meant the killing of a Norman. In the United States to-day lynch law is openly tolerated in many States. And in a recent case in Kenya a white woman, sister of an Anglican dean, escaped with a few weeks' imprisonment after having a native flogged to death for the theft of some cow bells worth a few shillings. In less obvious ways the same truth holds. There is little to prevent the rich poisoning the poor through the systematic adulteration of food, and the permanent scandal of " coffin ships " shows to what lengths the bourgeoisie are prepared to go in their search for profits.

There is, of course, another side to the question. While the bourgeoisie are able, through their control of the State machine and of the apparatus of persuasion, to impose their morality upon the workers, they are unable to prevent the latter from developing a revolutionary morality of their own. Above all, the proletarian virtue of solidarity can never be extended, despite the efforts of certian " labour leaders," to include solidarity with their exploiters. On the contrary, it can only exist in the form of solidarity against their exploiters, and the stronger it grows quantitatively the more does it become qualitatively the most powerful lever for the overthrow of the bourgeoisie and the whole class system. Closely associated with it is the virtue of proletarian anger. When Connolly wrote :

> *The slave who breaks his slavery's chains*
> *A wrathful man must be,*

he was voicing one of the fundamental points in the proletarian morality which is about to overturn the world.

V. SOME PROBLEMS OF TRANSITION

When Lenin declared that " we deduce our morality from the facts and needs of the class struggle of the proletariat," he was speaking after the revolutionary seizure of power had already taken place in Russia. This seizure of power does not end the class struggle, but raises it to a new plane, and brings to the front a whole series of urgent problems of social morality. Prominent among them are the problems of freedom, of the relation between the State and the individual, of dictatorship, and of revolutionary terrorism. Few questions have been so wilfully mishandled by bourgeois apologists as this of freedom. Freedom was one of the main slogans of the bourgeois revolution, and was a means of rallying to its support the masses of town workers and of the petty bourgeoisie during the struggle against feudalism. But the bourgeois conception of freedom was of an extremely limited and negative character. It meant the abolition of those feudal restrictions which were preventing the full development of trade and industry—freedom to buy in the cheapest, and sell in the dearest, market, and freedom to exploit the labour power of the proletariat. For the proletariat it meant, first, " freedom " from any connection with the soil, and, secondly, " freedom " to make whatever terms they could in the disposal of their labour-power. At the same time a purely negative theoretical conception of freedom as absence of restraint was elaborated, freedom being regarded always as an affair of the individual.

Clearly, however, no individual in society can ever be free in this sense. For Marxism, freedom can only be conceived in terms of classes, and of the relation of man to his environment. Thus, a class is free to the extent to which it is able to pursue its proper class interests, and a society is free to the extent to which it is able to understand and control the natural forces in the midst of which it operates. The classical statement of the position has been made by Engels, in the *Anti-Dühring* :

" Hegel was the first to state correctly the relation between freedom and necessity. To him, freedom is the appreciation of necessity. ' Necessity is *blind* only *in so far as it is not understood.*' Freedom does not consist in the dream of independence of natural laws, but in the knowledge of these laws, and in the possibility this gives of systematically making them work towards definite ends. This holds good in relation both to the laws of external nature and to those which govern the bodily and mental life of men themselves—two classes of laws which we can separate from each other at most only in thought, but not in reality. Freedom of the will, therefore, means nothing but the capacity to make judgments with real knowledge of the subject. Therefore the *freer* a man's judgment is in relation to a definite question, with so much the greater *necessity* is the content of this judgment determined ; while the uncertainty, founded on ignorance, which seems to make an arbitrary choice among many different and conflicting possible decisions shows by this precisely that it is not free, that it is controlled by the very object that it should itself control. Freedom, therefore, consists in the control over ourselves and over external nature which is founded on knowledge of natural necessity ; it is therefore necessarily a product of historical development. The first men who separated themselves from the animal kingdom were in all essentials as unfree as the animals themselves, but each step forward in civilisation was a step towards freedom."[1]

So, for the proletariat after it has seized power, freedom means the freedom to consolidate this power, and to proceed to the further historical stage of the establishment of a classless society. It is free because it is acting in accord with the laws of historical development. But in following its interests as a class the proletariat serves the ends of each individual member of the class. Because this is a period of transition from a lower to a higher stage in social evolution, the period of transition shares some of the characteristics of both stages fused dialectically into something qualitatively different from either. Thus, although the State still exists, its function is no longer the repression of the great majority of the population. Consequently, the quantity of individual freedom enjoyed by the majority is far greater than under any form of bourgeois State, and even greater than that formerly enjoyed by the old ruling class.

[1] pp. 130–1. Engels's italics.

At the same time the progressive conquest of nature, and the spread of scientific knowledge, enormously accelerated by the overthrow of capitalism, which has now become a drag upon production, ensures to everyone a greater freedom through the understanding of natural laws and the possibility of making use of them instead of being controlled by them. It is these developments which " alone make possible a state of society in which there are no longer class distinctions or anxiety over the means of subsistence for the individual, and in which for the first time there can be talk of real human freedom and an existence in harmony with the established laws of Nature."[1] The proletarian revolution not only offers for the great mass of the people a real and immediate extension of freedom, but is the only way through which mankind can pass to a really free society based on the abolition of classes. Finally, the State itself passes with the passing of classes. Communists, despite a widely accepted myth to the contrary, do not deify the State. They see it merely as the outcome of the fact of the division of society into classes, and accept it as such. But the principal function of the proletarian transition state is to preside over its own liquidation into a society in which, because it is classless, the individual plays a rôle previously unknown in history.

In any society divided into classes freedom for one class inevitably involves the absence of freedom for the classes opposed to it. Under a proletarian dictatorship freedom for the bourgeoisie is just as impossible as is freedom for the workers in a bourgeois State. This is a fact which well-meaning people—idealists and humanitarians of all kinds—find peculiarly distasteful, and can never understand just because they are incapable of perceiving that society is basically composed of classes rather than of individuals. In consequence they fail to grasp the essential dialectic of history, which is the progress towards a classless society through struggle and through the victory of the ultimate exploited class. It is this victory which alone, as has been

[1] *Anti-Dühring*, p. 131.

said, makes possible the emancipation of mankind as a whole, and the possibility of this victory which makes the proletariat the custodian of the future.

It is therefore not only the right, but the absolute duty, of the proletarian State to repress, with any degree of force which may be necessary, every attempt of the former ruling class and its adherents to overthrow it or to retard its development. Neglect to do this is not merely a weakness, but a crime against the working class and the present and future happiness of mankind. The workers have been slow to learn this lesson. Over and over, in the Paris Commune, in Hungary, in Bavaria, at times in the early stages of the Russian Revolution, too great leniency and too much trust in the good faith of opponents have had disastrous results, and have had to be paid for many times over in suffering and blood. The bourgeoisie have never hesitated to take the fullest advantage of these weaknesses, and Red tolerance has led to White terror.

The lesson has been learnt, and while the victorious working class will never use violence as a means of revenge, or countenance the barbarous atrocities which have been the mark of White terrorists and Fascists everywhere, it will also never hesitate to take any steps which may be necessary to ensure that no counter-revolutionary group shall turn aside the stream of history. This is something quite different from the glorifying of violence for its own sake which has been a characteristic of some types of petty-bourgeois anarchist revolutionaries. In advocating the use of force, not as the most desirable, but simply as the only possible, way of achieving necessary ends, we differ fundamentally from such a theorist as Sorel, who elaborated revolutionary violence into a mysticism—and was one of the first to fall headlong for the even greater violence of the World War. Radek records how Dzerzhinski, in 1918,

" gave an interview to the representatives of bourgeois and petty-bourgeois newspapers which were still in existence. They asked if he was not prepared to admit that

MR

the Cheka might sometimes make mistakes and commit acts of injustice in individual cases. Dzerzhinski answered: ' The Cheka is not a court. The Cheka is the defence of the revolution, as the Red Army is. And just as in the Civil War the Red Army cannot stop to ask whether or not it may harm individuals, but is obliged to act with the one thought of securing the victory of the revolution over the bourgeoisie, the Cheka is obliged to defend the revolution and conquer the enemy, even if its sword by chance does sometimes fall upon the heads of the innocent.' For Dzerzhinski the safety of the revolution was the supreme law, and so he could find in his heart that unshakable rigour without which a victorious struggle against counter-revolution would have been quite impossible."[1]

Terrorism, like war, is just or unjust according to whether its objects are historically progressive or historically reactionary.

VI. MAN THE MEASURE

A luminous sentence in the *Programme of the Communist International* forecasts that " this new culture of a humanity that is united for the first time in history, and has abolished all State boundaries, will, unlike capitalist culture, be based upon clear and transparent human relationships." And it is these clear and transparent human relationships which will characterise the morality of man in a Communist society. Solidarity, which we have seen to be the essential virtue both for primitive man and for the exploited masses of all ages, will undergo a new dialectical change. In primitive society solidarity was a reflection of man's ignorance, and of his weakness in the face of natural forces. Among the exploited it was solidarity in struggle against the exploiters. In a fully developed Communist society, with an always increasing knowledge and control over

[1] *Portraits and Pamphlets*, p. 106.

natural forces, this solidarity will develop a more positive form, embracing the whole human race.

For the first time men will find it possible to approach each other as individuals with none of the artificial barriers which now divide them, and, having solved the problem of how to exist, will begin to learn how to live. With the ending of poverty, of exploitation, and of all inequality, morality will no longer be embodied in a code of crimes and penalties, but will become purely a system of personal relationships. This does not mean that moral questions will no longer exist. With each step forward new problems will arise from the social contacts into which men and women enter, problems about the exact nature of which it is probably idle to speculate. Mankind will always have problems to solve, and each solution will create fresh problems on a higher plane as well as equipping man more perfectly for each succeeding solution.

For long enough, of course, the legacies of the past will continue to act as a retarding factor. As Engels says :

" A really human morality which transcends class antagonisms and their legacies in thought becomes possible only at a stage of society which has not only overcome class antagonisms, but has even forgotten them in practical life."[1]

To-day we are forced to deduce our morality from the needs of the class struggle, while never allowing ourselves to forget that the objective of that struggle is the abolition of classes. The basis of all morality in the classless society can be summed up in the single phrase, meaningless now to all except revolutionary Socialists : " Man is the measure."

[1] *Anti-Dühring*, p. 109.

PART III

DIES IRÆ

I

THE ESSENCE OF FASCISM
by Karl Polanyi

VICTORIOUS FASCISM is not only the downfall of
the Socialist Movement ; it is the end of Christianity in all
but its most debased forms.

The common attack of German Fascism on both the
organisations of the working-class movement and the
Churches is not a mere coincidence. It is a symbolic expression of that hidden philosophical essence of Fascism which
makes it the common enemy of Socialism and Christianity
alike. This is our main contention.

All over Central Europe Socialist Parties and trade unions
are being persecuted by the Fascists. But so are Christian
Pacifists and Religious Socialists. In Germany National-
Socialism is setting up definitely as a counter-religion to
Christianity. The Churches are suffering oppression, not
for some unchristian rivalry with the secular power, but
because, in spite of all compromise with the world, they
have not ceased to be Christian. The State is attacking the
religious independence of the Protestant Churches, and,
when they succeed in asserting their independence, it
calmly proceeds to secularise society and education. Even
the Roman Church is under heavy fire in Germany. There
is reason to doubt whether the Lateran Treaty in Italy has
fulfilled her expectations. Where she seemingly holds her
own, as in Austria, her position is both politically and
morally more than precarious.

Our picture may seem to over-stress the importance of
the German developments and to ignore the fact that the

struggle between Fascism and the Churches is far from general. Undoubtedly, the Roman Church follows a different line of policy in different countries ; and even in one and the same country the attitude of the various Christian communities to the Fascist Party State varies. In the encyclical, *Quadragesimo Anno*, the Pope opened an avenue of compromise with Fascist sociology ; though this happened before the victory of National-Socialism, it left no doubt about the direction in which Rome was eventually prepared to take its bearings on the future. Its experiment with a kind of Catholic Fascism in Austria proves this conclusively.

But these instances of the Catholic will to compromise seem rather to enhance than to diminish the significance of the German Church conflict, the seriousness and the reality of which should not be underrated. It bears out our conviction that it is to National-Socialism we must turn to discover the political and philosophical characteristics of full-fledged Fascism. Parallel movements in other countries are but comparatively undeveloped variants of the pro-totype. Italian Fascism, in spite of Mussolini, has no distinctive philosophy of its own ; indeed, it is almost characterised by a deliberate lack of it. Corporative Austria is marking time. Only in Germany has Fascism advanced to that decisive stage at which a political philosophy turns into a religion. National-Socialism is, indeed, almost as far ahead of Italian or Austrian Fascism as Socialism in Soviet Russia is of the tentative Socialist policies of Labour Governments in Central Europe.

But, even so, there are objections to using the German Church conflict as a proof of the inherent antagonism of Fascism to Christianity. There is, for one, the patent lack of identity between Christianity and the Churches ; secondly, the traditional feud between the Socialist Move-ment and the Churches on the Continent.

Undoubtedly, it would be impossible to argue that he who attacks the Christian Churches is attacking Christi-anity. Only too often has the opposite been true in the course of history. Even in Germany to-day, Christian Pacifists and Religious Socialists are as far removed from the pale of the official Churches as ever ; the same applies to Religious Socialists in Austria. Not even common persecution could bridge the gulf between the live faith of Christian revolutionaries and organised Christianity. However, as long as the Church in Germany stands up against Fascism in defence of her Christian faith, in the universality of her mission the significance of her witness cannot be denied. Incidentally, in this an important difference between the fate of the Western Churches in Germany and the Orthodox Church in Russia is revealed, where the Church suffered persecution not because she was faithful to her Christian mission, but because she was not ; for who could deny that the Orthodox Church in Russia was the political mainstay of tsarist tyranny, at a time when the social ideal of Christianity was inherently on the side of revolution ?

This helps to clear up the second objection : the reference to the traditional feud between the Socialist Parties and the Churches on the Continent. From the rise of the working-class movement this hostility existed.

But the Russian example should be a strong warning from adducing it as an argument. For in the eyes of the masses, also, the Western Churches were far from embodying the ideals of Christianity. Though organised Christianity paid cautious lip service to the idealist aims of Socialism, it fought its advance with all its power. At the present juncture, however, the Churches, though predominantly reactionary, are unconsciously bearing witness to that Christian content which they have in common with Socialism. Thus, not in spite of its antagonism to Marxian Socialism, but in consequence of it, is National-Socialism attacking them. This, however, is precisely our contention.

On the face of it, the argument is really extremely simple. No attack on Socialism can be permanently effective that fails to dig down to the religious and moral roots of the movement. But at these roots lies the Christian inheritance. The Fascists setting out to deliver mankind from the alleged delusions of Socialism cannot pass by the question of the ultimate truth or untruth of the teachings of Jesus.

But politics does not deal with abstractions. That which may seem an insoluble contradiction in the realm of pure thought does not necessarily lead to a clash in reality. If Fascist Governments take great risks in order to infuse pagan elements into the Christian religion, they do this for compelling reasons of a purely practical order. What are these reasons ? Are they accidental only, or do they spring inevitably from the efforts of Fascism to re-cast the structure of society in such a manner as to rule out for ever the possibility of the development towards Socialism ? And, if so, why can they not eliminate this possibility without removing at the same time every vestige of the influence Christian ideals may have had on the political and social institutions of Western civilisation ?

It is to the philosophy and sociology of Fascism we must turn for the answer.

I. FASCIST ANTI-INDIVIDUALISM

The common complaint that Fascism has not produced a comprehensive philosophic system of its own is not altogether fair to Professor Othmar Spann of Vienna. Half a decade before the corporative principle can be said to have emerged in Italian Fascist politics he made this idea the basis of a new theory of the State. In the subsequent years he amplified this theory into a philosophy of the human universe, and dealt, in detail, with politics, economics, sociology as well as general methodology, ontology, and metaphysics. But that feature of his system which makes it peculiarly relevant to our enquiry is neither its priority nor its comprehensiveness. It is the manner in which its author laid down as its basis the idea which in one form or another has become the guiding principle of all Fascist schools of thought of whatever description : the idea of *anti-individualism*.[1]

[1] " Moral decay in Liberalism, cultural paralysis through Democracy, and final degradation by Socialism," are then inevitable.

After having first broadly established this fact, we will enquire more closely into its less obvious implications.

Spann, the prophet of counter-revolution, starts on his career amid the middle-class ruin and despair of 1919. It is his belief we have come to the eleventh hour. We must make our choice between two world systems : Individualism and Universalism.[1] Unless we accept the latter, we cannot escape the fatal consequences of the former. For Bolshevism is but the extension of the individualist doctrine of the natural rights of man from the political sphere to the economic. Far from being the opposite of Individualism it is its consistent fulfilment. In spite of Hegel, Spann contends, Marx remained thoroughly individualist. In his theory of the State he is individualistic to the point of anarchist Utopianism. " That in Marxism the ' State dies off ' is the outcome of its inherent Individualism which regards society as being, essentially, lack of domination of human beings by human beings, a ' free association ' of individuals." The Socialist ideal is definitely the " State-free " society. Historically, it is by way of Democracy and Liberalism that Individualism leads to Bolshevism. The " barbaric, brutal, and bloody " rule of Liberal Capitalism, as Spann himself terms it, prepares the way for a Socialist organisation of economic life, a transition for which representative Democracy supplies the political machinery. Once we allow the universalist principle of medieval society to be finally destroyed by the individualistic virus, no other outcome is possible.

The distinctive feature of Spann's system is the manner in which he attempts to locate this virus. Individualism is with him not a principle confined to social philosophy—it is a formal method of analysis. Basically it is responsible for the vicious causational approach to natural phenomena in modern science, and thus, ultimately, for the atomistic Individualism in terms of which we have, to our undoing,

---

[1] The meaning of this term with Spann has nothing in common with its accepted use as current with the Christian Churches to-day.

come to conceive of society. Spann's " Universalism "[1] professes to be the counter-method to this inclusive concept of Individualism.

The deep conviction of the individualistic nature of the forces working for Socialism to-day pervades Fascism in all its forms. Ernst Krieck, the leading German pedagogue, thus contrasts the National-Socialist revolution with the two stages of Individualism embodied in the last centuries of Western European development on the one hand, and Socialism on the other : from the time of the Renaissance, he says, " the People, the State, Society, Economic Life, were regarded as a mere sum of autonomous individuals. . . . With Marxism the dialectic move to collectivity supervenes. In Socialism the sum ranks higher than the component parts ; this is due to a coercive mechanism which lies, however, preformed in representative mass Democracy." Individualism, he asserts, is thus not overcome in Socialism ; there is only a shifting of the centre of gravity. In short : Socialism is preformed in Democracy. For Socialism is but Individualism with a different emphasis.

There is the same insistence amongst Italian Fascists on the individualist and Liberal origins of Socialism. Take Mussolini himself : " Free-Masonry, Liberalism, Democracy, and Socialism are the enemy." Or the Catholic Fascist, Malaparte : " It is originally Anglo-Saxon civilisation which has recently triumphed in democratic Liberalism and Socialism." Finally, the reactionary aristocrat, the Baron Julius Evola : " The Reformation supplanted Hierarchy by the spiritual priesthood of the Believers, which threw off the shackles of authority, made everybody his own judge and the equal of his fellow. This is the starting-point of ' Socialist ' decay in Europe."

But an identical attitude is apparent also in political National-Socialism. To quote Hitler : " Western democracy is the forerunner of Marxism, which would be entirely unthinkable without it." Similarly, Rosenberg : " Democratic

---

[1] The term Universalism is generic ; the specific term given by Spann to his philosophy is " Totalitarianism " (*Ganzheitslehre*).

and Marxian movements take their stand on the happiness of the *Individual*." And Gottfried Feder's semi-official commentary to the Party Programme curtly speaks of " Capitalism and its Marxian and bourgeois satellites "—a syncopated form of speech which hides under its apparent paradox a tactically well-considered amalgamation of Individualism and Socialism.

This unanimity is impressive. For a generation or two, Socialism has been assailed by its critics as the enemy of the idea of human personality. Although sensitive minds like Oscar Wilde discovered the fallacy, it remained a favourite charge with the writers of the day ; that Bolshevism is the end of personality is almost a standing phrase in middle-class literature. Fascism disclaims all solidarity with this facile school of criticism. It is too deadly serious in its will to destroy Socialism to afford to use as its weapons charges so misdirected as to be ineffectual. It has fixed upon a true one. Socialism *is* the heir to Individualism. It *is* the economic system under which the substance of Individualism can alone be preserved in the modern world. Hence the efforts to produce a systematic body of knowledge that could provide a background to a distinctively Fascist, i.e. radically anti-individualist, philosophy. It is under this heading that most of the work of psychologists like Prinzhorn, ethnologists like Baümler, Blüher, and Wirth, philosophers of history like Spengler, are relevant to our problem. It would be safe to say that the invisible border-line dividing Fascism from all other shades and variants of reactionary anti-Socialism, consists precisely in this irreducible and extreme opposition to Individualism. No spiritual ancestry of this idea, however august, is safe from the ruthless onslaught of the Fascist, and invariably he will found his attack on the charge that Individualism is responsible for Bolshevism.

The new State-supported religious movements in Germany, whether based on racial or tribal or only national and super-patriotic tenets, turn against Individualism even when they do not profess to have discovered a complete dispensation from ethics. Thus, Friedrich Gogarten's *Politische Ethik*, the non-nationalist trend of which was very far from foreshadowing the subsequent rôle of its writer in the German Christian Movement, was aimed at redefining social ethics in a pointedly anti-individualistic sense. No wonder that even the Catholic Church, which of all Christian persuasions is known to be least inclined to overstress the individualist elements in its teachings, complains of the unchristian leanings in Fascism predominantly on the grounds of the lack of appreciation in Fascism for the human individual as such.

The German Faith Movement, lastly, is free from all the embarrassing ambiguities inherent in the German Christian position. It is German, not Christian. It prides itself on its choice between these self-styled alternatives. It can thus proceed to proclaim the fundamental inequality of human beings in the name of religion. Thus the ultimate aim is reached. For obviously the democratic implications of Individualism spring from the affirmation of the *equality of individuals as individuals*.[1] This is the Individualism on which Democracy is based, and on the destruction of which Fascism is bent. It is the Individualism of the Gospels.

We are back to our starting-point again. We noted Spann's insistence that Democracy is the institutional link between Socialism and Individualism. This singles out representative Democracy as the point of attack for Fascism. It is of signal importance to realise that the underlying political belief is solidly founded in fact.

In Central Europe, if not in the whole of Europe, universal suffrage increased enormously the impact of the industrial working class on economic and social legislation, and, whenever a major crisis arose, Parliaments elected

---

[1] Wilhelm Stapel, in his " Theology of Nationalism " (as the subtitle of *Der Christliche Staatsmann* runs), proves an almost injudiciously frank despiser of ethics, which, as he propounds, " are indebted for their existence merely to the sentimentality of those who are not yet capable of surrendering illusions." Even Ernst Krieck contends, in his handbook on *Education*, that " we cannot allow any imperative ethics to lay down for us the values and laws upon which we should act."

on a popular vote invariably tended towards Socialist solutions. The steady progress of the Socialist Movement, once representative Democracy is allowed to stand, is the dominating historical experience of the Continent in the post-war period. It is the main source of the conviction on the Continent that, if only the authority of representative institutions is left unimpaired, Socialism must come. Thus, if Socialism is not to be, democracy must go. This is the *raison d'être* of the Fascist movements in Europe. Anti-individualism is but the rationalisation of this political outlook.

But the anti-individualist formula meets also the practical requirements of this movement most adequately. By denouncing Socialism and Capitalism alike as the common offspring of Individualism, it enables Fascism to pose before the masses as the sworn enemy of both. The popular resentment against Liberal Capitalism is thus turned most effectively against Socialism without any reflection on Capitalism in its non-Liberal, i.e. corporative, forms. Though unconsciously performed, the trick is highly ingenious. First Liberalism is identified with Capitalism ; then Liberalism is made to walk the plank ; but Capitalism is no worse for the dip, and continues its existence unscathed under a new alias.

II. ATHEIST AND CHRISTIAN INDIVIDUALISM

But we are not primarily concerned here with politics. We hope to have succeeded in establishing the fact that anti-individualism is, broadly speaking, the cue of all Fascist schools of thought. But what exactly is the Individualism at which the Fascist attack is aimed, and what is its relationship to Socialism and Christianity ?

The answer which we will try to extricate from Spann's argument is of a highly paradoxical character. It is, in short, that the Individualism on which Socialism fundamentally rests, and against which Spann's attack must necessarily be aimed, is an entirely different Individualism from the one against which his actual arguments are directed. Thus, as a critical contribution to Fascism, Spann's argumentation is a failure. Yet incidentally it reveals the true nature of the problem with exceptional clarity, i.e. that meaning of individualism which Socialism and Christianity have in common.

Spann's indictment of Individualism is based on the double assertion that its concepts both of the individual and of society are fictitious and self-contradictory. Individualism must conceive of human beings as self-contained entities spiritually " on their own," as it were. But such an individuality cannot be real. Its spiritual autarchy is imaginary. Its very existence is no more than a fiction. The same would hold good of a society that is made up of individuals of this kind. It might or it might not exist—according to whether the individuals decided to " form it " or not. This, again, would depend upon the more or less fortuitous circumstances of their feeling more sympathy or antipathy towards each other, whether they took a rational or irrational view of their self-interest, and so on. A society thus conceived must lack essential reality.

Nobody can deny the strength of these arguments. Indeed, they are conclusive. And yet they prove exactly the opposite of what they are intended to prove.

Spann's criticism of Individualism is vitiated by a fundamental ambiguity. What he is *aiming* to disprove is the Individualism which is the substance of Socialism. It is essentially Christian. His *actual* arguments are directed against atheist Individualism. Both these forms of Individualism are theological in origin. But the reference to the Absolute is negative with the one and positive with the other. In fact one is precisely the opposite of the other. No valid conclusions can be reached if we confuse them.

The formula of atheist Individualism is that of Kiriloff in Dostoevsky's *The Possessed* : " If there is no God, then I, Kiriloff, am God." For God is that which gives meaning to human life and creates a difference between good and evil. If there is no such god outside myself, then I myself am god, *for I do these things.* The argument is irrefutable. In the novel, Kiriloff resolves to make his godhead actual and real by conquering the fear of death. He proposes to achieve this by committing suicide. His dying proves a ghastly failure.

Dostoevsky's ruthless analysis of Kiriloff leaves no doubt about the true nature and limitations of the spiritually autonomous personality. The Titanic Superman is the heir to the gods Nietzsche had proclaimed dead. In the mythological figures of Raskolnikoff Stavrogin, Ivan, from whom Smardjakoff also derives, but, most forcibly of all, in Kiriloff, Dostoevsky provided us with an almost mathematically exact refutation of this concept of human personality. Spann's criticism of Individualism is but a belated attack on Nietzsche, with whose position Dostoevsky had dealt half a century earlier.[1] Historically, both Nietzsche and Dostoevsky had been anticipated by the lonely genius of Soren Kierkegaard, who, in a unique dialectic effort, had a generation before them created and wiped out again the Autonomous Individual.

But Othmar Spann does not only force open doors, he also gets through them into the wrong apartments. By his effective, though superfluous, attack on atheist Individualism he refutes what in corporate Capitalism he eventually intends to uphold : the Individualism of Unequals, and upholds unwittingly what he started to refute : the Individualism of Equals. For the latter is inseparably bound up with Christian as the other is with atheist Individualism.[2]

Christian Individualism arises out of the precisely opposite relation to the Absolute. " Personality is of infinite value, because there is God." It is the doctrine of the

---

[1] Partly, indeed, prior to the actual publication of *Zarathustra* itself.

[2] Titanic Individualism derives the value of personality from the assertion that there is no God. It is not to be confused with the Individualism of Luther or Calvin or Rousseau, the Individualism prescribed under its different aspects in the rise of Capitalism. It is the atheist Individualism of Kierkegaard's Seducer, of Stirner's Only One, of Nietzsche's Superman, the philosophy of a short transition period in which Liberal Capitalism was triumphant.

Brotherhood of Man. That men have souls is only another way of stating that they have infinite value as individuals. To say that they are equals is only restating that they have souls. The doctrine of Brotherhood implies that personality is not real outside community. The reality of community *is* the relationship of persons. It is the Will of God that community shall be real.

The best proof of the coherence of this series of truths lies in the fact that Fascism, in order to rid itself of one of the links finds itself constrained to renounce them all. It tries to deny the equality of Man, but it cannot do this without denying that he has a soul. Like different properties of a geometrical figure these statements are really one. The discovery of the individual *is* the discovery of mankind. The discovery of the individual soul *is* the discovery of community. The discovery of equality is the discovery of society. Each is implied in the other. The discovery of the person *is* the discovery that society is the relationship of persons.

For the idea of Man and the idea of Society cannot be dealt with separately. What Fascism is contending with is the Christian idea of man and Society as a whole. Its central concept is that of the person. It is the individual in his religious aspect. The consistent refusal of Fascism to regard the individual in this aspect is the sign of its recognition that Christianity and Fascism are completely incompatible.

The Christian idea of society is that it is a relationship of persons. Everything else follows logically from this. The central proposition of Fascism is that society is *not* a relationship of persons. This is the real significance of its anti-individualism. The implied negation is the formative principle of Fascism as a philosophy. It is its essence. It sets to Fascist thought its definite task in history, science, morals, politics, economics, and religion. Thus Fascist philosophy is an effort to produce a vision of the world in which society is *not* a relationship of persons. A society, in fact, in which there are either no conscious human beings or their consciousness has no reference to the existence and functioning of society. Anything less leads back to the Christian truth about society. But that is indivisible. It is the achievement of Fascism to have discovered its whole scope. It rightly asserts the correlatedness of the ideas of Individualism, Democracy and Socialism. It knows that either Christianity or Fascism must perish in the struggle.

At first sight it seems almost inconceivable that Fascism should have undertaken a task which to our conventional minds seems so utterly hopeless. And yet it has. That its assertions and propositions are more startling than anything which Radicals of the Left have ever produced ought, however, not to surprise us. Revolutionary Socialism is but a different formulation and a stricter interpretation of truths generally accepted in Western Europe for almost two thousand years. Fascism is their denial. This explains the devious paths which it has been driven to explore.

III. THE SOLUTIONS

Let us restate the problem. How is a society conceivable which is not a relationship of persons ? This implies a society which would not have the individual as its unit. But in such a society, how can economic life be possible if neither co-operation nor exchange—both personal relationships between individuals—can take place in it ? How can power emerge, be controlled, and directed to useful ends, if there exists no individuals to express their wills or wishes ? And what kind of human being is supposed to populate this society if this being is to possess no consciousness of itself and if its consciousness is not to have the effect of relating him to his fellows ? In human beings endowed with the type of consciousness we know such a thing seems frankly impossible.

Indeed, so it is. Fascist philosophy deliberately moves on to other planes of consciousness. Their nature is suggested by the two terms : Vitalism and Totalitarianism. As a biocentric philosophy Vitalism derives from Nietzsche, Totalitarianism from Hegel. But both terms are intended to convey here vastly more than mere systems of thought. They point to definite modes of existence. The Vitalist philosophy of Nietzsche has been carried by Ludwig Klages to an appalling extreme. It is usually referred to as the Body-Soul theory of consciousness. Hegel's philosophy of the Absolute Mind has been used in an equally extreme manner by Spann. It is known as the Totalitarian philosophy, sometimes also referred to by the wider term Universalism. It is in some ways an analogy to Hegel's theory of the Mind Objective, but with Totality instead of the Mind as the central principle.

As social philosophies Vitalism and Totalitarianism define different, or, rather, opposite, types of human existence. Vitalism represents the animal plane of a darker and more material consciousness ; Totalitarianism implies a vaguer, more shadowy and hollow consciousness. The substance of Vital consciousness is curiously enough called the " Soul " (a term introduced by Klages) ; that of Totalitarianism, the Mind. As a rule Fascist thought moves to and fro between the two. It is in the terms of the struggle of these two concepts that the partial insights and the fatal contradictions of Fascist philosophy can best be understood.

IV. "SOUL" *VERSUS* MIND

Let us begin by a broad contrast.

The first type of consciousness is the " Soul " ; it belongs to the plane of vegetative or animal life. There is no Ego. No movement towards self-realisation emerges because there is no self. The tide of consciousness does not reach out towards the faculty of intelligence ; its climax is in ecstasy. No vapour of the Mind hovers over the surface of the Soul and drives the wedge of the Will into the

tissue of animal instinct. Neither power nor value have
crystallised in the day-dream of tribal existence. Life is
immediate, like touch :

> *Touch comes when the white mind sleeps*
> *and only then.*

> .   .   .   .   .   .

> *Personalities exist apart ;*
> *and personal intimacy has no heart.*
> *Touch is of the blood*
> *uncontaminated, the unmental flood.*[1]

Whether it is the rule of womanhood or that of manhood
is doubtful ; in either case it is the communities of one sex
alone which determine the flow of life whether in the
clubs of the young men, or in matriarchal " sororities."
The urge of sex runs like a thin thread through the rich
flux of homoerotic emotionalism. Blood and soil are the
metaphysical nourishment of this almost corporeal body-
soul, which still adheres to the womb of nature. Such is
the structure of consciousness in undiluted Vitalism.

The alternative type of consciousness is as far removed
from this as can be imagined. The Mind is the chief actor in
producing that other plane of existence in which there
is society which is not personal relationship. Society
which is the realm of Totality has not persons for its units.
The Political, the Economic, the Cultural, the Artistic,
the Religious, etc., are the units ; persons are not related
to one another except through the medium of that sphere
of Totality which comprises them both. If they exchange
their goods they are fulfilling an adjustment Totality, i.e.
the Whole ; if they co-operate in producing them, they are
relating themselves not to one another, but to the product.
Nothing personal has here substance unless it be objectified,
i.e. has become impersonal. Even friendship is not an immediate relationship of two persons, but a relation of both
to their common Friendship. What the individual person

---

[1] D. H. Lawrence, *Pansies.*

is supposed to contain as a subjective experience in himself, he thus encounters as colourless semi-translucent objectivity outside himself. Society is a vast mechanism of intangible entities, of Mind-stuff; the substance of personal existence is merely the shadow of a shadow. We are in a world of spectres in which everything seems to possess life except human beings.

The details of this broad contrast are more or less arbitrary, each of the opposites being the compound of the spirit of a whole school of thought. Yet the values and methods presented in them ultimately derive from Nietzsche and Hegel respectively. They are biocentric in the system referred to in the first picture, i.e. survivalist, amoral, pragmatist, mythological, orgiastic, æsthetic, instinctive, irrational, bellicose, or apathetic; logocentric in the second picture, i.e. the values and ideas are related and graded, hierarchic, orientated on reason, a realm of the objective existence of the Mind and Spirit.

Both Nietzsche and Hegel were thinkers of great intellectual passion. But their present embodiments, though inferior in stature, surpass them by much in the capacity for a one-sided line of thought. Klages is Nietzsche without the Superman. Spann is Hegel shorn of his dialectic. Both omissions are so vital that they suggest a caricature rather than a portrait. But as with Klages so with Spann the change serves only to increase the reactionary effect. Nietzsche rid of anarchist-individualism; Hegel deprived of revolutionary dynamics; the one reduced to an exalted Animalism, the other to a static Totalitarianism: obviously the change enhances greatly the methodical usefulness of their systems from the point of view of Fascist philosophy.

V. SPANN, HEGEL, AND MARX

Spann's method in using Hegel's concept of the Mind Objective without his dialectic tends to produce a new kind of metaphysical justification of Capitalism.

This can be readily seen when contrasted to Marx's criticism of Capitalist society.

Marx starts from primitive Communism as the original state of mankind. Human relationships in daily life are here immediate, direct, personal.

In a developed market-society distribution of labour intervenes. Human relationships become indirect ; instead of immediate co-operation there is indirect co-operation by the medium of the exchange of commodities. The reality of the relationships persists ; the producers continue to produce for one another. But this relationship is now hidden behind the exchange of goods ; it is impersonal : it expresses itself in the objective guise of the exchange value of commodities ; it is objective, thing-like. Commodities, on the other hand, take on a semblance of life. They follow their own laws ; rush in and out of the market ; change places ; seem to be masters of their own destiny. We are in a spectral world, but in a world in which *spectres are real*. For the pseudo-life of the commodity, the objective character of exchange value, are *not* illusion. The same holds true of other " objectifications " like the value of money, Capital, Labour, the State. They are the reality of a condition of affairs in which man has been estranged from himself. Part of his self is embodied in these commodities which now possess a strange self-hood of their own. The same holds true of all social phenomena in Capitalism, whether it be the State, Law, Labour, Capital, or Religion.

But the true nature of man rebels against Capitalism. Human relationships are the reality of society. In spite of the division of labour they must be immediate, i.e. personal. The means of production must be controlled by the community. Then human society will be real, for it will be humane : a relationship of persons.

In Spann's philosophy it is precisely the self-estranged condition of man which is established as the reality of society. Thus pseudo-reality is justified and perpetuated. Social phenomena are universally represented as thinglike :

yet, it is denied that there is self-estrangement. Not
only the State, Law, the Family, Custom, and the like
are " objectifications," as with Hegel, but so is every kind
of social group function and contact, including economic
and private life. This leaves no foothold for the individual ;
man is entrapped in his condition of self-estrangement.
Capitalism is not only right, it is also eternal.

The anti-individualist implications of this position go
far beyond Hegel. The reason for this is easily found. His
apologia for State-Absolutism and his glorification of the
semi-feudal Prussian State are restricted, after all, to the
sphere of political ethics ; they do not affect the person.
He proclaimed the State, not society, as " the Divine Idea
as it exists on Earth." But the State is itself, for Hegel,
a person, and as such can never entirely rid itself of the
metaphysical substance of freedom—self-realisation. In
order to eliminate the concept of freedom from man's
world altogether, society—not the State—must be made
supreme. In fact this is precisely the point of difference
between Spann and Hegel. Spann relegates the State
to a most modest position in his system (which, incidentally,
is in accordance with medieval organic conceptions),
and reserves Totality to society as a whole. By this subtle
move he eliminates the very possibility of freedom. For
even a slave-state is a State, and thus can become free.
But a slave-society which was so perfectly organised that
it could exist without the coercive power of the State could
never become free ; it would lack the very machinery of
self-emancipation. Thus, in spite of the use of the Hegelian
method, the world of man in its totality is not a person ;
it is a helpless body devoid of consciousness. There is no
freedom and there is no change. It may be doubted whether
a more complete absence of self-determination in society
was ever conceived.

VI. KLAGES, NIETZSCHE, AND MARX

If the Mind Objective suggests a kind of consciousness in human individuals which does not link them up in personal relationships, Vitalism implies human beings with no rational consciousness whatever.

It was the philosophy of Ludwig Klages which presented the lure of this startling line of thought to the younger generation in Germany.

Klages derives his thought from Nietzsche. But of the two different visions present in Nietzsche's mind, he follows up only one ; and with the utmost consistency. Nietzsche had, if unconsciously, divided his allegiance between the Superman and the Blond Beast ; Klages decided for the latter. He sums up both the greatness and the limitations of his master thus : " Nietzsche was the philosopher of the Orgiastic ; the rest was no good." The " rest " means Zarathustra, Titanic Individualism, the Superman.

Klages is appalled at Nietzsche's inconsistency. He rails against Christianity—this feeble-nerved, vile, and cowardly religion of slaves in rebellion against the laws of Nature and Life, and yet refuses to comply with these laws himself, fatuously pursuing the phantom of some " higher " and " nobler " form of existence. Nietzsche, for all his passionate aversion to Christianity, Klages suspects, never quite overcame the Christian superstition that animal life was not enough. His philosophy of Natural Values is contaminated by spiritual elements. Klages made it the task of his life to decontaminate it.

He deduced from Nietzsche's orgiastic line of thought an anthropology comprising a theory of consciousness of human character, prehistoric culture, and mythology. J. J. Bachofen's antithesis between the chthonic and the solar principles in prehistoric culture inspires much of this work.

The core of Klages's anthropology is between the *Body and the " Soul "* on the one hand, the *Mind* on the other.

Body and "Soul" belong together; for the "Soul" signified with Klages not *anima*, but *animus* : the physiological companion of the Body. The Mind stands apart; it is the principle of consciousness. It is an inimical irruption into the Body-Soul world ; in fact, a disease. Before this fateful intrusion occurred man remained in animal harmony with his environment, a life-pervaded part of Nature. With its occurrence, consciousness starts. The Ego emerges. The " Soul " is gripped by the Mind, becomes a person—a form of parasitism on Life in which the " Soul " is reduced to a mere satellite of the Ego. But the main form in which the Mind takes hold of Life is the Will ; for domination is inherent in the Mind ; it is the source of all Will to Power. The urge of animal instinct is not purposive ; it is more akin to the forces at work in parturition : like the ἀνανκή of the Greeks. Conscience and ethics are the symptoms of a Mind-process of which Christianity is the most pernicious form. That which it calls the Spirit is poison to the " Soul " ; it is Will to Power bent on the destruction of life. When it has succeeded, the end of mankind will have come.

For Klages, psychology is emphatically not a theory of consciousness. Life is unconscious. He distinguishes six fundamental concepts in psychology ; only two of which are conscious. The Body finds expression in the process of sensation and the impulse to movement ; the " Soul," in the process of contemplation and in the impulse to form (i.e. the magical or mechanical realisation of images) ; the Mind, in the act of apprehension and the act of volition. The first four relating to the Body and " Soul " can take place without consciousness ; they are " genuine " processes which in their totality constitute animal and human vitality. Apprehension and Will are conscious ; they are the product of that extraneous and life-destroying principle, the Mind.

This is a far cry from Nietzsche's voluntarism. According to Nietzsche volition is a natural function of life ; the Will to Power, the very embodiment of vitality. With Klages, the Will is a product of the Mind ; but the Mind is not a genuine part of vitality, it is the parent of that deadliest of all parasites of life, the Spirit which Nietzsche himself denounced in Christianity as the enemy.

Here, then, is the Source of all the inconsistencies in Nietzsche. In vain did he try to oppose the Will to Power to Christianity, for fundamentally they are akin. In affirming the Will to Power, Nietzsche unwittingly reaffirmed Christianity in disguise. In the ethics of Love, the danger is not in Love, but in the Ethics. Yet, are the ethics of Zarathustra no less ethics for being antichristian ? Personality is a parasite of Life, whether it is the personality of man or the Superman. Thus a mistaken psychology leads from contradiction to contradiction. For either we must accept Will as a natural expression of vitality—and then we must affirm what Nietzsche refuses to affirm, moral conscience and ethics—or we must deny, like Klages, that the Will and the Mind are natural to man, and then we can consistently refuse, as he does, to submit to domination of the Christian " Spirit " of Love over life. Fundamentally it is the choice between two concepts of man : man endowed with consciousness and man devoid of it. The position of Vitalism cannot be doubtful : natural man and natural society do not involve the individual consciousness. The reality of man lies in his capacity not to be a person.[1]

Two theories of community can be said to be in accordance with Vitalism. The one is based on Karl Schmitt's " Enmity " principle : Politics, according to him, is a category based on the phenomenon of enmity. The State being the foremost institution of a political kind, its precondition is the acknowledged necessity of the physical destruction of the enemy. The State is thus synonymous with an instrument of armed struggle. It exists only in so far as this is its hypothetical task. A world-State is a

---

[1] The formation of images by the still uncorrupted " Soul " is a central part of this anthropology. It is part of a theory of the Eros which is presented as an emotional ecstasy of a universal and essentially non-possessive nature, only superficially related to sexuality.

contradiction in terms, for such a State could not be at war for lack of an enemy. Ethical or economic alternatives to war are conceptually excluded from politics.

Schmitt's theory of politics fits in well with the Tribalism inherent in the social approach of the Vitalist.[1] It is a typical product of that *morale close* which Bergson has shown to be the expression of the instinctive tribal morality of fear. The counterpart to it is the *morale ouverte* of Christianity.

But the enmity theory of politics does not account for the undoubtedly existing content inside human community. Even though the killing of non-nationals be the logical justification of the national State it cannot be denied that there are also elements of harmony in community. Hans Prinzhorn, Klages's chief disciple, explains this phenomenon thus : The animal instincts of man refer us to an order of things in which perfect harmony reigns. Every animal is certain to end in the belly of another animal. This is the existential background to that pervading feeling of complete assurance which is a feature of all animal life in its natural environment. The principle of a " fixed sequence of devouring " together with lack of consciousness are the natural preconditions of that state of bliss which is associated with the memory of original community.

This theorem of the nature of human community suggests that Klages was not unsuccessful in his efforts to disinfect Nietzsche of his alleged Christianism. Eventually, he removed from Nietzsche every vestige of Individualism. The vast influence of Nietzsche on modern National-Socialism is due to a considerable extent to the conviction induced by Klages's life work that Nietzsche's Vitalism can be—logically, must be—detached from Individualism. Thus it can serve as the other alternative to a society which is not a relationship of persons.

The rediscovery of Bachofen by Klages deserves some notice. It is always a suggestive fact when a line of thought

---

[1] We do not wish to imply that Karl Schmitt himself belongs to the Vitalist school.

unconsciously takes off at a point that proves to be a cross-road.

Bachofen's work on matriarchy was, apart from Morgan, the main source of the Marxian vision of primitive society. Marx and Engels might have been as much fascinated as Klages himself by its poetic emphasis on the alleged unity of human existence in prehistoric times. But their impulses lie in opposite directions. Nietzsche's Dionysian principle and Klages's Body-Soul represent a move backwards to the blissful regions of undeveloped harmony. Marxism represents the move onward towards a higher replica of the primeval harmony of man with his environment. Thus, Socialism and Fascism appear for an instant on the same plane, representing alternative roads, as it were, to the conditions of closer human community. But the reactionary road is illusionist. Regression—but how far back ? German Nationalists proposed to go back beyond 1918. Reactionary romantics like Moeller van der Bruck made it 1789. Spann and the German Christians proclaimed a counter-Renaissance, thus extending the recession to half a millennium. The German Faith Movement realised that unless we put back the clock by full two thousand years there is neither safety nor permanence in reaction. It is Klages's achievement to have shown that the destruction of Christianity is not enough ; ten thousand years is nearer the mark !

The revolutionary solution was based on realities. The counter-revolutionary one leads to an endless regression.

Let us return to Vitalism and Totalitarianism. There is no need to regard them as logical alternatives. Yet their striking contrast proves that there is more than a superficial opposition between them ; it suggests some measure of polarity. Vitalism is preconscious and prehistoric ; Totalitarianism is post-conscious and post-historic. With the one, history has not yet started ; with the other, " it has been." With the one, there is no necessity of change ; with the other, there is no possibility of it. With the one, the " Soul " is the reality, the Mind is a fatal deviation ; with the other, the Mind is the reality, and it is the vestiges of the " Soul "

that cause the trouble. With the one, the person is not yet
born into society ; with the other, he has already been absorbed in it. With the one, there is no dialectic, because the
" Soul " is undialectical ; with the other, there is none because Capitalist society does not lead onward to a higher
personality, but back to the unconscious social organism.
The one flees from the present into an animal past ; the
other is an apotheosis of the inhuman present. Indeed, the
Vitalist's vision of a life sapped and destroyed by impersonal entities of the Mind-world is not entirely fictitious ;
it is that condition of things in a market-society which is
seen in Totalitarianism. But in a highly developed
society of the machine age there is no alternative to Capitalism but Socialism. Consistent Vitalism is the end of civilisation and culture of any kind whatsoever. Totalitarianism
thus signifies the perpetuation of the loss of freedom in self-
estrangement and unreality ; Vitalism, the return to the
fumbling blindness of the cave. If there is one thing which
could justify either of them, it is the appalling alternative
presented by the other.

VII. RACIALISM AND MYSTICISM

Actual Fascist thought is in continuous oscillation between
the two poles of Vitalism and Totalitarianism. Both succeed
in establishing that which is the main requirement of
Fascist philosophy—the concept of a human society that
would not be a relationship of persons. They attain this end
by presenting us with a vision of man's existence which, if
accepted, would force our consciousness into a different
mould from that which was created by the doctrine of the
Brotherhood of Man. Yet, the trend in Fascism is distinctly
towards Vitalism. It is in this tendency that the deepest
roots of its irreducible enmity to Christianity become
apparent.

It is in the German scenery that Fascism reveals its
Vitalist bent most consistently. Racialism and mysticism

are the corollaries of this development. They enable
Vitalism to meet two essential requirements of corporative
Capitalism which in itself it fails to satisfy, i.e. technological
rationality and nationalism.

It is a curious fact that both Vitalism and Totalitarianism
leave in their conceptual structure but scant room for
nationalism. Klages claims the discovery of anthropological
laws of the general validity ; Spann's method of the Mind
Objective cannot stop short of mankind. Indeed, both
Nietzsche and Hegel were emotionally anti-nationalist.

However, with the help of a fiction, the idea of the nation
can be easily fitted into the materialist pattern of Vitalism.
The concept of the race acts as a common denominator to
tribal reality and the artificiality of the modern nation.
National-Socialist philosophy is Vitalism using the race as a
substitute for the nation. The pivotal character of race
and nation in Fascist thought will emerge later on.

The need for rationality raises deeper issues. It is its reality,
not its concept alone, which must be secured if modern
machinery is to be run in corporative Capitalism. In producers of all grades there must be use of the intellect and the
Will directed towards achievement, i.e. the organised consciousness of the psychological Ego. But Vitalism is an
affirmation of the non-conscious functions of life ; it seeks
the reality of man in his capacity not to be a person ; and it
is precisely this principle which singles it out as the philosophy of Fascism. Yet how can rational-consciousness be
re-introduced without re-establishing the person ? And
how can the Ego emerge without a responding Thou ? The
need for rationality inseparable from technological civilisation endangers the whole fabric of Fascist philosophy.

The problem is obviously a religious one. Indeed, it is
the philosophic problem of Fascism in its religious form. It
is this : Is it possible to give a meaning to my life without
finding it ultimately in that of the other ?

The Fascist solution is in pseudo-Mysticism. True
Mysticism is a product and proof of faith ; not a substitute
for it. Without it Mysticism degenerates into a formal state

of a mind, which can be filled with almost any æsthetic or religious content. Such a Mysticism does not belong to the sphere of the Spirit but to that of the Soul. Whether it is the orgiastic Mysticism of paganism or the fashionable Mysticism of modern æstheticism, it is psychological, not spiritual. The use of this method in order to assert the reality of the Soul (or even the animal body) against the Spirit is pseudo-Mysticism. From the point of view of religion, which is inherently social, it is a negative phenomenon. For mysticism is the communion of God and Man ; thus it is also the separation of man from man by God. Mystic man has God at hand ; he is separated by Eternity from his fellow. Mystic experience encompasses the whole Universe except my neighbour ; the mystic Ego has no human Thou to correspond. Thus, in reaffirming medieval German mysticism, only this time as an alternative to faith, Fascism uses mysticism as an outlet for religious and æsthetic emotions, that is safe against any aberration into ethics. In the mystic state of mind the most exalted valuation of reason and will, a very deification of the faculties of the soul, is coexistent with a complete dissolution of personality itself. But the rationality and will thus mystified remain essentially unsocial. In Eckehart's Christian faith mysticism was the expression of the yearning of the medieval soul to continue in his seclusion in spite of a new world calling imperatively for contact and wider companionship. In National-Socialism it serves to build an artificial centre of rational consciousness for the individual without establishing him as a social unity. For in the mystic system of Eckehart God Himself is born in the human soul ; its laws govern God Himself—no stronger safeguard for the rationality of Nature is conceivable. Thus pseudo-Mysticism meets perfectly the requirements of a curiously circumspect irrationalism which combines extreme rationality in the relations of man to nature with a complete lack of rationality in the relations of man to man. Eventually the adoration of the blood and the race provides for this mystic vessel a content closely homogeneous to Vitalist philosophy which is transformed thus into a faith. It is National-Socialist religion in the making.

VIII. VITALISM VICTORIOUS

The tendency of National-Socialism to produce a political religion is manifest in Rosenberg's work. He calls this creating a mythus. His efforts mirror all the different aspects of Fascist thought with which our analysis has made us familiar : the double dependence upon Vitalism and Totalitarianism ; the adaptation of Vitalism to the needs of the machine age ; the trend towards vitalist supremacy ; and anti-individualism as the final test of adequacy.

Rosenberg tried to define his own philosophical position by rejecting both the systems of Klages and Spann. Yet there is an important difference to be noted : while, in spite of his criticism of Klages, Rosenberg remains himself deeply committed to Vitalism, his rejection of Spann cuts very much deeper.

Rosenberg turns sharply against Klages's " pessimistic outlook on civilisation." " The forces of pre-civilisation cannot be pressed into the service of super-civilisation," he comments. He is fully aware of the hopelessness of the attempt to run modern Capitalism on the basis of a human consciousness fashioned on the pattern of paleolithic man. Neo-Vitalism, he complains, has not improved on Nietzsche by proscribing also the Will to Power as Nietzsche also had done with the Gospel of Love. He is conscious of the debt of gratitude National-Socialist thought owes to Klages's discovery of the original unity of Body and Soul, and of that state of " complete assurance " in which the human animal enjoys a harmony untroubled by moral conscience. But, apart from Klages's reactionary prejudice against progress, Rosenberg protests against his obnoxious tendency to set up general laws of human development. This is entirely contrary to the basic tenets of racialist philosophy, which holds that nothing is good or bad, but race makes

NR

it so. Rosenberg proceeds to recast Klages's anthropology on racialist lines. According to him, both the harmony of the Body and Soul which Klages attributes to primitive man and the radiant qualities of the Mind and Spirit, which in other races are so destructive of that harmony, should be credited to the Nordics. For with them the higher forms of consciousness never degenerate into those pathological excretions of the Mind with which Christianity presents us. These are the outcome of the bad blood of the lower or mixed races such as inhabited Asia Minor, Syria, and the Mediterranean basin in historic times. The mind of the Nordic " is naturally Vitalist " ; his religion is Sun-worship—a sound persuasion which never falls a victim to Oriental magic, wizardry and superstition.

However, Rosenberg finds it difficult to suit Klages's anthropology to the needs of Aryan mythology. There is more than a suspicion that the idealised " Soul " of complete natural assurance and harmony was deduced by Klages from the religious, mythological, poetic, and archeological documents of the peoples of Asia Minor in the pre-Hellenic days, i.e. precisely that " Syrian " race and " Mediterranean medley " so despised by the anti-Semite and anti-Catholic ideology of Rosenberg. Also, Klages happened to believe in Bachofen's theorems on primitive matriarchy. Rosenberg believes in patriarchism for the Nordics ; he is adamant on this point.

Rosenberg's own philosophy is essentially. Vitalist. " Truth is that which the organic principle of life determines as such." Or : " The highest values in logic and science, in art and poetry, in morals and religion are but the different aspects of the organic truth of the race." His theoretical and practical aims are perhaps best summed up in the phrase that " all true civilisation is but the shaping and moulding of consciousness according to the vegetative and vital characteristics of the race." It is important to note that this concept of the race is not in itself necessarily a biological one. Although as a rule the race is identified with blood, it is just as often regarded as consisting of various different elements, of which ancestry is only one, even if the dominant. Thus, not the Body but the " Soul " is the bearer of the race—an extension of this concept which makes it very much easier to graft Nationalism on the race theory than would otherwise be the case.

But while Klages's system is banned only to triumph as the unconscious basis of Rosenberg's own philosophy, the latter's rejection of Spann is infinitely more downright. Rosenberg turns with hate and scorn against Universalism. The Old Testament and the Jewish mind, the New Testament and the Christian mind, the Roman Church and Marxian Socialism, Pacifism and Humanism, Liberalism and Democracy, Anarchism and Bolshevism are all in turn denounced as Universalist. This series includes almost everything the author despises from the Psalms to the Sermon on the Mount and the *Communist Manifesto*. An understanding of the precise meaning Rosenberg attaches to this term is almost indispensable to a full grasp of that passionate hostility to Christianity which is apparent in the Vitalist line of Fascist thought.

To start with, it has nothing in common with Spann's " Universalism," the general term by which the Vienna philosopher describes his own Totalitarian system. Universalism, in Spann's terminology, denotes a method of logical analysis inspired by the Aristotelian, " The whole is before the parts," or the Hegelian, " The truth is the whole." When Rosenberg describes this system as Universalist, he uses the term in an entirely different sense. Indeed, his meaning roughly corresponds to the accepted use of the term as current, e.g. with the Churches, when they denounce racialism for its implied denial of the Universalism inherent in their Christian mission. Negatively, Universalism is thus more or less synonymous with non-racialism. Its positive meaning, as deduced from the most extensive use Rosenberg makes of it in his *Mythus*, is that of an idea implying the concept of mankind. In other words, it is the claim of an idea to apply to mankind as a whole, i.e. to all individuals or groups of individuals constituting it. In fact it is the strict opposite of the racialist principle which makes the different value of different races axiomatic, and thus implicitly denies both the concept of the equality of individuals and of the unity of mankind alike. In this sense, Universalism and Individualism, far from being opposites, are correlative terms. Accordingly Rosenberg proclaims that the ultimate antagonism in philosophy is that between the racial-national principle on the one hand, the individualist-universalist principle on the other.

This explain Rosenberg's criticism of Spann's Totalitarian philosophy. He arraigns it as being " Individualist because it is Universalist." This may sound astonishing when we remember that Spann made anti-individualism the guiding principle of his system. However, Rosenberg rightly contends that no line of thought which refuses to accept the racial-national principle (as Spann does) can entirely escape the individualist implication of human equality. What Spann refutes is only the rationalist, materialist Individualism of the nineteenth century, not Individualism as such. Indeed, we used exactly the same argument ourselves when attempting to show that Spann's attack missed its object : the refutation of Christian Individualism.

A clear-cut anti-individualist philosophy must reject the concept of mankind in any but the barest zoological sense. Hence the vehemence with which Fascists of all shades inveigh against its very ideas. The racial-national principle is thus entrusted with the double function of resisting both the individualistic and the universalistic poles of the idea of humanity as a community of persons. The Fascist denial of Internationalism is but the counterpart of its denial of Democracy. Corporative Capitalism is both authoritarian and nationalist ; it asserts the inequality of individuals and the inequality of nations alike. "Internationalism and Democracy are inseparable," announced Hitler, in his still insufficiently noticed Düsseldorf speech on the foundations of National-Socialism.

The racial-national opposition to the individualist-universalist principle goes to the heart of the religious problem. The race or the nation is the supreme value in Fascism, whether National-Socialist or otherwise ; the individual and mankind are the two poles of the Christian ideology in the sphere of the human world as a whole. Accordingly the consciousness of the inevitability of the oncoming religious conflict was apparent with National-Socialism from the start. If the original programme of the party declared for positive Christianity, events have shown that this plank in its platform was not to be adhered to more strictly than other planks since entirely dropped. Hitler's own philosophy did not only include racialist convictions that were obviously contrary to Christianity, but also an endorsement of the principles of Machiavellian tactics, which allowed him to act upon those convictions, while continuing to do lip service to positive Christianity, without being seriously open to the charge of insincerity on this account. Indeed at a comparatively early date Gottfried Feder's comments on the party programme referred to the eventuality of the emergence of a new religion inside the orbit of the National-Socialist movement. This hint at a possible mental reservation with the authors of the programme was followed by what amounted to a declaration of war on " positive Christianity " in Rosenberg's *Mythus*. He ingeniously termed the Christianity of the Gospels " negative Christianity "—suggesting by this simple device to bridge the gulf which divides an undertaking to uphold Christianity from a policy directed towards its deliberate substitution by a new form of paganism. Rosenberg's appointment as " the Führer's Commissioner in matters relating to the philosophy of life " took place at a time when the *Mythus* had revealed to the whole of Germany the philosophic outlook of its author. It is doubtful whether the existing differences in tone and shade between the public expression of Hitler's and Rosenberg's views are not mainly accounted for by their respective positions and functions. The religious wars of the seventeenth century that turned Germany into a wilderness are, for Hitler, the true analogy to that cleavage of minds and spirits which is the feature of our time ; blood and nation, strife and survival are the ultimate realities with the one religion, while the other is their persistent denial in the name of the pernicious delusions of human equality and the unity of mankind. The Commissioner reiterates his conviction that the morbid strain of pacifism and humanitarianism engrained in the European mind is due to the Christian virus. He rightly traces the inveterate internationalism of Russian Communists to that spirit of infinite devotion to the service of mankind which is apparent both in Tolstoi's and Dostoevsky's poetic embodiments of the Christian inspiration, For the Socialist Russian Revolution in Russia is for him but a new eruption of that " spirit of the desert " which has sapped the lifeforce of the West during the course of its history : a remission into the spiritual plague that has stricken the heathen soul of Teuton Europe—Christianity.

The Churches, in bearing witness to Universalism, stand for the essence of their faith. But so do, also, the German Fascists in denying human equality to the last. The battle is engaged between the representatives of the religion which has discovered the human person and those who have made the determination to abolish the idea of the person the centre of their new religion.

IX. THE SOCIOLOGY OF FASCISM

Fascist philosophy is the self-portrait of Fascism. Its sociology is more in the nature of a photograph. The one presents it as it is mirrored in its own consciousness ; the other in objective light of history. How far do the two pictures correspond ?

If the philosophy of Fascism is an effort to create a vision of the human world in which society would not be a conscious relationship of persons, its sociology proves it to be an attempt to transform the structure of society in such a manner as to eliminate any tendency of its development towards Socialism. The pragmatic link between the two is found in the political field ; it lies in the necessity of the destruction of the institutions of Democracy. For, in the historical experience of the Continent, Democracy leads to Socialism ; thus if Socialism is not to be, Democracy must be abolished. Fascist anti-individualism is the rationalisation of this political conclusion. It is thus essential to Fascist philosophy to regard Individualism, Democracy, and Socialism as correlated ideas deriving from one and the same interpretation of the nature of man and society. We had no difficulty in identifying this interpretation as the Christian one.

However, in this order of things there is not only the sociological nature of the Fascist Movement, but also that of the Fascist System to be considered. Obviously Fascism must aim at more than the mere destruction of Democracy ; it must attempt to establish a structure of society which would eliminate the very possibility of its reversion to Democracy. But what is the precise nature of the tasks entailed in such an attempt? And why does it compel Fascism to continue in that attitude of radical anti-individualism which is the necessary ideology of its militant phase ? The answer entails at least a cursory view of the nature of the Corporative State.

The mutual incompatibility of Democracy and Capitalism is almost generally accepted to-day as the background of the social crisis of our time. Differences of opinion are confined to formulation and emphasis. Mussolini's *Dottrina* has it succinctly that Democracy is an anachronism, " for only an authoritative State can deal with the contradictions inherent in Capitalism." In his conviction the time of Democracy has passed, but Capitalism is only at the very beginning of its career. Hitler's Düsseldorf speech, to which we have already referred proclaims the utter incompatibility of the principle of democratic equality in politics and of the principle of the private property of the means of production in economic life to be the main cause of the present crisis; for "Democracy in politics and Communism in economics are based on analogous principles." Liberals of the Mises school urge that the interference with the price system practised by representative Democracy inevitably diminishes the sum total of goods produced ; Fascism is condoned as the safeguard of Liberal economics. It is the common conviction of "Interventionist" and of "Liberal" Fascists that Democracy leads to Socialism. Marxian Socialists may differ from them on the reasons but not on the fact that Capitalism and Democracy have become mutually incompatible ; and socialists of all creeds denounce the Fascist onslaught on Democracy as an attempt to save the present economic system by force.

Basically there are two solutions : the extension of the democratic principle from politics to economics, or the abolition of the Democratic " political sphere " altogether.

The extension of the democratic principle to economics implies the abolition of the private property of the means of production, and hence the disappearance of a separate autonomous economic sphere : the democratic political sphere becomes the whole of society. This, essentially is Socialism.

After abolition of the democratic political sphere only economic life remains ; Capitalism as organised in the different branches of industry becomes the whole of society. This is the Fascist solution.

Neither the one nor the other has yet been realised. Russian Socialism is still in the dictatorial phase, although the tendency towards Democracy has become clearly discernible. Fascism proceeds but reluctantly towards the setting up of the Corporative State ; both Hitler and Mussolini seem to think that a generation which has known Democracy cannot be trusted to be ripe for corporative citizenship.

Roughly the sociological content of Socialism is the fuller realisation of the dependence of the whole upon individual will and purpose—and a corresponding increase of responsibility of the individual for his share in the whole. The State and its organs work towards an institutional realisation of this end. Encouragement of the initiative of all producers, discussion of plans from every angle, comprehensive oversight of the process of industry and of the rôle of the individuals in it, functional and territorial representation, training for political and economic self-government, intensive Democracy in small circles, education for leadership, are the characteristics of a type of organisation which aims at making society an increasingly plastic medium of the conscious and immediate relationship of persons.

The sociological content of Fascism is a structural order of society which rules out the dependence of the whole on the conscious will and purpose of the individuals constituting it. If this is to be achieved, such a will and purpose must not come into being. The objection is not to the form of Democracy, but to its substance. Whether it takes the form of universal suffrage and parliamentary Democracy ; of organised public opinion based on Democracy in small groups ; of the free expression of thought and judgment in municipal and cultural bodies ; of religious and academic freedom guiding society through channels peculiar to this kind of influence; or any combination of these—in Fascism they must equally disappear. In this structural order human beings are considered as producers, and as producers alone. The different branches of industry are legally recognised as corporations, and endowed with the privilege to deal with the economic, financial, industrial, and social problems arising in their sphere ; they become the repositories of almost all the legislative, executive, and judicial powers which formerly pertained to the political State. The actual organisation of social life is built on a vocational basis. Representation is accorded to economic function ; it is technical and impersonal. Neither the ideas and values nor the numbers of the human beings involved find expression in it. Such a structural order cannot exist on the basis of human consciousness as it is known to us. The period of

transition to another type of consciousness must be necessarily long. Hitler measures its length in terms of generations. The Fascist Party and State work by all means towards an institutional realisation of this change. Unless
they succeed in achieving this end, an abrupt transition of
society to Socialism is almost inevitable.

A bare outline of the objective nature of Fascism thus
tends to support our interpretation of its philosophy. The
Fascist system has to carry on persistently the task begun by
the Fascist Movement : the destruction of the democratic
parties, organisations, and institutions in society. Fascism
must then proceed to attempt to change the nature of
human consciousness itself. The pragmatic reasons for its
clash with Christianity are due to this necessity. For a
Corporative State is a condition of things in which there is
no conscious will or purpose of the individual concerning
the community, nor a corresponding responsibility of the
individual for his share in it. But neither such a will not
such a responsibility can pass from our world altogether so
long as we continue to conceive of society as a relationship
of persons.

II

MORAL SANCTIONS AND THE SOCIAL FUNCTION OF RELIGION

by Bruno Meier

I. CALVINISTS, ANABAPTISTS, AND THE ASCETIC MOTIVE

OF ALL THE EXISTING Christian Churches the denominations derived from Calvinism have the deepest roots in modern society ; so we start our investigation with a discussion of their origins and their present function.

They came into existence in connection with the growth of capitalist society and consequently are best adapted to it. They alone brought out the real meaning of the Reformation by giving it a real and living application to contemporary life. The reformation of the Church had become necessary as a consequence of the breakdown of the traditional feudal social bonds at the end of the Middle Ages. There is no necessity to construct "economic" explanations of the religious crisis in the sixteenth century. Under the feudal system man was treated as a child, materially and spiritually. In his secular life he was under constant supervision, by his lord in the village, and by the guild in the town ; his work was ritualised by ancient traditions ; his leisure canalised into public feasts. His spiritual life lay under the direction of the priest, who took away all responsibility for moral decisions by his authoritative counsels and allayed the sense of sin through the confessional and absolution. The spiritual infancy corresponded exactly with the secular one. With the dissolution of the feudal system the secular infancy became impossible. Innumerable individuals became detached from the traditional bodies their ancestors had belonged to, and had to face life on their own account, deprived of the protection, as well as of the supervision, of any authoritative body. Thus the modern independent individual came into existence. Spiritual infancy could not exist together with secular adulthood. While belief in God remained unshaken for most people, men now stood face to face with God without any mediator. A thing unknown in any former period of history had come into existence—individual moral responsibility. This is the essential fact of modern spiritual life, of the ideological superstructure of modern society, as Marx would call it. Calvinism has given it its clearest expression, and therefore has sent its deepest roots into our modern world.

Moral independence of small groups was not entirely unknown to earlier centuries, but it was always confined to the ruling stratum of society. In order to make individuals of the ruling class capable of moral independence they had to undergo a special training. That is the meaning of the strict and far-reaching ritual of good manners in Confucianism, of the highly developed habits of self-control in late Greek and Roman Stoicism (Epicureanism was unacceptable to the governing Roman aristocracy because of its lack of such a training), that was also the aim of the ascetic discipline of Christian monasticism. Whatever the psychological foundations of these attitudes, training for moral independence was their function in social life. Calvinism has been described as asceticism in secular life. This is correct if the comparison is with the asceticism of the monastic orders. But it would be better to describe it as *mass asceticism* in opposition to the asceticism of selected groups which alone was known in former times. And again, it is not asceticism which is the main feature of Calvinism, for this is only the means of moral training. Ascetic training for moral independence, needed until then only by the ruling classes, became necessary for the masses with the break up of feudalism.

It is worth while to look once more at the formation of this mass asceticism. Seen from our times the formation of the new moral attitude seems almost providential. Without it capitalism could never have come into existence. The dissolution of feudalism, without its being replaced by capitalism, would have meant retrogression into barbarism. The more fortunate issue of events was, however, by no means due to prevision. As feudalism broke up, the corporative feeling towards one's fellows also dissolved, and submission to social superiors was undermined. But this breakdown of existing morals might just as well have led to a breakdown of all morality, and to a considerable extent this is, indeed, what it came to mean. The desire to get rid of all moral restrictions was prevalent in that section of society which backed the Renaissance movement, and from the middle of the sixteenth century materialism and so-called " libertinism " became the avowed belief of the leading European Courts. The Jesuits, with their lax moral doctrines, gave official justification for it as far as Catholic countries were concerned. Far from seeing in these movements the most important influence in the formation of the modern world, as the nineteenth century believed, we regard it as the mere resultant of the dissolution of feudal morality, which, had it not been checked, would have led to the dissolution of European civilisation. Ethical nihilism has always been characteristic of the extreme sections of society, of the richest and most powerful group on the one side, and of the *déclassés* on the other. The labouring masses, who have nothing to gain by the release of uncontrolled passions, as a rule hold fast to the old moral traditions even if they have become obsolete. This, too, was the case to a very large extent at the beginning of modern times. Their conservatism gave strength to the Catholic revival, but, as is common in turbulent situations, it turned into furious reaction which largely changed its real meaning. The most striking example of this reactionary fury is the " French " League. Later on, however, Catholicism returned to the calm conservatism characteristic of the modern Catholic political movement. The important fact, as far as the coming of capitalism is concerned, is that sixteenth-century society did not divide itself exclusively into the camps of Conservatives and Libertines. A third force interfered, born of the creative power of the lower aristocracy and the handicraftsmen ; this was the movement towards moral reform—in other words, the Reformation. This was neither a merely intellectual movement nor a movement for the defence of the economic interests of these two classes. It gathered only a minority out of both classes, and this minority was in the strongest opposition to the majority. It changed, however, the whole outlook of spiritual life. Christianity originally meant confidence in the approaching deliverance of believers by the Coming of the Messiah. In the time of the Fathers it meant salvation of the members of the Church by belief in the mysteries of the Trinity. In the Middle Ages it meant the salvation of the Catholic by the power of the Church to dissolve and to bind. Now, after the creation of the spirit of individual responsibility, it meant salvation of the believing individual, taking for his guidance the genuine observance of the Law of God. These four attitudes are entirely different, and not only the Marxist, but even the critical historian cannot admit the existence of one and the same Christian creed throughout the history of the Church. He is compelled to acknowledge, however, that there is one notion that has passed from the time of the Fathers into the modern Churches, and that is the idea of Original Sin. The transition from medieval Catholicism to modern Calvinism cannot be understood without it.

This study is not intended to give either a social or a psychological interpretation of these beliefs any more than it attempts to deal with the origin of Christianity itself. All we are concerned with is the indubitable fact that for the late Middle Ages the deep feeling of guilt pervading the

whole of society is already a matter of tradition. In medieval
Catholicism the terrors of conscience were allayed by the
rites of the confessional, by belief in the intervention of the
saints, and by the magical aspect of the whole religious life.
Manning, in a fine study of practical religion in Wyclif's
time, has shown that the average man in the fourteenth
century got practically no religious education at all, but
believed simply in the magical powers of the unintelligible
Latin formulæ of the Mass. When these magical beliefs
disappeared, the sense of guilt behind them showed itself
in all its strength. This alone could give to the new moral
attitude its imperative and absolute character. We see,
then, that the breakdown of feudalism exerted a triple
influence on spiritual life. It set the average individual
free from the feudal and corporative links, and consequently
created the necessity of a new mass morality based on individual moral responsibility. It broke the magical attitude
towards religion, and consequently opened the way to a
renewed sense of guilt. It eventually forced upon the lower
aristocracy and the handicraftsmen a difficult process of
adaptation to new conditions. Which of these effects still
remain in our times ? The ascetic attitude of the masses
clearly does not. It served as a means to enforce the new
moral attitude of individual responsibility, and declined gradually as soon as the latter had become habitual. But we
cannot be satisfied with the statement that the Reformation
created the morals of individual responsibility. It is the concrete meaning of this moral responsibility which matters.
This concrete meaning has, to-day, lost its religious basis,
although it still prevails. In order to understand it, we must
turn back once more to the early days of the Reformation.

II. LEGALISM AND A CORRUPT
SOCIAL ORDER

Quite early on, the Reformation split into the three
main sections of Lutherans, Calvinists, and Anabaptists. We

do not intend to deal at length with Lutheranism, which
is an adaptation of the Reformation to the needs of autocrats
ruling small States in the most backward parts of Germany
and Scandinavia. But the strife between the Calvinists and
Anabaptists is essential for the understanding of the Reformation, and of the real meaning of religion in modern
life. Hardly ever have more opposite ideas sprung from one
single movement. The Anabaptists originally firmly believed
in the immediate possibility of the Kingdom of God on earth ;
consequently they wanted to realise it. They identified
the Kingdom of God with the mode of life they believed
to have been that of the original Christian community,
and desired to introduce absolute brotherhood and the
community of goods as the basic rule of society. With the
Anabaptists, Christianity became a revolutionary creed.

The Anabaptists have several times been accused by eminent German theologians of Catholic propensities. The
charge in one sense is more justified than appears at first. The
Anabaptists had, in common with medieval Catholicism, the
belief in the possibility of living on earth in accordance
with the Law of God. Only, this belief is relative for Catholics, but absolute for Anabaptists, conservative for Catholics,
but revolutionary for Anabaptists. Thomas Aquinas, the
representative thinker of Catholicism in the feudal period,
had taught the identity of the existing forms of society
with the Law of God. He believed that all natural instincts
were good when satisfied in a reasonable manner, and that
sin was only an incidental, though unavoidable, deviation
of man from his real being. Man is essentially good. So
he is for the Anabaptists ; but according to them society as
a whole must be transformed in order to bring about
conformity between the social organisation and the moral
demands of human nature. The achievement of this
purpose would introduce the millennium, and mark the end
of the times. But the similarity of Catholic and Anabaptist
optimism is only apparent, for the Anabaptist Chiliastic belief
has beneath it a deep conviction of the profound corruption of the existing world which leaves no room at all

for a life according to the precepts of Christ. The will
to realise Christ's teachings on earth becomes revolutionary,
because a religion of love and brotherhood is impossible
if existing institutions continue. The social reason for the
impossibility is evident. It had by no means always been
impossible, but the dissolution of the corporate bonds of
feudal society, the introduction of ruthless competition
in economic life, the abandoning of customary law by the
despotic princes, made a Christian society impossible.
When all the elements of brotherhood are destroyed in
existing society, the will to live in a brotherly community
must take revolutionary forms.

This fact becomes evident even in the development of
Catholicism. It was not by chance that the Jesuits got hold
of the Catholic Church, and that all tendencies to apply
strictly the rigorous morality of the previous age (as was
the essential aim of Jansenism) were crushed. The Catholic
Church was determined to defend the existing religious
organisation and its dogma, but it could not defend the
vanishing moral code. It, too, had to renounce the idea
of brotherhood, and to cover this surrender under casuistry
and probabilism.

Calvinism was the one religious movement which
accepted frankly the new situation. Its theology starts from
the idea that the whole world is utterly corrupt. Everything
man does by his own strength is sin, and nothing but sin.
Nature, in itself, is sin, and original sin is identified with
human nature as a whole. Such remnants of natural
morals and natural reason as Adam had possessed before
the Fall were still to be found in human nature, but they
were like scattered sparks in the dark, unable to give any
effective light. The theory of predestination must be
understood in this context. Predestination itself was not
a new teaching introduced by Calvin. It was taught by
St. Thomas, and is in fact a direct consequence of belief
in the omnipotence of God. The new idea of Calvin is that
predestination has no connection with the merits of the
individual, for beings who are utterly corrupt cannot

merit anything. Moreover he believes in the damnation
of the great majority of men, an idea entirely unknown
to the mild creed of the high Middle Ages. Calvinist morals
are built on this belief in the profound corruption and
incorrigibility of the world. In Catholicism, as well
as among the Anabaptists, there is an intimate connection
between individual and political morals. Rules for a
society according to the Law of God are put forward first,
and the duties of the individual members of such a society
are derived from them. Calvinism, on the other hand,
disrupts individual morals and social ethics. Society in
itself is a Realm of Evil, as inevitably corrupt as anything
else which man may build up. The individual, therefore,
has to follow the precepts of the Scriptures without any
concern for the depravity of the community he lives in.
One possible outcome of such an attitude would be the
formation of a group of professional ascetics, but it is not
meant to have this consequence, for Calvinism does not
believe that any person can really attain sanctity. Again,
scriptural holiness is not to be confined to the few, but is
obligatory for all. But in an essentially depraved society
the morals of the individual cannot consist in anything but
the observance of strict, positive rules. These rules may be
very numerous and extremely rigorous ; they may cover
practically the whole of life, as in Puritan times they really
did, but they never can be a system of morals intended to
lay the foundation of a good society ; they always remain
a set of concrete, unconnected, positive rules which cannot
form a social ideal. Hence the stress laid by Calvinism
upon the decalogue, and upon the literal interpretation
of the Word of God.

The legalist side of Puritan morals is, however, not the
only one. It is, of course, the side nearest to the theological
dogma of Calvinism. Puritanism has been called "pre-
cisionism" on account of its legalist aspect. The morality of
corrupt individuals in a corrupt society cannot, as a matter
of fact, be anything but legalistic. But legalism, on the other
hand, was unable to give satisfaction to the Puritans. The

simple application of positive rules could not, and was not meant to, overcome the feeling of guilt. But this feeling of ineradicable guilt lay at the bottom of the legalist attitude, and at the same time drove the Puritan movement beyond it. Man was corrupt ; he could not merit his salvation, but he wanted certainty about God's mercy towards him, about his predestination to eternal life. This desire was a direct consequence of the basic attitude of Puritanism. No human being could stand the terrors of the conviction that he merited damnation without seeking the means to avoid it. The Puritans therefore strove to get proofs of their predestination to eternal life. This meant that they tried to overcome the sense of guilt by achieving holiness. A more paradoxical attitude can hardly be conceived. The very essence of the Calvinist creed was the negation of the possibility of holiness. Its legalist attitude was the consequence of this negation, and yet the Puritan saints tried to achieve holiness within the framework of this legalism by the strictest execution of every conceivable precept of the Law of God. It was a struggle for an ideal never to be reached.

An unbridgeable gulf lay between the belief in the corruption of human nature and the task of living a sinless life. Only the continual approach to, the continual struggle for, the ideal was possible, never its achievement.

We believe the essentials of all modern morals whatsoever to be hidden in this aspect of Puritanism. Therefore we must enter still further into its character. Even apart from the impossible moral idealism implied in Puritanism there is a deep contradiction at its root. If man is utterly corrupt, how can he possibly fulfil, even formally, the precepts of God ? Calvinist theologians may have replied that it was only a purely external obedience, but even external obedience asks for a psychological motive. If man does not consist of anything but concupiscence, if morals are really completely foreign to his soul, no moral attitude can ever be effective in this regard. The contradiction between the real importance of morals in Puritan life and the theory of the profound corruption of man is of enormous importance. This theory, however, gives expression to a reality, namely to *the reality of the struggle of man against man in a capitalist society.* It is the same fact which Hobbes has expressed in his famous sentence : " *Homo homini lupus.*" Hobbes's axiom would have been as meaningless in medieval society as Puritan morals and Calvinist dogma. It is perfectly understandable after the collapse of feudalism.

We have tried to give, in the briefest space, a sociological interpretation of the development of the moral and religious attitude of Calvinism. We now summarise again :

The dissolution of feudal society is the cause of the whole social and religious transformation.

It creates the necessity for individual responsibility.

It demands the ascetic training of the masses, a training which until then had been the privilege of only sections of the ruling class.

It strengthens the sense of guilt.

These tendencies are strongest among the handicraftsmen and lower aristocracy who cannot enjoy the new possibilities afforded by commercial capitalism in a life of moral freedom. They are tendencies in the direction of moral reform.

They are dictated by the fact that brotherly social life is no longer possible in society. Consequently their struggle for moral reform leads to legalism and to moral idealism.

As far as this tendency to moral reform touches the lowest strata of society, it takes the form of the revolutionary movements of the Anabaptists.

Where the resistance against the coming of capitalism is strong, Catholicism is maintained, but its former moral attitude becomes impossible.

III. THE PESSIMISTIC-IDEALISTIC ATTITUDE

This short sketch of the meaning of the Calvinist religious attitude is intended to show that many of the problems of Calvinism are identical with the problems of the individual in any modern capitalist society. The basic fact of modern life is the paradox that social life is bound to be the most direct expression of the egotistic instincts, where the advantage of the one is necessarily the damage of the other, while at the same time society not only needs strict legality, but even a continual strife for the moral and material progress of the community. This paradox is not only the paradox of all modern religions, it is also the basic problem of modern philosophy. It found its clearest expression in the system of Kant. The arguments of Kant have often been judged to be rather abstruse, and it is also true that the *Critique of Pure Reason* is built upon the axioms of the Newtonian system, which present science rejects. But it is not Kant's arguments which are important. The real meaning of Kant's philosophy cannot be grasped by considering the *Critique of Pure Reason* alone. The real object of Kant becomes evident only in opposing the *Critique of Practical Reason* to the *Critique of Pure Reason*. This opposition was intended by Kant, who strictly opposed the realm of norms to the realm of nature, the realm of morals to the realm of instincts. Nature acts by causes. As far as a man is a natural being he is subject to causality, i.e. to his inherited character and the external influences which work upon it. No free will is conceivable in the framework of causality, and consequently no moral action. Moral action takes place outside the realm of causality, and is not conceivable under its laws. It is, however, a fact, and takes its origin from the categorical imperative, i.e. from the innate principles of conscience. The proof of the morality of an act lies in the complete absence of any hedonistic motive behind it. Such complete absence of egotism, of course, cannot be found in

natural man. Therefore man's nature is the " radical evil."
This is the Puritan conception of Original Sin translated
into philosophical language. The moral rule which Kant
opposes to man's natural tendencies is purely formal. Acts
are immoral in so far as they are incompatible with the performance of similar acts by other individuals. The categorical imperative does not care whether society is organised
for the happiness, the æsthetic satisfaction, or any other concrete concerns of its citizens. It simply demands that no
action of any individual hampers equal actions of other
individuals. These actions may be egotistical and completely
devoid of utility or beauty, but as long as they do not in-
fringe on the rights of other individuals they are not
immoral.

Kant's morality is as legalistic as Puritanism. Kant certainly lays weight not upon the legality of acts, but on the
morality of motives ; but these motives are themselves
legalistic in so far as they are not concerned with the building up of a good society but exclusively with the keeping
of the formal rule of equality between individuals. But, as
in Puritanism, legalism in Kant is completed by moral
idealism. The strict rule of the categorical imperative not
being found in nature, the categorical imperative remains
fictitious. On the other hand the compulsion exerted by
conscience is an undeniable fact which has to be taken into
account. There is a gap between these two, the one denying
the other. It is the struggle between earthly happiness and
peace of the soul which Schiller, Kant's disciple, has sung
in touching verse. How, then, can the gap be bridged ? In
reality there is no possibility of doing so. We can strive
continuously to moralise our whole life, but we have to
acknowledge that the struggle between nature and the spirit
continues unabated. This continual struggle between concupiscence and the spirit is the main content of a true Puritan life. It is also the real meaning of Kant's ethics. This
struggle ought to be infinite and inextinguishable, but we
may hope that in an infinite development we shall more
and more approach the point where the gap between

instincts and moral law will be finally bridged and morality shall have become a motive in the realm of causality. The primary data of human life in Kant's conception remain, of course, unchanged by this hope. Here again, Kant's morals are identical with the morals of Puritanism. Puritanism also, and especially its sectarian developments, has cherished the belief in the moral improvement of humanity. But it is essential in Puritanism as well as in Kant that this belief has nothing to do with any change in the basic facts of human life. It is assumed that man is naturally driven towards evil, but that he will gradually overcome his instincts. This concept of the natural corruption of man is, however, linked up with one special structure of society— with a society of free competition. In a society really built upon corporate principles, where the interests of every individual are identical with the interests of the community to a very high degree, the strict antagonism between egotism and morality would no longer exist. (This identity, of course, must be a real one. To proclaim it only in words will not do. This is what Italian Fascism does, with its idle talk of the "corporative system.") No such change of society is envisaged either by Kant or by Puritanism. Therefore the only possible change is for them not a change in social structure, but a change in the souls of individuals.

It is difficult to decide whether Kant's attitude is religious in the ordinary acceptance of the term. It is clearly not so in the Puritan sense, for it ignores the direct influence of God on the fate of the individual. The idea of predestination, of course, is quite foreign to it. On the other hand, it acknowledges the necessity of belief in God and in eternal life as the basis of morals, though refusing to state anything concerning the objective reality of either. Kant was a deist, as were most leading scholars of the eighteenth century, but in Kant this religious attitude is characterised by one peculiarity—God, for him, is not so much a necessity in the natural as in the moral order of things. In this respect his God is nearer to the God of Pascal than may appear at first, for he, too, wants a "God sensible to the heart," or at least to the moral sense. But this transformation of God from a real almighty being to a mere hypothesis, necessary as a foundation for the moral sense, is only the prelude to the complete disappearance of belief in God. It would be easy to prove that this hypothetical idea of God underlies the most important systems of modern philosophy from Descartes and the English empiricists to Hegel. Even religious personalities of the high quality of Pascal could not conceive of God in any other way. They all know and feel that there must be a God if moral idealism is to be justified in a profoundly corrupt world. But they equally know that the very existence of such a corrupt world is inconceivable if such a God exists. They feel the contradiction between direct interference of God in human life by special predestination and moral idealism as an attitude based on belief in free will. There is no deep difference between moral idealism logically based on a purely hypothetical belief in God and moral idealism put forward as a belief in itself without any regard to metaphysical theories.

IV. POSITIVISM AND NON-RELIGIOUS MORALISM

Many attempts have been made to overcome the hybrid conception of this God who does not exist in nature but only in morals, and to replace it by an autonomous idea of secular moral idealism. The French Positivist school, whose ideas have been so important for the ideology of the Third Republic, is one of the best examples of the inevitable failure of such attempts. Comte started with the task of eliminating metaphysics from human thought, and ended by proclaiming his own system as a religion and introducing a Church organisation. In fact there is no essential difference between the strictly religious idealism of, for instance, the Society of Friends, the deist moralism of Kant, and the atheist idealism of the French Positivists and many similar schools in France and other countries. For the main fact is the paradoxical coexistence of the acceptance of the world driven exclusively by causality, which means driven by concupiscence in religious terminology, and the equal acceptance of moral ideals as a motive of one's own practical actions. Modern society, however, could not exist without this paradoxical coexistence of both. The pessimistic-idealistic attitude which originated in the Reformation as a spontaneous reaction of a special class of men in a particular situation has since become an indispensable element in the modern body politic and economic. Its elimination would mean an immediate breakdown of society. It stands in modern life as a given fact, inexplicable but necessary.

We used the term " pessimistic-idealistic attitude " ; we have to explain it still further, being convinced that the understanding of this attitude leads directly to an understanding of the position of religion in modern society. We shall best understand it if we hold in mind that it is profoundly individualistic. Society itself may have its laws and its necessities, which belong to the amoral realm of individual, class, and national egoisms ; but the individual in his own conduct, though he may take these laws into account, must, as far as his motives are concerned, ignore these amoral requirements. It is for him to act as if it were possible to moralise social life throughout. His acts are to be judged by standards of individual morality, for no other kind of morality exists. In reality, of course, his moral idealism will not change the laws of social life, and it would be insincere not to acknowledge this fact. But, knowing the inevitability of the eternal contradiction between his ideals and the realities of social life, he has to follow his ideals. He may know, for instance, that periodical use of violence is a necessity in present society, and that to renounce it under certain conditions may issue in serious damage to the causes he is most attached to, but non-violence is a rule of individual morals, and he has to live up to it under all circumstances. This spirit guides the Society of Friends, which is undoubtedly one of the bodies in which religious belief is most genuine to-day. It must to-day guide any community as far as its religious attitude is sincere. It ought to guide even Kantian moralists, but the sociologist may suggest that in the decisive moments of social life no philosophic conviction in the average man will prove sufficient to enforce such an attitude. Only religious belief will be strong enough to do so. Kantians, who used to read with enthusiasm Kant's *Treatise on Eternal Peace*, joined the army without reluctance when war broke out ; Quakers became conscientious objectors. (But such strength of religious convictions is exceptional in our times.) Moral idealism imposes itself categorically wherever sacrifices are demanded, but no identity of individual and social interests can be achieved. Consequently wherever such a situation arises some sort of religious attitude is bound to appear. In our day the toiling masses in Russia must build up, under enormous sacrifices, a modern industry whose fruits they themselves will probably never enjoy. Before this they had to undergo the tremendous hardships of a civil war with an uncertain issue. They believed, first of all, that the transitional periods of suffering would be short. Their attitude, therefore, was heroic and enthusiastic. But it would not be true to call their belief that the liquidation of a ruling class would bring them the highest possible degree of happiness a religious belief. Menshevik intellectuals, who for their part were not devoid of religious feelings, reproached the Bolsheviks with their complete lack of moral sense. They felt sure that no one ought to be allowed to give rein to violent instincts in order to bring about a social change, even if this outbreak of hatred and violent blood-lust were combined with the highest achievements of heroism and sacrifice. In November 1917, Menshevik moralism stood against the amoral political sense of Bolshevism. These proved to be incompatible. But later on, as the achievement of success receded into the background, Bolshevism itself entered a religious phase. Nowadays it has its God, its Holy Scriptures, its Church, its dogma, its inquisition, and its heretics.

Similar tendencies exist in Fascism. It asks for enormous

sacrifices, and it gives very small or practically no satisfaction to the masses, consequently it must build up an
idealistic morality. But religion in the old sense is not strong
enough, and not sufficiently in accord with the aims of
Fascism. So a pseudo-religious nationalistic enthusiasm,
mainly built on an adaptation of the aggressive group
instincts, has to take its place.

V. RELIGION AND THE SOCIALIST MOVEMENT

We can now get some idea of the importance of the
religious attitude in the Labour Movement. As far as democratic Socialism is concerned, its outlook in morals is
much the same as that held by various shades of pessimistic
idealism. As a matter of fact, it is irrelevant whether a
given moral attitude is combined with religious beliefs
or not. The moral attitude of democratic Socialism is the
same in most countries, and it is a minor concern whether
their moral idealism is built on a religious foundation or
a non-religious foundation. One could, of course, express
the same idea by stating that even the non-religious
Continental Labour movements are really religious in their
moral attitude.

But if we compare movements of a different moral
attitude the question of the rôle religion plays in them
becomes at once very important. The Russian movement
may be, and is in fact, as idealistic as the English one,
though the one is largely composed of "ethical," and even
religious, people while the other consists of staunch materialists. But it is a different sort of idealism. The Russian
idealism is much nearer to the attitude of the original
Anabaptists than is the morality of the English movement.
It is a very superficial and purely contingent fact that the
faith of the Russian movement has not taken the shape of a
religious eschatology, but of Marx-Leninism transformed

into a religious creed. Bolsheviks may argue that a religious attitude could not assist men to grapple realistically with the modern political world, as they claim Marx-Leninism does. We, on the contrary, believe that Lenin's practice was separated to a considerable degree from his own theoretical convictions. No doubt he was one of the most ingenious politicians of all times, and it seems to us that his special gift was a highly uncommon capacity for feeling the concrete needs of every situation. But never in history has religious enthusiasm as such hindered leaders from being excellent politicians. Marxism supplied Lenin rather with a creed that gave to all his actions the necessary firmness than with a guide for practical decisions. Just the moral attitude which Marxism required—this ineradicable belief in revolutionary action—was of the highest importance for the achievements of the Bolshevik Party. In this sense, but only in this sense, Sorel's theory of the " Social Myth " is right.

But one has to acknowledge that the rôle of any given religion in social life cannot be predicted. Religious belief in revolution was an important element in achieving it, but it is also powerful in conserving all its mistakes and in justifying its decadence.

In our times religious attitudes have a threefold function. The main body of modern religious life is pessimistic-idealistic. Its purpose is to maintain individual moral struggle without concern as to the corruption of the society in which it exists. Its second form, modern Catholicism, is conservative. It gives sanction to old traditional habits, largely sparing the individual any moral responsibility. Its third element is enthusiastic, and stands for different political and economic changes. Taking the concept of religion so broadly, we have to acknowledge that religion is still prevalent throughout the modern world. It has only loosened its connection with the metaphysical concepts of God and immortality. But that does not mean that its strength is diminishing. One must be blind to the signs of the times to deny that we are in the presence of a religious revival, though not in the

framework of the old denominations. This is but a consequence of the tremendous amount of dangers and sufferings
that humanity is undergoing to-day. To believe that the
spread of rationalistic science in itself leads to the disappearance of religious feelings and ideas, as the thinkers
of the Enlightenment pretended, and Bolsheviks, unaware
of their own mind, pretend to-day, is a gross misconception
of the real nature of the human soul.

Are we bound to conclude that we have only the choice
between different religious attitudes ? To a certain extent
no other conclusion is left. It is clear that any movement
which has to call for present sacrifices in order to secure
remote achievements must have one kind of idealism or
another. It is a very important question which sort of idealism
we want to prevail in our movement. But that is only one
side of the question.

We showed in our analysis how modern religion grew
out of the acceptance of the capitalistic system. An attitude
which sets individual moral effort against social conditions
is clearly incompatible with Socialism. But what about
an attitude which sets the enthusiasm of common revolutionary action against existing social evils ? Such an
attitude is surely preferable from the Socialist point of
view. But this fact is not sufficient, and the reason is
essential for the understanding of the rôle of religion in
modern life. Why were the original Anabaptists religious
enthusiasts and not simply revolutionary Socialists ? It
was because their desires were in evident contradiction
with the social realities of their time. In their religious
belief is hidden again the essential feature of the Reformation creeds—the setting of individual moral effort against
social facts. The Anabaptist was driven by his social ideal
to accept any suffering including death. He was constrained to confess his creed, to refuse any sort of compromise. He had to regulate his behaviour, not according to
expediency in the service of the political cause he served,
but according to the duty of uncompromising fidelity
to his truth. Enthusiasm may be a good thing—even a

necessity—in the day of decisive battle. On that day it may be indifferent which motive underlies it, but it is a very dangerous thing in the years of preparation and in the years of constructive effort. Anybody who knows the history of revolutionary movements is aware of the damage it ordinarily does at that time. It is indispensable as a psychological force, but it is quite unfit to be a guide to subsequent development.

This, of course, does not apply to modern religion alone. It is a general feature of religion as a whole, inseparable from its essential function in society. Religion steps in where knowlege and common sense prove to be insufficient to cope with life. It lays down irrational principles where rational principles will not do. In former periods, it had a wide field in relations of men with the forces of nature, but its influence in these matters has considerably narrowed since we know how to handle natural forces at large. It is still, in one form or another, inevitable in human life, to deal with such matters as death, the wide gap between effort and success, the inevitability of unrewarded sufferings, and with moral restraints. Even with the rapidly growing difficulties of social life it is likely to extend its influence in these matters still further. But the very fact that it appeals to irrational emotional beliefs makes it an inadequate means for rational handling of social matters. It is indispensable in society, but it is incalculable in its effects, and, consequently, unreliable as a means of action.

As a matter of fact, even men who believe themselves to be thoroughly irreligious are seldom found to be completely devoid of the sort of enthusiasm which is found in religion, whenever they undertake something grand and uncertain in its results. That applies to Socialism as well as to other lofty aims of mankind, and without it no great work could be done. Its favourable or detrimental influence upon the activity of men mainly depends on the degree in which it handicaps a clear and sober outlook on things. It always does so to a certain extent. The formalistic morality of pessimistic idealism forbids certain actions which may be unavoidable in order to secure victory. You then have either to renounce victory or to cope with your religious beliefs by one or another sort of casuistry. The Chiliastic enthusiasm of the Bolshevist religion does not draw formalistic boundary lines between acts allowed and forbidden, but takes their efficiency for the purpose of the "dictatorship of the proletariat" as a moral criterion. In this sense Bolshevism is less handicapped by formalism, without losing the emotional impetus proceeding from religious impulse, than is the more puritanical attitude of the Western Labour movements. This state of things has certainly contributed to its efficiency, but, unfortunately, what Bolshevism gains in ruthless unconcernedness it loses in clear insight. Moral restrictions in Western society are practically independent of all beliefs, and can go together with any appreciation of facts. They do not handicap thorough-going research into their real character. Bolshevism, on the other hand, has re-established a credo, a set of religious beliefs, which define appreciations of the real world on an emotional basis. Consequently it is unable to have an unbiased outlook on them, and its leaders over and over again run their heads against a wall as soon as facts do not fit into their dogma. There may really be something in human nature which makes man unable to balance sufficiently emotion and intellect.

III

SCIENCE, RELIGION, AND SOCIALISM

by Joseph Needham
Fellow of Caius College, Cambridge

I. INTRODUCTION

THE PROBLEM of the relationship between the traditional religion of the European West and the coming new world-order, as yet in its details uncertain, seems at first sight to have little to do with the preoccupations ·of the scientist. Whether the old forms of theology and liturgy disappear, whether the new social order is, or is not, more just than that which is breaking up, whether he has to live and work in the corporate or in the classless State, might seem to be matters of indifference to him. Nevertheless such a view would be remarkably superficial. The moment a scientific worker begins to reflect upon the nature and methods of his science, he will find himself involved with the history and philosophy of the subject, and hence with its relations to economic and intellectual historical factors. The moment he begins to reflect upon the ends to which others are putting the results of his work, he will find himself involved with the current economic and political questions of his time. Even some hypothetical scientist who aimed at the most complete neutrality with respect to the world in which he lived could not long escape the ultimate argument of economic forces, and would be induced to think over his relation to his fellows when he found himself unemployed after some sudden restriction of scientific effort.

In my previous contribution to this book of essays, a description was given of the beginnings of the scientific movement in the seventeenth century. Acquisition of personal wealth, the fundamental motive of capitalist enterprise, acted then, and for a long time afterwards, as the most powerful stimulus and support for scientific research. But the indiscriminate application of the scientific method to natural things bursts in the end these limitations. It shows us not only how to make textiles and cheese, but also how, if we will, a high degree of universal physical and mental well-being may be achieved. In so doing, it goes beyond the facts which any single group of men can lay hold of with the object of acquiring private riches. And it dictates to the scientific worker a new allegiance, a separation from his allies (or masters) of three centuries' standing.

II. THE POSITION OF THE SCIENTIFIC WORKER

The position of the scientific worker in the world of to-day is indeed a very difficult one. Owing to the gradual permeation of our entire civilisation by the practical results of scientific thought and invention, the scientific worker has in some measure succeeded to the semi-oracular tripod previously occupied by the religious thinker, whether enthusiastic saint or prudent ecclesiastic. That ancient separation of life into secular and sacred, which arose out of the acquiescence of the early Christians in their failure to transform the human society of their time into God's kingdom on earth, still reigns in our civilisation. Owing to the increasing intellectual difficulties which the ordinary man of our time feels with respect to the theology of the traditional form of Western European religion, he turns more and more to the scientific worker, expecting to hear from *him* sound doctrine about the beginning of the world, the duty of man, and

OR

the four last things. The scientific ascetic in the laboratory is the monk of to-day, and is tacitly regarded as such by the ordinary man. Conversely, the secular power, the medieval *imperium*, has been succeeded by the power of the owner—the owner of factories, the owner of newspapers and propaganda agencies, the owner of land.

In a new guise, then, the sacred and the secular are still at war. We may study their antagonism best by observing the fate of the concept of *Regnum Dei*, the Kingdom of God —always the surest indication of the relative power of priest and king. Roughly speaking there have been, in the history of the Christian Church, two separate doctrines about the Kingdom of God, two separate interpretations of the Kingdom-passages in the Gospels.[1] Firstly, there was the identification of the Kingdom with a purely spiritual mystical realm of beatitude, either to be reached after death by the faithful, or attainable here and now through the methods of prayer and ascetic technique, or existing in the future in Heaven after the last judgment. This has been perhaps the commonest theory. It has flourished whenever the secular was strong, since it discountenanced any attempt to improve the conditions of life on earth. As an instance, one could mention the mystical theology of Lutheranism, whose founder held the world to be utterly bad and irredeemable, a realm of Satan, from which the only escape was by means of religious exercises within the organised body of Christians.[2] But, secondly, in every age there have been those who have interpreted the Kingdom as a state of divine justice in the future and in the world, to be attained by unceasing effort on the part of men and women. This struggle was the outcome of their thirst for social justice, and gave meaning to all martyrdoms since the beginning of the world.

But if the scientific worker is the modern representative of the medieval cleric, he finds himself in a relatively much

---

[1] Cf. Robertson, A., *Regnum Dei*, London, 1901.
[2] *See* Pascal, R., *The Social Basis of the German Reformation : Martin Luther and His Times*, Watts, London, 1933.

worse position. Science in our time is not able to dictate its terms to capitalist " captains of industry " and the governing class in general ; on the contrary, it is in utter bondage, dependent upon their fitful and grudging support, split up itself by dangerous national boundaries and sovereignties. In such a case we should expect that many scientists would interpret the concept of the Kingdom (though none of them, of course, would dream of referring to it under that name) as something spiritual, something harmless, something incapable of any affront to a capitalist world.

This is exactly what we find. Nothing could better illustrate the point than the Huxley Memorial Lecture of A. V. Hill, and his subsequent controversy with J. B. S. Haldane —two of England's most distinguished biologists.[1] The discoveries of science, said Hill, whatever mistakes may be made, do gradually build up a structure which is approved by all sane men ; in the last three hundred years, the experimental method, which is universal, has produced results beyond all previous human achievements. This universality of its method and results gives science a unique place among the interests of mankind. But " if scientific people are to be accorded the privileges of immunity and tolerance by civilised societies, they must observe the rules." " Not meddling with morals or politics ; such, I would urge," he went on, " is the normal condition of tolerance and immunity for scientific pursuits in a civilised State." Nothing would be worse than that science should become involved with emotion, propaganda, or particular social and economic theories. In other words—" my kingdom is not of this world," must be taken as meaning not *in* this world either. Let unemployment, repression, class justice, national and imperial wars, poverty in the midst of plenty, etc., etc., continue and increase ; nothing is relevant to the scientific worker, provided only his immunity is granted—immunity

[1] Hill, A. V., Huxley Memorial Lecture, 1933 ; abridged version : " International Status and Obligations of Science," *Nature*, 1933, *132*, 952.

Hill, A. V., and Haldane, J. B. S., Correspondence, *Nature*, 1934, *133*, 65.

to pursue his abstract investigations in peace and quiet.
Here we substitute for the kingdom-concept of mysticism
a kingdom-concept of mathematics, equally sterile with
respect to human welfare, equally satisfactory to the powers
of this world.

" The best intellects and characters, not the worst," continued Hill, " are wanted for the moral teachers and political governors of mankind, but science should remain aloof
and detached, not from any sense of superiority, not from
any indifference to the common welfare, but as a condition
of complete intellectual honesty." Haldane was not slow
to point out that Hill's sterilisation of the scientific worker
as a social unit arose from the facile ascription to him of
no loyalties save those of his work. In so far as he is a citizen
as well as a scientist, he *must* meddle with morals and
politics. But Hill's point of view can be attacked more
severely from a deeper standpoint. Science does not exist
in a vacuum ; scientific discoveries are not made by an
inexplicable succession of demiurges sent to us by Heaven ;
science is, *de facto*, involved with " particular social and
economic theories," since it exists and has grown up in a
particular social and economic structure. Here there is no
space even to outline the marks which theoretical and
applied science bears revealing its historical position. I
merely wish to point out that it is not altogether surprising
that the ordinary man expects some lead from the scientific
worker in his capacity of citizen. In the Middle Ages,
life was ruled by theology, hence the socio-political
influence of the theologian ; to-day it is ruled by science,
hence the socio-political importance of the scientific
worker.

III. THE TREASON OF THE SCHOLARS

Hill's conception of the Kingdom as a realm of truth and
exact knowledge far removed from the affairs of human life
has been most clearly formulated in recent years by Julien

Benda, in his book, *La Trahison des Clercs*.[1] The betrayal of our generation by the clerks—that is to say, by the scientists and scholars which it has produced—he conceives to consist in the fact that whereas the medieval clerk was wholly devoted to the working out of the implications of a transcendent truth, the modern clerk has no similar task, and therefore engages without hesitation in the political struggles of the time. " Our century," says Benda, " will be called the century of the intellectual organisation of political hatreds. That will be one of its great claims to fame in the history of human ethics." But does not Benda misread the attitude of the medieval clerk ? Preoccupied by transcendent truths he might certainly be, but he was also very much concerned about economic relationships, and by virtue of that fact alone, he *was* politically minded in the modern sense of the words. For modern politics bear no relation to the politics of the medieval world. A thirteenth-century theologian might well leave on one side the quarrels of petty princes about territorial jurisdiction or feudal honours, but he, on his own assumptions, could not, and did not, leave on one side the detailed economics of the commerce and finance of the time. Benda fails to realise that in our days there is no longer any distinction between politics and economics. What are the violent nationalisms which he describes with such force but devices engineered and operated by interests which do not wish co-operation and friendship between the common peoples of the world ? What is modern patriotism but a word designed to out-shout the call to union of the *Communist Manifesto* ?

The medieval scene was supremely characterised by its subordination of other interests to religion. We may call it a period of religious genius, when all poetry, literature, learning, and music was co-opted into the service of this primary preoccupation of men. And since this was the case,

[1] Benda, J., *La Trahison des Clercs*, Grasset, Paris, 1927. The word clerk meant originally any man who could read, an attainment chiefly confined in the Middle Ages to ecclesiastics major and minor. Cf. the Book of Common Prayer : " the priest and clerks."

no human interests could be regarded as outside the sphere of theology, least of all the interests of the market-place, where every economic transaction was a possible opportunity for the snares of the devil, or, alternatively, could, by right arrangement, be turned into an exercise of spiritual profit. The life of man on earth was regarded not as an end in itself, but as the preparation for a fuller life in heaven —a fuller life which could not be entered into without the passport of justice, temperance, and piety. It was the province of theology, therefore, to regulate public economic affairs just as much as those of individual devotion. The most important means by which this was done were, firstly, the principle of the just price, and, secondly, the prohibition of usury. Every commodity had its just price, based on the cost of its production, and allowing to its producer a margin of profit sufficient for him to live in that degree of comfort which was considered appropriate to his class. It was unchristian to force prices up in a time of scarcity, and thus to take advantage of the necessity of others ; unchristian to allow prices to fall in time of glut, and so defraud honest merchants. Usury was prohibited alike by civil and canon law. And the names of many other long-obsolete misdemeanours, such as Regrating, Forestalling, and Engrossing, remain to show how the theologian guided medieval economic transactions.[1]

What would happen to our present social structure, we might ask, if by some miracle the medieval Church were to have full power again, and all usury were prohibited, the principle of the just price exacted, and the restriction of profits renewed ? We should, of course, observe a very spectacular collapse. And if we were to define a collectivist society as one which tended towards a maximum of social

[1] Regrating was the practice of buying goods in order to sell them again in the same market at a higher price, and without adding to their value. Forestalling was the purchase of goods on their way to the market, or immediately on their arrival, or before the market had properly opened, in order to get them more cheaply. Engrossing was the medieval counterpart of cornering—the buying up of the whole, or a large part, of the stock of a commodity in order to force up the price.

justice, we should have to call the Middle Ages collectivist. But obviously this form of society was fundamentally non-equalitarian ; each group of workers, ecclesiastical, military, or commercial, held a distinct place in a system of cells possessing different degrees of social prestige. And although it was true that each cell had definite duties towards the other cells, not excluding even the proletarian or peasant basement of cells, it was equally true that these obligations were frequently unfulfilled.

" The clerk can only be strong," says Benda, " if he is fully conscious of his nature and his function, and if he shows us that he is conscious of it—that is to say, if he declares to us that his kingdom is not of this world. This absence of practical value is precisely what gives greatness to his teaching. As for the prosperity of the kingdoms of this world, that belongs to the ethic of Cæsar, and not to his ethic. And with this position the clerk is crucified, but he has won the respect of men and they are haunted by his words." Yet if one of Julien Benda's medieval clerks were placed in our modern world, would he not denounce the fantastic system of economics under which we live ; would he not criticise the laws which cause food to be destroyed because people are too poor to buy it ? It is well that Benda castigates the modern clerk for lending the weapons of his intellect to nationalism, but there are other forces than nationalism at work in the political world of to-day. He can, of course, remain inactive, adopting the position of absolute neutrality laid down by Benda, and urged, as we have seen, by distinguished representatives of science, refusing to take any part in the political and social struggle, and finally perishing, like Archimedes, at his laboratory bench during the next war. But what differentiates the position of the modern from the medieval clerk is that, if he wished to be active, the latter had no choice in his allegiance, while the former has a choice, and must make it. Thus there are two ways open to the scientific worker at the present time. All the backward pull of respectability and tradition urges him to throw in his lot with the existing capitalist order, with its corollaries of nationalism, imperialism, militarism, and, ultimately, fascism. On the other hand, he can adopt the ideals of social justice and of the classless State : he can recognise that his own best interests lie with the triumph of the working class, the only class pledged to abolish classes ; in a word, he can think of the Kingdom *literally* and can work for its realisation. A kingdom not of this world, but in this world.

IV. THE CONCEPT OF THE KINGDOM

The concept of the Kingdom is of such importance for every aspect of the relations between Christianity and Communism that I must amplify a little what I said above about the forms which it has taken in Christian thought. We may divide the logical possibilities into four. The Kingdom of God has been thought to exist :

(1) Here and now ;
(2) Here but not now ;
(3) Not here but now ;
(4) Not here and not now.

Clearly the most fundamental distinction lies between those who have looked for the Kingdom on earth, whether now or in the future, and those who have interpreted it as meaning an essentially invisible and other-worldly State. The extremest division was between the second and third alternatives, for they had nothing in common.

The early Church, which for this purpose must be taken as meaning up to the end of the third century in the East and the end of the fourth in the West, was almost wholly devoted to the second of these interpretations. It was believed that the second coming of the Lord, which was thought to be imminent, would inaugurate a visible reign of complete righteousness, in which the saints would administer until the last judgment a society based on love

and justice. This doctrine, known to theologians as Millen-
arism, Chiliasm, or "realistic eschatology," found its
canonical authority largely in the Apocalypse of John,
and its intellectual defenders in such men as Justin,
Irenæus, and Tertullian. It was attacked, as time went on,
by three principal factors. Firstly, there was the necessity
of adapting the prophetic vision of a world made new to a
world in which the expected leader did not return. Secondly,
there was the influence of Hellenistic mysticism and allegori-
sation, which in the hands of Origen and other more thorough-going neo-Platonists, tended to emphasise the third
interpretation, i.e. that the Kingdom was a purely mystical
idea, existing now but elsewhere, wholly in the world
of the spirit. Thirdly, there was the increasing organisation
of the Church, and the acceptance of this by the secular
power in the time of Constantine ; this invited men to
diminish their ideals of love and justice, and to identify
the Kingdom with an actually existing society. This led
to the interpretation No. (1). The Kingdom was "here and
now," either in the form of the Eastern Empire or the
Latin Church, which after Augustine, and still officially
to this day, claimed to be itself the Kingdom. Lastly in
all the ages of Christianity there have been supporters
of the fourth and most utterly remote interpretation,
namely that the Kingdom means only the reign of God
after the last judgment.

Thus have decayed the first bright hopes and visions
of the Christians. In a most interesting passage, Robertson
reveals the class character of the opposition to Millen-
arism. "Intense as was the Christian instinct to which
millenniarism gave articulate form, it was in some respects
in latent antipathy to the ecclesiastical spirit, and waned
as that spirit gathered strength. Its rejection by rational
theology, and by the *trained theologians* who filled the more
important places in the Greek Churches in the third and
fourth centuries, had practically the effect of ranging the
clergy in opposition to it. In fact, millenniarism, by virtue
of its direct appeal to minds of crass simplicity, was a creed

for the lay-folk and the simpler sort. When religious interest was concentrated upon it, it would indirectly undermine the interest felt in doctrines requiring a skilled class to interpret them. The apocalyptic spirit is in fact closely akin to the spirit of unregulated prophesying, and the alliance has been apparent, not only in the second century, but in medieval and modern times as well." Crass simplicity —might we not almost say, inferior economic position? A skilled class—perhaps a privileged one too?

Of the hopes of the "simpler sort" we get a glimpse in that very interesting fragment of Papias, preserved by Irenæus[1] and believed to be an authentic saying of Christ himself—" The days will come when vines shall grow, each having ten thousand branches, and on each branch ten thousand twigs, and on each twig ten thousand shoots, and on each one of the shoots ten thousand clusters, and on every cluster ten thousand grapes, and every grape when pressed will give twenty-five firkins of wine. And when any one of the saints shall lay hold upon a cluster, another shall cry out, ' I am a better cluster ; take me ; bless the Lord through me.' And in like manner, that a grain of wheat will produce ten thousand stalks, and each stalk ten thousand ears . . ." and so forth. It has often been said that the Communism of the early Christians was purely one of distribution, not of production. Here, however, we have, as it were, a dream of the abundance of natural wealth latent in the world's productive forces, and to be unloosed by science so many centuries later. But the inevitable answering note is struck. Asceticism comes to the aid of the possessing classes, and when we turn to Augustine we find—" The opinion that the saints are to rise again would at least be tolerable if it were understood that they would enjoy spiritual delights from the presence of the Lord. We ourselves were formerly of this opinion. But when they say that those who then arise will spend their time in immoderate carnal feastings —in which the quantity of food and drink exceeds the

[1] See *Apocryphal New Testament*, ed. M. R. James, O.U.P., 1924, p. 36.

bounds not only of all moderation, but of all credibility—such things cannot possibly be believed except by carnal persons."

Whatever happened in later centuries, then, it is certain that the Christians of the primitive Church put their Kingdom on the earth and in the future. To this belief of "crass simplicity" let us return. We reach the paradox that Marx and Engels would have been more acceptable to the martyrs and the Fathers than the comfortable theologians contemporary with them, seeking to excuse and support the phenomena of class oppression. For the Kingdom of Marx and Engels was not of this world, but in this world.

Yet Benda goes on : " I regard as being able to say ' my kingdom is not of this world ' all those whose activities do not pursue practical ends—the artist, the metaphysician, the scientist in so far as he finds satisfaction in the exercise of his science and not in its results. Many will tell me that these are the true clerks, much more than the Christian, who only embraces the ideas of justice and love in order to win salvation." Here he adopts, as I think, a quite unjustifiable separation of these activities from practical affairs. In science, at any rate, the closest relations exist between practical technology and pure research. Biology would be in an etiolated condition if it were not bound up at every point with stockbreeding, agriculture, medicine, the fisheries, and sociology. With physics and chemistry the case is even more obvious. " Historically, the sciences grow out of practice, the production of ideas arises out of the production of things."[1] It is true that in science we must not set out, in general, to solve problems *because* the answer will afford us some new invention, but it is often the technical practice which suggests the problem. The great difference which we must recognise between medieval theology and modern art or science, is that an economic structure was directly and logically derivable

[1] Bukharin, N., *Theory and Practice from the Standpoint of Dialectical Materialism*, Kniga, London, 1931, p. 5.

from the former, and no clear guide can in such matters come from the latter. The former incorporated a system of ethics, in the form of moral theology. The latter does not.

Where, then, is the moral theology of to-day ? The only possible answer is that Communism provides the moral theology appropriate for our time. The fact that a doctrine of God is apparently[1] absent from it is relatively unimportant in this connection : what it does is to lay down the ideal rules for the relations between man and man—to affirm that the exploitation of one class by another is immoral, that national wars for markets are immoral, that the oppression of subject races is immoral, that the unequal distribution of goods, education, and leisure is immoral, that the private ownership of the means of production is immoral. It dares to take the " love of our neighbour " literally ; to ensure that by the abolition of privilege each single citizen shall have the fullest opportunities to live the good life in a community of free and equal colleagues. It continues and extends the historic work of Christianity for woman, setting her on a complete equality with man. Its concept of leadership is leadership from within, not from above.

Only because Christian theology three centuries ago gave up the attempt to apply a very similar ethic to human affairs has this state of things come about. The essential weakness of the modern clerk resides in the fact that vast progress in art or science is *theoretically* equally compatible with national capitalism or with international Communism. The economic doctrines which he must adopt are not a direct consequence of his own fundamental axioms, but embody themselves in a social theory external to his own work. Hence the dual character of the scientific worker, as scientist and as citizen. Hence the temptation

---

[1] I say " apparently " because (a) dialectical materialism may be compatible with a Spinozistic theology ; cf. *Moscow Dialogues*, p. 55 ; (b) the immanence of the Christian Godhead as Love is better provided for in Communism than in any other order of human relationships. Future Communist Clements of Alexandria will have the task of codifying the *præparatio evangelica* of the Christian centuries.

for him to shirk his public responsibilities and as " pure clerk " to speak no word save the exact results of his own researches.

We may remember the words said to have been prefixed by the mathematician, G. H. Hardy, to a book on pure mathematics : " This subject has no practical value—that is to say, it cannot be used to accentuate the present inequalities in the distribution of wealth, or to promote directly the destruction of human life."

V. PHILOSOPHY, HISTORY, SCIENCE, ART, AND RELIGION

From general philosophical and historical studies we can only claim one result that seems to us certain, namely that there is a kind of fundamental validity attaching to the five great realms of human experience, philosophy, history, science, art, and religion. It seems, too, that each of these have their enemies—those who are deeply concerned to deny their validity, or their right to exist, or their right to play the part which they do play in our civilisation or our individual lives. Let us consider some of these factors in relation to the main theme of this book.

VI. AGAINST PHILOSOPHY AND SCIENCE

Against philosophy come many opponents. Particularly the mathematical logicians point out to us that there are few, perhaps no, metaphysical propositions which can be translated into the exact language of mathematical logic. Philosophy on this view is an art, a sort of music gone wrong. Among these opponents, however, Marxist ethics and orthodox theology cannot be numbered. They, at least, cannot be accused of undervaluing philosophy.

Against science come many influences, some of which are equally opposed to philosophy. The whole anti-intellectualist movement, so protean in its manifestations in our time, acts in this direction. From the mystical point of view represented by D. H. Lawrence and his followers at one end to the folky-brutal atmosphere of Nazism at the other, we have a thoroughly anti-scientific front. For these minds, if so they can be called, scientific internationalism has gone far enough; the feeling for racial oneness must step in, and true patriots must think with their blood. Nothing could be more valuable for the armament manufacturers than these manifestations ; nothing could be more in line with the almost pre-feudal vestiges which have for centuries lingered on in the army-officer class. In this way we are witnessing at the present day a wholesale frustration of science.[1] To the capitalist, scientific research is useful, but only relatively in comparison with other and perhaps even cheaper ways of obtaining profits. It is only when these fail that the capitalist now needs the scientist. Again, the conditions of profit-making forbid the introduction of safety measures and the application of labour-saving devices which could greatly increase world-production while at the same time equalising leisure in the form of a five-hour day under a planned Socialist system. Or improved technical methods may be used for actually destroying a part of the produced material, such as coffee or rubber. Or the area of land sown may be compulsorily restricted. Perhaps worst of all is the continuing and increasing use of science in war preparations ; the development and application of the most diverse scientific researches to rendering the killing of individuals more effective, cheaper, and possible on a still larger scale than ever before. " It does not need much economic knowledge," writes Bernal,[2] " to see that a system of which the essential basis is production for profit, leads by its own impetus into the present highly unstable and dangerous economic and political situation, where plenty and poverty,

---

[1] *See* the book of essays, *The Frustration of Science*, by Sir Daniel Hall, J. D. Bernal, J. G. Growther, E. Charles, V. H. Mottram, P. Gorer, and B. Woolf ; Allen & Unwin, London, 1934.
[2] Bernal, J. D., " National Scientific Research," *Progress*, 1934, 2, 364.

the desire for peace and the preparation for war, exist side by side ; but it does require far more knowledge to see how an alternative system could be built up, and yet unless scientists are prepared to do this they must accept the present state of affairs and see the results of their own work inadequately utilised to-day and dangerously abused in the near future." Thus the figures of the annual Government grants speak for themselves. In 1933 the Medical Research Council received £139,000 and the Department for Scientific and Industrial Research received £443,838, while the Research grants for the Army, Navy, and Air Force together were £2,759,000, i.e. five times as much as the whole total for civil research.[1]

Another of the great influences which are working in our time against science is the outcome of modern psychology.[2] An argument nowadays need not be answered ; it is sufficient to trace it back to the previous psychological history, and hence the prejudices, of the person who propounds it. Some exponents of Marxism, with its insistence upon the class basis of science, are not free from this accusation, but here it is perfectly legitimate to apply the class theory of history to the history of science, and the results are frequently not unconvincing. Far less respectable is the Fascist struggle (especially in Germany) against " objective science," for the racial theory of history, on which this struggle is presumably based, is infinitely inferior to the class theory in point of intellectual power and verisimilitude.

VII. AGAINST ART AND HISTORY

Art does not pay. No further enemy is needed. History, as eminent capitalists have assured us, is bunk.

---

[1] Budget Estimates.
[2] Cf. Joad, C. E. M., *Guide to Modern Thought*, London, 1933 ; and *Under the Fifth Rib : An Autobiography*, London, 1932.

VIII. AGAINST RELIGION

Against religion come so many forces that it is almost impossible to count them. The general trend from religion to science which took place in the Hellenistic age and the late Roman Empire repeated itself again in our own Western European civilisation from the Renaissance onwards. Religion has had to face the great pretensions of the medieval secular power, the mechanical philosophies of the seventeenth century, the enlightened atheism of the eighteenth century, and the Victorian agnosticism of the last age. Bourgeois agnostics and proletarian atheists have attacked it from all sides. It is surprising that there is anything left of it. And few people seem even to know what it is. Thus an anonymous writer recently began an article on agnosticism with the words : " The essence of religion is faith, the ability to accept as a truth a hypothesis for which there is no positive evidence."[1] Or again, in *Moscow Dialogues*, Socratov says,[2] " We are rather at a loss to point to anything of a positive character in religion. If you can suggest anything positive, I shall be glad to hear it " ; and the bishop (very conveniently) replies, " Well, first of all, the Church has always stood, even in its darkest days, for law and order." The first of these writers was confusing, as is so common, theology with religion. Theology has to accept hypotheses for which there is no positive evidence, because in a system so unlikely as the universe, of which there is only one, no comparisons can be made by which to test the credibility of anything. This is no argument in favour of theology, which may or may not be a necessary evil, but on the other hand, it does not discredit religion. The second was erecting an episcopal man of straw in order to have the pleasure of hearing the opium merchant give himself away red-handed. But the statement is not historically true ; when Irenæus, Clement, and Tertullian

---

[1] *New Statesman*, 1934, *8*, 332 (15th Sept.).
[2] Hecker, J., *Moscow Dialogues*, Chapman & Hall, London, 1933, p. 191.

were alive, the Church was not on the side of law and order. Christians were able to imagine a better law and a juster order than the established system of the Roman Empire.[1]

The clearest understanding of religion has been given, in my opinion, by the work of Rudolf Otto,[2] a German theologian, who described it as the sense of the holy. In primitive communities we see this " numinous sense " applied to all kinds of worthless or even degrading objects and rites, but in the great religions of the world it forms the essential backbone of the experience of their participators. In Christianity, where the ethic of love found its greatest prophets, the numinous sense has become attached to the highest conception of the relations between man and man that we know. The Christian who becomes a Communist does so precisely because he sees no other body of people in the world of our time who are concerned to put Christ's commands into literal execution. If for 1,800 years the Church has tended to put allegorical constructions on the Gospels, we know that the Christians of the first two centuries did not do so.

That religion has been, and largely is, " the opium of the people " is plainly undeniable. Proletarian misery in this world has been constantly lightened by promises of comfort and blessedness in the world to come—an exhortation which comes well enough from the ecclesiastical ascetic who does not spare himself, but very ill from the employer of labour or the representative of the propertied classes. But the conclusion usually drawn, namely, that religion could have no place in a Socialist State, where no class-distinctions existed, does not seem to follow. Because religion has been used as a social opiate in the past, there seems no reason why this should be so in the future. " Religion would continue to

---

[1] On the Socialism of the Apostolic Fathers, see the essay of Charles Marson in the collective work by Tom Mann and others, *Vox Clamantium*, ed. Andrew Reid, Innes, London, 1894 ; and also his *God's Co-operative Society*, Longmans Green, London, 1914.

[2] *See especially* Otto, R., *The Idea of the Holy*, O.U.P., 1923.

exist," writes A. L. Rowse,[1] " in the Socialist community, but on its own strength. It would not have the bias of the State exerted in its favour, as it has had so strongly in England up to the present, and in greater or lesser degrees in all Western countries." It may be said that religion is " the protest of the oppressed creature,"[2] and that therefore when social oppression, in the form of the class-stratified society, is done away with, the private need for religion will vanish as well as the class which profited by it. This, however, is to forget what we could call " cosmic oppression," or creatureliness, the unescapable inclusion of man in space-time, subject to pain, sorrow, sadness, and death. Shall we substitute for the opium of religion the opium of science? It has always been the tacit conviction of the social reformer and the person occupied with the practical application of scientific knowledge that by man's own efforts, not merely minor evils, but the major evils of existence may be overcome. This is expressed in that great sentence: "Philosophers have talked about the universe enough ; the time has come to change it." But the problem of evil is not capable of so simple a resolution. So long as time continues, so long as change and decay are around us and in us, so long will sorrow and tragedy be with us. " Life is a sad composition," as Sir Thomas Browne said ; " we live with death and die not in a moment." Or, in the words of the *Contakion*, " For so thou didst ordain when thou createdst us, saying, ' Dust thou art, and unto dust shalt thou return ' ; wherefore all we who go down into the grave make our song unto thee, sighing and saying, Give rest, O Christ, to thy servants with thy saints, where sorrow and sighing are no more, neither pain, but life everlasting." The whole realm of thought and feeling embodied in these phrases is fundamentally natural and proper to man, and there is little to be gained by trying to replace it by a eupeptic opium, derived from too bright an estimate of the

---

[1] Rowse, A. L., *Politics and the Younger Generation*, Faber, London, 1931, p. 194.
[2] Marx, K., *Introduction to a Critique of Hegel's Philosophy of Law*.

possibilities of scientific knowledge. Driven out, it will return in the end with redoubled force.

Fundamentally natural and proper to man—the sense of the holy is as appropriate to him as the sense of beauty. I said just now that the moral theology of Communism lacked apparently a doctrine of God. If this should be so, it does not seriously affect the existence of the sense of the holy. For the theology of the Gospels was, after all, not very complicated—Jesus, as another of the essayists says, did not meet disease and hunger by persuading people that blessedness was already theirs if they would accept an intellectual dogmatic system, but by curing sickness and distributing bread. This was the practical aspect of his teaching about love. In the motives of atheist members of the Communist Party we detect that which is worthy of numinous respect, since they work to bring in the new world-order.

Those who deny the importance of the sense of the holy are in an analogous position to those who cannot appreciate music or painting. It is an attitude towards the universe, an attitude almost of respect, for which nothing can be substituted. " The problem of death," it has been said,[1] " is not a ' problem ' at all, it is due simply to the clash between an idealistic egoistic philosophy and the disappearance of the individual, not in the least to the fact of death." On this view, science reveals facts to us so clearly as to reconcile us to them. But no matter how much we know in the classless State about the biology of death, we shall still suffer when some fellow worker that we have loved is suddenly killed. The question then reduces itself to a matter of taste ; shall we bury him with coarse speed and a callous reference to the unimportance of the individual ? Or shall we remember, as we fulfil the rites of a liturgical requiem, that this is the common end of all the sons of men, and so unite ourselves with the blessed company of all faithful people, those who earnestly looked and worked in their generation for the coming of the Kingdom ?

[1] Pascal, R., *Outpost*, 1932, *1*, 70.

It is true indeed, as Merejkovski has said, that whether we believe in Christ or not, we must certainly suffer with him. And, indeed, it is my opinion that, if the ancient Christian modes of satisfying this numinous sense are discontinued (Eliot's " *vieilles usines desaffectués* ") other liturgical forms will have to be devised to play their part in attempting to express that which cannot be expressed. This we already see in such cases as the tomb of Lenin himself, and the Red Corners. It is absurd to say that " with the denial of an objective creator, Socialism forgets the problem of evil." In whatever society man arranges himself he must take up some attitude towards the universe, and, in this attitude, the sense of the holy must be an element.

IX. SCIENTIFIC OPIUM

Not to be awake to the iniquity of class oppression, then, is religious opium. Scientific opium would mean not being awake to the tragic side of life, to the numinous elements of the world and of human effort in the world, to the worship of a God. Scientific opium seems to have been made an integral part of orthodox Marxism, but for us the question is how far the contribution of England and the West of Europe to the socialisation of the world need be essentially irreligious. In this connection there are two considerations which seem relevant, but which do not appear to have been yet discussed. In the first place, is it not a mere historical coincidence that Marx himself and the early Marxists adopted *en bloc* the anthropological and psychological arguments against religion which were fashionable at the time ? And, if so, are not these arguments wholly insufficient ground for condemning one of the greatest forms of human experience ? The anthropological arguments all confuse origin with value, as if primitive barbarism were not in the end responsible for science, art, and literature just as much as for religion. To say that the concept of God is derived from, or modelled on, the relation of primitive exploiting lord to primitive exploited slave is to say nothing about the religious value of the concept in a society where exploitation has been abolished ; still less about religion itself as opposed to theology or philosophy. For religion does not know what God is ; it only knows Him to be worthy of worship—a God comprehended would be no God—and it does not know why the universe is as it is, but only that there is sacredness in it. No doubt an excess of mystical religion engenders an attitude of inactivity against the external world, but why have an *excess* of mystical religion ? Must we have prohibition in the classless State because some people drink too deeply to-day ? In the end, there is but one end, and Communism can overcome the last enemy no more than any other of man's devices. It is difficult, no doubt, to be both scientifically " proud " and religiously " humble," but the best things are often difficult.

In the second place, the Byzantine nature of Eastern Christianity is relevant. From the very beginning the Byzantine Church showed a speculative rather than a practical tendency.[1] The East enacted creeds, the West discipline. The first decree of an Eastern council was to determine the relations of the Godhead ; the first decree of the Bishop of Rome was to prohibit the marriage of the clergy. Eastern theology was rhetorical in form and based on philosophy ; Western theology was logical in form and based on law. The Byzantine divine succeeded to the place of the Greek sophist ; the Latin divine to the place of the Roman advocate. The Eastern Church, therefore, occupied with philosophy and theology, made little or no pretensions to control of economic affairs, no attempt to subordinate the secular power to itself in the interests of a particular theory as to how the mercantile life should be lived. The Patriarchs, chosen from a monastic order remarkable for its detachment from secular business, left all economic questions to the chamberlains and officials who thronged the imperial

---

[1] *See* Milman, H. H., *History of Latin Christianity*, Murray, London, 1867 ; and Stanley, A. P., *Lectures on the History of the Eastern Church*, Dent, Everyman edn.

Court. After the fall of Byzantium, this same tradition of complete other-worldliness transferred itself to the Church of Russia. The Russian Orthodox Church had no pope, no Hildebrand, to impose a theological system of economics on Russian society. It had no scholastic philosophers, no " medieval clerks " to dictate to kings and rulers what measures they should take to secure social justice. It had nothing corresponding to our seventeenth-century High Churchmen, or to our nineteenth-century Anglo-Catholics, reviving those traditions and reminding men of the ideals of a pre-capitalist age. When capitalism, in the time of Peter the Great, reached Russia, it found a perfectly virgin soil for its operations, and had no such uphill task as it found in the West. In three generations it enslaved a population which could make no appeal to any distinctively Christian social theories. Such an appeal would have been vain, for the Orthodox Church had no such theories, and had never developed the first beginnings of them. On the contrary, it had become completely identified with the process of exploitation of the Russian people. But the contrast between this situation and our own is remarkable. Why should not the contrast between the theological aspect of Russian Marxism and that of English Marxism be equally remarkable ?

X. "CHRISTIAN THEOLOGY THE GRANDMOTHER OF BOLSHEVISM"

Important for the decay of religion in our time is the general and increasing domination of the scientific mind, or, rather, of a popular version of the state of mind characteristic of the scientific worker. The constantly growing power over external nature leads to a tacit belief in the possibility of solving the problem of evil by what might almost be called a matter of engineering. The principle of abstraction leads to a weakening of that attention to the individual and the unique which must always be an integral part of the religious outlook. The principle of ethical neutrality leads to a general chaos in the traditional systems of morals, and hence to decay in the religious emotion formerly attached to the performance of certain actions. The emphasis laid by the scientific mentality on the quantitative aspects of nature runs diametrically counter to the emphasis which religion would like to lay on the other aspects of the universe. And, above all, in actively interfering with the external world, in persistently probing its darkest corners, science destroys that feeling of creaturely dependence upon, and intimate relation to, a transcendent and supernal Being, which we must admit as one of the profoundest characteristics of the religious spirit. In the modern world, Epicurus and Lucretius have come into their own.

But here we find, paradoxically enough, that Communism and the Christian religion are again on the same side. If these effects of the domination of science were to operate alone, we should have a truly soulless society, such as is depicted by Bertrand Russell in *The Scientific Outlook*,[1] and by Aldous Huxley, satirically, in *Brave New World*.[2] This is what we shall certainly get if capitalism can establish itself anew and overcome the forces of fanatical nationalism which threaten to disrupt it. For capitalism has a fundamentally cheap estimate of the value of human life ; mine disasters and wars alike are but passing incidents in a society where the only principle recognised is that might is right. Communism and Christianity, on the contrary, estimate life highly. Ultimately the distinction here resolves itself into what kind of human society we wish to aim at, and the choice may be, at bottom, æsthetic. The logical continuation of the capitalist order would be the tightening and stabilisation of class-stratification, which seems to be the essential mission of Fascism. This could then, in time, be further fixed as biological engineering becomes more powerful, either by mating-restrictions, or by the quicker method plausibly suggested by Huxley, of producing large

[1] Allen & Unwin, London, 1931.
[2] Chatto & Windus, London, 1932.

numbers of low-grade workers of precisely identical genetic constitution from one egg. Here the biology is perfectly accurate ; in the case of armadillos, sea-urchins, and parasitic insects, we already know the process well, and the difficulties for the mammalian egg are almost purely technical. Successful experiments are even now being made on the *in vitro* cultivation of small mammals. In such a civilisation, then, where an abundance of docile workers of very limited intelligence was available, the class stratification would be absolute, and the governing class alone would be capable of living anything approaching a full life.[1] But the important point is that biological engineering would have done what mechanical engineering had failed to do, and flesh and blood would have been adapted to machinery rather than machinery to flesh and blood. Nevertheless the converse process is equally possible, i.e. a continually increasing automatism of machine operations, and hence an increasing liberation of man from the necessity of productive labour. With the increase of leisure would come an enormous increase in the beneficial and pleasurable occupations available for the workers. This is what is meant by the readiness to sacrifice the bourgeois liberty of to-day for the much greater liberty of the classless State. And these two alternatives are even now offering themselves to us, with capitalism on the one side and Christianity and Communism together on the other. It is a pity that Spengler's aphorism is not more widely known : " Christian theology is the grandmother of Bolshevism."

This train of thought leads us finally to consider on what ground Communism can stand as against Nietzschianism or other doctrines of the " Superman." These may be, for all we know, perennial, if they derive primarily from specific psychological types, and may appear long after the classless society has been established. Thus if it be

---

[1] It is of much interest that the similarity between Fascism and the ancient caste-system of India is expressly admitted in *Sanatana Dharma*, an advanced textbook of Hindu religion and ethics, published by the Central Hindu College, Benares, 1923, pp. 240 ff. Both are said to be based on the doctrine of immortality.

claimed that the fulfilment of the personality of one sort of individual necessitates the injury or exploitation of others, on what ground does Communist theory refute the claim ? The ethical superiority of social equality is in fact at issue. Barbara Wootton well points out that " every type of economic organisation will turn top-heavy unless it is quite definitely and deliberately weighted in favour of the weak, the unfortunate, and the incompetent." What justification can there be for this, except the ἀγαπη του πλησίου of the Gospels, one of the two commandments on which hang all the Law and the Prophets ? And this leads us to ask whence came the noble hatred of oppression found in Marx, and whence arises this passion in all the Communist confessors and martyrs of the present century ? It cannot be a coincidence that Marxist morality grew up in the bosom of Christianity after eighteen Christian centuries. The phœnix of the Kingdom is rising from the ashes of the Church's failure.

IV

CHRISTIAN POLITICS AND COMMUNIST RELIGION

by Reinhold Niebuhr

Professor of Ethics, Union Theological Seminary, New York City

I. INTRODUCTION

CHRISTIANITY is a religion with an ethic so pure that it has difficulty in coming to terms with political realities ; for in politics moral ideas are inevitably compounded with the practical necessities of conflict and coercion. With its religio-moral ideal of perfect love, it is not quite certain how to approach and what to do with the stubborn realities of the political order ; whether it should compromise with them, flee them or be indifferent to them.

Communism is a political idealism with religious over-tones. Its political realism is crowned with the hope of a perfect society in which a pure morality will devour politics ; for the uncoerced justice of its ideal society will dispense with the necessity of the conflict and coercion which have characterised political life through all the ages. The anarchistic note in the ultimate Communist hope is one of several marks of its religious temper. Communism expects to use political measures and techniques in order to create a world in which all human relations will be moral rather than political.

Thus the conflict between Christianity and Communism is a contest between a religion with an inadequate political strategy and a social idealism which falsely raises a political strategy to the heights of religion.

The Christian moral ideal is that of love. The Christian

love ideal is individual rather than social in the sense that it springs from a profound analysis of the conflict between egoism and sacrificial passion in the inner life of the individual. Its primary concern is not the establishment of justice in society, but purity in the life of the individual. It is naturally not oblivious to the social consequences of human egoism. It knows that the moral life of the individual is not developed in a social vacuum. It realises that human selfishness leads to the exploitation of human life : and it knows that the achievement of perfect love means the attainment of social relations in which life is related to life in terms of mutual harmony. But it does not approach the problem of social harmony directly. In the Christian religion each individual soul feels the tension between human egoism and the ultimate ideal of sacrificial love as an individual problem. Human evil and sin is therefore recognised primarily as an individual fact, and only secondarily as a social fact. This individualism is both the virtue and the vice of Christian morality. It is a vice because it is difficult to make the purest individual moral ideal relevant to the necessities of social life. It is a virtue because profound Christianity, by discovering the root of social evil in the egoism of each individual soul, discourages the hypocrisy and brutality of political relations which derive from the fact that men know the egoism of their foes without recognising their own.

Whether a virtue or a vice, the ideal of Christian love is not an artificial ideal, superimposed upon human life by a canonical revelation. The drama of the cross in Christianity has a perennial power in human life, because it corresponds to the profoundest aspiration of the human spirit. Every human soul is a part of the whole of life. The high degree of self-consciousness, which distinguishes human from other life, makes it at one and the same time more sensitive of its obligations to all life as such, and more persistent in affirming its individual existence against the needs and claims of all other life. The problem of human sin is given in the facts of human self-consciousness. Man

is at once more selfish and more conscious of the sin
of selfishness than the beast. His higher degree of self-
consciousness raises nature's will to live into forms of self-
assertion, egoism, and imperialism which heighten the
impulse to survive to the very point of defeating it. On the
other hand the capacity for self-transcendence in man's
consciousness makes it possible for him to view his life in
relation to all human life, and even to all living creatures;
and to feel the assertion of his peculiar interests against the
claims of others as sin and rebellion against life and God.
The religious belief that all life is created by God is a natural
and inevitable expression of the feeling that all living forms
have an ultimate significance and sanctity beyond the
utilitarian purposes and obvious uses which these forms
of life serve. A religious interpretation of life, therefore,
sharpens the sense that egoism is sin, and creates an uneasiness about even the most inevitable utilitarian uses of
other life for the benefit of self.

Secularism regards this religious sense of sin as morbid ;
but a secularism which dispenses with this religious check
upon egoism inevitably involves itself in unwarranted and
dangerous forms of egoism and imperialism. It tends not
only to subordinate human life too immediately to the
specialised human ends of State, class, and race ; but it
also tempts to an unwarranted sacrifice of non-human life
to the purpose and caprices of human beings. Moral
sensitivity towards the rights and interests of human
beings can never be maintained at its highest without
an overtone of reverence for all life as such.

The effort of Christian orthodoxy to explain, or at least
to establish the fact of, sin in terms of the myth of the Fall
and the doctrine of original sin is not the result of mythical
caprice and fantasy. It springs just as naturally and inevitably out of a profound analysis of the human moral
problem as does the Christian ideal of love. The Christian
myth of the Fall simply establishes the fact that human
egoism is something more than the impulses of nature set
against the obligations conceived by reason. It expresses

the idea that human selfishness is a defect of the spirit and not a defect of natural impulse. It is because man is spirit and not merely nature that he is a sinner : for it is through the powers of his self-consciousness that man both conceives his obligations to life around him and violates those obligations. There is thus a mystery in human evil which cannot be comprehended in either the dualism of neo-Platonism, which derives evil from the world of matter and nature, or the modern naturalistic monisms, which identify sin with ignorance. The orthodox Christian belief that there is a mystery in sin which can be expressed more perfectly in mythical than in purely rational terms is warranted by the fact that the same spiritual capacities which enable man to see his own life in relation to all of life also tempts him to the pretension of subordinating all life to his own ego. The Christian ideal of love and the Christian recognition of the sinfulness of egoism are thus two poles of a spiritual tension which is bound to develop wherever life is profoundly analysed and its heights and depths fully understood.

II. THE INADEQUACY OF CHRISTIAN POLITICS

The virtue of these Christian insights into the innermost problem of the human spirit does not, however, prevent Christianity from finding it very difficult to come to terms with the social and political problem. The social and political order lives under the tension of the ideal of justice and the facts of injustice. The difference between justice and injustice is more relative than the difference between egoism and love ; but it is in some respects more immediately relevant to the weal and woe of most people. To approach the relative problems of justice in the realm of politics from the absolute perspective of the Christian ideal is a little like judging the merits of house-painting by canons of art which guide a Rembrandt.

The orthodox Christian Church, both Catholic and Protestant, has taken the position that the law of love is not fully applicable to the world of politics, since politics is concerned with the establishment of justice in a " world of sin." The Church has admitted, in other words, that, however much egoism must be chastised as sin, it must be taken for granted in man's collective behaviour. If the elimination of egoism was not to be hoped for, the Church was bound to draw the conclusion that justice in politics must be established by conflict and coercion. Conflict is necessary because relative justice depends upon setting interests against interest in the hope of achieving a degree of equality and stability between conflicting interests. Coercion is necessary in order that organised society may prevent the expression of inordinate egoism on the part of individuals and groups. This political realism in the viewpoint of orthodox Christianity stands in wholesome contrast to the romanticism of liberal Christianity, which imagined that it had, in the law of love, a moral ideal which would painlessly transmute the realities of politics.

However, the political realism of Christian orthodoxy did not guarantee an adequate political strategy. Having disavowed the ideal of love as a possibility in the political order, it lacked an effective source of criticism for the injustices of politics and economics. In part this deficiency was supplied by the incorporation of the Stoic idea of the *lex naturæ* into Christian teaching. The lesser, but more relevant, ideal of justice was substituted for the purer ideal of love. But the Christian re-interpretation of the Stoic natural law led to several deplorable consequences. The very absolutism of the Christian ethic made for a pessimism so deep that the justice set up as an ideal was something less than the equal justice of Stoic doctrine. Christian orthodoxy may have been right in its pessimistic assumption that equal justice is beyond the possibilities of attainment in human society ; but by sacrificing the ideal of equality entirely—or, to be more exact, by transmuting it from a socio-moral to a religio-moral ideal without relevance to social problems—it lost an effective source of criticism for a given situation in the political order. Conceptions of justice which are not disciplined by ideals of equality inevitably sink into the sand of complete relativism or contemporary conventions.

The conception of justice which Christian orthodoxy substituted for the Stoic ideal borrowed heavily from the conventions of feudal society. The hierarchical structure of this society was taken for granted. Justice meant merely that social relations should be ordered and decent within terms of the presuppositions of this society. Sometimes the inequalities of feudalism were given added sanctity by the suggestion that they were God's punishment for sin, and His way of holding sin in check. This doctrine helped the Church to adjust its conscience to slavery. The moral confusion resulting from such a doctrine was aggravated by the fact that the Church was not at all clear whether God intended to punish the victims or the beneficiaries of inequality in the social scheme by permitting its continuance. In the Thomasian elaboration of Catholic ethics it was quite natural that Thomas's heavy indebtedness to Aristotelianism should prompt him to support feudal inequalities with Aristotle's aristocratic ethics. The patriachal social ideals of the Old Testament gave further support to this general scheme. Thus strongly buttressed on the side of both philosophy and theology, Catholic social ethics gave religious sanction to the feudal social structure ; and that sanction continues into the modern day. Catholicism, particularly in the Latin countries, maintains an essentially feudal politics. The deleterious effects of this political orientation of Catholicism are particularly obvious in the contemporary political situations of Spain, South America, French Canada, and Mexico. France paid a heavy price for its political progress in the eighteenth century because of the too intimate relation between Catholicism and feudalism. Even in England many a country parson and country squire still sanctions the feudal politics of his toryism by " Christian " presuppositions. Only in Germany, and, to a lesser degree, in the thoroughly bourgeois America, is the Catholic Church really emancipated from feudalism. It is interesting to find very stubborn remnants of feudalism in the social ethics of so modern a (Greek) Catholic thinker as Nicholas Berdyaev, in spite of the strong Marxian influences upon his thought.

The defeatism and pessimism which Christian orthodoxy derived from the very rigour of its ethical ideal, and which betrayed it into a premature acceptance of the social inequalities of a given society, were further accentuated by the force of religious piety and reverence at work in every religious institution. Vital religion is compounded of both piety and spirituality, to borrow Santayana's phrase. Spirituality sees the given situation from a high perspective, and is therefore critical of it. Piety sees the given situation as a revelation of Divine purpose. Of the two dominant religious emotions, gratitude and contrition, the former is clearly the fruit of piety as is the latter of spirituality. In Christian orthodoxy piety and spirituality have unfortunately led frequently to a common sanctification of the *status quo*. An acute spirituality led to the pessimism which regarded the world of politics as essentially unredeemable. A reverent piety uncritically included the relativities of a contemporary social situation in the " order of creation " which had its source in God, and toward which grateful acceptance was more Christian than critical analysis. As a result a given social *status quo* was removed from the realm of moral criticism both because it was hopeless and because it was God-given. Christian orthodoxy did not combine these two forces as baldly as they are united in this sentence. Nevertheless that was its total effect upon politics. There has been no age in which the Christian ideal of love has not had a leavening effect upon individual morality. But not only did it fail to influence the attitude of the Church toward politics, but Christian orthodoxy failed to find an adequate substitute for it as a source of moral criticism of political realities.

Protestant orthodoxy shares many of the political characteristics of Catholicism, but also reveals significant distinctions. It agrees with Catholicism in its acceptance of the *lex naturæ* as the basis of political judgment, and it maintains the same complacency toward social inequality both because it represents God's punishment upon a sinful world and because it belongs to a God-given order of creation. Luther's sharp distinction between a spiritual kingdom and an earthly one, used against the revolting peasants, when the latter foolishly took some of the equalitarian implications of the gospel ethic seriously, revealed the depth of his pessimism in regard to politics. There is, in fact, a striking similarity between Luther's and Machiavelli's interpretation of the political problem. The very. violence of Luther's opposition to asceticism tended to a depreciation of the absolutism of the gospel ethic in the Lutheran social and political ethic.

The Protestant compromise with the realities of politics did not, however, lead to a sanctification of feudalism as in the case of Catholicism. Though Luther's attitude toward business and banking, toward the problem of usury and profits, was essentially feudal rather than modern, both the Lutheran and the Calvinistic reformation movements were ultimately swept into the bourgeois movement. This was not due to any superior moral insights in Protestantism, which might have given it a superior detachment from the presuppositions of feudalism. It was due to the coincidences of history which made the rise of Protestantism contemporaneous with the development of modern commerce and industry : so that the religious movement was drawn into the orbit of the bourgeois political and economic development and made to do service for it. The individualism of Protestantism, as against medieval ecclesiasticism —particularly its emphasis upon the right of each individual to approach God without intervention of priest or Church —was derived from purely religious considerations, but it contributed to the disintegration of the authority of medieval social institutions, and was therefore made

PR

relevant to the bourgeois insistence upon political and economic liberty. Protestantism thus gradually drifted into an intimate relation with the bourgeois, democratic, capitalistic social order, very similar to the too intimate relation between Catholicism and feudalism.

In some respects the relation of Protestantism to capitalism is more grievous than the intimate embrace of Catholicism and feudalism. The capitalistic world is a mechanical rather than an organic one. It is held together by means of production and communication rather than by social sentiment and traditional loyalties. The rapid changes produced by a technical civilisation require more constant and thoroughgoing changes than were necessary in the more stable feudal and agrarian economy. When religious piety sanctifies such a world, and tempts men to regard its relative and shifting social arrangement as a part of the " order of creation," it commits a more grievous fault than the suggestion of a similar attitude toward an agrarian social order. The stable and organic feudal world was, after all, a more fitting object of religious reverence—at least in the period of its health—than the impersonal and mechanical social structure of modern civilisation.

A more serious weakness of Protestantism in comparison with Catholicism was, and is, its attitude towards the State. In both types of orthodoxy the coercive, and even violent, methods which the State invariably used to preserve social cohesion and maintain its authority were justified in spite of the anarchistic and pacifistic implications of the gospel ethic. But no Catholic theologian leaned quite as heavily upon the scriptural sanctification of government as an ordinance of God (Romans xiii.) as did Luther. Furthermore the Catholic effort to maintain the authority and prestige of the Church as superior to that of the State prompted a critical attitude toward the limitations of government, even though many Catholic teachers taught that the ruler must not be resisted under any circumstances. In Catholicism at its best the Church was the vehicle and instrument of an ethical universalism, from the perspective of which the dangers of international anarchy, arising from morally autonomous States, was recognised. In Protestantism this perspective was lost, and as a result Protestant Churches have tended to become ignoble servants and tools of nationalism. If the State was ordained of God to preserve a sinful world from anarchy, no Protestant teacher seemed to have concerned himself very profoundly with the problem of avoiding the anarchy which results from the conflict of wills and interests between powerful and morally self-sufficient States and nations. Whatever the limitations of the medieval papacy, it was an international authority, the very existence of which symbolised the necessity of limiting the moral autonomy of each nation. For this fact and symbol Protestantism has never had an adequate substitute. What has been done in recent years to establish an inchoate society of nations owes its impetus to secular Liberal movements in politics. Protestantism has frequently hailed these efforts with enthusiasm (sometimes with uncritical enthusiasm), but it did not inspire them.

Not only has orthodox Protestantism failed to deal adequately with the violence of the State in its relation to other nations, but it has failed, also, to develop a discriminating attitude towards the use of violence by the State in its task of maintaining domestic order and tranquillity. Modern pacifistic Liberalism criticises the State for its use of violence, and even its use of coercion, under any circumstances. The recognition on the part of Protestant orthodoxy of the necessity of coercion in maintaining social cohesion is politically more realistic, and therefore justified. Its great weakness lies in the fact that it is completely uncritical toward the use of coercion by the established government while it rigorously prohibits every type of rebellious coercion and violence. Luther's political ethic was particularly flagrant in its moral confusion upon this point, for he enjoined the purest pacifism upon the citizen in his relation to the State while he absolved the rulers of every moral scruple in their use of violence. He declared,

" I will side always with him, however unjust, who endures rebellion and against him who rebels, however justly." Calvin was hardly less confused. " If we are cruelly vexed by an inhuman prince," he said, " or robbed and plundered by one prodigal and avaricious—let us remember our own offences against God which doubtless are chastised by these plagues." Calvin followed Luther also in enjoining a pure Christian ethic of non-resistance upon the subjects, and allowing the rulers *carte blanche* in the use of the sword. " The use of the sword ought not to be permitted any private individual, to make resistance to evil : for the arms of Christians are prayer and meekness, to possess their lives in patience and to overcome evil by doing good according to the doctrine of the gospel.—But to condemn the public use of the sword, which God hath ordained for our protection, is blasphemy against God Himself.—The sword is placed in his hands to punish malefactors. Since God orders him to do this, who are we to hinder him ? "

All this represents moral confusion which borders on perversity, and justifies much of what radicals have said about the deleterious effect of religion upon the political attitudes of the victims of political and economic injustice. Fortunately, later Calvinism, enlarging loopholes left by Calvin himself, found ways of justifying political rebellion against injustice, provided the lower magistrates led the rebellion against the higher magistrates (the kings), and thus guaranteed the public rather than private character of the use of force. Thus Calvinism became intimately related to the democratic movements which helped to destroy the old feudal order. In the case of an Oliver Cromwell we find the rebel against the monarch armed with a sense of the religious sanctity of his task equal to that of any king who believed himself to be a ruler by Divine right.

In spite of the qualified endorsement of rebellion against injustice in later Calvinism, the weight of orthodox Protestant teaching, both Lutheran and Calvinistic, has been on the side of established authority and against rebellion. The effect of this moral and political doctrine is still apparent in contemporary Christian thought ; for the modern Church always has more pacifistic scruples against the use of force by a political group which is protesting against social injustice than against the violence of the State when it engages other nations in combat.

In so far as this viewpoint is not dictated by purely economic and class interests but springs from an honest pessimism, which believes that the achievement of any social order is so difficult that it ought not to be lightly challenged and endangered, even though it fails to attain perfect justice, it must be allowed a measure of justification. It is easy to imagine a more perfect scheme of justice than can be found in any established social order. But there are greater perils of anarchy in the disintegration of an old order than most radicals realise ; and their perfect schemes of justice will be more seriously impaired by the inertia of concrete reality than their Utopianism allows them to believe. Nevertheless there are times and seasons (such as the one in which we live) when old social orders disintegrate because of their own weaknesses, and when a frantic effort to maintain the old against the logic of history will create more anarchy and confusion than a frank espousal of a new order. The Churches of Germany, and the middle classes which were under their influence, learned too late that a Fascist revolution creates more tyranny and anarchy than a Socialist one ; and nothing is gained for the terrible price that is paid for Fascism but the unstable preservation of a dying social system beyond its day.

The degree to which religious pessimism and realism may lead to moral confusion, when an undue reverence for established authority is combined with the recognition of the need and inevitability of conflict and coercion in political life, may be clearly seen in some of the modern German theological literature.[1] Any realistic analysis of political life is bound to recognise the inevitability of conflict and coercion in man's collective enterprises. If the

[1] *See,* for instance, Gogarten's *Politische Ethik,* or Stapel's *Der Christlicher Staatsmann.*

Christian ideal of love is to influence this realism in any degree, it must create a profound uneasiness among those who feel themselves compelled to use force for the attainment of certain specific ends. The use of force is always an evil, and invariably runs the risk of aggravating tyranny and accentuating injustice. But these perils are no less when established government avails itself of force than when impatient rebels appeal to the arbitrament of the sword. Lazy and corrupt Governments always have a tendency to seek the elimination of social discontent by violence rather than by removal of the causes of social friction. They also incline to drift into wars with other nations whenever they feel the necessity of allaying domestic social unrest by arousing a unifying and blinding patriotic emotion. The uncritical justification of violence by Governments and the equally uncritical prohibition of violence by rebels in Christian orthodoxy are therefore a constant source of moral and political confusion.

The radical may feel that it is unnecessary to disclose the religious sources of this confusion, since he regards the religious institution as a mere instrument of class domination and the religious discouragement of rebellion as an invariable betrayal of class interest. The Christian Church, however, must try to correct the tendencies in the religious life which tempt the Church to justify acquiescence in injustice by a confused appeal to its absolutistic ethic on the one hand and by exploiting the force of religious piety for an established order on the other. A realistic religion cannot commit the pretension of traditional religion and assume that the religious institution transcends economic and political interests, and is free of the temptation of sanctifying class interests. Genuine religious realism, by its very consciousness of the prevalence of human sin, knows that every institution—the religious as well as other cultural institutions—may easily become the tool of special class interests. All institutions, whatever their cultural and religious pretensions, have a sociological locus. This locus will partially determine their political and social attitudes. If they are robbed of the opportunity of rationalising these attitudes by certain types of theological doctrines, they will find others to do the same service. It is, nevertheless, important to track down error and dishonesty wherever it reveals itself. The political and moral confusion of Christian orthodoxy may have been partly derived from the special social interests of the classes which are preponderant in the religious institutions ; but they were also derived from the misapplication of certain emphases in the Christian faith and certain inevitable attitudes in the religious life. These, once discovered, may be corrected.

Naturally a religion with as uncompromising and rigorous a love-perfectionism in its canon and at the heart of its interpretation of life as Christianity could not make the compromises with the realities of political and economic life, which the Orthodox Church made, without prompting some groups in the Church to challenge the compromises and seek to realise the absolute ethic. In the medieval Church the monastic movement made this effort. In the Protestant Church it was made, along somewhat different lines, by the sects.

The fact that the absolutism and perfectionism inherent in the Christian religion should have resulted in ascetic rather than revolutionary movements is a proof of the predominant individualism of the Christian ethic. Asceticism seeks to achieve a higher degree of individual purity— particularly emancipation from egoism—by mystic discipline of the individual soul, and by withdrawal from the ordinary social relations. The ascetic withdrawal from family, property, and political relations is a proof of its realism. It understands the perennial paradox of man's social life. The most unselfish individual is drawn by his very loyalty to a social group, whether family, race, or nation, into an expression of collective egoism. Individuals may run the risk of annihilation always involved in the practice of complete non-resistance ; but it is questionable whether they can justify the same risks when they are dealing with the interests of a group. Perhaps it is even more important that the impulses of both survival and the will to power are too strong in the social group to bring a policy of complete non-resistance into the realm of possibilities in collective relationships, even if it could be morally justified. The effort to realise the perfectionist ideals of Christianity can be carried through literally and absolutely only upon an ascetic basis. Thus only can the individual separate himself sufficiently from both the entanglements and natural obligations of broader social life to seek individual purity without being betrayed into either compromise or perversity.

The fact that the ascetic life remains, on the whole, an irrelevance to the broader socio-moral problems of human society, and that it easily results in a morbid pre-occupation with self rather than emancipation from egoism, does not completely invalidate it. No community of the ideal can ever be fully conscious of the ease with which natural and inevitable human loyalties are transmuted into sinful and socially dangerous forms of imperialism, if a portion of the community does not, by the ardour of its discipline, reveal the subtle peril and the stubborn inertia of egoism in even the most natural and praiseworthy collective enterprises. The complete scorn of modern Liberalism and Radicalism for the asceticism of the past is merely a proof of the incapacity of modernism to understand the persistence and power of egoism in all human relations. While there is, therefore, a place for asceticism in the institution of religion, it offers only a slight and a very indirect contribution to the social problem. Human society, as such, must always be more interested in the attainment of a basic justice in all relations than in an individual perfection, which can be achieved only by monastics who cultivate their spiritual excellencies while they live parasitically upon the rest of society.

The protest against the compromises of the Orthodox Church in Protestantism was presented by sectarians, rather than monastics, i.e. by Anabaptists, Levellers, Brownists, Diggers, Mennonites, and Quakers, etc. The sectaries differed from the monastic in that they did not disavow the ordinary relations of life in order to strive for perfection. They either believed it possible to transform the whole of society into a community of the love ideal, or they regarded the whole world as sinful and damned, and themselves as called upon to realise perfect love in their lives. Some form of perfectionism characterises every type of sectarian Christianity. Sometimes the chief emphasis is upon equalitarianism ; at other times it is upon non-resistance. It is significant that occasionally the equalitarian emphasis prompts a revolutionary rather than pacifistic strategy ; but usually Christian sectaries have been pacifistic.

While the perfectionists sects of Protestantism have not espoused celibacy, but continued in their ordinary family relations, and while they substituted the ideal of simplicity and absence of luxury for the ascetic ideal of poverty, they have on the whole been forced into asceticism in regard to politics. They have been unable to relate an ethic of complete non-resistance to the obligations which fall upon those who organise political relations. In the case of such groups as the Mennonites the eschatalogical hope was powerful enough to absolve them completely of political responsibility. The perfect community of love could not be established, according to their faith, by human striving, but only through the grace of God. Meanwhile the community of God would live by His laws as best it could in an evil world. Among the Quakers there has always been a larger admixture of the Liberal faith in the gradual redemption of the world through moral action. Their willingness to assume a larger share of political responsibility than the Mennonites involved them inevitably in coercion and social conflict. They were willing to participate in various forms of social pressure as long as these were not violent. They were therefore able to carry most political responsibilities, except those associated with warfare.

The difficulty with this type of qualified intra-mundane asceticism is that it makes a too rigorous moral distinction between forms of violent and non-violent coercion. Violence ought no doubt to be discouraged in society on pragmatic grounds. But every effort to establish an absolute moral distinction between violent and non-violent forms of pressure and social conflict creates moral confusion, particularly by giving an undue moral advantage to those classes in society which need not resort to violence because they possess all the economic power, the instruments of propaganda, and the authority of the State by which non-violent pressure is exerted. The tendency of the Quakers to claim the authority of the gospel ethic for their emphasis upon non-violence, though the gospel ethic is clearly one of unqualified non-resistance, leads to particularly serious moral confusion in the world of commerce and industry. Unlike the Mennonites, who devoted themselves almost exclusively to agriculture, Quakers engaged in commercial and industrial pursuits, and prospered in them. They have undoubtedly conducted their business enterprises with a higher degree of honesty and sympathy for the workers than any other group of business men. They have nevertheless failed consistently to realise to what degree business is as essentially coercive as politics, and have erroneously imagined themselves to be practising an absolute ethic within the relativities of economic life. The moral confusion which may arise from this type of qualified non-resistance justifies some of the cynicism of radicalism against pacifism. Pacifism may have an honest religious source ; but it can be easily appropriated by privileged classes to obscure the economic and political realities from which they benefit.

The modern Liberal Protestant Church has tried to eliminate the compromises of the Orthodox Church by accepting and diluting the ethic of sectarian Christianity. The optimism and rationalism which it inherited from the Enlightenment gave it confidence that the gospel of love needed only to be adequately preached to be universally accepted. It therefore envisaged a new society, achieved by gradual evolutionary process, and practically identical with the Kingdom of God of the gospel. It failed completely to understand the inertia of sin in human history, and the inevitability of conflict, tyranny, and injustice in economic and political life. Having accommodated the Christian faith to the naturalism of the era, it had little understanding for the fact that the purest ideals of perfection always transcend the world of nature and history. In its naïve optimism it destroyed the ascetic elements which persisted in the ethic of the sects. It thought of the Christian ethic of love as a prudential rule of conduct which needed only to be applied to prove its practical efficacy. As a result the modern Liberal Church, while imagining itself in the possession of a " gospel " and an ethic which completely transcended the interests of a capitalistic civilisation and corrected the errors and the defeatism of the Orthodox Church, really reduced the rigorous love perfectionism of the gospel to a morality which could hardly be distinguished from the prudential morality elaborated by a commercial civilisation. By preaching the ideal of love without revealing the depth and persistence of the egoism, which frustrates both the ideal of individual perfection and the goal of social justice, the modern Church has obscured rather than revealed the moral and social realities of our day, and has compromised more seriously with the prejudices and interests of a commercial civilisation than did the Orthodox Church. The gospel ethic is too rigorous and uncompromising to be used as a practical guide for the social problems of our or any other civilisation. The effort to put it to such a use destroys its usefulness as a source of criticism for the practical morality of expedience, which informs the life of every society and of every individual who is in organic and responsible relation to his society.

If we summarise the efforts to elaborate an adequate political ethic from the absolute ethic of Christianity, we discover that the very perfectionism and rigour of the Christian ethic have betrayed the Church into grave difficulties and errors when dealing with political problems. (1) The Orthodox Church is tempted to acquiesce in social injustice prematurely because its pessimism, derived from its perfectionism, and its reverence for established social forms, emerging from its piety combine to discourage radical social readjustments. (2) The ascetic protest against the compromises of the Church with the world has only a slight relevance to the social problem. (3) The semi-asceticism of the sectaries either shares the irrelevance of asceticism or creates political confusion when it accepts political responsibilities. (4) The highly diluted perfectionism of the modern Church obscures the realities and necessities of the political and economic order by promising to establish justice by pure love when every evidence of history points to the necessity of achieving justice through a contest of power and a conflict of wills. The perfectionism of the Christian ethic, whatever its genuine merits for any high morality, tends, in other words, to either a defeatism which regards the world of politics and economics as so sinful that the Christian must be satisfied with a very minimal justice in it (orthodoxy), and must seek genuine perfection outside of it (asceticism) ; or it tends to a naïve optimism (semi-asceticism and modern Liberalism) which promises the triumph of the love ideal in the whole of society.

III. COMMUNISM AS A RELIGION

The political failure of Christianity has encouraged the emergence of a new religion in the Western world, which is strongest where Christianity is weakest (in the analysis of the political realities), and is weakest where Christianity is strongest (in plumbing the depths of the individual's soul). The emergence of a politically oriented religion in such a day as ours is significant. The intensity and extent of modern social cohesion have made the social and political problem particularly urgent, and the disintegration of our capitalistic civilisation has made the failure of our historic institutions to deal with it particularly tragic. It was natural, therefore, that a religion should emerge which would attack the total human situation from the centre of the political problem. Though Communism is avowedly irreligious, its significant attitudes are religious. Unlike modern Liberal rationalism its interpretations of life and history are dogmatic rather than scientific. Like all vital religion it engages the entire human psyche and offers its interpretation of life and the world in order that it may challenge to action in conformity with its " truth." Irreligion is a luxury which only those may allow themselves who observe life rather than live it. Those who live vitally must base their life upon an act of faith that life has meaning, and seek to conform their actions to that meaning.

In the Communist religion the significant drama of history is the conflict of classes, and the most redemptive action is therefore the avowal of that struggle. As in all great religions the ultimate outcome of the drama of history is preordained ; yet it is necessary for the individual to affirm what is ordained in the dialectic of history (God). It is ordained that the perennial social struggle in human history shall finally culminate in the victory of the exploited classes ; and by that victory a classless society will be established in which perfect justice is guaranteed. In Communism there is thus an interesting combination of cynical political realism with a religious hope. Its political realism is in one respect no different from that of a Hobbes or a Machiavelli. It knows that politics and economics is a contest of power and interest, and that no pure moral idealism will ever establish justice in the world. But its religio-social hope transmutes this realism. It is not interested in the mere technique of power politics. It believes rather that God (the dialectic of history) can use the wrath of man to praise Him, and that out of the disintegration of an unjust social system the victims of injustice may build a perfect society. The perfect society is on the one hand the creation of the proletarian class, and on the other hand it is a fruit of the historical dialectic, without which the weakness of the industrial poor could not achieve the strength which is promised them in the new order.

Both in its belief that something more than the moral

effort of the believer is necessary to establish a new social
order and in its type of social perfectionism, Communism,
and Marxism in general, is a version of the old Jewish
prophetic hope. It is a secularised version of this hope.
Jewish prophecy is one of its parents, and eighteenth-
century naturalism and optimism is the other. While it
shares the hope of eighteenth-century Liberalism, in the
goodness of human nature it does not share modern
Liberalism's confidence in evolutionary progress. It believes,
rather, with the prophet Amos, that the day of the Lord
will be darkness and not light ; and, with the prophets in
general, it knows that judgment precedes mercy. Interpreted in modern terms it does not expect the creation of
a new social order until the old one has destroyed itself by
its own "inherent contradictions." The Communist
analysis of the self-destruction of capitalism can be put in
ethical terms, though orthodox Communists usually prefer
a purely economic analysis. But in moral terms the Communist thesis is that capitalism destroys itself by its own
injustices. The oligarchs of capitalism, who own the
productive processes upon which the weal and woe of all
people depend, take too much for themselves out of this
process, depriving the general public, and particularly
the worker, of the consumption power by which the markets
for goods are kept open. Thus capitalism suffers from increasingly serious crises of overproduction, unemployment, and depression. The efforts it puts forth to save itself
from these crises (tariffs, import quotas, currency depreciation, etc.) actually aggravate its difficulties in the end. They
reveal the international anarchy of capitalism as clearly as
the depression itself discloses the domestic anarchy of
capitalistic production.

The catastrophic interpretation of the destiny of modern
society, supplied by Marxism, is validated by so many facts
of contemporary history that the stubborn optimism of the
middle-class community must be regarded as a rationalisation of its interests rather than a sober judgment upon
historical processes. The Liberal Church shares this

optimism on the whole, and proves thereby that its senti-
mentalised version of religion is incapable of understanding
the tragic elements in life and the necessity of judgment in
history. The God of Liberal Christianity is a God of mercy,
but not of wrath, because it has followed modern secularism
in denying the reality of sin and is oblivious to the destruction and self-defeat of egoism. The Marxian interpretation
of contemporary history is therefore superior to the optimistic interpretations of modern Liberalism. It is not only
truer to the facts, but in greater accord with the insights
of profound religion. In one of its aspects Marxism is therefore a modern application, rather than a modernised version, of Jewish prophecy and eschatology. With Jewish
religious thought it shares the hope of a redeemed society
in historical time, and resists the individualistic temptation
of Greek thought to find redemption in a realm above
history. Its perfectionism expresses itself in the hope of a
redeemed community. Since its hope is predominantly
social, its social ideal is the ideal of equal justice rather than
the Christian ideal of love. Justice is as inevitably the
highest ideal for social life, as love is the highest ideal of the
pure soul. Furthermore, equal justice is the inevitable
symbol of perfect justice. Perfect equality may be as
unattainable in history as perfect love ; yet it must remain
the regulative principle of justice and the perspective
from which every concrete achievement in justice is
assessed.

Marxism, therefore, has much to commend it, both as a
political strategy and as a religion. Its political strategy is
based upon a realism which the facts of human nature and
history justify on the whole. As a religion it supplies some
insights into life and history which have been neglected
in modern Christianity, and sets a moral and social goal
for the ethical life which is relevant to the necessities of
modern society. Nevertheless Marxism is an inadequate
religion, and it is not a completely adequate political
philosophy for the Western world.

Its inadequacy as a religion is due to its effort to solve

the total human problem in political terms, and its limitations as a political philosophy and strategy are derived
from its religio-dogmatic over-simplifications. Marxism
attributes practically all ills from which the human flesh
suffers to the capitalistic social order, and promises every
type of redemption in a new society in which the productive
process is socially owned. It does not realise that the
political and economic order can never do more than
establish a basic justice, and that this basic justice will
always be a rather rough justice and will require every
refinement which reason and goodwill can elaborate.
Marxism is led to its illusions by its essentially romantic
estimate of human nature, which is in turn an element in
its naturalistic philosophy. While the Communist can be
brutally realistic in discounting moral pretensions and
penetrating to the actual egoistic economic motives revealed in a contemporary social situation, he gives himself
to the unwarranted illusion that a new order of society will
eliminate egoism and socialise men to such a degree that
the problem of justice will be practically solved and
eliminated. His anarchistic Utopianism persuades him that
the dictatorship of the proletariat is only temporary, and
that the State will gradually wither away. He believes
that a classless society can maintain social cohesion without coercion. His ultimate dream and hope are, in other
words, very similar to the expectations of the Utopia of
uncoerced co-operation which eighteenth-century thought
has made familiar. His Utopianism blinds him to the
perennial nature of the political problem. This problem
can be briefly stated in the following form : (1) Social co-
operation on a large scale requires a measure of coercion.
(2) The instruments of coercion are always wielded by a
particular social group, whether capitalistic industrialists
or communistic oligarchs. (3) The natural force of human
egoism tempts these oligarchs to use the instruments of
power for their own advantage rather than that of the total
society. The result is therefore always something less
than perfect justice. (4) The problem is to place the most

effective possible inner moral and external social checks upon the centres of social power in society in order that the perennial tendencies toward injustice in society may be retarded. The recognition of this problem does not mean that the substitution of Socialism for capitalism would not represent a solid gain for justice. The social power which inheres in the ownership of the means of production is so irresponsible and so irrelevant to the necessities of a technical civilisation that its destruction has become a primary prerequisite of social health ; but its destruction will produce something less than the paradise of goodwill of which orthodox Marxians dream.

The orthodox Marxian is tempted into another grave error by his faulty religion with its mistaken analysis of the problem of human sin. By attributing all injustice to the capitalistic social structure it lifts the class of rebellious victims of injustice into the category of the only redemptive and Messianic community. The proletarian class is in fact the counterpart of Messianic nation or community in early Jewish eschatology. But the Marxian idealisation of this class represents a kind of religious primitiveness ; for its claims for this class are as unqualified as were the claims of Israel, before the prophets criticised and refined this tribalism in religion. The consequence of this religious sanctification of the peculiar insights and needs of a particular class and group is the same that it has always been in history : fanaticism and brutality. If you are certain that your opponent is an instrument of evil, and that you are a vehicle of God's grace, you may allow yourself every cruelty in " liquidating " the enemy. One of the pathetic aspects of Marxian religion is that its interpretation of history allows it to see the relativity and imperfection of the cultural values and pretensions of all other classes and groups ; but the characteristic social attitudes and political objectives of the proletarian are made absolute. As a result the Marxian may pursue the foes of his ideal without pity or forgiveness. The worst cruelties and tyrannies in political history always result when religion and politics are thus unwholesomely compounded and absolute significance is claimed for the relative values of a particular social group.

If Marxism sloughs off its religious pretensions it could make a very convincing claim for the peculiar destiny apportioned by history to the industrial workers and the victims of capitalistic injustice. Once the power of owner-ship disintegrates, the men who actually run our modern machines will possess the most significant social power. Since these are the same men who suffer from the injustices of the present system of ownership and social organisation, they, more than any other social class, are driven by their experience and their need to seek a new society. Possessing both the strongest incentive for social change and the most significant social power in a technical civilisation the pro-letarian class is bound to be the most creative in bringing about fundamental social change. The creative force in society must always come from below. The upper social layers of society always represent hard crusts, hardened by the interests which they are defending. The religious realism of the prophets and Jesus recognised this. Hence their blessings upon the poor. Rationalistic and moralistic ages and classes are blinded to this obvious fact, and speak fearfully of the lack of intelligence of the poorer classes, and of their lack of any peculiar virtues which would give them the right of political leadership. Political leadership, however, is determined not by personal virtue, but by social cohesion and organisation and a strong sense of mission and direction.

Marxian orthodoxy tends to transmute this rightful and necessary sense of mission into a demonic pretension. Human life grows demonic whenever the impulses of nature are falsely mixed with spirit, and absolute claims are made for the values of a social group or cause which are bound to be relative and partial. Thus Marxism always hovers on the brink of primitive tribalism in which a single social group pretends to the eternal sanctities and excludes all other life from the area of a meaningful existence.

In prophetic religion the peculiar destiny of a particular

group is alternately affirmed and denied. Thus the prophets in one moment assured Israel, " You only have I chosen," and in the next moment denied any special significance in the mission and destiny of Israel, saying, with Amos, " Are ye not as the children of the Ethiopians unto Me ? saith the Lord." In the same manner John the Baptist deflated the Messianic consciousness of his nation, and declared, " Think not to say within yourselves, We have Abraham for our father : for I say unto you, that God is able of these stones to raise up children unto Abraham " (Matt. iii. 9).

A prophetic religion must alternate between discovering the special and unique mission of different classes and peoples at various junctures of history and setting bounds to the pretensions created by their special calling. Somewhere in high religion there must always be the sense of an ultimate good which reveals the partiality and relativity of all human values and all social forces. It was such a sense which prompted Jesus to say, " Why callest thou Me good ? no one is good save God." An exclusive emphasis upon this thought, as in the modern Barthian theology in Germany, is, however, as enervating as the lack of it is a basis for false religion and fanatic politics. The dialectic theology of Germany is perilously near the dualism of neo-Platonism in which all historic reality and concrete existence is robbed of meaning.

Perhaps one of the reasons why labour politics in England, though held in contempt by the more orthodox Marxians of the Continent, may yet succeed in its social task to a greater degree than it has on the Continent or will in America is because radicalism has never completely broken with the Christian tradition. It is rightfully in rebellion against the Church which uses religion to sanctify a *status quo* and the privileges of the upper classes. But the discipline of what is best in Christianity remains in its heart, and prevents it from elaborating profound political impulses into tribal and demonic religious pretensions.

Unfortunately the limitations of Marxism as a religion

also corrupt its politics. When it confuses its shrewd political realism by religious claims for its own social group, it introduces dogmas into politics which blind it to the realities of modern society, and of Western society in particular. The struggle in Western society is, as Marxism claims, primarily a struggle between owners and workers. But the social situation is confused and the struggle complicated by many neutral and semi-neutral classes—the farmers, the lower middle classes, and the professional groups. Marxian intransigeance forces these classes into the arms of reaction. Communism helps to create Fascism. Marxism cannot be held responsible for the inclinations of the owning classes to resort to force and violence in order to maintain their rule. Any disintegrating oligarchy is bound to seek the perpetuation of its rule by force alone. The rebellious classes would have to renounce their fateful mission in modern society to prevent the tendency towards Fascism. But Marxism is partly responsible for giving the industrial oligarchs such substantial numerical allies as the lower middle classes. Failure of Marxian fanaticism to deal sympathetically with the cultural inheritance, with the national sentiment, and with the legitimate individualism of these classes forces them into the abortive and fatal effort of trying to save their spiritual goods by maintaining a dying capitalism. The strategic significance of the lower middle classes in Fascist ventures is clearly revealed in recent German history. Contemporary German politics makes it equally clear that the political confusion and ineptness of these classes are not entirely responsible for their susceptibility to Fascist propaganda. They are driven into the Fascist camp, in part, at least, by the dogmatic political religion of Marxism, which fails to do justice to the complexities of Western civilisation, and which, in its blind *furor*, makes enemies out of potential allies.

In spite of the weaknesses of Marxism as a religion, and as a political strategy, it may conquer Christianity and become the dominant religion of our industrial civilisation ; and it will undoubtedly contribute, as a political philosophy and strategy, to the destruction of capitalism and the reconstruction of our society. If it conquers both as a religion and as a political philosophy, the new social order which it will build will not only fall short of the dreams of Communist Utopians, but it will in some respects represent a return to barbarism. A culture which represents emancipation and construction to the senile feudalism of Russia may bring decades of civil war and social confusion to the Western world. Certain social forces of the Western world, which Communism fails to comprehend in its simple religious dogmatism, have more power than they had in Russia, and they will therefore make a more desperate effort to save themselves from extinction. There is little possibility that pure Marxism can become the centre of a new culture and the organising principle of a new society in the Western world. It is more probable that its religious pretensions will prevent the Western world from achieving a workable and stable system of social ownership for some decades to come.

The ominous possibility of the success of Marxism as a religion in the Western world and its consequent failure as a political strategy is partly due to the failure of Christianity to develop a political ethic, consistent with the perfectionism of its gospel on the one hand, and relevant to the political necessities of our day on the other. The pessimism of the Orthodox Church has lamed the moral impulse to achieve a more perfect justice in society, and the optimism of the Liberal Church has obscured the social realities of an unjust civilisation. The Orthodox Church is satisfied with any political order which avoids anarchy, and the Liberal Church gives itself to the illusion that the political order is being gradually transmuted by the moral forces in society into a society of perfect justice. The victims of contemporary social injustice will naturally have nothing of either this pessimism or this optimism. They need a view of life and history which is pessimistic enough to do justice to their actual experiences but does not rob them of the hope of ultimate emancipation.

IV. TOWARDS A CHRISTIAN
POLITICAL ETHIC

There is no reason why Christianity should not have a
political ethic which inspires men to the attainment of
justice without sacrificing the values of its love perfectionism. The ideal of perfect love must remain the most
ultimate ideal of morality. It is the very ideal which discloses the imperfections of every concrete moral achievement by revealing the alloy of egoism which expresses
itself in every act of history, particularly in every collective
act. But this very fact means that the ideal of love is really
beyond the possibilities of history. It may be approximated
in individual life, and only very roughly approximated in
collective relationships. The most significant approximation
of the ideal of love in politics and economics is justice.
The kind of justice which is possible in the economic and
political world is, however, something less than the justice
of free mutuality. Justice in the larger relationships of life
can be established only by a contest of power which creates
a fair equilibrium of power. In our own day this means the
destruction of such dangerous and anachronistic centres of
social power as are maintained through the private possession of social processes. The Liberal Church need only to
consult the political realism of the Orthodox Church to
overcome its squeamishness about the necessities of politics.
The Orthodox Church must combine its political realism
with a hope for, and a will to establish, justice as a more
legitimate approximation of love than its sterile principle
of " order."

In so far as both pessimism of the Orthodox Church and
the optimism of the Liberal Church are rationalisations of
class interest, and do not spring honestly from religious
convictions, this advice is, of course, futile. The Christian
Church is undoubtedly badly enmeshed with, and seriously
compromised by, the social groups which are trying to
maintain the old social system. Yet there is a force in vital

religion which helps it to transcend the interests of particular groups and classes. This force has been vitiated in
the contemporary Church, partly by class interests as such,
and partly by moral and political confusions, derived from
faulty interpretations and applications of the Church's
perfectionist ethic. If the Church corrects these errors, it
will have a political ethic which will borrow from, and
affirm, the validity of many of the basic tenets of Marxian
politics. And such an ethic will relate the heights of its
pure religion to the depths of the political and economic
realm. It would be an ironic, but tragic, justice if the
Church were forced to capitulate to the error in Marxian
religion because it had scorned the truth in Marxian
politics.

It would be well for Christian critics of the more demonic
aspects of Marxism to remember that these aspects are,
on the one hand, the natural consequences of the failure
of Christianity, and, on the other hand, revelations of
human weakness which Marxians share with all human
beings. They are the consequence of the failure of Christianity, because a religion which falsely claims the authority
of God for the particular interests of a portion of the human
community (as historic Christianity has consistently done)
challenges the portion of the community which has been
left out of this process of sanctification to make counter-
claims equally monstrous. Since historic Christianity, both
Protestant and Catholic, has failed to find a rightful place
in its scheme of things for the industrial proletariat, and
has failed even more completely to understand the fateful
mission of this class in modern society, it is natural that this
neglect should be revenged by a self-assertion on the part
of this class in which its high mission in modern society
should lead to unqualified (and therefore demonic) pretensions.

Unqualified pretensions by, or on behalf of, the workers
are the revelations of a common human weakness as well
as the consequence of the sins of the privileged. What gives
all human life its tragic character is that finite men are

always usurping the place of God, i.e. the centre of the meaning of existence. If the workers of the modern world commit this religious pretension, they are not the first, but the last, of all social classes to do it. They are not committing a new, but a very old, human sin. It will be more justly judged by the whole community if it is recognised that it is a sin which the potent class of the hour shares, on the one hand, with all humanity, and to which it has been driven, on the other, by the religious pretensions of its enemies.

V

COMMUNISM THE HEIR TO THE CHRISTIAN TRADITION

by John Lewis

Lecturer in Social Philosophy under the
Cambridge Extra-Mural Board

I. PRIEST AND PROPHET

RELIGION never appears in history as a uniform and balanced system. While in thought we may construct a finished whole, treating heresy and schism as regrettable lapses from an ideal unity, in reality religion always manifests a struggle between two opposite forces, and stability is never possible.

This conflict is most clearly seen in the struggle between Priest and Prophet.

The strength of priestly religion lies in its cast-iron theoretical and organisational system, by means of which it creates the very categories in which men think, so that its gods, its heaven, its hell, its priestly powers, are not mere theories, but objective realities. The world is seen in terms of the mythology and theology of the Church. This type of religion stands for discipline and fixed codes of conduct. Authority is vested in a hierarchy, and great stress is laid on legality and validity. Criticism and change are feared and resisted.

The prophet, on the other hand, proclaims that life and reality have drained out of the forms of religious life, while the moral code constrains men to be less than moral. In him the spirit, which bloweth where it listeth, appears outside the organisation and in opposition to it, undermining authority, irreverent before institutions and officials. The prophet is unimpressed by validity and legality. He opposes his intuitions to the orthodoxy of the priests ; daring to set one man's vision against the creeds of the ages. On the other hand, he is subjective, impracticable, and Utopian. Faced with the practical task of organising the community, prophecy is irresponsible. Its strength is destructive and critical.

It has been argued that this conflict is due to the existence of two psychological types which go to extremes, so that if we fail to balance these two tendencies we shall proceed zigzag fashion, as first one and then the other is predominant. Others have explained that religion is a gradual apprehension of unchangeable truth, approximating to it by alternate movements of fresh discovery and subsequent embodiment in institutions.

Neither approach gets to the heart of the matter. Both the type and the movement depend less upon intellectual or temperamental one-sidedness than upon the evolution of society as a complex of economic, political, and historical factors.

Society develops by alternate periods of consolidation and reconstruction. After a forward step it halts for a time and elaborates a civilisation. But the new structure creates conditions of strain and instability in the process of its development. The result is a period of movement and reconstruction which is also a period of advance. At this stage, and in the period which precedes it, unrest and criticism are to be expected. The prophet, the satirist, the dreamer are ahead of their time. They foreshadow the coming disintegration. When things get more serious the movement becomes a radical criticism of existing institutions which are proving inadequate to the new conditions. Changes, some of which may give a lead in the right direction, are sketched out in Utopian fashion and in great variety. Eventually these forces of change become organised and constructive, while both the pressure of external circumstances and the internal strain steadily increase. Then follows a period of revolution and reconstruction, and a new order supervenes.

At a succession of moments in this process, a cross-section will reveal conflicting tendencies at various stages of development. At an earlier period the old categories are still valid, but later they are so hopelessly inadequate that to all intelligent people they are mere dead forms, contradicting reality. This is not a mere development of ideas, it is an interaction of ideas and events. Events develop not only in themselves, but because men understand them and manipulate them accordingly. On the other hand, interpretation is strictly conditioned by the facts and concrete possibilities.

A classical example of the eternal conflict in religion and its dependence upon social development is found in the history of the Hebrews. The prophetic protest covered a period of a hundred years from the disconnected utterances of Amos, the herdsman of Tekoa, to the elaborate written discourses of Jeremiah and Isaiah II. Four great prophets criticised priestly religion and social injustice, and foresaw the collapse of the Hebrew monarchical system. The reconstructed Jewish State embodied many of the more ethical and democratic principles of the prophets, and these became embodied in a new temple ritual, a new theology, and a new code of taboos and morals. Subsequently the growth of the world empires of Greece and Rome submitted the new Jewish State to intense strain. This, combined with its internal development, led to the condition of political and economic distress responsible for the despair of Jewish apocalyptic.

Jesus was the child of His age. He did much to hasten the disintegration of society in this period of decline by His devastating criticism of the now outworn forms of conduct and religion, but He also foreshadowed a new Kingdom of a distinctly Utopian kind. In fact when the time became ripe for the foundations of a new social order to be laid, medievalism was compelled to degrade His lofty ideals to something altogether more practical and politically workable. Eventually Christianity became "categorical" rather than idealistic, and continued as a priestly rather than a prophetic system until the social and economic changes of the Renaissance.

Religion in the critical and prophetic phase will possess the defects of its idealistic qualities. It will be pure, but it will also be abstract. On the other hand, when its turn comes to mould the world to its heart's desire and it enters the priestly phase, it will suffer some worldly contamination, but it will, at any rate, become more concrete. This is the source of the unending conflict between Prophet and Priest.

The religious struggle, moreover, is not the only ideological expression of the dialectic of social development. Philosophy also reflects it. The period of organisation and consolidation is a period of rationalism and monism, while the period of disintegration and reform sees a movement in the direction of pluralism and empiricism.

Conservative rationalism forces content into form. Radical empiricism breaks the forms as inadequate to the richness of experience and the movement of a living world. The new wine bursts the old bottles.

II. SECULAR AND SACRED

In this eternal contradiction of form and matter we have the clue to the conflict of the Secular and Sacred.

Secularism is the tendency to accept the concrete, supernaturalism to accept the ideal. The supernatural ideal of the Kingdom of God suffers progressive degradation as it embodies itself in the medieval social system, but at the same time it organises society. We thus have the paradox of medieval Christianity which at one and the same time upholds the spiritual in the form of an other-worldly religion, and debases and secularises it.

Man was made God in order that God might become human. This humanising of the Divine ideal compels the Church to compromise in its endeavour to be practical.

Hence, as the inevitable reaction to this secularisation, idealism and supernaturalism are driven into sharper antithesis to the semi-Christianised world, and appear as monasticism, mysticism, the perfectionist sects, the ascetics, the saints, and in an intense other-worldliness.

Neither side is in the right or in the wrong. If supernaturalism completely succumbs to the secular programme of the Church, we get the political-ecclesiastic, and religion becomes simply another counter in the secular game. If supernaturalism wins, the world is left unredeemed, and society goes to the devil. The saints go into a monastery or disappear into their seventh heaven, while supernaturalism itself tends to dissolve the solidarity of temporal and eternal, of body and soul, and thus degenerates into an utterly unchristian, dualistic asceticism.

In the face of this dilemma there is only one way out ; the saint and the politician have to join forces in an unstable and uneasy combination. Often, indeed, these opposite forces will be found in one man, the ecclesiastical statesman, or the prophetic social reformer.

The business of the saint is to urge the doctrine of self-denial, the hollowness of earthly satisfactions, the supremacy of spiritual ends, loyalty to " another world," more real and of infinitely greater worth than this one. The Church cannot allow itself to be absorbed by a State it may be compelled to rebuke. The ideal of Hildebrand was :

" A throne of judgment, different in its origin and authority from all earthly thrones ; a common father and guide of Christians whom all acknowledged, and who was clothed with prerogatives which all believed to come from above ; a law of high purpose and scope, embodying the greatest principles of justice and purity, and aiming, on the widest scale, at the elevation and improvement of society ; and administration of this law, which regarded not persons and was not afraid of the face of man, and told the truth to ambitious emperors and adulterous kings and queens." [1]

[1] Church, *St. Anselm.*

Yet, as Dante saw so clearly, ultimately the secular State must be absolute, depending on spiritual government neither for its being, nor for its force and authority, nor for its power of action. The statesman must govern, and government imposes its inexorable demands. It requires laws which can be enforced. It requires sanctions. It must contract alliances with economic and political forces. Policy must be determined not by what we wish for, but by what it is possible to get.

Out of this contradiction springs the age-long struggle between the practical reformer and the transcendentalist. The religious reformer claims that the social order should glorify God, that right human relations should manifest the Divine, that pity, fellowship, and equality are sacred. He wants to conform the real to the ideal, believing that as the reluctant material is subdued to the vision so it becomes the medium of the Divine. He is a Platonist in that he believes that the Divine cannot make itself known except in so far as the material world participates in it. This is a doctrine of incarnation. The eternal purpose, the ulti-mate goal, always present in the mind of God, slowly operates in and upon the evolving world ; it penetrates, and is apprehended by, the mind of man, and thus be-comes conscious. It attains full self-expression in Jesus, who knows of what man is capable and that his destiny is to constitute with his fellows a perfect society. Man is only truly himself in an ideal society. Therefore it is in the Beloved Community that the Ideal is realised, that social evolution achieves its goal.

In Christianity this ideal first comes to full consciousness. It remains for all men to come up on to the level first reached by Jesus, and on that level to bring their social relations into conformity with the demands of the sacred fellowship. So long as society falls short of this ideal, religion must maintain its separate identity in ecclesiastical and mystical forms, but as society approximates to it these forms will disappear, giving way to the " extension of the incarnation " into society itself. True religion becomes seeing God in your fellow, and being knit together in the holy communion in which we no longer live, but Christ liveth in us.

The long continuance of ecclesiasticism is due to the fact that this task cannot be accomplished prematurely, but awaits that post-capitalist stage in social development in which a classless society is for the first time possible. The secular reformer is therefore in unending conflict with the transcendentalist. He is suspicious of every form of religion which postpones the Kingdom to the next world, or which projects its ideal into a transcendental sphere and abandons the stern task of conforming life to the will of God. He is acutely conscious of the danger of religion becoming a substitute for righteousness instead of a force making for righteousness. His gospel is rooted in the old prophetic denunciations of priestly formalism, and in Jesus's stern criticisms of the Pharisees and the Temple.

On the other hand, the transcendentalist sees that the more the reformer becomes immersed in the petty details of his task, and is compelled to work with all kinds and conditions of men, the more does his ideal contract and his method conform to expediency. Therefore, he never ceases to remind the reformer that only the ideal has absolute authority, that works without faith are of no avail, that a purified spirit is the first essential of effective reform, and that spiritual values are superior to material. The true mystic pins his whole faith in God and not in man. The Kingdom comes in God's time, not in ours ; in God's way, not in our way ; in God's strength, not in man's. It is not for us to strive and cry in the streets, " in quietness and in confidence shall be your strength, in returning and rest shall ye be saved."

On the purely intellectual level there is no solution to this problem. Victory can be awarded to no side, nor can some synthesis be found which will do justice to both tendencies. We are in the painful position of the Indian in the legend. When the Gods gave him a wife, he found life intolerable, but when the Gods relented and took her away again, he found things still more intolerable. He could neither live with her nor without her. Thus also secular society can neither live with religion nor without it. It is only the movement of history which brings us to a solution, and changing circumstances which can soften the harshness of the antithesis.

Something like this seems to happen in the life of Jesus. He fulfils the Law and the Prophets, He does not destroy them. His strength lies not in His giving the victory to secularism over religion, or to religion over secularism, but in His unique orientation of the problem. He seems, at any rate for a moment, to do justice to both sides by lifting the whole question on to a new level.

Thus in Jesus we have an apocalypticism which is both God-dependent and a call to urgent and immediate action ; a mysticism which touches the absolute, but sanctifies the present duty. The Holy Communion was at one and the same time a sacrament to endue a suffering, waiting Church with grace, and an achieved fellowship in which no man said that aught of the things which he posesssed was his own, but they had all things in common. Holy Communion was Holy Communism.

Thus the old controversy becomes meaningless, but the synthesis is premature, and the postponement of the Second Coming forces the Fellowship to become a Church in which the old antithesis develops again in a new form.

But Christianity was not merely a fresh start. It was Jewish society moving on to a new organisational form. The nation decays, the Temple falls, the synagogue of the dispersion encounters the gentile world, European society is in the melting-pot, and a new type of religious society is born. It is the culmination of all that went before it. It grows out of historical Judaism—not merely out of its ideas and literature, but out of its life, its kingship, its government, its customs and experience, its flesh-and-blood people. But at the same time it is a new compound, not a mixture. It is Judaism plus Græco-Romanism. Finally, it does not merely happen of itself, it is created by Jesus and is inconceivable without Him.

As Stalin once said :

" It is men who make history. But of course, men do not make history according to their imagination, as pictured by their minds. Every new generation encounters certain conditions which existed in completed form already at the moment this generation was born.

" And great men are only of value in so far as they know how rightly to grasp these conditions, to understand how they are to be changed. If they do not understand these conditions and seek to change them according to their own imagination, then these people find themselves in a position of Don Quixote."[1]

In any synthesis there are three factors : tradition, the present circumstances, the man of genius. This does not say that given a certain objective situation there is only one possible outcome. It does insist that the next phase is demanded by the previous development and is limited by it. But there will be no development without the insight and initiative of the human genius who brings it about.

III. RELIGION AND SCIENCE

Since the Renaissance, religion has been compelled to surrender large sections of human life to secular control, especially in science (including medicine), art, and economics.

So long as we do not understand nature, and therefore cannot control it, we are constrained to accept a supernatural or animistic explanation of events, and to attempt their control by magic and prayer.

But the more we know, and the more we can control

[1] Newspaper report of an interview with Stalin, June 7th, 1932.

events for ourselves, the more the area of science expands and the province of the miraculous is contracted. To-day not even fundamentalists expect miracles to happen in connection with the electricity supply, or the railway service, or the operations of a factory, a blast-furnace, or a chemical works.

When men do not know, and think they cannot know, they fall back on mythology and magic. Mythology eventually becomes poetry. The poet will give us, by intuition, a cosmology which *appeals* to us as true. This is its only criterion. There are still many people who will accept an imaginatively conceived philosophy of life simply because it *feels* true. Many religious ideas rest on that basis. They are imaginative hypotheses which explain the apparently contradictory and confusing facts by fitting them into a pattern or a story—perhaps a story with a happy ending. It is not necessary to *prove* that such an explanation is true, it is true *because* it explains so much. Christian theology itself is frequently defended on these grounds, though it is not realised that by so doing the rational basis of theology is destroyed. The fallacy is a fatal one. We cannot logically conclude from the conditional proposition that *if* certain things are true then the facts as we find them would be the consequences, that such consequences *prove* those things to be their cause. It is no more than a possibility, and twenty other circumstances might equally as well have been the cause. You cannot prove cause from effect until you have shown that the effect could be produced by no other cause. It is not claimed for these poetical explanations that they conform to such conditions.

The area of tested cause and effect, however, is rapidly growing. Science does not know everything, but it does not exclude any phenomena from its enquiries, or admit that there can be, from a scientific point of view, an uncaused event. Where science is not yet complete—as in medicine, and, to an even greater degree, in economics and sociology —magic and mythology still occupy the field. Medicine is an interesting case in point, because we can actually watch the rising tide. The more ignorant sections of the population still rely on quacks and prayer, but the more enlightened communities trust medical science almost completely, and, even where medicine has failed, they believe that the remedy is not to substitute magic for science, but more and better medical science.

Religion is thus being driven into departmentalism. Instead of covering the whole of life, influencing the secular and redeeming the material, it retreats into an enclave, where it cultivates specifically religious emotions and fosters a direct mystical contact with God.

The result is religious degeneration. When religion is an attempt to sanctify life, communion with God involves a real effort to find and to do His will in the secular sphere. When religion turns from life, then God Himself becomes a mere spiritual existence in a universe which He has ceased to control. Religion may even become a refuge from a world too sordid to be anything but the enemy of the religious spirit. The guarantee of objectivity vanishes as God is driven from the secular. " I had fainted unless I had believed to see the goodness of the Lord in the land of the living." Healthy, objective religion roots its faith in the judgments of God, in the discernment of His purpose in history, and in a Divine significance in events. If God is not here at all, but only in religious experience, we have nothing at all to validate that experience. It may be pure illusion. The psychologist confronted with this confessed abandonment of the secular world is compelled to diagnose it as a clear case of the flight from reality. Such religion becomes the absorbing pursuit of the few—a mere cult of ecclesiastically minded Churchmen and vague pseudo-mystics.

Nothing could be less " catholic " or more remote from the religious activities of the Hebrew prophets and the Christian statesmanship of the great Churchmen.

This degeneration of religion into other-worldliness is more closely connected with life than it knows.

It is a refuge from its growing perplexities, and the more

social collapse ends in tragedy for countless lives the more will religion of this sort be needed.

It is also a way of personal holiness in a wicked world, and the less possible it is to be just and generous in one's social relationships the more necessary it is to find a way of being good in isolation from one's fellows.

Finally, it is an outlet for individuality when normal opportunities for self-development are diminishing. It enhances the sense of personal worth in a world which is increasingly regardless of the individual.

This type of religion is no cure for the diseases of modern society, it merely prolongs it. It is, in fact, part of the disease.

IV. RELIGION AND REFORM

But religion also develops in the opposite direction in the numerous movements which have attempted to Christianise the social and political order. This, as far as it goes, is a real continuation of the prophetic tradition and the struggle to redeem the secular. But its end is not essentially different from the lapse into other-worldliness. In its early days it is earnest, searching, and courageous, but the closer it gets to grips with the real world the more anxious it is not to identify itself with any particular remedy, least of all with one political party. This is rather like a religious campaign for protecting child life from diphtheria which would shrink from " taking sides " on the question of whether the milk should be purified. It is obvious that in such a case if the Church is serious it is just the effective method of prevention which needs its unqualified support. Indeed, assistance which falls short of this, or asserts that it is too controversial for the Church to take sides about, is doing serious harm.

It may be said that this begs the question, since Socialism is not so certain as the conclusions of preventive medicine. But that is also begging the question ! Perhaps Socialism is the only remedy and the scientific solution, in which case the Church must reach this conclusion or be a dangerous delaying force to progress.

The psychology of the Christian Social Movement is interesting. When it dawns on the more alert among the clergy that mankind has reached the limit of endurance under the profit-seeking order, they are quick to see that men will turn to the most promising political or economic way out unless they can be persuaded that Christianity is the alternative. They do not find it easy to conceive that Christianity itself might lead to one of these more concrete proposals ; perhaps because in that case it might seem that, after having guided men to the truth, there was no further use for the Church, and the task of reconstructing the world could be safely left with some new political movement. But even if Christianity could indicate such a movement, and could safely leave the task of economic reconstruction in its hands, it might still find itself playing an indispensable part in the movement in purifying men's motives and maintaining a flame of consecrated devotion to the sacred cause of which it was the instrument. The more closely the ideal and the practical are welded the more necessary is it to maintain the supremacy and purity of the ideal.

The clergy would appear to shrink from such a function, fearing perhaps to see church-going and devotion falling into a secondary place, or even disappearing. We therefore find them very reluctant to admit that any cure for our social ills is to be found in the great social movements of our time, and inclined to claim that Christianity by itself, acting through the Churches, will do all that they promise, and do it better. The Church has therefore given many the impression that, while it may wish to develop a social conscience, it is only as a substitute for a social programme.

The Christian Social Movement was more impressive when it was farther from the end of its enquiries and when Socialism itself was a remote contingency. To-day it is definitely less Socialist than it was, and in many cases has committed itself to other alternatives (notably the Douglas scheme). It gives the impression of trying to sound heroic while meaning as little as possible. Even the socialistically inclined in the Church are vague and evasive in their social diagnosis, and tend to substitute rhetoric for serious analysis. An inhibition prevents them ever getting as far as the brutal truth. They are more dangerous than the downright reactionaries, because they draw after them a following of earnest people who are profoundly dissatisfied with the social system, persuading them that they are joining a crusade for Christian Socialism, and then stopping short of decision on every crucial issue. Thus they satisfy the discontent and idealism of their followers, and successfully hold them back from going on to Socialism—as many of them undoubtedly would.

V. DUALISM IN PHILOSOPHY AND RELIGION

Dualism is the common-sense philosophy. There appears to be something in the universe which thwarts our desires. If the world were wholly good or wholly bad, no problem would arise. We could not be otherwise than perfectly at home in it. But if the universe is good, where did the evil which mars it come from? If the universe is purposeless or evil, where did the good come from?

The problem has never been better put than by Plato, in his image of the two steeds dragging the chariot, and in his dialogue on immortality, where he declares that the body is a hindrance to the soul, not suffering it to acquire truth and wisdom, filling us with longings, desires, and fears. We are not to suffer ourselves to be polluted by its nature, but must purify ourselves from it, until God Himself shall relieve us.[1]

The heart of the problem, however, is not the purely intellectual difficulty of reconciling the oneness of the

[1] *Phædo*, p. 66–7.

universe with the obvious multiplicity of experience, or explaining the existence of an alien tendency in the universe, but the more urgent difficulty of coping practically with the evil in the world. Therefore it is not a case of proving irrationality to be more apparent than real, or evil to be but the shadow cast by the light: evil has not so much to be explained as abolished. The movement towards unity is a practical one, and not a mere movement of the mind in a static world.

The ritual and mythology of religion, as well as the theories of philosophers, express this conflict, and endeavour to resolve it. Religious mysteries dramatise it, and the theologies rationalise it, but at bottom it is the fight against cold, hunger, disease, death, devils, ill-luck, fate, the furies, bodily lusts, and even matter itself.

Thus religion is at first an impulse to abolish evil practically, and make life more harmonious by extending control over nature and the selfish impulses of man. But, unfortunately, it may attempt to achieve its aim prematurely by leaping over contradictions and resolving dualism in thought and imagination only. Monistic philosophy on the one hand, and mysticism on the other, must be held to be guilty of this shirking of the real task. The first, by an effort of reason, tries to show that the universe must always have been perfect, and that both change and evil are the illusions of a partial point of view ; reconciliation being therefore rather an effort of thought than the turning of irrationality into rationality by changing events. For Hegel the changes of history represent the movement of partial ideas towards greater completeness and unity, but in reality the goal is already attained. The mystic, for his part, claims to reach by intuition an identity with God, in whom the distinction between good and evil is transcended. Time, history, and struggle *sub specie æternitatis*, are seen to have an illusory character. In the ecstasy of union with God, the mystic is granted the vision of what life really means for all men if they would only see it. No matter what man's earthly lot the bliss of joyful acquiescence might be his present possession. Therefore the way out of trouble is to tread the path of purgation to the state of mystic contemplation of, and rest in, the Absolute Good.

We need not doubt the bliss, but we have every reason to doubt its explanation. The mind may be stilled, as by an opiate, but the contradiction remains for the more realistically minded to overcome by deeds. We may note that Jesus did not, either by example or precept, meet disease and hunger by persuading people that blessedness was really already theirs, but by curing sickness and distributing bread.

There is only one sane way to overcome dualism, and that is by eliminating the evil. In so far as hygiene and medicine abolish disease, there is actually less evil in the world. In so far as divergent economic interests are removed, and the class division between owners and disinherited vanishes in common ownership, there is actually more unity and rationality in the universe.

This is not only the product of idealistic effort, but of social evolution. In this fact we find the grain of truth in absolutism, but the evolutionary process whereby contradictions are resolved is not a mere unfolding of the given, but an actual movement of history. Naturally the logical unity of our conception of a more highly developed order is greater than that which reflects a more chaotic period. It is only in this sense that thought attains its quest and reaches harmony. Furthermore the successive steps do not happen of themselves. Only a clear apprehension of the hopeless contradiction involved in some particular form of social organisation, coupled with an equally clear apprehension of the immediate practicability and desirability of a certain definite reorganisation, will enable the necessary steps to reform to be made.

Evolution also means that there can be no hurrying of social development, least of all can the whole historical sequence be skipped. Rationalisation and harmonisation proceeds through conflict, through patient effort, and along the line of successive stages.

As it succeeds, the universe actually changes. Here is a flat contradiction of absolutism. The world of 1934 is quite different from the world of 1834. It contains motor-cars, wireless-sets, steamships, and electricity. Its economic structure is different ; its social relations are different ; its values have altered. But change may be in the direction of unity and more good. If evolution proceeds according to our hopes, the unity is an achieved unity, and the evil has been actually eliminated and replaced by good, though this does not follow inevitably. Therefore, when we ask, " Is the universe rational ? " we cannot answer on the assumption that it is eternally either one thing or the other : it may be irrational to-day and rational to-morrow, *if we succeed in making it so.* The problem of evil is not whether there is eternally more evil in the world than good, or whether that evil is real or apparent, or whether it serves some purpose, *but how to eliminate it.*

VI. THE ECONOMIC BASIS OF DUALISM

" Why should the almost immeasurable increase in productive power and the possibility of universal abundance result in universal impoverishment and lowering
standards ? This is the question that confronts the whole
human race, that is becoming a life-and-death question
for nineteen hundred million human beings, to which
these hundreds of millions must find the answer or go
down in catastrophe."[1]

A growing consensus of economic opinion endorses the Marxian judgment that the capitalist economic system can-not but lead to conditions of confusion and intolerable paradox. But the system itself depends on the relations of the two main classes of society—those who, in the main, own the means of production and for whom the world's oyster is opened, and those who are employed by them and

[1] Dutt, R. P., *Fascism,* p. 15.

can produce nothing and get nothing until some " owner "
will employ them, and who, as employees, do the whole of
the world's productive work and create its wealth. This
state of affairs is what is rightly called a class society. It is
clear that such a society, with its muddle and strain, is not
an easy one to live comfortably in. Men are baffled, per-
plexed, reduced at last to hopeless despair. The world appears a thoroughly irrational place. As the economic consequences of private ownership work themselves out, and
the period of permanent crisis is entered, the darkness
deepens, and to the thoughtful mind irrationality appears
rooted in the very nature of reality. In consequence philosophy takes an irrationalist turn. As reason falls into contempt, superstition revives and strange cults have a new
attraction. Even in the physical sciences men turn to mysticism, and begin to speak of the bifurcation of the universe,
a partial rationality, but outside it a penumbra, non-
rationally apprehended, incalculable, indeterminate, mind-
created. Professor Blackett says, shrewdly, of this new
mysticism :

" I really do think that this type of philosophic attitude is
   just one of the reactions to the muddle of our social
   structure. It seems to me a ' flight from reality ' in the
   sense that it seeks a purely personal and intellectual
   satisfaction in a world of emotional ideas."[1]

Man's failure to understand the economic situation, and
to control it, has therefore increased the unintelligibility of
the universe and deepened the problem of evil. Just as the
Hebrews in their decline turned to child sacrifice and the
" dark gods," and a great wave of superstition swept over
them, so we are witnessing a revival of superstition, of belief
in Divine intervention, and of the notion of an irrational
element in human affairs. Thoughtful men see that science
is baffled by the vagaries of the human will, by anti-social
instincts, by intractable social and economic forces. This
may develop into blank pessimism, or into cults which foster

[1] Broadcast address, *Web of Thought and Action* series, 1933.

an intense spiritual life in some little corner of a distracted and evil world.

In these circumstances, man cannot dispense with the consolations of religion. Life would become absolutely unbearable.

" Religious misery is, on one hand, the expression of actual misery, and, on the other, a protest against actual misery. Religion is the sigh of the oppressed creature, the kindliness of a heartless world, the spirit of unspiritual conditions. It is the people's opium.

" The removal of religion as the illusory happiness of the people is the demand for its real happiness. The demand that it should give up illusions about its real conditions is the demand that it should give up the conditions which make illusions necessary. Criticism of religion is therefore at heart a criticism of the vale of misery for which religion is the promised vision.

" Criticism has torn away the imaginary flowers with which his chains were bedecked, not in order that man should wear his chains without the comfort of illusions, but that he may throw off the chains and pluck the living flowers. Criticism of religion disillusions man so that he may think, act, and shape his reality as one who is disillusioned and come to full understanding, so that he may move on his own axis and thus be his own sun. Religion is but the false sun which revolves around him while he is not yet fully self-aware."[1]

It is useless for modernists and rationalists to demonstrate the baselessness of these superstitions ; as fast as they are destroyed they will spring up, for they are a product not of the weakness of man's intellect, but of the disintegration of the social order in which he is condemned to live.

To destroy these illusions, one must first of all abolish the social evils out of which they spring. Now society not

[1] Marx, *Introduction to a Critique of Hegel's Philosophy of Law.*

only descends into the abyss, but simultaneously the forms of a new order are maturing in the womb of the existing world. The same circumstances which hasten us to destruction prepare our deliverance. Everything conspires to a resolution of the fatal dilemma of a class society. The working class begins to demand the complete abolition of the private ownership of productive apparatus. They claim that it is their historic mission, for which their very sufferings have prepared them, to be the instrument of emancipation. Meanwhile the imminent danger of the collapse of capitalism drives the employing class on to make cruel onslaughts on working-class standards in a last effort to reduce costs, recapture trade, and stave off disaster. This onslaught only serves to precipitate the counter-attack of the workers, and the monopoly of ownership is wrested from a class and transferred to the community. Under these conditions " the relations between human beings in the practical everyday life would assume the aspect of perfectly intelligible and reasonable relations as between man and man and as between man and nature."

Therefore, the moment this becomes possible the religious institution is confronted with an altogether new crisis. Hitherto it has stood for an unrealisable ideal, and has alternated between secularisation and transcendentalism. It now becomes possible to enmesh the ideal in the material world without loss. So long as the social and economic organisation was of such a character that it could not permit the realisation of ideals, the idealist was steadily forced to accommodate his principles to its inexorable demands in so far as he decided to live and work in society and not dream. On the other hand, if he determined to keep his ideals intact, then he could not grapple effectively with reality, and he was compelled to become a hypocrite (making the best of both worlds) or a mystic. But when social development reaches the stage when ideals are realisable the struggle becomes capable of a successful issue. It is not settled, but it is no longer condemned to futility by the very nature of the conditions.

As a consequence the whole structure of religion changes. The ecclesiastical, devotional, and mystical forms proper to a dualistic period become obsolete. Religion has been adapted to the needs of a class society ; it must now suffer complete transformation as the classless world approaches.

To some this spells the death of religion and blank materialism ; but to others it is what they had always sought. The prophet should be able to welcome the new age. Now, at last, it is possible to manifest the will of God in social relations and show forth the glory of His purpose in the common ways of life.

" In that day shall there be upon the bells of the horses, Holy unto the Lord. . . . Yea, every pot in Jerusalem shall be holy unto the Lord of hosts." "This is the law of the house . . . the whole limit thereof round about shall be most holy. Behold, this is the law of the house." (Zech. xiv. 20, 21 ; Ezek. xliii. 12.)

The sacred is far from being the " wholly other," it is the quality of the secular raised to its highest power and consecrated to the noblest purposes. As each part of life is integrated into the social organism it finds itself, and takes on the special quality that belongs to a part of a new whole —just as a note of music is transformed by being in its place in a musical composition.

On the other hand, transcendentalism withers away. It is no longer necessary to project into another world the order, the justice, and the beauty which we cannot achieve in this. The life process of society loses its veil of mystery when it becomes a process carried on by a free association of producers, under their conscious and purposive control.

It is no longer necessary to explain famine and disease and war as due to the inscrutable will of God, or to offer the consolations of religion and a recompense hereafter as a substitute for justice and the chance of a full life here and now.

VII. RATIONALISM AND IRRATIONALISM IN ETHICS

(1) As long as a class society exists, *ethics must be arbitrary and authoritative.* Under capitalism you must not ask why property rights are sacred. It is a categorical imperative, rooted in the Divine Will or in the very nature of things. An uncorrupted conscience will intuitively recognise the validity of this moral law.

But the real reason why this moral law must not be questioned is that it is irrational and has no basis other than the need to perpetuate a class society. It is instinctive simply because it is one of the categories of such a society, it is part of the pattern of that sort of world. This moral code is enforced by religion, education, dramatic art, and literature. It is sacred tribal custom, hedged by taboo. The supernatural or mystical sanction of morality is necessary so long as morality does not bear rational investigation.

Benjamin Kidd restates in the language of modern science what had been more crudely put by those religious leaders who in the eighteenth century interpreted the message of religion as a summons to the poor to adapt themselves to the inconveniences of life with pious gratitude.

Wilberforce had urged, in 1798, that Christianity made the inequalities of the social scale less galling to the lower orders by teaching them to be diligent, humble, and patient. " This," explained Wilberforce, in a letter to Pitt, " is the basis of all politics." Benjamin Kidd argued that :

" A religion is a form of belief, providing an ultra-rational sanction for that large class of conduct in the individual where his interests and the interests of the social organism are antagonistic, and by which the former are rendered subordinate to the latter in the general interests of the evolution which the race is undergoing."[1]

This puts the matter very neatly. It was formerly supposed

[1] Kidd, Benjamin, *Social Evolution*, chap. v., p. 111.

that the individual participated in the welfare of the whole, and could therefore be rationally persuaded to subordinate himself to the community. Evolution and the law of the survival of the fittest has shown the folly of this. It can no longer be pretended *in a capitalist society*, since it is obvious that under competition one class suffers in order that another may enjoy special privileges. What is to be done about it ? Religion, which foolish rationalists have sought to destroy, is obviously intended for this predicament.

All rational grounds for exploiting the individual having disappeared, irrational, or, shall we say, " ultra-rational," grounds must be found. We must be in the position to say to the worker, " We can offer you nothing but suffering, we propose to sacrifice you to the community. The struggle for existence renders the interests of the social organism and of yourselves antagonistic " ; " they can never be reconciled ; they are inherently and essentially irreconcilable."[1] Religion shows us that self-immolation is an inescapable obligation. It is right, not because it is reasonable, but because God has revealed it. Believe it because it is impossible. Religion alone can provide the ultra-rational support which the perpetuation of such a social system requires. As Kidd further demonstrates, Christianity does not preach this doctrine to everybody. It balances self-assertiveness and subordination. But it has been a mistake to suppose that these impulses are to be reconciled in the lives of individuals. The antithesis finds its solution in the class theory of the State. *One class is to manifest the self-assertiveness, the other class the self-sacrifice.*

Kidd is right in challenging the identification of individual and social welfare under capitalism. He is right in seeing the imperative need for supernaturalism if a class society is to be perpetuated.

But in a classless society morality has the possibility of becoming rational. It is reasonable for the individual to participate in an order the single aim of which is to secure the maximum advantage to its constituent members.

[1] Kidd, Benjamin, *Social Evolution*, chap. iii., p. 84.

The question of morality really disappears into the question of ways and means. It becomes the economy of balancing our goods and deciding how best to achieve them.

(2) A divinely ordained *hierarchical authority* is necessary in a class society, because unquestioned subordination is required in order that privilege may be maintained. This can only be secured by a caste system based on purely irrational and supernatural sanctions. With the disappearance of class ownership of the apparatus of production, caste privilege also vanishes. Differentiation of function implies no privilege and needs no Divine sanction.

VIII. TRANSITION

The end of an era is inevitably a period of extreme difficulty and distress.

> *They walk to and fro in darkness ;*
> *All the foundations of the earth are moved.*

There are two kinds of change. Readjustment and revolution. All sensible men would prefer that under all circumstances the conservatism of Burke were possible.

" In what we improve we are never wholly new ; in what we retain we are never wholly obsolete. The disposition to preserve and ability to improve, taken together, would be my standard of a Statesman."[1]

Unfortunately there come times when change goes down to the roots of things. This is not of the will of man except in so far that no change is possible apart from profound understanding and deliberately willed reconstruction. It is understanding of an objective situation, as when the subsidence of a low sea-coast compels its inhabitants to abandon it and withdraw into the interior high lands.

Change is fundamental to-day because the subsidence of capitalism requires the final and complete abandonment of

[1] Burke, *Reflections on the French Revolution.*

private ownership of land and capital. On these foundations our whole social structure is reared, and, if they go, not a thing remains the same. Art, philosophy, religion, customs, and morals, class distinctions, science itself, everything, " suffers a sea change, into something new and strange."

The world is seen and constituted by means of certain forms and categories. Form and content are normally inseparable. The network of relations in which a thing exists makes it what it is. From the point of view of organism, a part of the body is constituted by its relations to other parts and to the whole. From the point of view of our categories, the earth is for us a revolving sphere, the blood circulates in the body, soul and body interact, a man can " own " a coal-mine. Are these theories or facts ? Both. They are ways of perceiving, and at the same time things perceived objectively. There was a time when the world was different ; the time is at hand when it will again be different. It is as though the faculty of sight were taken away and another faculty given us through which we felt some new essential quality in things—some fourth-dimensional aspect, neither solidity nor colour, but quite as real. So the world dissolves and is remade. All the landmarks are altered, and we cannot comprehend things in the old terms any more.

Such a period was the end of Judaism, with the dissolution of Temple worship and the Law. It is crucifixion and death, that rebirth may follow. The chrysalis becomes the butterfly, the grain of wheat dies, is buried, and is reborn. Yet the new grows out of, and is determined by, the old. It is not only change, but fulfilment. The essence of evolution is continuity, development, identity. But the essence of evolution is also discontinuity and real, not apparent, change. A new pattern emerges with totally new behaviour, new laws, new characteristics, even though no new substance has been injected, only the original material has gone to the making of the new, and only the original forces have created the new organisation.

In our day the theological, devotional, and ecclesiastical

forms which have functioned since the Reformation are in
dissolution. Up to the present they have constituted an
essential element in the complex of society. A flat earth,
a starry firmament, phlogiston, corpuscular light, a feudal
society—all these modes once obtained and we lived by
them. In so far as they served us, they were partially true.
When they became inadequate, we dropped them or
modified them. Religion, too, was a way of organising and
dealing with our world and ourselves, but its day of change
has also come. The Church will bitterly resist as Judaism
did. The end of Law and Temples, from its point of view,
is the end of religion itself. Because it cannot separate form
and content, the winding up of the old institution will
seem pure loss. That legally constituted channels of
supernatural grace, a divinely constituted and infallible
Church, the propitiatory sacrifice, the way of prayer and
purgation, should become obsolescent is a terrible thought
to some. Bertrand Russell has pointed out that philosophies
are never overthrown, they fade out. The old controversy
becomes meaningless and ceases to interest. The world
has moved on. So we are moving beyond the religion of
yesterday and to-day. Very soon the hotly canvassed questions of current religious controversy will have but an
historical interest and will awaken no spark of heat.

During the period of transition, however, we must
expect the most bitter divisions. " Suppose you that I am
come to give peace on earth ? I tell you, No; but rather
division. From henceforth there shall be five in one house
divided, three against two, and two against three. And the
brother shall deliver up the brother to death, and the
father the child. Think not that I am come to send peace
on earth : I came not to send peace, but a sword."

We may be quite certain that practically the whole body
of clergy and religious laymen will resist the inevitable
change. It is tragic, even pitiful, but it is not an occasion
for bitterness or cynicism. The new wine needs new bottles.
Jesus knew well enough that this Second Coming would
find men unprepared, would sift them as wheat. " At

such an hour that ye think not," and in such a manner, and in alien guise, the Lord comes. Only the elect recognise Him, and they are Samaritans, Roman centurions, publicans and sinners, outcasts, heathens and harlots. The Church still solemnly reads these passages (and how very many of them there are), but it has not the slightest comprehension of what it is reading.

When the Kingdom dawns the whole force of organised Christianity will be mobilised to resist it. But in vain. Birth is irresistible. The child must come forth. When the leaf matures and the cincture grows, the leaf must be nipped off and fall. Decay is irresistible too.

But, since it is a step in emergent evolution, we may expect all of value in the old to be conserved. There is no real loss. Religion in its pre-Socialist phase remains apart in order that it may serve a necessary function which no other organisation fulfils. Society at this time needs its God, its Saviour, its Heaven, its Sacraments. But this particular need passes with the age. It becomes unnecessary to have an apparatus for crystallising the unattainable, a vehicle for the unrealisable ideal. Dualism dies a natural death. But all that religion existed to preserve has been preserved, and is now embodied in the secular as its very soul.

The new age of the Kingdom can say to a dying Church :

> *All which I took from thee I did but take*
> *Not for thy harms,*
> *But just that thou might'st seek it in My arms.*
> *All which thy child's mistake*
> *Fancies as lost, I have stored for thee at home :*
> *Rise, clasp My hand, and come !*

On the other hand this is no victory for a barren secularism. The new world is not materialistic, but realistic. Spiritual values are supreme, but they are the values of material things. Music is the spiritual value of its material conditions, and is inseparable from them, even though it is distinguishable. The secularism of the nineteenth century, in its anxiety to escape the contamination of superstition, was overcome by a barren rationalism which made change impossible, and so was forced to deny the emergent realities of spirit, virtue and beauty. To-day we can gratefully accept the critical spirit and the stern monistic naturalism which secularism so courageously championed, but we can also reject its limitations. Its atomism, its anarchical determinism, sprang from the philosophy of competitive individualism in which social results were the outcome of the blind interaction of unconscious elements and forces.

The capitalist era sees atomistic secularism organised in one camp and spiritual idealism organised in another, both defective, both children of their age, and both necessary.

The Socialist era sees the death and rebirth of both movements and their synthesis in an entirely new orientation of life and thought.

Some of the world's profoundest thinkers have anticipated such a consummation. In the twelfth century Joachim of Flora taught that the age of dualism, of the contrast between the Church and the world, was over, the Age of the Spirit had dawned. This meant the end of ecclesiasticism and of special sacraments and the institution of world Communism of a monastic type. Joachim was no obscure scholar or neglected prophet, but the founder of one of the most widespread and influential movements of the Middle Ages.

Eckhart from a very different point of view dissolved the idea of a separate transcendent Deity into the conception of the potentiality of being, rather after the fashion of Whitehead. God is unknowable only because all the potentialities of life are not yet realised. *There is nothing more Divine than the human soul.* Is this materialism of the Marxist type ? If we remember that Marxism never attempts to reduce spirit to matter, but, on the contrary, declares that spiritual activities are the highest functions of matter, we shall see how near the great mystic is to the secularism of Communism. But neither philosophy affirms that man as he is to-day is Divine. The potentiality has yet to be realised.

In our own times, in that little-known drama, *Julian the Apostate*, Henrik Ibsen foretells the coming of " The Third Religion."

" The reconciliation between nature and spirit, the return to nature through spirit, that is the task for religion. The third kingdom shall come. The spirit of man shall take its inheritance once more."

The coming of the third age of man, however, will not be by a quiet unfolding, a slow, almost imperceptible ripening. It will be catastrophic and marked by the violent destruction of old and outworn social institutions together with an equally violent disruption of the philosophies and religions which justify and support them.

The Communist philosopher does not welcome this overturning of foundations and dissolution of society any more than the prophet Jeremiah rejoiced over the destruction of Jerusalem.

He stands dismayed and agonised before the spectacle, but unable either to deny its inevitability or to avert it.

IX. APOCALYPTIC

We live in the apocalyptic times foretold by the New Testament, the day of the coming of the Son of Man. Religion is faced with the alternatives of fulfilment or apostasy. Fulfilment means the carrying over into Communism of the age-long struggle to sanctify the common life and concretise the Divine ideal. But if that Second Coming is rejected, " the glory is departed," and the Church is finally cast out. The result is not a mere falling short, a worthy and progressive effort that does much good, though not as much as it might, but a rapid degeneration of every part. Judaism crucifies its Messiah, and the Church its Christ. The Mass, as it were, becomes a Black Mass.

Prayer becomes a psychological disease, spirituality an escape mechanism, moral idealism moral evasion. Sometimes blatantly, as in the papal encyclicals against Socialism with their call to a crusade on behalf of private property and authority, sometimes very subtly as in the sickly philosophisings of a Berdyaev, the Church moves into closer alliance with the dying world that lieth in the Evil One. The reunion of Christendom may be in the last ditch of Fascist resistance to Socialism.

The more the world gets out of hand and incapable, on accepted lines, of being reduced to order, the more world-denying faith flourishes and men take refuge in the spiritual. Religion becomes the cult of death, the spiritualisation of despair, a sweetened opiate. It ceases to be the spiritual order underlying the concrete world, the truth of *things*, the guiding power behind statesmen and men of action ; it becomes a perverted cult and lapses into quietism. The Church of the Middle Ages had its world-denying aspects, its mysticism, its appalling moral defects, but it never lost its intellectual integrity, its realism, its indissoluble bond with the world, with politics, industry, art, and life. Therefore religion was alive. Even its supernaturalism was an integral part of the real world, not an irrational dualism like that of Eddington or Inge or the modern Catholic. But in our day, religion in its decadence, marked by psychological disintegration and instability, exerts no moral power and offers no enlightenment. This neurotic spirituality is heightened by the desperate sickness of society which we refuse to cure. The Gods of our fathers become the idols of our own generation, the piety of yesterday the superstition of to-day.

The great religious leaders of the past would repudiate this perversion, but particularly would they condemn it for missing that great flood-tide of the spirit which sweeps forward in the Socialist movement of our time. In their day they were quick to ally themselves with the world movements which claimed their allegiance. To-day they would be ill at ease in the Churches, but at home in the class war, which is the world's growing-point as well as its storm-centre.

Religion, when it is alive, belongs not to the backwater but to the open sea, not to the effete legislatures and timid counsels of reaction, or to the frozen impartiality of a cautious ecclesiasticism.

" *The Church is on the rocks, and breaking up. I told him it would unless it headed for God's open sea.*" (Shaw.)

" The test of a true faith," says Principal Oman, " is the extent to which its religion is secular." That is blasphemy to modern religion, but, because it is so, such religion is itself condemned. Men and religious bodies are revealed for what they are by their reaction to the Son of Man as He stands before them veiled in the carpenter and his friends, in the child asking for a cup of cold water, in the traveller fallen by the wayside. The Divine which confronts us is always incarnate. " Watch therefore for you know neither the day nor the hour when your Lord comes. Let your loins be girt and your lights burning ; and be yourselves like men that wait for their Lord. For in an hour that ye think not the Son of Man cometh." The religious tragedy of Judaism was that when its Messiah stood before it, it could only crucify Him. The religious tragedy of Christendom is identical.

The judgment is the same. The invited guests make the great refusal and the feast is spread before those from the highways and the hedges.

" Therefore I tell you the Kingdom of God shall be taken from you, and given to a nation that brings forth the fruits of it.

' There shall be weeping and gnashing of teeth when you shall see Abraham and Isaac and Jacob and all the prophets in the Kingdom of God, and yourselves thrust out ; and from east and west and from north and south many, I tell you, shall come and sit down in the Kingdom of God, but the children of the Kingdom be cast into outer darkness ; and lo ! there are last who shall be first, and there are first who shall be last."

The reaction will argue, as they did of the message of Jesus, that Communism is not religion at all, that it is a perversion of the facts to claim that Jesus and the prophets endorse the anti-religious movements of our time, and mere special pleading which links religion to social reform. That may well be true of modern religion, even though it is not true of religion in the past. In that case, if religion is no longer the recognition of the sacred in the developing purpose of history, if it is no longer the gospel of the Kingdom, it is wholly of the decadence, it is world-denial, delusion, and the cult of death, " the opium of the people."

It may well be that the time has come for religion to dissolve like an insubstantial dream and leave not a wrack behind, dying to be born again as the Holy Spirit of a righteous social order.

VI

CHRISTIANITY AND COMMUNISM: TOWARDS A SYNTHESIS

by John Macmurray

Grote Professor of Philosophy, London University

IN SPITE OF large divergencies of opinion and of approach, the contributors to this volume have one thing in common. All of them take Christianity seriously. All of them consider that Communism and Christianity are relevant to one another. This is as true of those who are professing Communists as of the others. The orthodox Communist is committed by his theory to the view that Christianity is the major subjective influence in the capitalist world determining its opposition to Communism, and in his practice, therefore, to a militant effort to eradicate religion. The success of this effort is for him a *sine qua non* of the triumph of Communism. The sincere Communist, therefore, takes Christianity very seriously indeed—more seriously, in fact, than most professing Christians. The rest of us agree in this at least. In spite of our own differences of outlook we all agree that we must take Christianity seriously, and that to do this we must relate it directly to the social issues of our own time. We must recognise it as a social force determining human life in its contemporary changes. It is clearly impossible to take Christianity seriously in this way without relating it to contemporary Communism, whether by way of opposition or otherwise ; and it is impossible to regard the issue as a purely theoretical one. We are not convinced, however, that the orthodox

Communist view of this relation is correct. We do not feel convinced that it is impossible, for example, to accept the social analysis and the political attitude of modern Communism without becoming atheists. This does not imply that we all do accept the Communist position, either wholly or partially, with the exception of its attitude to religion. We should admit that many Communists have found their rejection of religion the mainspring of their political activity. But we do not think it proven that there is any practical incongruity or any logical inconsistency between being at once a convinced Communist and a sincere Christian. I have no authority to speak for anyone but myself, but I think that I am interpreting their contributions rightly when I say that the non-Communist contributors would agree, with greater or less decisiveness, that the Communist case against Christianity has not been made out. Some of us would concede more and some less to the substance of Communist theory, but we would agree that it has not been conclusively shown that Communism and Christianity are in the nature of the case irreconcilable adversaries.

It will be clear to all who read the book that no concluding chapter could reasonably attempt to reconcile the conflict of views which it contains, or even to judge between them. The book itself is not an argument. Each writer has expressed his own view, in his own way, on the aspect of the subject which he has dealt with. This final contribution must similarly be judged on its own merits, and in no sense as a conclusion which carries the agreement of even a number of those who have taken part in the production of the book. It has, however, been designed as a conclusion, after careful consideration of the various points of view that the rest of the book expresses, and it is written in relation to them. This is the most that it can claim, unless the personal conviction of its author be counted an advantage— that the contemporary opposition between Christianity and Communism is a dialectical opposition which admits of, and, indeed, demands and necessitates, a synthesis.

There is one very strong reason for suggesting that Christianity cannot stand in such essential opposition to Communism as most Christians and nearly all Communists suppose. It is the fact that Christianity stands in precisely such an essential opposition to Fascism. In an earlier part of this book Dr. Polanyi has dealt with this opposition at length, and there is no need to repeat his exposition. Now every Communist will admit that the real objective of Fascism is the defence of capitalism against the threat of a Socialist revolution. He will insist that Fascism is the only alternative to the socialisation of the means of production. If, then, capitalism cannot maintain itself beyond a certain point without accepting Fascism, and if Fascism cannot establish itself without coming into fundamental opposition to Christianity, how is it possible that Christianity and Communism are inherently contradictory? How, at least, can the Communist be right in holding that Christianity is the natural ally of capitalism in its resistance to Communism? The Fascist would like to use religion for his own purposes, no doubt, and he is aware that Christianity has already been used to support a capitalist society. But he discovers in experience that this is only possible for a capitalism which is able at least to do lip service to certain ideas which are inherently bound up with Christianity—which are, indeed, the creation of Christianity. Amongst these are the ideas of freedom, of equality, and of progress. But in its Fascist stage capitalism can no longer tolerate these ideas. It can no longer compromise with them as it could when it was itself a progressive force. It must openly repudiate them as mistaken and vicious. It must seek to root them out of men's minds. For these ideas have passed into the keeping of the Socialism it must prevent at any and every cost. The practical Fascist discovers in his effort to construct the Fascist State what the more intelligent Fascist theorists had already foreseen—that Christianity breeds Liberalism, Liberalism breeds Socialism, and Socialism breeds Communism. Fascism, therefore, though it might be compatible with some form of religion, and may stand in need of some religious movement to support its claims, cannot look to any form of Christianity for support. The structural ideas of Christianity and of Fascism are in such point-blank contradiction that neither could assimilate the other without openly and completely denying its own essence.

Orthodox Communism is in no position to deny *this* relation to Christianity ; and its theory, as I understand it, does not do so. The Communist opposition to Christianity is not of the same type at all. The main structural principles of Fascism are totally incompatible with those of Christianity. The main structural principles of Communism are either identical with, or implied in, those of Christianity. I cannot understand why any intelligent Communist should wish to dispute this. His quarrel is not with the ideas, but with their religious form, and with what he considers to be the inevitable social consequences of holding them in this form. It is not merely that throughout its history Christianity has tended to produce communist theories, and attempts to organise societies on a communist basis. This is true and important, and the objection that modern Communism is totally different because it depends upon the development of machine production is true, but irrelevant. It merely explains why the earlier Christian efforts to establish communism could not have succeeded. There is a patent and direct historical relation between the modern Communist movement and Christianity. Hegel maintained that he had embodied in his philosophy the full content of Christian doctrine. After his death the Hegelian school divided on the question whether their philosophical position was compatible with theism. The left wing of the school decided, in my opinion rightly, that it was not. Consequently they rejected the belief in God, and became materialists. They were thus committed to the task of disentangling the essential content of Christianity from its religious form. In particular, it led Feuerbach to call his chief philosophical work *The Essence of Christianity*. Its aim was to restate the content of Christianity in purely

humanistic terms. This work was a turning-point in the
development of Karl Marx, who went so far as to say that
no one could reach the true Communist position without
being baptised in the Fire-brook.[1] Against Feuerbach,
Marx maintained that he had failed to carry the process to
completion. His philosophy still remained tainted with
sentimental idealism and imperfectly realistic because it
was not rooted in the recognition of labour—of actual,
physical work—as the determining factor in human experience. It was left to Marx to complete the process of
restating the sentimental religious idealism of Christianity
in the form of a practical materialistic humanism. Thus the
Marxian sociology, which forms the essential background
to the special economic theories of modern Communism,
is the end-product of a historical process in which the
essential human content of Christianity is maintained
through a change of form. The critical point in the change
is the rejection of the idea of God. With this the essential
human content of Christianity is released from its religious
expression. The completion of the change depends on
discovering the empirical human reality from which it
springs, and to which it properly refers, and applying it to
that. This is an account of the historical relation between
Christianity and Communism which no Communist need
quarrel with, and which, I am convinced, Marx himself
would willingly have accepted. It explains why Marx
could say that " from a certain point of view, Christianity
is the truth of all forms of religion " ; and also why Mr.
Lewis can maintain the thesis so convincingly, in the
previous essay, that Communism is the heir to the Christian
tradition.

Marx, however, would have gone on to insist that for this
very reason the rejection of the belief in God, and consequently the total rejection of religion as such, is an essential
condition of the acceptance of Communism, or even of a
proper understanding of its theory. When the truth about
humanity has emerged from its religious chrysalis, the

[1] The name Feuerbach in German means Fire-brook.

wrappings that concealed it are of no further value, however essential they may formerly have been to its growth and preservation. Indeed at this stage any effort to preserve the religious form is necessarily an effort, conscious or unconscious, to prevent the truth from emerging in its proper form. It is necessarily obscurantist and reactionary. And since the continued existence of religion depends upon the success of this effort, all religious organisations and their supporters are committed, by the mere fact of their existence, to a reactionary and anti-Communist *rôle* in the transition of society from capitalism to Socialism. This seems to me to be the proper answer of the orthodox Communist to the contention that it is Fascism, not Communism, that is the direct antithesis of Christianity. He can admit it ; he can admit, also, that the truth that is implicit in Christianity, disguised under its religious form, becomes explicit in Communism. And he can still maintain that in spite of this the whole force of the Christian religion will be used to defend capitalism, in the struggle of the transition, against Communism—even if in doing this it is warring against its own truth, and allying itself with its opposite to its own undoing. For its only hope of a continued existence, even if it be a desperate hope and a precarious existence, is bound up with the continuance of capitalism. The only alternative, to accept Communism and fight in defence of its own truth against a capitalism which is driven beyond the limits of possible compromise, would involve its own self-repudiation as a religion. In a Communist society religion would disappear, not because it was incompatible with the principles of the society, but because it would be a hopeless anachronism, without any human significance. And at the end of the capitalist era the Communist is driven into militant opposition to religion, because religion can only hope to preserve what human significance it still possesses by resisting the forward march of the workers' movement. For organised religion any other policy would be suicidal. For the Communist to accept an alliance with Christianity, even if it were sincerely offered, would be to compromise the conditions of his own success.

No one who believes, as I do, that this conclusion is a mistake can afford to dismiss it lightly. It is a serious argument, and it makes out a very strong case. Moreover, it is a case that does not merely rest on speculative interpretations, but is supported by a considerable amount of practical experience. The various Churches, with negligible exceptions, are so bound up with the existing social order, and so unaware of the character of the crisis which they are facing, that it would be a miracle if they did not rally to the support of contemporary law and order against any real attempt to revolutionise its property basis. What Christian Socialist, however optimistic, has ever dreamt of claiming that he had the Church behind him ? And what Conservative statesman, planning the defence of the existing tradition against the threat of Socialism, has ever lost sleep through the fear that organised religion would move into opposition ?

One has therefore to begin by admitting that organised Christianity, as at present constituted, could not survive the transition to a Communist society. So far as the Communist is expressing a practical and empirical judgment upon the spirit and social attitude of contemporary Christianity, as exhibited in its organised forms, he is justified—at least for all practical purposes. To be compatible with a truly Socialist form of society, modern Christianity would have to submit to a reformation comparable only with the one which closed the medieval epoch. The synthesis of modern Christianity and modern Communism which I believe to be not merely possible, but urgently necessary in the interests of both, as well as of humanity, could leave neither unaltered. It would transform Christian practice in a way that would make it much more nearly the expression of its own professed ideals ; and it would transform Communist theory in a way that would much more adequately express the actual nature of the form of practical life that it seeks to realise.

In admitting this, however, we must remind ourselves

that such an attack upon contemporary Christianity is
fully in line with Christian experience and with Christian
teaching. Because it is a religion, and is rooted in the eternal
aspect of human life, Christianity has a substance which is
independent of the temporary forms of social organisation
through which it expresses itself. It has existed, and does
exist, under all the forms of social organisation of the
historic period, though it tends to their transformation.
It has persisted throughout the series of revolutionary
transformations, unique in human history, which constitutes the progress of European civilisation. It is itself
the major source of the developing consciousness which has
made this progress possible. It has assisted at the transition
from one stage to another, and the transition has always
involved its own transformation. Christianity has therefore
behind it a long experience of self-transformation, which is
bound up with general social change. On the strength of
this experience any Christian would be justified in expecting
that, in the transition from a capitalist to a socialist order
of society, Christianity itself would necessarily undergo
profound changes of form, and that those changes would
involve a rediscovery of its own inherent substance. But
the teaching of Christianity, from the beginning, has shown
itself aware of the danger of compromise with the organisation of worldly power. The New Testament, while promising
that one day the Kingdom of Heaven would come, with
power, on earth, enjoined upon all its adherents the policy
of keeping themselves separate from the world, and of
refusing the temptation to achieve worldly power and
influence even as a means to establishing the new society.
The Church was to bear witness to the new order that was
to take the place of the existing order in the fullness of time,
and in the interim to abstain carefully from any alliance
with the established powers which would compromise its
witness. However much this part of the Christian teaching
may have been slurred over, or neglected in practice, it has
always remained part of the Christian doctrine. As a boy,
I was myself taught that any Church which compromised

with the State, or with the order of " worldly " society, was on the high road to apostasy, and would assuredly be confounded and destroyed. On the same grounds, therefore, as those practical grounds on which Communists judge that contemporary Christianity must perish with the order of society with which it has allied itself, the Christian might, in terms of the Christian tradition itself, come to the same conclusion. But the Christian would recognise the issue not as the destruction of Christianity, but as the penalty paid by an apostate Church, and as a chastisement recalling Christians to their true allegiance.

Thus to the empirical argument that the contemporary character of organised Christianity allies it with capitalist society, and so makes it incompatible with Communism, the Christian can answer that in that case contemporary Christianity is incompatible with true Christianity. He may even feel certain that it is ready for destruction, and that the new form of his religion which will arise in the new order of Socialist society will find that new order much more compatible with its own teaching than any that has preceded it. The Communist case cannot, therefore, be made out in such empirical terms. So far the historical facts are susceptible of either interpretation, though the historical analogies tend to support the view that Christianity will persist into Communist society through a change of form. This view, moreover, is strengthened by the historical connection and the similarity of content between Christian and Communist social doctrine which we have already discussed.

The Communist attitude to Christianity rests upon its conception of the nature of religion. It does not rest upon the empirical facts of history, but upon their interpretation in terms of a sociological theory. It rests upon the conviction that, with the coming of Socialist society, religion as such must disappear, because the conditions of its existence have disappeared, and it no longer has any human function to perform. Indeed, the Communist might reply to the argument of the last paragraph that in a sense it is true

RR

that Christianity will persist into Communist society through a change of form ; but that the change will be such that the form will be no longer religious. If the Communist conception of the nature and function of religion is correct, this would, in my opinion, be the truth. It is with this conception of religion that the Christian must come to grips. It is its concentration upon this central aspect of the whole question which gives its peculiar significance to Dr. Reinhold Niebuhr's contribution to this book. If it is possible to be a Communist and remain a Christian, then the Communist interpretation of religion must be mistaken.

The core of the Communist view of religion is the conception that religion is essentially idealist, and that idealism is inherently dualist. This dualism is natural and inevitable in any form of human society except the Communist form. It arises from a discrepancy between the essential nature of Man and the environmental conditions of his actual existence. Man is a developing organism, and the forms of human consciousness are part of his nature and develop with it. Our consciousness is not exempt from participation in the development ; neither is the development merely, or even essentially, the development of consciousness. Our development is unitary. It is the development of human nature as a whole, and in its actual unitary reality. Now it is only in and through our relation to physical nature that we can actually exist at all, and therefore it is only in and through our relation to physical nature that human development can proceed. This is the root of the perfectly proper insistence in Communist theory upon the economic aspect of human life as holding the clue to the form of the process of human development. In the earlier stages of human development the environmental conditions of life make it impossible for Man to reveal, and therefore to recognise, his essential nature in his actual ways of living. It is only through the process by which Man gradually achieves the mastery of his material environment, ultimately, therefore, only through the development of machinery, that the conditions can arise in which the actual expression of the real nature of Man in his ways of living can become possible. Until the establishment of Communist society there is, therefore, a necessary discrepancy between the actuality of human life—which is always life in society—and its own essential nature. The reality of human nature can only be manifested in actual forms of social life at the end of a long historical process.

It is interesting to see the identity of substance between Communism and Christianity on this issue, through the change of form. St. Paul, for example, writes as follows : " I reckon that the sufferings of the present time are not worthy to be compared with the glory that shall be revealed unto us. For the eager expectation of the creation waiteth for the revelation of the sons of God. For the creation was subjected to vanity (not willingly, but by purpose of him that subjected it) in hope ; because the creation itself also will be set free from the bondage of corruption into the freedom of the glory of the children of God. For we know that the whole creation groaneth and travaileth in pain together until now, and not only it, but ourselves also, though we have the firstfruits of the Spirit, we ourselves also groan within ourselves, waiting for adoption, the redemption of our body. For in this hope we are saved ; but hope that is in sight is not hope ; for what any seeth, why doth he hope for it ? But if we hope for what we see not, with steadfastness we wait for it."[1] If we take this together with the insistence of Jesus that it is impossible for a rich man to enter the Kingdom of Heaven except by a miracle, we find the whole substance of the Communist position on this fundamental point. Even the exception reappears in the changed form. Marx, while maintaining that the capitalist bourgeoisie is incapable of creating a Socialist form of society, allows also that, as the crisis of capitalism deepens, a certain number of the bourgeoisie will desert their own class and make common cause with the workers.

[1] Romans viii. 18–25 (Cunnington's translation).

For this discrepancy between his essential nature and his actual existence Man finds a compensation in the activities of his imagination. He turns to the realisation of his true nature *in idea*. In idea he constructs another world—a world congruous with his impulse to self-realisation. Frustrated in his actual life by the conditions under which he must labour, he seeks fulfilment and consolation in the imagination of a life of complete self-realisation in a world completely adapted to his impulse. Religion is the social organisation of this tendency. By maintaining the idea of another world in which the hopes and aspirations of the members of society are fulfilled, and in which the maladjustments and injustices and hardships of actual society are put right, it blunts the edge of the despair and anger which would otherwise make social life impossible. It persuades men to accept conditions which otherwise would goad them to revolt. Thus religion forms the major subjective defence of the existing social order.

It is important to remember that this does not in itself, for intelligent Communist theory, amount to the condemnation of religion. So long as the existing order of society is the best that is possible under the existing conditions, it is to the interest of all its members that it should be safeguarded against threats to its stability, from inside as well as from outside. It is only in revolutionary periods, when the process of development demands that the existing form of social life should be replaced by a more adequate form, that religion becomes the instrument of reactionary conservatism. When the historic task facing a society is a revolutionary self-transformation, when the advance in man's control of the conditions of his life has reached a point at which a new form of society will mean a lessening of the discrepancy between his actual life and his essential nature, then any influence which tends to divert men's minds from the effort to carry this task through is to be deplored, and becomes a strong weapon in the hands of any section of society which is interested in preventing the change from being made. To this we must add that, when the point in the development of human society is reached at which the mastery of the conditions of life is sufficient to allow of a form of social life which corresponds with the essential nature of humanity, there will no longer be a need for diverting men's minds from the actual life they lead to an ideal world. The social need for an escape-mechanism will have disappeared. For the Communist this means that religion ceases to have any social function with the establishment of a Communist order of society.

The crux of this view of religion lies in the implication that religion can only perform its consolatory function through dualism. It must set the ideal world in strong contrast to the actual word, and it must make the ideal world the real world by attaching man's emotional interest to it. But this it can only do by withdrawing his interest from the actual world, so that the actual world and man's life in it are felt and thought to be unreal and of no importance. Yet, in fact, the ideal world draws its reality from the actual world, because it is constructed by imagination as a compensatory contrast to it. It has meaning and significance only in terms of this contrast. The heaven of the poverty-stricken has its streets paved with gold. The true meaning of the ideal other-world lies in its reference to the actual world ; yet the dualism necessitates the suppression of this reference. This is the essence of idealism in the sense in which Communism attacks it, and rightly attacks it. It makes the world of ideas, which is the world of the imagination, real in its own right, and independent of the actual world. To achieve this it must reduce the actual world, in the thought and feeling of men, to a quasi-illusory status. The actual world has to be represented as relative to, and drawing any relative reality and significance it may have from the ideal, imagined world.

The answer which the Christian must make to this position is that its identification of religion with idealism is false, and that this identification is the underlying premiss of the whole argument, without which it ceases to have any relevance to the discussion. But, before dealing with this final point, it will be well to point out that, even if it were true, the argument is not conclusive. It would only prove that religion would cease to have any human function when the discrepancy between the essential nature of humanity, and the actualities of human existence had disappeared, or, to put it in Christian terms, when man had been completely redeemed. The belief that religion must disappear with the establishment of a Communist order of society involves the assumption that the sum total of the conditions responsible for the frustration of human reality will be removed once and for all by the socialisation of the means of production. This assumption is an extreme example of that naïve Utopianism which the Communist continually, and rightly, denounces. The Communist may reply that the change does once and for all establish an order of society which corresponds to the inherent nature of man, and that no further revolutionary change in the social order will be necessary. That may be granted. We may even insist, with the Communist, that this is the urgent and unavoidable issue facing contemporary society. But it is quite irrelevant to the present question. If the Communist revolution is the final revolution of the form of society, then with its achievement all reason for fearing and attacking religion must disappear. If religion inherently acts as a force for the conservation of an existing order, and against all revolutionary tendencies, then in a Communist society, on his own showing, it could only be an unmitigated blessing. It would be the major subjective influence working for the preservation of the *true* order of human society against any tendencies making for inner dissension and disruption. At the most, therefore, the Communist could reasonably maintain that there would be no need for it, though if there were it should be welcome. But what real grounds are there for thinking that there would be no need for it ? The Communist is too apt to think that the form of social organisation is the whole of human reality, whereas it is not even its substance. Even in its efforts to console men for the hardness of their lot, the most idealistic forms of religion have been forced to concentrate upon those problems which centre round the factors in human life which are quite independent of the forms of social organisation—such as love and death. These aspects of life are eternal, and will be substantially the same in a Communist order of society as in any other, and a good half of the sense of frustration which has turned men to bitterness and despair and hatred of their kind has its source in them. Religion has always been specially bound up with the fear of death in particular, and it seems to me that only a mad idealist could suggest that the socialisation of the means of production will make an end of that fear and of the ramifications of its effects. And if it will not, then the need for religion remains. To this Communists are apt to reply that these things belong to the private life of the individual. I have never been able to understand how this answer can even seem relevant to the question. If it were so, it would only mean that religion was concerned with the private life of the individual, which no religious person would be likely to deny. The answer could only be relevant if it were taken to imply that the private life of the individual was of no social importance. But the Communist cannot mean this, because it would follow that religion was of no social importance, which is just what his theory of religion denies.

But this answer does reveal the Communist tendency to lapse into a new form of the dualism which he attacks. The dualism between the individual and society is one of the effects of idealism which is particularly prominent in capitalist democracy. This antithesis is, indeed, the basis of individualism, but only the rights of the individual are held to take precedence of the rights of society. If this emphasis is reversed, and the rights of society are asserted to take precedence of those of the individual, we reach a denial of individualism which rests upon the same antithesis. A Communist theory which develops in this way remains still infected with idealism, and logically implies the doctrine of the totalitarian State. In practice, that is to say, it leads to Fascism, which denies explicitly the rights

of the individual against organised society. So long as social
theory is stated in such terms a true Communist theory is
impossible. The only logical alternatives are capitalist
democracy and capitalist Fascism. The attempt to formulate a theory of Socialism in terms of the antithesis of society
and the individual will result in a vacillation between a
Utopian anarchism which looks for the abolition of organised social authority and a pure authoritarianism which
denies the rights of the individual, and consequently
repudiates all individual freedom. Neither of these two
poles expresses properly either the practice or the inherent
meaning of the modern Communist. What is required as
the basis of Communist theory is a synthesis of individual
and society, not the assertion of one or the other term
against its opposite. It is the dualism of individual and
society which is at fault, and consequently not one or other
of the alternatives which may be derived from it, but both.
Pure collectivism is just as false as pure individualism, and
for the same reason. And it is the error common to both
which leads to the misunderstanding and rejection of
religion. For it leads to a confusion between individualism
and the religious and Christian insistence upon the supreme
value of the individual, which is in no sense individualist,
though it is sometimes described by the contradictory
phrase " religious individualism." Religion cannot be
individualist because it is grounded in the fact and the idea
of communion, and is therefore concerned always with the
individual in his relationships with others.

The individual, isolated from, and contrasted with,
society, is a pure myth. Christianity, Communism, the
Hegelian idealism from which Marxian theory derives, and
Fascism are all agreed on this. It is almost the one important point on which they are all agreed. Society, isolated
from, and contrasted with, the individual, is equally mythical, since it consists of individuals in relation. Individual
and society are correlative terms. There is no such thing
as an individual life which can be contrasted with social
life. Similarly there can be no social life which is not the

life of individual people in their relations to one another. If we are to take this obvious fact seriously, we must cease to think in terms of a distinction between individual and society. If we try to do this, however, we soon become aware that the distinction referred to in the contrast between individual and society is a real one, even if it is falsely formulated in these terms. The reason for this is that the term society is ambiguous. The term may be used in a general and abstract sense to refer to that aspect of life which expresses, in any of its forms, the inherent relatedness of human beings. When it is used concretely, it may refer to any of the concrete manifestations of this essential relatedness. Of these there are three which must be distinguished for our present purpose. The term society is used to refer to the State. In this case membership of society is defined by common citizenship. This use of the term is formal only —that is to say, the relations of citizens as citizens are legal and institutional only, and so, in the strict sense, accidental, not substantial. The State is a complex of institutions maintained and secured by law. Membership of the same State is compatible with conflict of interests, with individual and class animosity, rivalry, and struggle, with differences of status, race, and nationality. The substance of human relations lies outside the legal sphere of the State, however much the legal form may affect or be affected by it. From this we must distinguish the substantial relations in which people co-operate for the purposes of life. Now, since the basic needs of life are material, society in this sense is defined primarily by the forms of economic co-operation between its members, and it is these forms that determine the actual way of life of its members in its daily substance. This distinction is fundamental to Communist theory. It enabled Marx to explain how a society could be formally democratic, since its members were legally free and equal citizens, and at the same time substantially undemocratic, because its forms of economic co-operation were not compatible with the real freedom and equality of the persons co-operating. It enabled him further, when taken in

conjunction with his study of the process of economic development, to show that the discrepancy between the formal and
the substantial structure of society could not be maintained
beyond a certain point, but must in the long run produce
a revolution which would bring them into harmony.

Now it is on this distinction between the formal character
of society as legally or politically defined, and its substantial
character as economically defined, that the social theory of
Communism rests. It is this that makes the economic factor
the determining factor in the process of social development.
So far as it goes, it is correct, but it still rests upon an incomplete analysis. There is a third reference of the term
society which has been overlooked. It applies also to those
relations of human beings which cannot be defined either in
political or in economic terms, but which rest upon the
impulse to achieve fellowship and human community for
its own sake. It is this aspect of life, in the last analysis,
which is indicated by the contrast between the individual
and society. And it is here that Christianity diverges from
modern Communist theory. Christianity maintains that
these relations are the essence and reality of human life,
and not the economic ones ; while Communist theory either
ignores them or treats them as subordinate to, and derivative from, the relations of economic co-operation, as part
of the " superstructure " of social life.

In trying to understand the nature of human society we
must begin by distinguishing between the direct and the
indirect relations between the individuals who compose it.
Marx has pointed out that the introduction of money
destroys the simplicity of primitive Communism, by making
the relation of producer and consumer indirect. But this
distinction of direct and indirect relationship in the exchange of the products of labour, though important, is still
subordinate. In a deeper sense all economic relationships
are indirect, because they are mediated by the goods ex-
changed, and based upon the individual needs of the persons so brought into relation. Members of a primitive tribe
may be in direct relations of exchange with those of another

tribe as well as with one another, but it is only with one another that they are in direct human relation. Thus economic relations, however direct, do not in themselves suffice to establish community between human beings. To these there must be added a mutual recognition of one another as fellows in the sharing of a common life.

I call indirect all relationships which are mediated by something external to themselves, and which are not, therefore, maintained for their own sake. In particular, all forms of relation which are determined by, and which can be defined in terms of, a common purpose, or end to which they are the means, are indirect. Indirect relations are therefore relations of co-operation for the achievement of a common end ; and for this reason they admit of organisation. They are functional and organic. On the other hand, direct relations are not organic, but personal, and they cannot be organised, since there is no purpose beyond themselves in terms of which they can be determined. They are the direct expression of the inherently mutual or communal nature of man.

All human community is a structure of direct relations between human beings. Community cannot be constituted by indirect relations, or defined in terms of them. It cannot be organic, because it exists, when it does exist, as an end in itself, and there can be no purpose beyond it which can determine it. On the contrary, it generates and determines common purposes. This is immediately evident from the fact that all indirect relations are in principle compatible with a complete absence of community between the persons concerned. I say *in principle* because in practice no set of human relationships that was purely indirect could have any permanence or stability. The positive reason is that, in the absence of a positive impulse to maintain direct relations for their own sake, society would be completely individualist. All motives would be self-regarding, and individuals could only co-operate for the satisfaction of their individual needs.

It follows that human society cannot be determined

essentially by economic motives, since economic relations are indirect. The organised form of society, however, is necessarily economically determined, since only indirect relations are susceptible of organisation, and of these the economic relations are fundamental. Modern Communist theory may provide an adequate and complete account of the nature and process of social organisation, but it gives no account at all of the essential nature of human community itself. For community is grounded in the essential mutuality of human nature, and therefore in the direct relations of persons in their personal character. And the field of direct relations is the field of religion.

This can be more conveniently stated from the standpoint of the motives which determine human action. These are of two types, which can be subsumed under the ideas of hunger and love respectively. The hunger-type determines actions in which an individual appropriates the external world to his own use. These motives are individualising and ego-centric, and they are basic to all purely economic activity. Motives of the love-type determine actions in which the individual gives himself to the external world and, in particular, to his fellows. They are basic, therefore, to the creation and maintenance of community, as well as to all creative activity in which the individual transcends his self-centredness and gives himself to life. Now human society is only possible through the combination of both types. They presuppose one another. The co-operation of men for economic purposes would be impossible apart from the impulse to enter into community. The love-motives can only determine action by creating and maintaining co-operation. Indeed, no strictly human action is possible which does not involve both types of motive.

We can now deal with the final charge against religion—that it is inherently idealist. Religion is primarily concerned with the direct relations of human beings, and with the love-motives which govern them and make them possible. Its function is to create and maintain, throughout the process of human development, the universal conditions of direct community. Now idealism is the product of dualism ; and dualism is the result of a dissociation of the two types of motive. If the love-motives are dissociated from the hunger-motives, they lose all material reference, and can no longer determine action. They are therefore diverted into an ideal world created by the imagination. To the degree in which they are so withdrawn from the control of material action they cease to function as determinants of community and co-operation. So long as this dissociation persists, any advance in social development is impossible. If religion is involved in such a dualism, it will necessarily become idealist, and will refer all the love-impulses to an " other world." Supernaturalism will set in. But, in so becoming idealised, religion becomes unreal *as religion*. Now European society has been involved in dualism for centuries, and Christianity, so far as it has accepted the organisation of this society, has inevitably been forced into idealism. The essence of Christianity is so much the truth of all forms of religion, as Marx recognised, that it cannot accept, and be accepted by, any society which is not substantially—that is to say, economically—democratic in its organisation without being vitiated. The effort to maintain itself without a continuous struggle against social forms which are its negation must make it unreal. For it is an attempt to make the forms of direct relationship between men universally real and true without altering the forms of indirect relationship in terms of which alone they can find a material expression. This is to accept the dissociation of love and hunger, through which hunger determines economic life as a universal struggle for existence, and love becomes sentimental and ideal, a matter of imagination and feeling ; and the self-transcendence which is its natural property is turned into a glorification of self-sacrifice for its own sake, divorced from the material co-operation in creative social activity which is its natural expression, and in which alone it is real and meaningful.

Thus from the tangle of half-truths in which an idealistic Christianity and a materialistic Communism are equally involved there appears the outline of their necessary synthesis. The Communist is right in demanding the disappearance of idealistic religion. He is right in holding that there is no longer any place in human life for supernaturalism. But he is wrong in thinking that religion is necessarily idealist, or that its reference is necessarily to an " other world " of superhuman experience. That is merely the perversion of religion through dualism. The true reference of religion is to the field of direct human relationships, and these are as much a part of ordinary social experience as any other. Indeed, they are its human core. The Christian is right in holding that a merely economic interpretation of human society is like *Hamlet* without the Prince of Denmark. It denies the core of all human experience. But he is wrong in imagining that it is possible to cure the ills of humanity by a spiritual regeneration that leaves the organisation of economic society out of account. Love in dissociation from hunger is purely sentimental. Hunger in dissociation from love is purely anti-social. The direct and the indirect relations of men in society are inseparable. Communism must learn to take account of the direct love-relations if it is to realise its own meaning and overcome the dictatorship of mere organisation. Religion must reject supernaturalism, and refer its ideal truth to the world of material reality, or be destroyed by the organised material injustice to which it turns a blind eye.

But if religion rejects supernaturalism, must it not reject God and cease to be religion ? Not at all. Either God is natural or religion is nonsense. The idea of Nature which excludes God is itself the product of dualism. God is no more supernatural than Matter. Both are infinites, and lie beyond all their finite manifestations. God is infinite personality ; and personality dissociated from matter in idea is purely ideal—that is to say, non-existent. God is real ; and therefore he is the ultimate synthesis of matter and spirit, of Nature and Man.